PAIN AND GRACE

STUDIES

IN THE HISTORY OF RELIGIONS

(SUPPLEMENTS TO *NVMEN*)

XXXVI

ANNEMARIE SCHIMMEL

PAIN AND GRACE

LEIDEN
E. J. BRILL
1976

PAIN AND GRACE

A study of Two Mystical Writers
of Eighteenth-Century Muslim India

BY

ANNEMARIE SCHIMMEL

LEIDEN
E. J. BRILL
1976

ISBN   90 04 04771 9

Whithersoever ye turn there is the Face of God
Koran, Sura 2/109

The veil on our Friend's Face
   that's we ourselves:
We opened our eyes, and
   no veil was left.

      Mir Dard

One castle and a hundred doors,
   and windows numberless:
Wherever you may look, o friend,
   there you will see His Face

      Shah Abdul Latif

To
Pir Sayyid Hussamuddin Shah Rashdi
in gratitude

TABLE OF CONTENTS

FOREWORD

Eighteenth-century Islam is something that is usually neglected by the historians of religion. Histories of Sufism in general end with the thirteenth, at the best the fifteenth century; the following period is, then, shortly classified as decadent. Certainly, there were many decadent mystics and would-be Sufis as they are criticized in Hijazi's satire which, published by A. J. Arberry, has apparently given the impression that most of them were so degenerate as to be almost outside the pale of Islam, or else, that their works were nothing but epigonic repetitions of what had been said better in previous centuries.

However, mystical thought and poetry flourished during the eighteenth century from Morocco to Islamic India. Suffice it to mention the beginnings of the Tijaniyya in North Africa, the oft-quoted prolific Sufi writer Abdul Ghani an-Nabulusi in Syria; Ibrahim Hakki Erzerumlu, the author of the highly interesting Marifetname, and Ghalib Dede, the last great Mevlevi poet, in Ottoman Turkey; and eventually the great theologians of Delhi such as Shah Waliullah, Mazhar Janjanan, and Mir Dard. Besides, we notice the amazing amount of mystical poets who sang in the regional languages of the Indo-Pakistani subcontinent. Without studying the works of the mystical writers during the pre-modern period it will be difficult to appreciate the developments that set in, during the following century, for the rejuvenation and reform of Islam. Thus, my interest in Khwaja Mir Dard (1721-1785), the saint of Delhi and first truly mystical poet of the Urdu language, developed during my studies on Muhammad Iqbal's work and was deepened when I was working on Mirza Ghalib's (1797-1869) poetry. It became clear that the Delhi school of mysticism contributed more to the formation of Indo-Muslim modernist thought and poetry than is usually realized. Besides, it is rare that a mystic offers his readers such a deep insight into his spiritual formation as does Mir Dard. Although I am well aware that he constitutes only one facet in the multicolored scene of eighteenth century Delhi I feel that he is important enough to attract the interest of historians and, even more, psychologists of religion.

Approximately at the same time when Mir Dard appeared in
my studies, that means, in the late 1950 ies, I felt attracted to
the greatest mystical poet of the Lower Indus Valley, Shah
Abdul Latif (1689-1752), in connection with my study of the
Sindhi language. In his case a much greater amount of material in
both Sindhi and English was available for the study of his poetry
than is the case with Mir Dard who, strangely enough, has never
attracted a scholar in the West, and only a few Urdu writers, who
mainly discuss his poetry, not his theology.

As different as the two eighteenth century mystics may appear
at first sight, they have two important features in common: both
were Indian Muslims, deeply steeped in the tradition of Sufism,
particularly in its Persian expression; both produced exquisite
mystical poetry in their mothertongues; both were fond of music
and knew the effect of the celestial harmony on man's heart.
Both receded into the depths of their own hearts, closing their
eyes to the outward world at a time when 'the world' seemed to
illustrate the truth of the Quranic sentence: 'Everything is perishing save His Face' (Sura 28/88).

Poets who write in such 'esoteric' languages as Sindhi, Urdu,
and Persian are liable to be misquoted by those who cannot read
their works in the original, and from a superficial study of their
writings such conclusions can be drawn as may or may not prove
wrong in the long run. It would have certainly been easy to
compare the sayings of both Mir Dard and Shah Abdul Latif to
many expressions of mystical poets inside and outside Islam and,
in the case of Shah Abdul Latif, particularly to the verse of
Kabir; but I have tried to rely largely upon the poets' own words
without introducing too many parallels or attempting at developing a closed system. My intention was to offer a picture of two of
the most fascinating Islamic mystics in eighteenth-century India,
of two men who stand before us as representatives of various
trends inside Indian Islam at a crucial point of its history.

The title of these studies, 'Pain and Grace', alludes to the
names of the two mystics: *Dard*, 'Pain', and *Abdul Latif*, 'The
Servant of the Gracious', as we may translate it. At the same time
it sums up the central ideas of both writers, ideas which they
have expressed in various forms, i.e., that suffering is the prerequisite of spiritual bliss, and that the Divine grace will descend
upon those who rejoice in the tribulations which they undergo

while travelling through the constantly shifting sand dunes of this
created world, hoping for the city of God at the end of the road.

1. Advent 1975   ANNEMARIE SCHIMMEL

ABBREVIATIONS

In order to facilitate the printing we have avoided the diacritical marks in proper names; they appear only in the indices in full scientific transcription. The footnotes, too, have been reduced as much as possible. Instead, the main works of Mir Dard and Shah Abdul Latif are mentioned in abbreviations in the text. Books by and about Dard are quoted as follows:

K. *ᶜIlm ul-kitāb*, Delhi 1310 h/1892-3.
N. *Nāla-yi Dard* ⎫
A. *Āh-i sard*   ⎬ Bhopal 1310 h/1892-3.
D. *Dard-i dil* ⎪
S. *Shamᶜ-i mahfil* ⎭
U. *Urdu Dīwān*, ed. Khalil ur-Rahman Daʾudi, Lahore 1961.
P. *Dīwān-i fārsī*, Delhi 1309/1891-2.
NA. *Nāla-yi ᶜAndalīb*, Bhopal 1308/1890-1, 2 vols.
F. Nāṣir Nadhīr Firāq, *Maikhana-yi Dard*, Delhi 1344/1925.

The titles of the thirty *Surs* (chapters) in *Shāh jō Risālō*, ed. Kalyan Adwani, Bombay, 1957, are abbreviated from the list given on pp. 154 ff.

CHAPTER ONE

THE INDIAN SCENE IN THE EIGHTEENTH CENTURY

In the tides of history, the eighteenth century is usually considered to be the time of lowest ebb for the Islamic peoples between the Balkans and Bengal. Almost no trace of the past glory of the Islamic Empires was visible any longer; the political scene was ruled by internecine wars on the one hand, by the strong encroachment of European colonial powers upon the Islamic lands on the other hand, and in the cultural field the dusty veil of stagnation seemed to cover everything, not allowing of new enterprises for redirecting the spiritual energy of the Muslims.

Contrary to this deplorable condition of the Islamic East the historian sees the glory of Europe who had gained her stand in world history and was just passing through the Age of Reason, and through political and economical developments which were to culminate, eventually, in the French Revolution and in the independence of North America. It was a time of highest cultural activity in literature, philosophy and music, to mention only the most important fields, a time in which the borders of an outlook centering on Christian Europe opened and the East was, for the first time, considered worthy of an objective study.

The general political and social climate in Western Europe brought forth a new world-consciousness, but also an economic and political trend to expansion. It was only this latter aspect of 18th century Europe with which the Muslim countries were confronted. These countries, however, went through an age of stagnation and wars. That holds true for the Ottoman Empire with its Arabic provinces and Iran, for North Africa and Central Asia.

India herself, once the marvel of the world, was shaken by constant wars between the weak Muslim rulers and the Mahrattas and Sikhs as well as their Muslim neighbors from Iran and Afghanistan. Thus, the British East India company was able to slowly extend its rule over larger parts of the Subcontinent after the successful battle of Plassey in 1757. The Portuguese and French tried to defend their positions in Southern India where the Muslim rulers of the Deccan fought partly with them, partly against them.

It was, indeed, the 'twilight of the Mughals.' Still, 'Agra and Lahore of Great Moghul,' which, as Milton says, were shown at the beginning of creation to the wonder-stricken Adam, kept some of their old charm. But Delhi, the capital of Muslim India since 1200, was nearly destroyed under the continuous blows of fate. When Mir Dard, in his poetry and prose, often speaks of the 'rose garden of manifestation of Divine power,' one should not forget that in Persian poetical language the red rose is connected not only with the idea of happiness or joy and love, but likewise with blood and wounds.

India had been under Muslim rule since the early Middle Ages: the Arabs conquered Sind, the southern part of present day Pakistan, in 711, and this province never ceased to be a center of Islamic studies and a seat of Islamic mysticism. From the year 1000 onward, Sultan Mahmud of Ghazna, descending 17 times from the Afghan Hills, conquered the northwestern part of the Subcontinent; thus, Lahore was to become an important center of Persian culture. The borders of the Muslim provinces slowly extended to the South and the East, and in about 1200, Delhi—with the magnificent building of the Qutb Minar—became the capital of the Muslim rulers, who from there, soon extended their influence to East Bengal and the Deccan. The Deccan, the Muslim kingdoms of Bijapur and Gujrat were independent for a long time, which resulted in special developments of Islamic culture and literature in the South.

The Mughal rule, which began in 1526 with Babur from the family of Tamerlane, is one of the most glorious epochs in Muslim history. Its beginning coincides with the high time of the Ottoman Empire (Sulaiman the Magnificent) and with the first decades of the Safawid rule that united Iran since 1501. The mid-16th and early 17th centuries are those periods when Muslim architecture from Adrianopel and Istanbul to Delhi and Agra reached its apex.

The borders of the later Mughal Empire included most of the Subcontinent. The last decades of the 17th century, however, were largely spent in wars with the Deccan states, where the Hindu Mahrattas tried to regain their independence. After Aurangzeb's death in 1707 the internal weakness of the vast empire became visible and the different national and religious groups, long dissatisfied, found an opportunity to revolt against the Mughal rule. For the Muslims themselves were immersed in constant struggles, the weak rulers being mere puppets in the hands of shrewd politicians without more than very personal ambitions. External powers, like Nadir Shah of Iran, took advantage of the situation; he invaded the country and eventually looted Delhi in 1739; about 30,000 people were killed. The once splendid city never fully recovered from this blow. Nadir Shah's successor, Ahmad Shah Durrani, came allegedly as a helper against the growing Mahratta threat and invaded the northwestern provinces time and again; his campaign in 1757 was a similar catastrophe, all the worse, since internal feuds and the misrule of the young minister Ghaziuddin had already impoverished the capital. Four years later, Ahmad Shah gained a decisive victory over the Mahrattas on the historic battlefield of Panipat; however, he did not use the fruits of his victory, and left Northern India to its fate. The exiled Mughal emperor Shah Alam II stayed for thirteen years in the Eastern provinces before he dared come back to Delhi in 1772, when the British and the Mahrattas had guaranteed his safe return. After sixteen years of reign in Delhi, he was cruelly blinded by Ghulam Qadir, a young leader of the Rohilla. This Afghan tribe that had settled north of Delhi and Rampur played an important role in internal politics during the mid-18th century especially since their intelligent leader, Najib ud-Daula was trusted by the Delhi orthodoxy and the Afghan invaders alike. The descriptions by both Muslim intellectuals and the British officers and administrators allow a glance at the hopeless condition of Delhi in those years. In 1803, the Mughal emperor was taken under British custody: his house continued ruling by name until 1857, the year of the so-called Mutiny.

The history of Indian Islam is, however, not only a history of political facts, of conquests and wars, of expansion and breakdown, but is a spiritual history as well. It is the history of the century-long conflict between the Islamic concept of *tauḥīd*, strict monotheism, and Hinduism in its different manifestations which constituted, in the eyes of the pious Muslims, the very essence of idolatry and polytheism which had been condemned by the Quran. Without the help of the religious specialists, the rulers would scarcely have been able to maintain their rule over the vast country with its various racial and linguistic groups. The decisive force was, in the Islamization of India, however, not the

activity of theologians and specialists in Islamic law and traditions who were sometimes attached to the court, but rather that
of the mystics who had settled in the Subcontinent as early as
the 11th century; the first Persian treatise on Islamic mysticism,
the *Kashf al-maḥjūb*, was written by Ali Hujwiri—called Data
Ganj Ba<u>kh</u>sh—(d.1071), whose tomb in Lahore is still a place of
pilgrimage for the people.

In the 12th and 13th centuries, mystical orders and brotherhoods crystallized out of formerly loosely united groups of disciples, who were introduced into the spiritualization of life by
their religious guide, the *shaikh* or *pīr*. The first representatives
of such brotherhoods reached India in the beginning of the 13th
century. Probably the most influential among them is Khwaja
Muᶜinuddin Chishti (d. 1236) from Eastern Iran, who settled in
Ajmer in the heart of Rajasthan, that had just been conquered by
the Delhi kings. His strong personality, his preaching of love of
the One God and love of the Prophet, reflected in love of mankind, won over considerable numbers of Hindus to Islam. His
disciples and later members of the order wandered through the
whole of India, from the Panjab (Fariduddin Shakarganj of Pakpattan, d. 1265) to the Deccan (Gisudaraz of Gulbarga, d. 1422).
One of the centers of the Chishtiyya was Delhi, where Nizamud-
din Auliya (d. 1325) spiritually guided the population during the
reign of seven rulers.

Baha'uddin Zakariya (d. c. 1265), the Suhrawardi master, settled in Multan, at the border of Sind and the Panjab: one of the
leading Persian mystical poets, Fakhruddin Iraqi, stayed with him
for 25 years. The Suhrawardiyya, not as austere in their practices
as the early Chishtiyya, sent their members throughout the country and gained disciples even in Eastern Bengal. But only in the
late 14th century members of the most important order in the
central Islamic countries, the Qadiriyya, reached India.

The orders, who helped in Islamizing the country, contributed
also to the development of literature and, partly, music: mystical
poetry in Persian, and later in the regional languages, was inspired
from their centers. The disciples wrote down the *malfūẓat*, the
words and sayings of their masters. They allow us some insight
into the spiritual, and also the social life of the Middle Ages, and
complete thus the outlook of the official chronicles, for the Muslim saints rarely completely agreed with the politics of the ruling

classes or the way of life of the feudal lords,—although, in later times, the borderline between the highly influential pir and the feudal lord was sometimes blurred, for spiritual influence not rarely resulted in political power.

Thanks to these groups, a number of classical works of Islamic mysticism were introduced in India. They were frequently commented upon, partly also translated from the original Arabic into Persian, or from Persian into Urdu. The ideas and poetical imagery of Fariduddin Attar (d. 1220) and Jalaluddin Rumi (d. 1273), the greatest Persian writing mystic, inspired generations of Sufis and poets so that allusions to their works are found in almost every mystical work composed in India. The work of Ibn Arabi (d. 1240), the Spanish-born mystic who had built a close system of mystical theosophy in his *Futūhāt al-makkiyya* and the *Fusūs al-hikam*, the 'Bezels of Wisdom', became known in the early 15th century, and taught the Muslims the idea of *wahdat al-wujūd*, the essential Unity of Being, according to which God and the creation can be understood as two aspects of one Reality. Thus, the central Islamic dogma of God's unity was overstressed and expanded into a Weltanschauung which has been called either 'pantheistic' or 'monistic.' Both terms, however, do not give full justice to Ibn Arabi's complicated system of thought. The terminology of the 'Great Master' has influenced, in the Islamic East, even those rejected his theories. The poets and, through them, the large masses interpreted his system in the simplified short sentence *hama ōst*, 'Everything is He.'

The idea of an all embracing unity made some Muslim mystics discover similar thoughts in the religious systems of their Hindu neighbors. The Mughal ruler Akbar (reigned 1556-1605), as most of his family attached to the Chishti order, was certainly influenced by such ideas when he undertook to promote a deeper understanding among the different religions in his empire by arranging discussions of their representatives and by having translated into Persian the main religious and literary works of Hinduism. His great-grandson, Dara Shikoh, the heir apparent of the Mughal Empire, and member of the Qadiriyya, tried to realize this unity. He even undertook the translation of the Upanishads—'a book that is hidden' (Sura 56/78)—into Persian.

The more orthodox circles did not approve of such a dangerous interpretation of Islam which seemed to blur the borders between the two religious communities. One should, however, never forget that even the most ardent defenders of *wahdat al-wujūd* agreed that the person of the Prophet Muhammad was the locus of the manifestations of the Divine Names, the 'Perfect Man' *par excellence*, the highest model of humanity whom to imitate is the first and foremost duty of the believer. And Islam remained for all of them the last and most comprehensive Divine revelation which comprises in itself, and hence abolishes, the laws brought by every previous Prophet. The 'tolerance' of Islamic mysticism consists of its embracing all religions under the crown of that final revelation which was granted to Muhammad.

It is characteristic of the situation in 16th century India that the protest against the widespread theories of 'Everything is He' was launched again by a mystical order, namely the Naqshband-iyya. This group had been given its rules by Baha'uddin Naqshband from Central Asia (d. 1389), and had deeply influenced life at the Timurid court of Herat where most intellectuals, including the great poet Jami, attached themselves to it. Babur, the first Mughal emperor, knew the order quite well, for one of its centers was located in his home province Farghana; there two rivalling branches of the Central Asian Naqshbandiyya were to play a decisive political role in the 17th and 18th centuries.

The activity of the Naqshbandis in the Subcontinent was limited during the first century of Mughal rule. More emotional orders played a greater role. Only toward the end of Akbar's days, Khwaja Baqi billah, one of the leading masters of the order, came to India and gained a number of disciples very soon. Among them was Ahmad Sirhindi (d. 1624), who tried to attract members of the Mughal court to the Naqshbandi path. Imprisoned for a year at Gwalior, he was soon released and eventually gained the favor of the emperor Jihangir. His aim was to go back to the pure teachings of Islam, which excludes a 'Unity of Being' but admits of the possibility of 'Unity of Vision,' *wahdat ash-shuhūd*. I.e., in the moments of highest bliss the mystic eye-witnesses absolute Unity but knows that no essential union between creature and Creator is possible, for 'The Lord is Lord, and the servant servant,' as the formulation of this school holds. 'I am His servant'—that is the highest station man can reach, for it is the station of the Prophet during his Nightly Journey (cf. Sura 17/1). The central thesis is not *hama ōst*, 'Everything is He,' but *hama az ōst*, 'Everything is from Him'—a formulation which is, indeed, much closer not only to orthodox Islam but to the theories of unity as professed by the early mystics (which had been interpreted, during the centuries following Ibn Arabi, in the light of *wujūdi*-theories).

Ahmad Sirhindi has been called, by the great philosopher Abdul Hakim Sialkoti, the *mujaddid-i alf-i thāni*, the 'Renovator of the 2. Millenium,' since he appeared at the beginning of the second millenium of the Islamic era in order to restore orthodox Islam; and he has been praised by his admirers even in Turkey as the *imām-i rabbānī*, the Divinely bestowed leader of the community. However, the claims of saintship and charismatic leadership which Ahmad Sirhindi uttered, are expressions of such a fantastic self-consciousness that he, with his theories of the restoration of the first *m* of Muhammad's name, and his claim to be the *qayyūm* by far surpasses the limits of what we would normally call 'orthodox Islam.' He saw himself and three of his descendants as divinely invested beings, higher even than the *quṭb*, the 'Pole' of the traditional mystical hierarchy, and destined to guide the Muslim people as *qayyūm*. This remarkable self-consciousness of the Naqshbandi leaders, together with their skill in politics made them more and more influential in India. Ahmad Sirhindi's successors and followers successfully worked to penetrate into the court circles. Shah Jahan's second son, Aurangzeb Alamgir, lent his ear to their advice, and fought against the ideals which led his elder brother Dara Shikoh to his attempts of mystical reconciliation between Islam and Hinduism. During Aurangzeb's reign, which lasted nearly half a century (1658-1707), music and fine arts were restricted. More than three decades after his death, members of the Sirhindi family still continued working behind the political scene, until the fourth *qayyūm*, Pir Muhammad Zubair, died a few months after the destruction of Delhi by Nadir Shah—his death coincides, so to speak, with the end of the third period of Mughal rule which was followed, during one more century, by constant decline.

The Naqshbandiyya also spread in other parts of India, for instance in the Lower Indus Valley.

The other orders continued their activities; some of them had split up, forming numerous sub-groups. Almost every poet and writer was connected in some way with a mystical order. Thus, the whole mystical vocabulary, as developed during centuries, was practically common stock for all members of the society, down to the lowest strata. Poetry and prose written during this period can be understood and enjoyed only with a certain knowledge of its mystical background; for whether the population of the unhappy country would accept tribulations patiently in the feeling that 'Everything is from Him,' or would believe in the all embracing Unity of Being which showed its strange manifestations in suffering and pain—the mystical way was, for most of them, the one source of strength which enabled them to survive during the afflictions which were showered upon Northern India in the 18th century.

All tribulations notwithstanding, literature, and especially poetry, remained alive in India. It flourished at the courts, but in its vernacular form it was the delight of the illiterate villagers. The Muslims produced a vast literature in the classical Islamic languages, Arabic and Persian, but also in Turkish, and the longer and more regional languages like Sindhi, Panjabi, and Pashto developed fascinating poetical forms, while Urdu inherited the Persian refined tradition.

There was no dearth of Arabic writing scholars during the Mughal time. Even Akbar's court poet Faizi produced an Arabic commentary on the Quran, composed completely of undotted letters, an amazing, though not very useful, achievement. During the 17th century the whole corpus of theological studies was in Arabic, thus the works on traditions and history by the leading traditionist of Delhi, Abdul Haqq Dihlawi (d. 1642), or those on logic and philosophy from the pen of Abdul Hakim Sialkoti (d. 1656). Here belongs also the important collection of legal decisions according to Hanafi law compiled during the rule of Aurangzeb Alamgir, *fatāwā-yi ʿAlamgīrī*, a comprehensive work in whose preparation a great number of excellent scholars were involved. Shah Waliullah of Delhi, the mystic, traditionist and politician of the 18th century, continued writing prose and even poetry in the classical language of theology.

One of the greatest contributions to Arabic lexicography, the dictionary *Tāj al-ʿarūs*, is the work of an Indian scholar, and pupil of Shah Waliullah, Sayyid Murtaza (d. 1787), who, like many of his compatriots, had migrated to Zabid in Yemen.

Arabic was likewise used for poetry. In the kingdom of Golconda, a school of rather traditional Arabic poetry blossomed during the early 17th century. In the 18th century the learned Ghulam Ali Azad Bilgrami (1704-1786) was tenderly called *'Hassān al-Hind'* because he composed many Arabic *qaṣīdas* in honor of the Prophet Muhammad, and thus became comparable to Hassan ibn Thabit, the Prophet's panegyrist. Azad's uncle, Abdul Jalil (d. 1715) had likewise excelled in Arabic poetry. Both scholars were prolific writers in Persian, too.

Azad Bilgrami was also well versed in Turkish, a language which was often used in the higher circles in Mughal India after the first Mughal Emperor Babur wrote his autobiography and several other works in his mother tongue, Chaghatay Turkish. Many of the Mughal generals and nobles who came from Central Asia continued in the use of their mother tongue—thus Bayram Khan (d. 1559), the faithful friend of the first three Mughal rulers, and his son Khankhanan Abdur Rahim, who both wrote poetry in Turkish. Already Amir Khosrau in the 13th century had boasted of his Turkish origin: Turk became synonymous with 'Muslim' and was also usually used in poetry as designation for the beautiful white, cruel beloved ruler as contrasted to the black Hindu slaves. Not few of the nobles around Delhi, even in the 19th century, claimed Turkish descendency.

The most important language for literary works, however, was still Persian, the official language of the Muslim rulers. They had settled in the northern part of the Subcontinent shortly after 1000. Lahore was, in the 11th century, a center of Persian culture, with poets and mystics writing in this language. Then the center of gravity shifted to Delhi, and although Persian was spoken and written even in Bengal and in the South, Persian literature proper was connected mainly with the northern plains of India.

It is impossible to enumerate the large number of historians who wrote their works, since in the 13th century, in the official court language, or the immense literature of Sufism which was composed from approximately the same period onwards.

The great master during the Delhi Sultanate was Amir Khosrau (d. 1325). He was a musician, poet, rhetorician, and his highly sophisticated style provides the reader with most intelligently put puns and precious images. His epical poems contain some interesting details about India. His younger contemporary Hasan Dihlawi (d. 1328), is sweeter and more tender, less artificial than he, but a more genuine mystic. In the Deccan the Chishti saint Gisu-daraz (d. 1422) wrote his exuberant mystical Persian poems, but is also the author of one of the first works in Dakhni Urdu. Numberless minor poets surrounded the rulers and the saints everywhere.

In the time of Akbar a great number of poets flocked from Iran to the art-loving Mughal court and influenced the style of the indigenous poets. Probably the greatest among them is Urfi of Shiraz (died at the age of 35 in 1591), whose *qasidas* in their glowing darkness and their majestic wording are reminiscent of heavily brocaded garments of purple velvet. His contemporary Faizi (d. 1595), more cerebral than he, is a master of every artistic form. Then follows the long line of the poets who have contributed to the development of the so-called Indian style: Naziri (d. 1612), and Talib-i Amuli (d. 1626), Kalim (d. 1651) and Ghani Kashmiri (d. 1661), Qudsi (d. 1646) and Fani (d. 1671) and innumerable others who praised in highly sophisti-cated words the world-encompassing strength and mildness of their rulers. Mughal miniatures of these decades often correspond to subjects described in their lyrics and panegyrics. They had to invent new figures of speech; for the outward forms of the Per-sian poem, the *qasida* and the *ghazal* with their monorhyme and their strict metrical rules as well as the *mathnawi*, used for didac-tic and narrative poetry, remained untouched. However, the im-ages were partly broken and put together in surprising patterns like the glass pieces in a kaleidoscope. Instead of the images of classical poetry which had in themselves a certain logic, pseudo-philosophical concepts, and artificial images became common. The spheres of hearing and seeing are strangely blended, and some new images taken from the material culture of the 17th century are used in this poetry which conveys the feeling that the poets were, at heart, nostalgic in the dazzling outward beauty of the 'Indian summer.' Were they homesick for Iran, or did they anticipate the gathering of those dark clouds whose lightning was to destroy the harvest of this whole super-refined culture? Or was it simply a convention that now words like 'shroud,' 'breaking,' 'blistered feet,' 'firestricken nest,' etc., were used much more frequently than in previous times; or that the poets compared themselves often to the trembling and melting dewdrop, or spoke of the firework of their burning hearts? The last master of this style is Bedil (d. 1721), the difficulty of whose poetry and prose is notorious. Still, his verses, contrary to those of many of his contemporaries, are often so filled with sentiment, and reach such a power of expression that one is tempted to translate them into very modern poetical language. Bedil and Nasir Ali Sirhindi (d. 1697), who later in life joined the Naqshbandi order, mark the limit which the Indian style could reach; 'his poems are more twisted than the curls of the lovely girls,' says one of Nasir Ali's admirers; but Persian-born poets, like Ali Hazin who reached India in the 1730's found the works of these two masters ridiculous and nonsensical.

However, the influence of Bedil and Nasir Ali (which proved dangerous for minor poets who were not endowed with a similar poetical vision) continued. In the 19th century Ghalib, the greatest Urdu and Persian writing poet of his time, remained, for a while, strongly under their spell. Even a modern writer of completely different mental stature, Muhammad Iqbal, admits his indebtedness to Bedil's poetry for the formation of his thought.

Still, Persian poetry had reached a kind of impasse; Persian prose remained, perhaps, alive longer. Ahmad Sirhindi's letters are an example for such prose, and so are the mystical writings of Prince Dara Shikoh, including his translation of the Upanishads. In the period of Aurangzeb not as many great works in Persian were produced as in the previous decades, for poetry had retired into the lofty corners of nearly incomprehensible stylistic difficulties. Miniature painting, too, slowly lost its glamour and music was forbidden.

One of the surprises in Indian cultural history around 1700 is, that members of the 'anti-artistic' Naqshbandiyya order were instrumental in the development of a new literary medium which was, after Aurangzeb's death, to supercede Persian and to become the typical language of Indian Muslims: that is Urdu.

A literature in the southern form of Urdu, Dakhni, had existed already since the Middle Ages. Here, too, the mystics had played a decisive role in developing the language, since they needed a medium for conveying their message to the large masses who were neither able to follow the theological Arabic nor the administrative and literary Persian. Among the Dakhni writing poets, the Qutbshah Kings of Golconda (1530-1687) and the Adilshahis

of Bijapur (1535-1686) occupy a prominent place. In the late
17th century, Wali Deccani elaborated his mother tongue in
poems, in which he uses all devices of classical Persian poetry.
Shortly after 1700, this poet was attracted to Delhi by the fame
of a Naqshbandi mystic and poetical preceptor, Shah Gulshan,
thanks to whom his poetry became famous in the capital of the
Mughal Empire. Apparently, the Muslims of Northern India, after
the breakdown at Aurangzeb's death in 1707, needed a new medium of expression which even the man in the bazaar would
understand. Thus, all of a sudden, a remarkable literature in Urdu
emerged in the first half of the 18th century in Delhi.

The situation in the literary field does, by no means, reflect
the deplorable state of the Indian Muslims. On the contrary, this
18th century is amazingly fertile in poetical expressions in all the
languages of Muslim India.

It is typical that even the great warrior, the 'liberator' of
Northwest India, Ahmad Shah Durrani, was a fine poet in his
mother tongue, Pashto. This language which had been used for
centuries in the border areas of India and Afghanistan had become a perfect instrument of poetical expression in the previous
century when the tribal chief Khushhal Khan Khattak (d. 1689)
composed numberless lyrical, epical and didactic poems which
reflect not only his large horizon and his vast range of interests
but also his stunning command over a language which was, until
then, only rarely used for higher literature (though the folk-
poetry of the Pathans is partly of touching beauty and, in the
genre of the three-lined *landay*, of almost *haiku*-like precise tenderness). Ahmad Shah Durrani does not reach the breadth of
variations found in the work of 'the father of Pashto poetry,' but
his poems, too, show an artistic feeling and his interest in the
mystical strands of Islam, and are counted among the finest products of the Pashto language.

The countries which were conquered first by Nadir Shah and
then by Ahmad Shah Durrani, Sind and the Panjab, could likewise boast of a rich literary heritage. In the Panjab, popular
mystical poetry may have emerged as early as in the days of
Fariduddin Shakarganj, the Chishti saint of Pakpattan (d. 1265).
Numerous folk songs and ballads existed but were never committed to writing. But the vast collection of Sikh sacred poetry as
preserved in the *Adi Granth* shows many of the features that

recur in Muslim Panjabi and Sindhi mystical songs. The golden age of Muslim Panjabi poetry is the late 17th and the 18th century, e.g., the time when the province was invaded one time after the other by Mahrattas, Sikhs, and, in between, by the liberating Muslim armies. After the short ecstatic poems of Sultan Bahu (d. 1691) the most famous of which are composed in the traditional form of *sīharfī*, 'Golden Alphabet,' Bullhe Shah's personality (d. 1752) looms large in the Panjabi poetry of the 18th century, so much so that he has even been called the 'Rumi of Panjab.' His poems are traditional in their forms, using *sīharfī*, 'Golden Alphabet,' *bārāmāh* (poems which describe the lovers' feelings during the twelve months) and others, and he has made use of the whole mystical vocabulary and imagery which had been inherited from classical times. He adds, however, to their beauty by combining them with the rural imagery of his homeland so that they could be understood by every villager and ploughman and sung by the large masses who would flock to the shrines of the saints, hoping for material and spiritual help in this time of deepest depression. Bullhe Shah is, like all the folk poets, a defender of the unity of Being. The same is true for Ali Haydar who died in 1785 near Multan. Shortly after his death the classical work of Panjabi literature was composed: Warith Shah's version of *Hīr Ranjhā* (around 1794). The story of the unhappy lovers was known since the days of Akbar, and had been turned into a popular tale in which the hero and the heroine undergo all kinds of tribulation and eventually are exiled, or die. Warith Shah has used this story as a vehicle for mystical thought, and interspersed it with mystical explanations; it is not told in logical sequence, for one expected everybody to know the contents, and the author could concentrate upon crucial scenes and dialogues, songs and prayers (just as it is the case in the Sindhi mystical versions of folk tales). Numerous variants of *Hīr Ranjhā* exist not only in Panjabi but also in Sindhi, Persian, and Balochi, but Warith Shah's version has never lost its attraction, and even today a Panjabi will be deeply touched when this moving story is sung.

In spite of the overall activity of writers, theologians, and mystics throughout Muslim India, two areas can be singled out as particularly interesting in the history of mystical poetry in the Subcontinent. They are, as is to be expected, the capital Delhi with its long history, and the Lower Indus Valley. Although both areas had to suffer under the breakdown of the Mughal Empire, and the invasions from their Western neighbors, they produced an amazing amount of mystical writings and poetry. Delhi, once the center of Persian literature in the Subcontinent, now became the place where Urdu poetry developed to its most beautiful expression. Shah Gulshan and his disciple Muhammad Nasir Andalib, Mir Dard's father, were prominent members of the group who encouraged the development of Urdu poetry. In poetical meetings the forms and figures of Urdu poetry were discussed, new words adopted, awkward expressions discarded, so that the language became polished and refined in a comparatively short time, and was able to express the different moods of the population of Delhi, and, later, of Lucknow, and eventually, of the whole of Muslim India. Most divergent types of poets are found in Delhi at almost the same time: besides the so-called *ihāmists*, who transplanted the ambiguous style of some of the Persian writing artists into Urdu, there lived in the first generation after Shah Gulshan and Khan-i Arzu (d. 1756), the 'four pillars of Urdu': Mir Taqi Mir (1724-1810), the love-poet, whose sighs still touch every heart, and who belonged to the close friends of Mir Dard, the mystic, who has in his turn written the most perfect Urdu mystical verses. Besides them we find the overpowering personality of Sauda (1713-1780), mainly praised as satirist, criticizing the social and political misery of 18th century India, but also an important religious poet of the Shiᶜa persuasion. The 'fourth pillar' is Mazhar Janjanan (c. 1700-1781). He was also a member and successful leader of the *Naqshbandi mujaddidi* school. Yet, more important for the history of Urdu literature than Mazhar is Mir Hasan (d. 1786) who, in his early youth, attended the poetical sessions of Mir Dard. He has gained fame by his *mathnawī Sihr ul-bayān* which, though not absolutely original in form or contents, is one of the loveliest products of Urdu narrative poetry, and whose atmosphere is somehow reflected in some of the miniatures from the later 18th century with their strangely bewitching style. Small wonder that the members of the Mughal court, long famous for its literary ambitions, became interested in Urdu poetry; the luckless Shah Alam II (1761-1806) wrote poetry under the penname *Āftāb*, 'Sun,' and attended the musical meetings of Mir Dard.

Delhi was also the place where three leading mystics lived and worked simultaneously, each of them claiming highest spiritual experiences, and trying in his own environment to ameliorate the situation of the afflicted Muslims of Northwest India. All of them were related in some way to the Naqshbandi order which, as we saw, was most influential among the poets, too. It is regrettable that we have barely any information about the relations among these three great masters, e.g., Shah Waliullah, Mazhar Janjanan, and Mir Dard. Among them Shah Waliullah has gained greatest fame as a reformer, as the translator of the Quran into Persian, and also as the politically minded leader of the community who did not hesitate to invite Ahmad Shah Durrani Abdali to fight the Mahrattas. Shortly after the third battle of Panipat, which took place in 1761, Shah Waliullah passed away in 1762, almost two decades before both Mazhar and Mir Dard. His political engagement has often overshadowed other aspects of his teachings, which are not easy to appreciate for a Western reader, since they are couched in a terminology very much his own, and which had to be explained by his grandson Ismail Shahid in a book called *'Abaqāt*. Waliullah's father, a Hanafi Jurist with mystical inclinations, had helped in the compilation of the *Fatāwā-yi 'Alamgīrī*. His young son, born in 1703, spent some time in Mecca, and returned to Delhi in 1730. For three decades he worked to help the Muslims of Delhi and all India by his writings and actions, for, as numerous revelations had told him, he had become the vicegerent of the Prophet 'in blaming.' Anything but modest, he claimed to have been granted the highest possible ranks in the religious hierarchy, and been taught *ḥikma*, wisdom, which is, in his theories, the last step before Prophethood: that he was promised to enter Paradise without reckoning is almost commonplace with later Muslim mystics. Shah Waliullah was certain that God had bestowed upon him the 'robe of *mujaddidiyya*' e.g., of renewing the Islamic faith and restoring it to its pristine purity, but he even claimed to have been invested with the robe of *ḥaqqāniyya*, the state of Divine Truth,[1] which deprived him of all logical understanding, so that he experienced 'how God talked upon my tongue.' His role as a 'blaming reformer'[2] is best expressed in a long address in which he scolds

---

[1]   At-tahfhīmat al-ilāhiyya II 53, 145.
[2]   Id. II 19.

the Muslims in holy anger: he attacks the scholars who have given up studying the Prophetic traditions but rather learn unnecessary things like grammar and Greek philosophy; the false Sufis; the perverted preachers; the kings who ought to fight for the extension, or at least the defense of Islam; the grandees who could not care less when wine shops, gambling dens or brothels are installed in the realm of their fiefs; soldiers who shave their beards and think only of amusements; artisans who indulge in drinking, adultery, and visits to allegedly sacred places, etc.[3] This piece, in its unusually straightforward language, shows best that Waliullah's interest lay in the purification of the Muslim community for a better life here, and even more in the Otherworld.

It is perhaps more than sheer accident that his main work in Arabic, *Ḥujjat Allāh al-bāligha*, was finished in 1740-41, shortly after Nadir Shah's invasion, that means, at the same time when Dard's father Andalib was composing his *Nāla-yi ʿAndalīb* in mourning Pir Muhammad Zubair, the last *qayyūm*. Shah Waliullah's attempts to bridge the gap between the different *madhhabs* in Islam, as well as the tension between the adherents of *waḥdat al-wujūd* and *waḥdat ash-shuhūd* can be understood from the situation in the country; in this respect he was a true mystical leader who relied upon the old Sufi maxim which is often quoted in his works:

> Our signs are different, but Thy beauty is one, and everything points to that Beauty.

Maulana Rumi's parable of the blind and the elephant was transformed by him into a story of blind men touching a tree, for truth is a big tree from which each person can grasp only one leaf, one branch, the bark, or one fruit. It was also this practical aspect of his teachings that led him to translate the Quran into Persian in order to bring people back to the original text, and avoid the useless study of too many commentaries which cover the sacred meaning rather than explain it. To live with the Quran, as it had been done by the Sufis of yore, was his ideal. A true Sufi has to live exclusively on the Quran and the Prophetic tradition. Therefore, he heavily attacks those Sufis who talk about 'what they think is truth,' seduce people by miracle mongering,

---

[3]   Id. I p. 281 ff.

and are nothing but *karāmāt furūshān*, 'sellers of miracles.' He sees in them the 'highwaymen and robbers of religion,' while his colleague Mir Dard uses the expression 'shopkeeper saints' for these characters, whom he even calls 'pig-natured.' The reformatory zeal of Waliullah leads him to even regard the Sufi books, 'which may have a wonderful effect on the elect, to be deadly poison for the ordinary people,' and would have liked to declare as infidels those who perform pilgrimages to sacred places: 'That is a sin, greater than murder and adultery.'[4] Utterances like this may be one of the reasons why the followers of his school were later often branded as 'Indian Wahhabis,' since the Wahhabis in the Arabian peninsula mercilessly destroyed all places of saint-worship.—Shah Waliullah tried to explain the secrets of religion in a way that is sometimes almost foreshadowing the 'naturism' of Sir Sayyid Ahmad Khan more than a century later. That is particularly true for his prophetology, where he now and then even explains miracles like the splitting of the moon (Sura 54/1) as a natural phenomenon. Prophecy, according to his view, shows itself in different ways by polishing the innate qualities of a people as beautifully as possible. The innate character of the nation is the raw material on which the Prophet works, be it a candle or a clot of earth. This kind of socio-geographical explanation of the various activities of the Prophets is for him also the reason why the mystical orders differ in their approach: the Turks, living in a cold climate, hence stronger in their 'bestial' powers, needed and indeed produced a *tarīqa* like the Naqshbandiyya, which is best for crushing the lower instincts.[5]

Shah Waliullah appears to us as a strange figure in the history of Islamic mysticism, combining great pride in his visions and his role as the true reformer of a rotten society with an extremely complicated web of thoughts, expressed in various linguistic means. He wrote poetry in Persian and Arabic, and a few verses in Urdu, his Arabic following the traditional models of devo-

---

[4]   Id. II 35. The text is interesting enough to deserve quotation:
   All those who go to Ajmer or to the tomb of Salar Mas⁽ ud or similar places for
· something they want from there: that is a sin, greater than murder or adultery.
   Is he not like someone who worships handmade things, or like those who called
   Allat and al-Uzza? But I cannot declare them clearly as infidels because there is
   no text from the lawgiver in this peculiar case.
[5]   Id. I 28-34.

tional verse, and his Urdu certainly not 'great poetry.' His many faceted character still awaits his biographers.

Waliullah's friend and colleague Mazhar Janjanan, who was highly respected in the Delhi community, and perhaps even better known to many of the pious in the capital, was a different character. This 'saintly, purified, dervish-like, scholarly, perfect, famous, incomparable person,' as Mir calls him, followed more closely the normal Naqshbandi line.

Born in 1699 in Agra as son of one of Aurangzeb's courtiers, Mazhar became the disciple of Nur Muhammad Bada'uni, a Naqshbandi saint, at the age of 18. His master was a disciple of Muhammad Ma^{c}sum's _khalīfa_. Then, the young man sought the instruction of Sa^{c}dullah Gulshan who, however, had entrusted his followers to Pir Muhammad Zubair, the _qayyūm_. Muhammad Zubair, in turn, sent Mazhar to Hafiz Sa^{c}dullah. Mazhar claimed also to be initiated, partly in _uwaisī_ succession, into the other orders. According to his own words, 'he began to sweep the dervish lodges at the age of thirty,' that is shortly after Gulshan's death in 1728.

Mazhar is recognized as one of the Four pillars of Urdu literature, although his output in Urdu is comparatively small. Everyone knows Sauda's remark about his 'mongrel' style, culminating in the Urdu proverb:

> It is the washerman's dog, belonging neither to the _ghat_ nor to the house!

But this satire may have been caused as much by rhetorical considerations as by religious prejudices, for Sauda, an outspoken Shia, naturally disliked the strictly anti-Shia attitude of Mazhar who followed, here, the ideals of the _Naqshbandiyya mujaddidiyya_. Mazhar went so far as to compose a defense of the Omayyad ruler Mu^{c}awiya, whose son Yazid is cursed by all Shiites as the murderer of the Prophet's grandson Husain in Kerbela; the Delhi mystic, however, wanted this just and successful ruler to be treated like any other companion of the Prophet. His uncompromising attitude even caused his death: at the age of 82 in 1781, he was killed when ridiculing a Muharram procession. Earlier in that century, Shah Waliullah too had protested against the celebrations of the Ashura Day, and although both Naqshbandi mystics were deeply attached to the Prophet and his family, they defended the view that the Sunnite faction is, for various reasons, the true form of Islam, whereas the Shia claims are vain (*bāṭil*).

Mazhar's letters addressed to his *khalīfa* Thana 'ullah in Panipat often deal with domestic problems, and with instruction in the path, but are much more sober and matter-of-fact than the high-flown words of both Waliullah and Dard. More than these two, Mazhar concentrated upon the leadership of his *tarīqa*, the Shamsiyya Mazhariyya, which seems to have flourished in Delhi and environment, for not less than 49 of his *khalīfas* are known by name. The stern Naqshbandi saint who was, in his youth, enraptured by the beauty of the young talented poet Taban, was extremely strict in keeping his ritual duties; he once remarks that one should pray not less than 60 *rakᶜas* (prayer units) during 24 hours; that is more than three times the prescribed number. His striving for perfection revealed itself in the fact that he married a perfectly intolerable woman in order to be polished by living with her; his letters sometimes point to his matrimonial difficulties.

It is interesting to see than Mazhar, his orthodox views notwithstanding, did not consider the Hindus as sheer *mushrikūn*, 'heathen,' but rather as followers of some sort of monotheism; but he, of course, maintained that Muhammad's revelation had put an end to all previous religions.[6]

Shah Waliullah and Mazhar seem to have been on friendly terms; some letters by the former reveal his admiration for his contemporary because of his faithful adherence to the Quran and the Prophetic tradition, and Mazhar used some of his colleague's writings in his instruction, as is understood from his letters. The relations were strengthened by Thana 'ullah Panipati who, besides becoming Mazhar's dearest spiritual successor, was Waliullah's disciple in *hadīth* and commented upon several of the master's treatises. Both mystics, too, admired and used ash-Shadhili's *Ḥizb al-baḥr*, to which Waliullah even wrote a Persian commentary: the famous prayer of the 13th century Egyptian Sufi belonged, for a long time, to the most cherished works of devotional literature, even in countries where the Shadhiliyya order itself had never taken deeper roots.

---

[6] Cf. Y. Friedmann's article 'Medieval Muslim Views of Indian Religions', in: JAOS 95/2, 1975.

It is difficult to judge the relations of Mir Dard with his two senior compatriots. He never mentions any of them by name in his writings, nor do they mention him or his father. Once, a friendly remark about Mazhar is found in a later source—'he recognized the light of saintliness in the face of one of Mazhar's disciples' (F 142)—and as much as the claims of Muhammad Nasir Andalib and his son Dard to represent the true Muhammadan Religion may have conflicted with Shah Waliullah's own claims, their *tariqa Muhammadiyya* remained important even after Dard's death, and was adopted by Shah Waliullah's grandson, Isma'il Shahid. Before detailed studies and comparisons of the three mystics and their theories are possible, one has to discuss them one by one. Their approach to life and religion is largely the same and can be summed up in a verse by Dard's father Muhammad Nasir:

> Strive to find the everlasting kingdom
> And that you'll find from the Muhammadan law (NA I 791).

All the three alike stressed the importance of the unmitigated Divine Law as the center of Muslim life; all the three attacked philosophy and fake Sufism, and refused to be called 'Sufis,' a term that had deteriorated during their days even more than before; all the three were poets in Persian and Urdu, and Waliullah also in Arabic—but while he has become the center of interest lately for his religious reforms and his political engagement, and Mazhar remains the model of a true Naqshbandi leader, Mir Dard, the youngest of them, is considered the most successful mystical poet in the Urdu language, and regarded himself as the elected leader of his community. It is he to whom we devote part of this study.

Ten years before Mazhar Janjanan, a man was born in the distant Indus Valley who was destined to become the greatest mystical poet in the Sindhi language. It is Shah Abdul Latif of Bhit (1689-1752) who died ten years before Shah Waliullah left this valley of tears.

Sind has always been praised as the country with a particularly strong inclination towards mysticism. A Sindhi author writes, and is the translator of the feelings of most of his compatriots:

> Sind has been flattened and has been in a state of negation. This is the
> cause of the many disadvantages from which it suffers; but it has been

also the cause of a great blessing, a great advantage of which other places in India cannot boast, something which is priceless in its value, something of which India is in need,[7]

namely, of the mystical tradition. From the day that Lal Shahbaz Qalandar settled in Sehwan in the 13th century, and Baha 'uddin Zakariya established the Suhrawardi center at the northernmost border of the country, in Multan, Sind had produced an immense number of mystics, whose shrines are scattered all through the Indus Valley, and who invented short songs in their mother tongue to express the mysteries of love and union. Perhaps the most typical story in this respect is that of Divan Gidumal, the minister of the Kalhoro princes, and his reaction to Ahmad Shah Abdali's invasion, which took place during Shah Abdul Latif's life time. He offered the invading monarch two bags which, as he said,

> contain the most valuable of Sind's gifts; they contain the holy dust from the tombs of numerous saints and Pirs of Sind.[8]

Sind was, since 1595, part of the Mughal Empire, and although representatives of the Delhi court came there, the indigenous rulers enjoyed much freedom. The first obvious sign of the struggle for power in the Lower Indus Valley becomes visible in 1717, when a mystical rebel was persecuted under the pretext that he tried to overthrow the established rule. The tragic story of Shah Inayat of Jhok, whose successful mystical preaching attracted many disciples from the mystical centers of the country, but also laborers from the neighboring big farms led his adversaries to denounce him at court; for during the confused situation in Delhi between the reign of Farrukh Siyar and that of Muhammad Shah it was easy to sow mistrust. The Kalhora clan from Upper Sind, particularly active in the struggle against Inayat, soon afterwards became independent in Sind. Shah Inayat was besieged in his Khanqah Jhok, and had to surrender to the overwhelming army that came from various places in Sind and Hind. He was executed in January 1718, and his fate has inspired many Sufi poets, Hindus and Muslims alike, to write touching poetry; he becomes 'the Hallaj of Sind' due to his death at the hands of the establishment,

---

[7] J. Parsram, 'Sind and its Sufis', p. 78 f.
[8] Id. p. 54.

and to his overwhelming mystical 'state.' It is possible that Shah Abdul Latif alluded to his fate in some of his verses; in any case he has quoted a Persian line usually connected with Shah Inayat.

At the same time, the 'Naqshbandi reaction' had set in in the Lower Indus Valley too, mainly led by Abu'l-qasim Naqshbandi, a follower of Ahmad Sirhindi's grandson Shah Saifuddin ibn Urwat al-Wuthqa Ma ͨ sum. By his disciples and friends, the first theological treatises in the Sindhi language are composed in the first half of the 18th century, beginning with the *Muqaddamat as-ṣalāt*, Preliminary discourse on Prayer, by Mian Abu 'l-Hasan (d. 1711). This treatise, written in 1700, deals with 130 questions concerning the ritual practices of Islam, and is the first major didactic poem in Sindhi. Of course, the rhyme-scheme is utterly simple, using the device of *alif-i ishbā ͨ* , which means the filling up of the last consonants with a long *a* so as to produce a rhyming effect. Here, Sindhi is for the first time written in the Arabic characters as they were to form, one and a half centuries later, the basis of the standard Sindhi alphabet as introduced by Sir Bartle Frere, and used up to our day in both India and Pakistan. Another prolific religious author in Sindhi was Muhammad Mu ͨ in, a mystically minded person; although he was a disciple of Abu'l-qasim Naqshbandi he was a great friend of Shah Abdul Latif, and it is said that he composed among others both a Persian *Risāla-yi uwaisiyya*, concerning the mystical introduction into the Path without the guidance of a living master: the initiation through the spirit of a deceased saint or through the Prophetsaint Khidr was considered valid in most Sufi circles. His Naqshbandi education did not prevent him from writing poetry in Persian (pen-name *Taslīm*) and Hindi (pen-name *Bairāgī*), and he loved music and mystical dance. That is why his works were attacked by his younger compatriot Makhdum Muhammad Hashim ibn Abdul Ghafur (1692-1761), the qadi of Thatta, which was still the center of the province of Sind. The Makhdum, who is buried on the famous Makli Hill near Thatta (the last resting place of 125,000 saints, as legend has it) was a prolific writer in Sindhi, Arabic, and Persian, and with the support of the Kalhora princes relentlessly fought against the innovations that had spoiled Islam in his days. Out of his more than 300 works some deal with popular customs exactly as those written by the great Delhi Naqshbandis, thus, when he attacks the Muharram celebrations, which were celebrated on Makli Hill. When he describes in his Sindhi poetry, *Qūt al-ʿāshiqīn*, the lofty qualities of the Prophet, he is exactly in line with his contemporaries in the capital. Commentaries of part of the Quran in Sindhi and of the whole Book in Arabic opened the way for his followers to comment upon and translate the Holy Writ into their mother tongue. Makhdum Hashim's Sindhi *Tafsīr Hāshimī* was usually the first book given to children in the Quran schools, and belongs to the first Sindhi books ever printed.

> In his time appeared so to speak a renovation of Islam, and every month some Hindus found salvation from the meanness of infidelity thanks to his laudable striving.[9]

Thus says the famous writer of Sindhi history, Mir Ali Shir Qaniʿ (1725-1789), who belonged also to one of the Naqshbandi families. His ancestors had reached the Indus Valley in the 16th century, coming from Shiraz. Qaniʿs work on the famous inhabitants of Sind (*Tuhfat al-kirām*), his biographies of poets (*Maqālāt ash-shuʿarā*) and his numerous works on the affiliations of Sindhi *ṭarīqas* show him as one of the most important writers in the Persian language in India during the 18th century. His *Maklīnāma* is probably the most charming account we possess about the famous Makli Hill near the capital; many of the buildings which are no longer existent, can be reconstructed from his remarks, and his notes about the festivities, the sessions of music and mystical dance, as they were held there in constant succession gives the modern reader a wonderful picture of popular mystical religion in 18th century Sind.

Another Naqshbandi mystic of Sind, and of quite a different formation, was Makhdum Abdur Rahim Girhori (1739-1778), the *khalīfa* of the famous saint Makhdum Muhammad Zaman who, in turn, was a disciple of Mian Abu 'l-qasim Naqshbandi and Mian Muhammad Thattawī. Girhori, contrary to the Naqshbandis of Thatta, was little interested in legal problems; the energetic man even threw an ink stand-at a scholar's head while attacking the 'dry trees of Makhdum Muhammad Hashim's school.' He completely relied upon Quran and tradition, and led a perfectly ascetic life, with long periods of fasting, which were made even more difficult since he used to take a purgative every third day.

---

[9] Qāniʿ, *Maqālāt ash-shuʿarā*, ed. H. Rashdi, p. 841 f.

Besides, he was a good writer who commented upon his master's Sindhi apophtegmata in Arabic, and composed poetical commentaries of several suras of the Quran. Most of his books were, however, destroyed during the Afghan raids in Upper Sind in 1781. Perhaps the finest expression of his mystical prophetology, which is in some way reminiscent of Dard's deep mystical love of the Prophet is his rhymed commentary on *Sūrat al-Kauthar*, the favorite theme of mystical veneration of the Prophet. A verse by him expresses also his admiration for Shah Abdul Latif, whom he may have met when still a child.

Girhori followed the truly mystical ideal of being killed on the way towards the beloved, as it was expressed in thousands of verses in Persian and Sindhi; but, for him, this longing took a particular form, e.g., he wanted to be a true martyr, shedding his blood for the defense of the true faith. Thus, he set out with 72 companions to destroy the Shiva idol in Hathungo, District Khairpur, and was killed there as he had hoped.

It would be wrong, however, to regard Girhori as a typical exponent of Sindhi Sufism. On the whole, there was 'a common basis of understanding, by Muslim and Hindu alike, of the mystical message of Islam,' as H. T. Sorley says correctly. To his analysis of the complex religious situation in 18th century Sind— which contains the 'almost incredible veneration for sayyids as such and a great accretion of superstitious practices in the belief of the multitude' we may add that the mystical understanding between the two great communities may perhaps have been facilitated by the activities of the Ismaili missionaries who came to Sind in the 14th and 15th centuries, after an Ismaili kingdom had existed in Multan around 900. Whatever the reason be that 'neither Hindus nor Muslims are orthodox in Sind'[10] and that still in the 1920's, there were 'numerous Hindus and amongst them some of the best brains of Sind, old and new, who are Sufi by religion'[11] —it remains a fact that a number of Hindus became devoted disciples of Muslim saints and did not hesitate to compose religious poetry in honor of Muslim saints and even of the Prophet of Islam. The most famous case is that of Shaikh Tahir, called by the Hindus Lal Udero, who is venerated by members of

[10]   Parsram, l.c. p. 75.
[11]   Id. p. 84.

both communities, and about whose ecstatic 'states' strange legends are told. [12] Shah Abdul Latif's admiration for the true Yogis belongs to this group of phenomena, and fits very well into the religious situation in the country.

Shah Abdul Latif was born into a family of mystics who lived near Hala; his father, Shah Habib, was a descendant of one of the first noted poets in his mother tongue, Shah Abdul Karim of Bulrri; about his mother's family the traditions are not unanimous. Yet, it is said that he (like Mir Dard) was a *sayyid*, his lineage going back to the seventh *imām* Mūsa al-Kāẓim. Shah Abdul Latif spent three years with a group of yogis, wandering through the country, up to the sacred mountain Hinglaj in Balochistan. [13] Later Latif settled in Bhit, where he died without issue in 1752, leaving behind him the collection of thirty Sindhi poems that has become known as the *Risālō*. That was the technical term for collections of poetry which are arranged according to the musical modes. Mir Ali Shir Qani[c] claims in his two major historical works that the mystical poet was *ummī*, 'illiterate;' but that is impossible to accept when one enters into the complicated web of thoughts displayed in the poems, and decorated with Arabic quotations, or allusion to Persian mystical poetry. Shah Latif was an excellent musician, who even invented a new type of tambura (drone instrument), and whose blending of traditional Indian *rāga* and Sindhi folk tunes enhances the beauty of his verses which ought to be sung, not analyzed, to enjoy their full charm.

Shah Abdul Latif's *Risālō*, written in Indian meters, contains a storehouse of legends, tales, and Sufi topics; but he never tried to rationalize or to systematize his thoughts, and it is not known that he should have written any theoretical statement about his mystical experiences. He lived his Divine love, and he sang of it—nothing else.

One of the Persian chronograms composed at his death and inscribed at the northern side of the dome says:

> When he became intoxicated by union from the goblet of 'Come back' (Sura 89/17).

---

[12]   About the 'complex religious history' of Sind see H. T. Sorley, 'Shah Abdul Latif of Bhit', p. 166, and Yusuf Husain, 'L'Inde Mystique', p. 15.

[13]   M. Jotwani has given as many biographical details as are available in his book, 'Shah Abdul Latif', New Delhi 1975.

> The hidden inspirer said: 'The year of his journey was *Ridwān-i Ḥaqq*,' (God's satisfaction) = 1165. [14]

Latif's tradition was taken up and developed by Sachal Sarmast (1739-1826), who met him when still a boy. His ecstatic poetry surpassed all limits of expression. In Shah's poetry, allusions and subtle images lead the understanding listener into the secrets of love, longing, and union; in Sachal's poems (he wrote in four languages: Sindhi, Siraiki, Urdu, and Persian) the mysteries of all embracing Unity are put openly before the listener, and his verse reminds the reader often of the enthusiastic folksongs by Turkish medieval mystics, like those of Yunus Emre (d. 1321).

Many more names of Sufis and poets could be enumerated when dealing with 18th century Sind so that Burton claims with full right in 1851:

> As regards the literature of the Sindhi tongue, it may safely be as-
> serted that no vernacular dialect in India, at the time of our taking the
> country, possessed more, and few so much, original composition. [15]

The problems of this part of the Subcontinent were almost the same as those that led to Delhi's breakdown: the collapse of the Mughal Empire after Aurangzeb's death, manifested itself in the internal struggle among the governors; eventually, the native Kalhoro dynasty took over the rule in Upper and later in Lower Sind, only to become the vassals of the invading Nadir Shah, who first conquered Sind and the Panjab before he reached Delhi in 1739. Almost the same situation repeated itself when Ahmad Shah Abdali invaded India, although his influence on the scene in Sind is not as important as it was in the northern areas of present day Pakistan. The Kalhoro dynasty, in turn, was overthrown by the former disciples of their saintly ancestor, Adam Shah Kalhoro, who had been executed by the central government in 1651. The Talpurs, who thus came to power in 1781, ruled the country until it was conquered by the British in 1843.

Just as the new spirit of Urdu poetry developed in 18th century Delhi, while the leading mystics looked for ways to lead their followers out of the darkness of the political situation, thus in Sind, too, the 18th century can be called the most important

---

[14]   Other chronogramms in Qāniᶜ, l.c. p. 428 f.
[15]   R. Burton, 'Sindh and The Races That inhabite the Valley of the Indus', p. 75.

period for the formation of mystical poetry and prose, and for the activities of many saintly persons whose works were meant to give spiritual nourishment to the suffering people. Thus, the 18th century, politically perhaps the most saddening phase of Indo-Muslim civilization, proves to be the most fertile period in terms of religious literature—very similar to the situation in the 13th century, when the larger part of the Islamic Empire was devastated by the Mongol hordes, and yet the greatest mystical poetry and theory was produced between Cairo and India: it is as though a strange balance of power produces such effects. Mir Dard would have seen here the constant interplay of the Divine manifestations of Wrath and Grace, which point, again, to The One; Shah Abdul Latif would have probably thought of the pearl which can be found in the very depths of the stormy, raving ocean, provided the oyster is patient.

KHWAJA MIR DARD OF DELHI

(1721-1785)

CHAPTER TWO

DARD'S LIFE AND TEACHING

Khwaja Mir Dard is buried in a small graveyard inside Delhi near Turkoman gate in what is now a slum area. Few people know the place, fewer visit it. And still, the man who has found his last resting place in this modest tomb was, in his time, one of the great mystical leaders of Delhi, and was, at the same time, the first to write mystical verse in Urdu. Those, who visit his tomb to recite a *fātiḥa* will probably more admire his poetical heritage than his achievements in mystical theology, but it is mainly the latter aspect of his work that concerns us here.[1]

For we have to remember that this influence worked under the surface upon the 19th century theologians of Delhi: Sir Sayyid Ahmad Khan was related through his mother to Dard; to trace these influences would be an interesting study that might contribute much to our knowledge of Indian Muslim revivalist movements.

EARLY YEARS

Towards the end of his life, Mir Dard wrote a chapter which sounds strange to a modern reader but reflects in a certain way some feelings of the Indian Muslims in the 18th century. Dard's contemporary Azad Bilgrami had tried to collect in his *Subḥat al-marjān* all those Prophetic traditions which pointed to Indian subjects, thereby proving that India is the real homeland of Islam, for Adam, the first in the line of prophets, came from

---

[1] Besides some articles by the present writer (see Bibliography) there are barely studies on Mir Dard available. The article by S. A. Bazmee Ansari in the EI, 2nd. ed., is valuable; Yusuf Husain Khan was the first to discuss Dard's theology in 'Glimpses of Medieval Indian Culture' at some length. In Urdu, Dr. Waheed Akhtar's study deals mainly with Dard's theology, and the long introduction into his *Urdu Diwan* by Khalil ur-Rahman Da'udi offers important material. Some of Dard's works are practically non-existent, like *Wāqi'āt-i Dard* and *Sōz-i dil*, which were published by the Matba'a Ansari from 1309/1891 onwards. Quite a number of manuscripts of Dard's poetry are available; the first edition was prepared in 1847 at the request of Dr. Alois Sprenger by Maulana Sahba 'i.

Paradise directly to Ceylon. Dard, however, finds another reason for the belief that his beloved country was blessed more than any other place by the sun of the Islamic religion, so that the traditional connotation of Hindustan, e.g., 'black,' or 'infidel,' as used since the Middle Ages in Islamic poetry and prose, was in his time no longer valid. He writes:

> True, other countries like ⁽ Iraq-i ⁽Arab and ⁽ Iraq-i ⁽Ajam are closer in distance to the radiant Medina than India and have been illuminated by the sun of Prophecy earlier due to their proximity, and this remained so as long as that Candle of Reality was shining in the visible world and the twilight of this sun (namely the time of the caliphs and the guiding imāms) lasted. But after the setting of this soul-enlightening sun from the visible horizon of humanity and the disappearance of its twilight from the eyes, India, which because of its outward distance, appeared like the dark night, became full of splendour from the light of this world-embracing sun thanks to the mirrorholding of the moon of the sphere of sayyidship and the Shah of the dynasty of the imāmat (namely the noble existence of the Exellence, the Prince of the Muhammadans) and thanks to the radiance of this moon which is the individuation (taᶜayyun) of the First of the Muhammadans, with strange subtlety of manifestations of Divine Beauty. Now, until the morning of Resurrection the spreading of the light of the spiritual bounty of the Muhammadan Path will firmly continue for the world and its inhabitants. And God and Muhammad are always Helper (Nāṣir) and friend, and everybody who has not found this light has, in fact, turned away his face from the Muhammadan light, for the light of the moon is taken from the light of the sun (D 275).

With these words, Dard introduces us to his theories about the ṭarīqa Muḥammadiyya which was founded by Muhammad Nasir, who was for him both real father and mystical leader, and to whom he owes his whole spiritual formation.

Khwaja Mir Dard's paternal family came, like many nobles, from Bukhara; they led their pedigree back to Baha 'uddin Naqshband, after whom the Naqshbandi order is named, and who was a descendant in the 13th generation of the 11th Shiᶜa imām al-Hasan al- Askari. Khwaja Muhammad Tahir reached Delhi in the 17th century. He was granted by Aurangzeb high offices; for the religious mentality had turned, at that point of history, in favor of the Naqshbandiyya; the time of 'intoxication,' the dream of a mystical religion which might bridge the gap between Hinduism and Islam was over; and the seed of Ahmad Sirhindi's teachings grew both in the Subcontinent and in Central Asia.

Khwaja Muhammad Tahir had three sons, two of whom married daughters of Aurangzeb's younger brother Murad. The third one, Khwaja Fathullah Khan (d. 1118/1707), married the full sister of Nawwab Sarbuland Khan, a *sayyid*, who was for a while Mir Bakhshi, Paymaster General.

Fathullah's son was Nawwab Zafarullah Khan, surnamed *Raushan ud-daula*, who played an important role in politics and war; and also swore allegiance to one of the leading members of the Chishti-Sabiri order, Miran Shah Bhik. He married the daughter of Sayyid Lutfullah ibn Sayyid Sher Muhammad Qadiri, and died of cancer, after a long and eventful life, in 1161/1748 at the age of 94 years. Among his children, Muhammad Nasir, born on 25. Shaʿban 1105/24.4 1691, played a decisive role. The chronogram of his birth is given as

> *wārith-i ʿilm-i imāmain wa ʿAlī*, the heir of the knowledge of the two Imams (i.e., Baha ʾuddin Naqshband and Abdul Qadir Gilani) and of Ali,

and he was a 'saint, possessed with a book' (K 137). Muhammad Nasir studied religious and profane sciences with his father and his grandfather (F 23). Then, like most sons of noble families, he joined the Imperial army, but apparently disliked the superficial life of the aristocracy. His descendant Firaq describes in his usual romantic style how the young officer would think of the thirst of the martyrs of Kerbela when he was offered delicious drinks, or would dream of the straw-mat of his ancestress Fatima when velvet and carpets were brought before him (F 23). He left the military service in the time of Muhammad Shah, i.e., after 1719, to devote himself to a religious life and perfect poverty, though we need not take too literally the detailed descriptions of his fasting and other ascetic achievements. As most members of the North Indian aristocracy, he was a Hanafi by creed, and adopted the *Naqshī mujaddidī ṭarīqa* (D 66), associating himself with two of its foremost leaders.

The feudal background of his education still looms large in the imagery of his main work, the *Nāla-yi ʿAndalīb*, which seems to consist, at least in some parts, of an autobiography: Its heroes are well versed in all those arts which were expected from a gentleman in later Mughal times: such as arrow-shooting, calligraphy, painting, and music (NA I 784), until they leave military service to become 'soldiers of God,' fighting the spiritual war against their lower selves (NA I 834).

Muhammad Nasir's masters in the Naqshbandi Path were Pir Muhammad Zubair and Shaikh Saʿdullah Gulshan.

Pir Muhammad Zubair was the fourth and last *qayyūm* in the family of Ahmad Sirhindi. The *qayyūm*, as he is described, 'is the dignitary upon whom the whole order of existence depends, and under whose control are all Names, Attributes, and things actual and potential. All things, whether they belong to the past, the present, or the future, up to the throne of God and the heavens with the signs of the zodiak are under his shadow. He is the vicar of God on earth.' 'The Absolute bestowes upon him a special essence, called *mauhūb*, given, on which depends the subsistence of the Universe.'[2] Even the *quṭb*, otherwise considered in Sufism to be the highest representative of the mystical hierarchy, is under his rule, nay, is his servant. Sirhindi's theory of *qayyū-miyya* surpasses by far the claims of most of the pantheistic mystics with the only, though important, difference that he does not speak, as did the pantheists, of *union* with God. Still, not many of the *wujūdī* mystics have claimed to be the depositary of Divine Mercy and to rule the universe. The second *qayyūm* was Ahmad's third son, Muhammad Maʿsum, surnamed *al-ʿUrwat al-Wuthqā*, to whom Prince Aurangzeb became attached. He is considered to be responsible for Aurangzeb's re-imposure of the *jizya* on the Hindus and to have been instrumental in forbidding music and *samāʿ*. Maʿsum's second son, Hujjatullah II, born in the year of Ahmad Sirhindi's death, 1624, followed him as third *qayyūm*; he, too, considerably influenced Aurangzeb. His grandson and disciple Muhammad Zubair, the fourth *qayyūm*, was born in 1093/1682; his birth was surrounded, like that of his ancestors, by miracles. He is credited with having uttered the profession of faith 'There is no God but God' 24,000 times during the 12 hours of the day; further, he repeated the name of God 15,000 times a day, retaining his breath according to the traditional Naqshbandi fashion. It is said (F 42) that these exer-

---

[2]   For the *qayyūm* cf. J. Subhan, 'Sufism,' and S. M. Ikram, 'Rūd-i Kauthar.' The Persian original of Ihsan's *Raudat al-qayyūmiyya*, the basic work about the development of the idea of the *qayyūm*, has not yet published; the ms. is found in the Library of the Asiatic Society of Bengal.

cises during his younger years resulted in a strong influence upon the Mughal rulers: after Aurangzeb's death in 1707, Pir Zubair sided with Prince Mu ʿazzam against Prince A ʿzam, the first-born son of the ruler. His protegee eventually succeeded in ascending the throne as Shah Alam Bahadur. Zubair probably continued playing an important role in the endless struggles and feudal strifes which caused the final disintegration of the Mughal Empire. Firaq's description (as usual, greatly exaggerated) tells how he was surrounded by large crowds when he rode through Delhi in pompous style, and how the princes spread velvet and brocade under his feet when he entered the Lal Qila. His death almost coincides with the breakdown of the Mughal Empire—he died in Dhu ʾl-Qaʿda 1152/Febr. 1740, not even one year after Nadir Shah had invaded India and pillaged Delhi where his soldiers killed about 30,000 citizens in a few hours. It is possible that some ideas which recur in Dard's work, especially those explaining the high spiritual rank of his father and the mystical graces bestowed upon himself, may have developed under the influence of some of the *qayyūmiyya* doctrines. But this assumption would need further clarification.

However, there was still another relation which impressed deeply Muhammad Nasir—perhaps even more deeply than the former one. It is his friendship with Shah Saʿdullah Gulshan, for whom he had an 'enthusiastic love.' The story that Gulshan did not accept Muhammad Nasir as disciple in mysticism but only in poetry because Nasir was superior to him due to his famous vision of Imam Hasan is historically incorrect, for Shah Gulshan died in 1728, and Muhammad Nasir's vision took place only in the mid-thirties (cf. F 34 f.).

Shah Gulshan, 'Rosegarden,' is known in Urdu literature as the mystic-poet whose fame attracted the Dakhni poet Wali Deccani to Delhi shortly after 1700 and thanks to whose influence Urdu became the fashionable language for writing poetry. Shah Gulshan, son of Khwaja Muhammad Saʿid (1005/1596-1080/1669), was a disciple of Bedil (d. 1721), notorious for the intrinsic difficulties of his poetry, and it is said that Bedil granted his pen-name to him. He was likewise a friend of the great poet Nasir Ali Sirhindi (d. 1696) who entered, in his later life, the Naqshbandi order to which Shah Gulshan was affiliated for a long time. Gulshan said of him that 'he was of melancholy temperament,

and beat the drum of 'I', and nothing else.' Shah Gulshan himself
is described by Dard as follows:

> He had a strange combination of outward and spiritual perfections,
> and his renunciations and solitude as well as his poetry and his virtues
> are so famous that everybody knows them. He has (composed) almost
> 200,000 verses, was a pilgrim to Mecca, and understood the science of
> music perfectly—in fact, he was a real Rosegarden of the roses of
> perfection (A 257).

But it seems that the poet-saint had also a good sense of humor
and though some miracles are attributed to him one of his biographers holds that he could not always stand the 'Divine moments' and therefore mostly devoted himself to poetry. Among
Gulshan's disciples we may mention the Hindu Bedraban Khush-
gu, the author of a useful collection of biographies, *Safīna-yi
Hindī*, further Farhat Kashmiri (d. 1138/1726) and Maimanat;
but his fame rests mostly upon his relation with Wali Deccani and
Muhammad Nasir Andalib.

The name *'Andalīb*, 'Nightingale,' was given to the young
Naqshbandi mystic by Shah Gulshan, and

> his guidance was spread in the world by Andalib, and the uproar of his
> spring reached everybody's ear through the Lamentation of the Night-
> ingale (*Nāla-yi 'Andalīb*, Muhammad Nasir's famous book).
> If this painful one (or: Lord of Dard, i.e., Muhammad Nasir) had not
> expressed such lamentations, who would have listened to the story of
> the rose and the nightingale? (A 257).

Shah Gulshan himself had been the disciple of the Naqshbandi
mystic Abdul Ahad Miyan *Gul*, 'Rose,' with the pen-name *Wahdat*, 'Unity' (d. 1126/1714), a grandson of Ahmad Sirhindi, who
lived in Kotla Firuzabad in Old Delhi and left a small collection
of poems. That is why Dard often inserts into his verses puns like
this:

> *Dard* (Pain) has so much become the *Nightingale* of the *Rosegarden* of
> *Unity*
> That the manifestation of the face of the *Rose* made him *ghazal*-sing-
> ing ...

Shah Gulshan died of diarrhea in Muhammad Nasir's house on
21. Jumada II 1140/3. Febr. 1728, when Dard was 7 years old.

Muhammad Nasir had married twice. His first wife bore him
one son, Mir Muhammad Mahfuz, and died soon. Mir Dard relates

that this brother was full of tenderness and guided him on the right path until 'he put the scar of separation on his heart' and died on 16. Rajab 1154/Sept. 1741 at the age of 29. Muhammad Nasir's second wife, Bakhshi Begum, called Manga Begum, (F 106) was the daughter of a prominent member of the family of Abdul Qadir Gilani, Sayyid Muhammad Husaini Qadiri ibn Nawwab Mir Ahmad Khan, called Mir Umda (F 30). This Sufi died on 2. Jumada II 1156/25.7.1743, at the eve of the celebration of an ⁽urs for his late wife, when a large number of noble guests had assembled in his house.

At the time of Muhammad Nasir's second marriage, the whole family lived in a suburb of Delhi, close to a place later called Barafkhane, outside of Shahjahanabad proper. Muhammad Nasir's father's stables and private houses were located in this area, and most of the pious people preferred to live there instead of staying in the city. A little canal watered the area; that is why it was called *Barāmda kī nāla*.

Here, Khwaja Mir, poetically surnamed Dard, was born on 19. Dhu 'l-Qa⁽ da 1133/13.9.1721.

Another son, born about ten years later, Sayyid Mir Muhammadi, who had shown remarkable signs of holiness already in his childhood, died on 5. Rabi⁽ II 1163/15.3.1750 at the age of 19. The youngest brother, Khwaja Muhammad Mir, with the pen-name *Athar*, 'Result,' was Dard's most faithful friend, companion and disciple in mysticism and poetry, and succeeded him after his death in the leadership of the order. He must have been born after 1740.

Mir Dard sometimes expresses a touching longing for his deceased brothers. He has also several times talked about the names he was given (K 84): Since the descendants of Baha 'uddin Naqshband are called 'Khwaja' and those of Abdul Qadir Gilani 'Mir,' his parents gave their first-born simply a combination of these two epitheta, calling him Khwaja Mir. Later he acquired the pen-name *Dard*, 'Pain.' Thus, he addresses himself in a soliloquy:

> You have been called Dard not because you should become pained by the pain of things besides God but because you should be completely exempt from corporeal pain and get the pain of the heart which is the means of salvation in both worlds; thus never act in negligence without pain, and become a remedy for all the servants of God ... (D 2).

The connection of his pen-name with those of his father and
Shah Gulshan is clear: the lamentation of the *Nightingale* in the
Rosegarden causes *Pain* in the heart, and this pain should become
the main subject of his poetry:

> For top to bottom 'Pain' rains from the word of our Khwaja Mir
> (P 15);

or:

> Our heart and breast are selling the roses of the scar of friendship—
> Our shop does not contain anything except Pain (P 7).

He also talks about his mystical names (see p. 83 f). Mir Dard's
greatest source of pride was the fact that he was a *sayyid* from
both sides. (Even today Indian *sayyid* families may consider
themselves as absolutely superior to any other human being and
will tell the visitor how fortunate he is to touch the threshold of
a descendant of the holy Prophet.) In this connection he liked to
refer to Abdul Qadir Gilani's verse:

> The suns of the first generations have set, but our sun
> Is eternally on the highest horizon and never sets (K 459).

The *sayyids*, children of Fatima, to which both of his parents
belonged were elected before all people and possessed the special
grace which God had bestowed upon their ancestor Muhammad.
And

> again after 1100 and odd years this special grace became visible from
> the interior fountain of (my father), the true *sayyid* and most true
> leader, the world illuminating sun of the sphere of sayyid-ship, the
> greatest luminary of the heaven of sanctity, the heir of the office of
> prophetic perfections, the vicegerent of Divinity, the master of the
> prayer-mat of proximity of the imāmat, the place of manifestation of
> the Muhammadan light, the master of the divine law, he who has
> attained Divine Truth, the expert of the path, the revealer of gnosis,
> the lord of divine wisdom, the protector of the nation of Mustafa, the
> enterprising one, the man of high rank, who is made indigent by
> Divine Greatness, the strength of the Naqshbandi and Qadiri progeny,
> who increased the Muhammadan path in value, the helper (*nāsir*) of
> the prophetic religion, the venerable Khwaja Muhammad Nasir
> Muhammadi ...

who unveiled all the mysteries of faith to his children and made
them, thus, both his external and real, i.e., spiritual, sons
(K 419).

Besides the numerous allusions to the high qualities of his father, Dard sometimes goes into details describing him. He constantly saw him before his eyes and tried to imitate the way how he acted with God and with human beings, for he belonged to that class of masters of spiritual conversation (those with 'living hearts') 'without meeting whom the whole spring of your life is autumn' (K 635). This spiritual conversation, ṣohbat, is regarded in the Naqshbandi tradition as one of the most important facets of mystical life. On the other hand it has deeply influenced the whole culture of Muslims in the later Middle Ages so that Mughal culture has been even called a 'culture of refined conversationalism.' To listen to the master, to be guided by his words, and to learn how to behave properly, to understand the hierarchy of values and the spiritual hierarchy among human beings was one of the most important educational contributions of the Naqshbandi order, rather of the mystical fraternities in general to Muslim cultural life. Not in vain uses Mir Dard in his writings the word bī-adab, 'without etiquette, ill-mannered,' as an expression of deepest abhorrence.

The story that he even rebuked the Mughal emperor Shah Alam II who attended his mystical gatherings, because he did not completely conform to the etiquette by stretching out his aching leg, shows the importance he attributed to the rules of behavior. The perfection of adab to the highest degree was revealed to Dard in his father—the perfect inward beauty of Muhammad Nasir was reflected in his outward beauty (A 73) so that everybody who saw him became bewildered, and people came to kiss his feet when he rode on horseback through the streets of Delhi, whether they knew him or not. The quality which particularly impressed him was his father's capacity to practice khalwat dar anjuman, 'solitude in the multitude,' a very important practice among the Naqshbandis, though, as a mystical attitude, mentioned in the earliest Sufi biographies. It means that the spirit of the mystic rests so completely in God that it cannot be disturbed by those who seek his company and guidance:

Though the door of guidance and the gate of visits for the sincere friends was permanently open, he used to sit constantly in the nest of 'solitude in the multitude;' and though he never became careless in his works of obedience and worship and did not neglect for a moment his supererogative prayers and the reading of the Quran and dhikr and

litanies (aurād), still he was a workshop, composing books and keeping conversation with his friends, and fulfilled the duties towards
those who were entitled to them; and though his body was outwardly
weak and frail, his inner strength and spiritual power was perfect to
such a degree that he was never and absolutely not affected by any
disrupture in the times of his sitting and getting up and in any part of
his daily routine (K 636).

Mir Dard claims that he was interested in religious problems
already in his early childhood—small wonder when we recall the
atmosphere of his paternal house, full of poetry and mystical
love. He may have been three or four years old when he was
puzzled, as many children of this age, by the question of his own
existence. But he (of course, in a back-projection which is typical
of old age) sees here already the specific religious interest which
was to characterize him throughout his life. That is why he describes his state of mind and tells how he was grasped by the
longing to swim in the ocean of Reality when he could scarcely
talk. Firaq, as usual, embellishes the story with touching details
and dates it back to Dard's second year (F 116 f.). Dard himself
tells how he spent most of the nights awake, and cried until his
nurse and the other servants became perplexed and worried and
tried all kinds of remedies on him. But he did not speak nor
answer any questions, until his 'noble mother,' his grandmother,
and his paternal aunt gathered and discussed the matter, thinking
that some misfortune might have befallen the child, or that he
might be afraid of something in sleep; tenderly they blew prayers
and four qul (Sura 112) upon him (even today it is common to
utter some prayers and 'breathe' over the sick part of the body).

> But when nothing worked they eventually brought the story to the
> blessed ears of the Venerable Qibla of the Worlds (i.e., his father), and
> that manifestation of Divine Mercy came down, and when I saw the
> perfect beauty of the Pir and leader towards truth, I jumped impa-
> tiently like mad from my bed, run about and rubbed my head and
> eyes on his necessarily fortunate feet and cried bitterly without con-
> trol. And I lamented: 'O venerable father, my breast is so narrow, and
> involuntarily tears come and come. I wish that the truth should be
> discovered unto me so that my heart may find consolation, for I do
> absolutely not understand the depth of my own reality—who I am and
> why have I been born and why do I live and whence, and where, and
> who is my creator, and the creator of all those things, and what is the
> goal of this creation?'

His father then slowly began to introduce him into mystical theology, and in this moment the close relation between father and son began, a relation which lasted as long as Mir Dard was alive, and waxed stronger day by day even after his father's death. The problem, however, 'Who am I?' never ceased occupying his mind, and he recurred to this question even in his last verses, his last sighs (see. p. 97 f.).

Mir Dard must have been busy studying the different branches of science (including Rumi's *Mathnawī*):

> In the middle of my youth I studied the formal sciences such as fundamentals of faith, and logics, and elements of law, and Sufism, and others as much as necessary, but I did not rub my foot in this path like the Mollas who cling to the husk, or the Sufis who do not understand and not see, for I did not leave that goal from my hand unless I understood it well, nor did I lift my foot from that place unless I could see it in details ... (D 216).

He did not become a *ḥāfiz*—but:

> God threw upon my heart clear signs (*āyāt*) though I do not know the Quran by heart (K 65).

It must have been during this period that his father was granted a revelation which was destined to reform Muslim mysticism. Dard tells in the *ʿIlm ul-kitāb* (85) that his father

> remained silent for seven days and nights and never turned to this world of humanity and did nothing of the necessities of human nature, like eating and drinking and the like, and remained lonely in his cell. We young boys attended the place at the time of ritual prayer so that he might lead us—but if I should write what events happened to us servants in those days when every time the door of the cell remained closed ... Then I fell alone on that threshold and lay down day and night on that floor and cried silently, bitterly, and did absolutely not turn to eating and drinking. Only once, on the command of the venerable mother who ordered me to be taken into her room and ordered me to eat in her presence I ate, forcing myself, a few mouthfuls for the sake of obeying her, and rushed again towards the cell, and the other family members and servants came at the time of prayer and then went to their own places. But I remained there, fallen on the floor, as much as my mother did not like that I remained there alone and downfallen, and was very agitated and ordered some men to remain close to me; but I did not allow anybody to come closer. And the bedspreads and cushions and whatever she sent I never used. And involuntarily I slept a bit ...

But when God eventually on the eighth day sent Muhammad
Nasir back to the world of humanity and he found his son in this
desperate state,

> the ocean of forgiveness became extremely agitated and the breeze of
> acceptance blew intensely, and he took me with his noble hand from
> the ground and embraced me full of grace and tenderness and kissed
> my forehead and kindly said many words of good tidings about me,
> which even now do not come unto my tongue ...

Mir Dard then asked his father about his experiences and was
introduced into the secrets which had been entrusted to him.
Thus he was the first to offer allegiance to this new path which
Muhammad Nasir gave to the world. He asked him how to name
the new *tariqa*, but his father answered:

> If my intention had been such, I would name the *tariqa* after my own
> name, as the others do. But all of us are children, lost in the sea of
> identity and drowned in one ocean. Our name is the name of Muham-
> mad, and our sign is the sign of Muhammad. Our love is the love of
> Muhammad and our claim is the claim of Muhammad. One must call
> this order the *tariqa Muhammadiyya*, the Muhammadan path. It is
> exactly the path of Muhammad, and we have not added anything to
> it. Our conduct is the conduct of the Prophet, and our way the
> Muhammadan way.

And thus, Dard writes 35 years later:

> Though this servant, who is less than a straw in his own view, is not
> more than a weak grass in the rosegarden of the Muhammadan path,
> yet the grace and acceptance of my venerable master Andalib has
> made this nothing more than all and made him the First of the
> Muhammadans, and the top-rose of the bouquet—and what sorts of
> favor did he open and what kind words did he say about me, the
> rebel ... (D 254).

The saintly spirit who had descended upon Muhammad Nasir
was that of the Imam Hasan, the grandson of the Prophet (K 85),
(who is, by the way, also regarded as the first *qutb*, 'Pole' in the
Shadhiliyya order). In Firaq's romanticizing account of this event
he addressed him, saying: 'My dear grandfather has sent me spe-
cially to you so that I may fill you completely with interior
knowledge and sanctity' (F 26). This story is taken from Athar's
Mathnawi about the family-saga. Dard became, thus, 'the threshold of the Muhammadan court,' or, with an expression usually
used for the relation between the Prophet and Ali ibn Abi Talib,

'the door of the town of knowledge' (K 587). Since the *tarīqa Muhammadiyya* is the focal point in Muhammad Nasir's main work, which was written in 1740, the event must have taken place sometime in the mid-thirties of the 18th century. Firaq is certainly right when he gives Dard's age at this event as being 13 years, but we doubt that the boy's fame as a saint immediately after his allegiance to his father was miraculously made known to the inhabitants of Delhi, and that he performed his first healing miracle the very next day (F 32).

The first fruit of Dard's new interest in religion is his booklet *Asrār as-salāt*, 'Mysteries of Ritual Prayer,' which he composed at the age of 15 during his seclusion in the month of Ramadan.

Shortly afterwards, at the age of about sixteen, Khwaja Mir Dard got married to a young lady of twelve (whose name, however, is not given by the sources; F 187), for, as his father says, 'a married dervish will be a hundred times superior to a single dervish' (NA I 895).

A number of later biographies mention that Mir Dard served temporarily in the Imperial army, but that may be due to a confusion of his and his father's biographies, for neither he himself, nor Firaq specify his occupations. He only says:

> A long time in my youth, as a consequence of youth and the strength of animal powers I had in my heart the search for natural and fleshly appetites and the wish of passion to gratify my desires; and a short while I was in the dress of wordly-mindedness and in the position of a man of the world; and when I began some work I looked up the lucky and unlucky days and in a certain way hoped from the sky for help. And since my mind was negligent and I was ignorant of the heart of the matter I kept my eye on things which came from the time-servers, and waited for the rise of wordly degrees and the gaining of my imagined goal which the people of this world carve in their heart. And whatever we possessed—*jāgīr* and high office—I considered a royal fortune. I tried to recommend myself to the great *amīrs* of the Emperor and those who were close to the ruler ... (K 473).

At the time of Nadir Shah's invasion, when Delhi was sacked in March 1739, Aurangzeb's daughter-in-law, Mihrparwar Begum offered shelter to Muhammad Nasir and Mir Dard, for she was afraid lest the houses outside the rampart suffer even more than the imperial town. The mystics, however, refused the offer, and 'thanks to the Muhammadan banner and the benevolence of Nasir' their place in *Barāmda kī nāla* remained outside the reach

of the looting soldiers. Nevertheless, they eventually accepted the
renewed invitation, and the princess built a nice compound for
them, comprising of houses, a mosque, a meditation room and a
large space for musical gatherings, the meetings for the celebration of ʿurs, and gatherings of poets. This compound in Chēluñ
kā kūcha remained in the hand of Dard's family for a long time;
its last traces disappeared after partition.

A few months after the fall of Delhi an event took place which
drew Mir Dard still closer to his father. It was the death of
Muhammad Nasir's spiritual guide, Muhammad Zubair, in Feb-
ruary 1740. Muhammad Nasir—as he states himself—had at that
time

> hoped to express a number of subtleties of the religious law like the
> rituals of pilgrimage into which not everybody's understanding can
> enter,

in an understandable way, but the news of his master's death
deeply shocked him. When his friends came for a condolence
visit, he

> told this story in Hindi language during three nights to them, and
> thanks to the Divine influence all those who listened to it were deeply
> impressed and started crying and weeping ...

Some of them even became enraptured and fell in ecstacy on the
ground, and many of them entered the ṭarīqa Muḥammadiyya.
The story which Andalib told to his friends in the language of
Delhi, 'Hindi' or 'Urdu,' was later on elaborated 'without difficulty in the Persian language.' In noting it down, Mir Dard was
his father's assistant, as Andalib states:

> And the happy and fortunate Khwaja Mir who is my middle son (and
> verily, about him the word 'The best things are those in the middle'
> came true) took paper and pen into his right hand and sat besides me
> and wrote down letter by letter (NA I 3).

At rare occasions Bedar, one of Andalib's disciples in poetry
served as secretary instead of Dard. The book which came thus
into existence, and comprises in its present print two volumes of
more than 900 pages folio size each, was completed in
1153/1741. It was called Nāla-yi ʿAndalīb, 'The Lamentation of
the Nightingale,' and its chronogram is formed from the words
nāla-yi ʿandalīb gulshan-i māʾst, 'The Lamentation of the Night-

ingale is our Rosegarden' (pun on the name 'Gulshan', Andalib's mystical master). It is an allegorical story of rose and nightingale, the representatives of love and beauty. (The story itself begins, though, only after ca. 600 pages). This traditional topic of many Persian and Urdu poems is elaborated in high Persian prose, and interspersed with many poems. As in most of these allegories one story develops out of the other, and again, wise words form the quintessence of the stories. The whole machinery of traditional Indian tales is mixed with allusions to Mughal history: there is the pious king and the wise merchant, 'Jupiter' and 'Sun,' musicians and dancers, the Hindu ruler converted to Islam, rebellion in the Deccan, white elephants and hunting parties; but every allegory is meant to explain the 'pure Muhammadan Path,' the 'behavior of the Muhammadans' (NA I 813). The nightingale, eventually, emerges as a symbol of the Prophet of Islam (NA II 712), who had so often been called by pious poets the 'nightingale of the higher spheres'. The stories are interspersed with detailed theological discussions, thus about the various schools of Sufism (NA I 789 ff., 882 f.) and the different *madhhabs* of Islam or Shiʿa imamology (NA II 583). Long paragraphs about the minutest details of ritual purity (Na I 446-49), fasting (NA I 842, II 217) and other problems do not lack. Dard's antipathy against the representatives of the theories of *waḥdat al-wujūd* can be understood from his father's attacks against this group of Sufis (cf. NA I 622, 797, 808 and more). Muhammad Nasir, however, is not as critical of Hallaj's famous word 'I am the absolute Truth' as his son; in fact, he even uses it in a charming story of an enamored gazelle who imagines himself to be a human being and calls 'I am a man' just as Mansur called 'I am God' (NA I 132).

Sometimes Andalib inserts Hindi *dhōras* into the story, and of special interest for the historian of religions are his allusions to Hindu philosophy and Hindu customs. He thus discusses in detail Yoga practices, which he considers to be a remarkable achievement but they are, of course, much inferior to the experiences the pious Muslim can reach through meditation, and by attaching himself completely to the Prophet.

For the Western reader who may enjoy some of the charming allegories, it is not easy to understand why Mir Dard called his father's work 'the billowing of the Divine wisdom ... inspired from God' (K 38). For the young mystic this 'excellent book' which he had heard word for word from his venerated father's mouth became, eventually, the only source of inspiration, as he often repeats:

> My gnostic knowledge (*'awārif*) and my learning do not come from reading the *'Awārif* [Suhrawardi's famous handbook on Sufism] and my knowledge of the realities exists not because of (Ibn Arabi's) *Fusūs* and *Futūhāt*—it is only from the abundant grace of the book *Nāla-yi 'Andalīb* that the door of all realities and subtleties was opened for my ignorant heart and I became part of the act, 'And we have taught him a knowledge from what is with us' (Sura 18/65) (D 216),

This book changed him completely, so that he gave up outward sciences. All the

> pictures of what is besides God became extinguished from my breast and always the cry 'O Nasir (helper), o Nasir' was in my heart and tongue, and my state and word are completely conformed to the *Nāla-yi 'Andalīb*, nay, even more, I am the speaking book of the sincere Muhammadans ...
> I read neither the *'Awārif* nor the *Futūhāt* or *Fusūs*
> The *Nāla-yi 'Andalīb* became my special litany;
> God made me a sincere Muhammadan—
> In me there is nothing, but sincerity (K 90)

Dard always acknowledges the superior merit of the *Nāla-yi 'Andalīb*, and even 'bent from age, the foot in the stirrup,' each sigh of his is 'O Nasir, o Nasir' (A 35). Muhammad Nasir himself considered this book to be the plain exposition of the Muhammadan Path, 'full of longing for the beloved,' but still, he thought it necessary to explain its narrative contents as allegorical with the classical simile 'lion'—'man':

> If, for instance, somebody calls a brave man in praising him a lion, nobody will look for claws and tail in him (NA II 900),
> and love of the idol is only a symbol of being caught by the love of the lightful and shapeful manifestation of the Lord (NA II 902).

The fact that Andalib tried to interpret his own poetry (which strictly follows classical imagery) is echoed in Mir Dard's numerous sentences about the relation between reality and poetry, and of poetry and mysticism. Andalib was absolutely certain that his book was extremely valuable, and recommended it for *tafā 'ul*, 'future-telling' (NA 902); his son, even more, stressed the divine quality of the *Nāla* (K 434) which yields marvellous predictions of the future (that is also true, as he held, for his own magnum opus, the *'Ilm ul-kitāb*). The modern reader will find, in its sweet style tinged with melancholia, a strange reflection of the vicissitudes of time under which Delhi and its unlucky inhabitants smarted in those years. Firaq recalls from his childhood (F 89) that the *Nala-yi 'Andalib*, whose original manuscript was destroyed during the Mutiny 1857, used to be read to the members of the family: the ladies, all acquainted with Persian, told their children the touching stories of the Rose and the Nightingale until they were able to understand their deeper meaning. It is surprising, though, that Mir Dard never mentions his father's second book, still extant in manuscript, e.g., the *Risāla-yi hūsh-afzā*, a book on 'mystical chess' which Muhammad Nasir composed to distract some of his disciples from chess playing: chess symbolism was common in Persian and Urdu poetry before him, and he has tried to explain the different events of human life in the terminology of chess (F 91), as his son, too, did later in his prose and poetry.[3]

If we believe Firaq, Muhammad Nasir must have invented a number of strange things (F 92), like the 'wandering tent,' and the 'bath for everywhere,' and the 'candle without tears' and similar items. His famous cane, called *an-Nāṣirī*, with the word Nasir engraved in it in an artistic *tughrā*, was for a long while in the family. Later, this peculiar type of *tughrā* was used by the members of the family for the sake of blessing (M 93 f).

Dard claims that, for a while in the blossom of his youth, he 'made run the mount of negligence in the arena of passion and lust,' but

> youth was still there when I drew off my hand from this passing and unstable world, and at the age of 29, I put on the garment of the dervishes ... (N 289).

---

[3] The imagery of chess was widespred in Persian poetry, the most famous example being a verse in Khāqānī's (d. 1199) *qaṣīda* on Mada'in/Ktesiphon. Andalib's *Risāla-yi hūshafzā* is found in the Library of the University of the Punjab, Lahore, written in a rather illegible *shikasta*. Andalib himself has used the chess imagery quite often, thus NA I 42, I 526:

Without fraud one cannot proceed in the chess of time:

The king must go sometimes crooked, sometimes straight.

In NA I 654 all technical terms of chess are used to express full obedience to the beloved's order. Dard, too has several verses in this style; in N 114 he builds up a paragraph on the imagery of *nard*, backgammon.

That was in 1750, two years after the lascivious king Muhammad Shah had died at the age of forty-five, and his son Ahmad Shah, addicted likewise to pleasure, followed him on the throne. The Mughal empire had broken into pieces—the Deccan, Oudh, the Rohillas in the Doab, the Bangashs at Farrukhabad did no longer recognize the central power; the Mahrattas controlled large territories, the Jats were virulent in Agra and its environments, and Sikh threatened the Panjab. The civil war between the rival wazirs Safdar Jang of Oudh and the young, ruthless Imad ul-Mulk in 1753 'when the two cities of Delhi were held by the rival factions and fighting went on ... for six months, paralysed the Empire ...' And Nadir Shah's successor, Ahmad Shah Durrani, invaded the Panjab several times, coming from his native Afghanistan. The useless king of Delhi was eventually deposed and blinded by his vizier and Alamgir II was put on the throne in 1754.

A certain period of alleged 'worldliness' notwithstanding Dard was not too much interested in things outside the path, and even before officially joining his father's *tarīqa* he devoted himself to the service of the convent, as he tells later (N 49):

> My disposition has been, from the beginning, such that never any wordly work came from me, and I was and still am completely inexpert in these things. But before, I was engaged for a while according to my own opinion in the affairs of the other world; and with pretention I served the brethren of the path and exercised the path and the writing down of a book and tried to be useful to people and to sweep the court of the 'Qibla of both worlds' and in the instruction and education of brethren and children and completion of assemblies and invitations of people and showing the people the way as far as I could ... But now I am by grace without reason exclusively drawn by special attention and brought to such a station that I am only the mirror-holder of 'God does what He wants and orders what He willeth' and traverse the road of 'And you do not want unless God wants,' for I have no longer remained myself that good or evil could appear from me, or something come out of my will.

Dard followed his father not only in the mystical path but also participated in the assemblies of poets which were frequently held in Delhi. He studied poetry with Khan-i Arzu, the 'Aristotle of Urdu literature' in the early 18th century. The mosque *Zīnat al-masājid*, built by Aurangzeb's daughter, Zinat un-Nisa, was a favorite place where mystical poets used to meet. In this mosque Muhammad Nasir Andalib, faithful to Shah Gulshan's instructions, used to arrange a *mushāʿira* (meeting of poets) on the 15th day of every month, his son accompanying him. During the sessions, he became friendly with the future master of Urdu love-poetry, Mir Taqi Mir, who was a few years junior to him. Mir himself tells in his *Nikāt ash-shuʿarāʾ* that Andalib had foretold him that he would become *mīr majlis*, 'master of the assembly,' and these words proved true. After Andalib's death, the organization of *mushāʿiras* was disrupted and Mir asked his friend Dard for the permission to continue the tradition, which permission was granted. Mir Dard himself took part in these meetings until they came to a close due to the political events which almost completely paralyzed the cultural life of Delhi.

It happened during these years, between Dard's entering the order and his father's death (1749 to 1758) that he was granted a number of inspirations. They were Persian verses and short sentences of wisdom in concise rhymed prose called *wāridāt*, 'things coming.' The genre of *wāridāt* is quite common among Muslim mystics, who feel that their words have been inspired by God; cases of 'inspired' writing in Turkey happen even today. Mir Dard had the opportunity to read these *wāridāt*—111 in number—to his father who very much appreciated them.

On the 'worldly' scene it was the time when the Afghans and the Mahrattas met in the Delhi plains, when Delhi was looted once more in 1757, this time by the Afghan 'friends;' two years of Ahmad Shah Durrani's military activity eventually culminated in the third battle of Panipat 1761, Jan. 6. The Mughal Emperor Alamgir II was assassinated in 1759 by Imad ul-Mulk; his heir had already flown to the eastern provinces of India where he reigned in exile under the title of Shah Alam II, and was recognized, in 1761, by Ahmad Shah Durrani, the victor of Panipat. In Delhi, the able Rohilla chief Najib ud-Daula was left in charge of the kingdom.

Muhammad Nasir Andalib died on 2. Shaʿban 1172/2.4.1759 and was buried in the graveyard near Turkoman Gate at a place which the Prophet himself had indicated to Mir Dard (F 96), for, as the quatrain on his tombstone says:

> He was the foot-print of the Lord of 'If thou hadst not been' (e.g., Muhammad).

Dard's close relation with his father is expressed in a daring
Arabic pun on letters in the beginning of the *ʿIlm ul-kitāb*:

> Praised be God who helped (*naṣara*) his servant and made him now the
> dot of the inside of the *n*, as he was previously the dot beneath the *b*,
> in order to unveil the hidden secret, and opened for him the door of
> the Town of knowledge and 'taught him a knowledge from Him' (Sura
> 18/65)

Dard claims here, as elsewhere, that he stands in the same
relation to his father Nasir as Ali, the 'door of the town of
knowledge,' stood in relation to the Prophet, and he continues in
explaining the word *ibn*, 'son':

> *Alif* is the divine connection, and *b* the blessing (*baraka*) of Muham-
> mad, and *n* the help of *Nāṣir*. When they are connected in special
> equality and combined in a particular way, then the form of *ibn* 'son'
> results from the gathering of those lofty roots; (*ibn*), in which there is
> contained what is contained, and who is a secret of his father, to show
> openly the Muhammadan Path (K 60).

In him, the 'son' of Nasir Muhammad, the divine, the prophetic, and the paternal qualities are hidden, and he is called to use
them in order to guide the people to these basic principles of
religion.

Dard's relation with Muhammad Nasir did therefore not end
with the father's death:

> Even though he has disappeared from the outward eye, yet in the
> inward actions there is (thanks to Divine grace and the attention of
> the holy spirits) not a single hair's breadth interruption in the relation
> with his presence. Nay, but every day the approximation became
> closer, and the company in speaking and hearing became better than is
> feasible in this visible world without real existence. And every mo-
> ment it is said with strange tongues without speech: 'Peace be upon
> you, o people of the tombs, and if God will we shall reach you.' And
> every moment the glad tidings of 'Do not think that those who are
> killed for God's sake are dead ...' (Sura 3/163) is heard by the corner
> of the ear that understands the inner meaning. God knows whether
> I—in consequence of the order 'Die before ye die'—have completely
> left this world and entered the world of spirits, or whether his High-
> ness has—according to 'Verily the saints of God do not die'—the ca-
> pacity of meeting and conversation without body, just like all the
> living beings, or whether these two acts come together so that I,
> thanks to Divine grace, have a bit of participation in the world of
> spirits and open the way to that world; partly, too, a certain connec-
> tion is still existent for those good spirits because of their friendliness

towards us who believe in them, for the sake of help, and they can come and go on the way 'without how' in this world. And o woe to me that in spite of all these signs of grace my heart, the seat of negligence, did not acquire these goods as its behoves, and the arrow of separation still sits in heart and liver ... (K 636).

This close and constant relation with his father notwithstanding, we see that Dard's stylistically beautiful lamentation about the loss of his parents (K 556) leads him again to accept the fact that the true faithful should turn to God, to Him who is kinder than seventy loving mothers and more merciful than the affectionate father.

Andalib's personality occupied the central place in Dard's thought, and his hope was to follow him soon (K 417), after bringing his life to a good end thanks to his constant spiritual blessing and the help of the Prophet. A few years after his father's death he was consoled by an audition as he tells in one of the last paragraphs of his last book (S 329), about twenty years after the actual event. God promised him (and here the words are 'translated' into Persian though otherwise the auditions are given in Arabic):

O Pain of my Beloved! (Or: O my beloved Dard!) and Lamentation of my Nightingale, we shall give you good tidings about three great and important things and soothe you with our special caress;
1) O Secret of the father and Pain with Result [i.e., Dard's brother Athar, ('result')], we shall make your resurrection according to the words 'It belongs to a person's happiness that he resembles his father' so much in the real form of your great father and high spiritual guide that absolutely nobody from among family and foreigners, and no one from among strangers and friends shall see a difference between you.
2) O Sign of God and Knower of God, we shall inform you beforehand about the year of your departure from the world and the state of your transfer from this place, and shall not send the messenger of death with the good news without damage without [previous] information in a [visible] form, whether you like it or not.
3) O Master of *tauhīd* and Confirmed by Support, a while before the days of death arrive and before the moment of passing away comes many clear miracles and strong supernatural powers shall appear from you, and numberless witnesses and clear evidences shall come so frequently and without interruption that involuntarily and indispensably friend and rival will acknowledge the stand of your right and title, and will obey and follow you, and the nature of family and strangers, present and absent, will not find the possibility of denying you.

This divine promise was almost fulfilled, when Dard wrote
these lines—he had reached the age of his father (66 lunar years)
and strange signs of Divine grace were showered upon him unceasingly so that he hoped for the end and for reunion with his
father.

Neither Muhammad Nasir nor his son did think much of mira-
cle-mongery. Yet, a miracle is connected with Andalib's tomb.
Mir Dard tells (K 495) that his father's tomb had no roof or
dome so as to be exposed to the weather. Nevertheless, twelve
years after Muhammad Nasir's death, the place had remained
always pleasant for the visitors: cool in summer and warm in
winter, so that those who visited it and kissed its threshold were
refreshed even during the hottest days of summer, when everywhere else the earth was burned. Everyone who has visited Indian
shrines in summer at high noon, walking barefoot through the
precincts will gratefully acknowledge Muhammad Nasir's kindness towards his disciples.[4]

Dard himself tells only one other miracle connected with his
father, although he says in passing that there are many. Once a
disciple of Muhammad Nasir travelled through Bengal when his
caravan was attacked by highway robbers. Suddenly, a most
beautiful knight appeared; he frightened the robbers so much
that they ran away and the caravan continued on its way. The
hero was Muhammad Nasir who, though in Delhi, had heard the
prayer of his disciple and helped him. Small wonder that most of
the travellers immediately entered the Muhammadan Path
(K 146)! Miracles of this kind are frequently attested in Muslim
hagiography and even in modern oral traditions: the mystic is
constantly in spiritual relation with his disciple and has the capacity to make himself visible, for a short while, when the disciple requires his help and intensely concentrates upon the master. Such a manifestation for healing or consoling purposes is by
no means unusual even today in Naqshbandi circles.

---

[4] I visited the tomb in September 1975; it is indeed open, and besides Andalib,
Mir Dard, his son Alam and his brother Athar are buried there; two small tombs in the
modest enclosure have no names. The ground is clay, and the location is situated on a
little hill—that may account for its 'coolness'.

MUSIC AND LITERATURE

After Muhammad Nasir's death, Mir Dard became his successor as the leader of the Muhammadan Path. He 'supported himself on the trust in God and did not lift his foot from his place,' as his friend Mir Taqi Mir says. He never left Delhi in spite of all misfortunes that came over the city; misfortunes and afflictions which caused most of the poets, musicians and scholars to wander East in search of livelihood. Dard, however, continued his preaching, writing, listening to mystical music, and instructing poets. In his mystical instructions, he strictly followed the rules of the *Naqshbandī mujaddidī* school, and besides explaining the theoretical foundations of his thought he describes many practical regulations in his different books. Likewise, his poetry is filled with classical expressions of Naqshbandi mysticism. In one point, however, he did not follow the tradition of the order, and that is his love of music; music and *samāʿ* are prohibited as religious expressions by the *Mujaddidī* school. One can understand this sober attitude of the 'orthodox' *ṭarīqa* better when remembering how the rulers of Delhi after Aurangzeb, especially Muhammad Shah, took to music and indulged in doubtful pleasures; but it is well known that from the beginning of Sufi history most theoreticians of mysticism have rightly suspected that the *samāʿ* sessions were only a pretext for many would-be mystics to reach a not always spiritual rapture.[5]

We have not got many explicit statements by Dard about his attitude towards music; his booklet *Ḥurmat al-ghinā*, 'Veneration of Music,' printed in 1843, is extremely rare. A few notes in *ʿIlm ul-kitāb* and *Nāla-yi Dard* allude to the fact that some of his pious colleagues did not approve of his inclination to music. We do not know, however, the source of this criticism. The way Mir Dard confesses candidly that musical sessions were frequently held in his house, seems somewhat amusing and (at least for a modern reader) not completely convincing:

> My *samāʿ* is from God, and God is every time witness that the singers come from themselves and sing whenever they want; not that I would call them and would consider it like worship to listen to them, as

---

[5] The Problem of *samāʿ* has been discussed from the time of Sarraj onward, see the bibliography in Schimmel, 'Mystical Dimensions of Islam', p. 178 ff.

others do; but I do not refuse such an act. However, I do not do it myself, and my creed is that of the masters (i.e., the Naqshbandiyya). But since I am imprisoned in this affliction according to Divine assent— what can I do? God may absolve me: for I have not given a *fatwā* that this should be licite, and I have not built the mystical path upon *samāᶜ*, so that the other masters of that path, who have absolutely no idea of the way of modulation, should have become dissonant and sing about me all those melodies which one should not sing, and open the lip of reproach without reason in my absence ... (N 35).

These attacks must have been particularly strong in the early 1770's, for Dard had noted down a few days earlier another sentence about those colleagues who weave like spiders the web of reproach and blame because of his inclination to music, although his creed is perfectly sound (N 25).

Some years later he tried to defend his interest in music as something rather theoretical. We may accept Firaq's statement that he had studied books on classical Indian music (even though he was probably not acquainted with Sanskrit, as this author claims, F 147); he had, as we are told, an amazing voice and an enchanting way of singing Indian *rāgs* and *rāgnīs* (F 148), an art, which he practiced, however, only in the company of some experts in music. Thus he writes:

My listening to melodies and songs is (neither) of that kind in which the adulterers and fornicators of passion and lust listen, for they are overcome by their animal natures; nor of that kind in which the Sufis and the Wayfarers listen with delight and love, for that is a sign that they are overcome by the mode of unity; but it is the same way as scholars and virtuous people study other mathematical sciences. For although the Muslims have no belief (which is) in accordance with the philosophers, yet they study all the natural, mathematical, and theological sciences and understand their real character and their subtleties well. Verily the science of music is most subtle and belongs among the mathematical sciences, and influences the soul, as he knows who knows this science. However, I am not so enthusiastic about these things as those who are completely absorbed in them, and I do not consider this whole act to be good, as the *samāᶜ* people among the Sufis think. But I do not consider it as bad as the husk-mollas suppose (it to be). In any case, God knows that I do not call the musicians and do not give relish to them, and if they would not come during my whole life I would never think of listening to them. And further, one does not know which wisdom God has put into my listening to them, that he sends all the perfect artists of this art to me without my will and makes me hear them as long as it is destined ... (A 77).

Dard's logic is, of course, infallible—since he does not call the musicians, and they still continue coming, it must be God's order—why, then, should he oppose it?

However, what ever 'the deeper wisdom' be, the musical sessions in his house were famous. This can be well explained: his father's master, Shah Gulshan had been called the 'second Khusrau,' alluding to Amir Khusrau Dihlawi (d. 1325), the Muslim poet and greatest musician in the Indian Middle Ages. Muhammad Nasir himself was also fond of music. This is obvious from the numerous allusions in the *Nāla-yi ʿAndalīb* which reflect his knowledge and understanding of music through the words of his heroes. Mir Dard, therefore, arranged for the memory of his father a *samāʿ*-meeting on every second and 26th day of each month, to which thousands of pious listeners flocked, enjoying the nightly music, kneeling as etiquette would have it, on both knees in perfect quietude. (F 46).

This love of music finds a literary outlet in Dard's poetical imagery. To be sure, musical imagery, and allusions to instruments and modes of singing are frequent in the work of his predecessors, particularly in Maulana Rumi's verse. In the case of Dard, the symbolism is more personal due to his being a practicing musician. He uses the symbol of the *ney*, the reed flute, favorite with poets since the days of Rumi's Prooem of the *Mathnawi*, and his advice to make oneself empty so as to become a true flute (P 23) is perfectly in tune with earlier images. His body is all complaint like a *ney* (P 122), and his conviction that his poetry was a divine gift was expressed frequently in comparing himself to the *ney*, touched by the Divine breath.

> *Sometimes the lamentation of the heart is the sound of the harp for me,*
> *sometimes my heart becomes narrow from the melody of the reed flute.*
> *There is no way out from the song of gratitude and complaint—*
> *as long as the string of breath exists, this harmony remains the same* (P 85).

He could compare himself to a *qānūn*, from whose different tunes the connoisseur may understand his *maqāms*—a clever pun on *maqām* which means both 'musical mode' and 'mystical sta-

tion' (P 82). It is therefore not surprising that even most complicated mystical definitions are couched in the imagery of music:

> The instrument of the degree of existence does not bring forth the
> sound of manifestation from itself, and the chord of its unity has no
> voice outside the harmony in itself (S 52).

Life is bound

> to the instruments of the body and tied to the chord of breath ... God
> Most Merciful may show the longing lovers behind every *parda* ('veil,'
> and 'mode') of branching out and behind every tune (*maqām*) the
> manifestation of reality without veil (*parda*) so that the voice of the
> one unique light comes through the multitude of high and low pitches
> and of every going up and down ... (S 24)

His Urdu verse that:

> *High and low are all alike in their own view,*
> *for in the instrument high and low pitch are alike* (U 15),

points to his favorite theme, the unity behind the multitude. He
felt that he belonged to his fellow beings and was yet distinct
from them, and when Mutanabbi (d. 965) has used in this connection the image of musk, which is part of the musk deer and
yet higher than it, or when Ghalib was to use the image of the
single long bead (*imām*) at the end of the rosary to express the
same feeling, Dard does it in a musical way:

> *We are among creatures, but we remain separate from all*
> *creatures*
> *Just as, in rupak tāla, the first beat is also outside the pat-*
> *tern of counting.*

(In the rhythmic system of Hindustani music, the rhythmic cycle
of seven beats known as *rupak tāl* is distinguished by having a
first beat that is not accented; while technically being counted,
this first beat is thus made prominent by its very lack of ac-
cent).[6]

And in this world, which is replete with confused sounds like a
kettledrum (P 77), the mystic felt that in his sayings:

> *I came out of myself like the melody* (P 121).

---

[6]   I owe this information to Dr. Brian Silver, Harvard University.

Perhaps the most touching expression of his state is that of a 'painted tanboura' without sound—

> Silences are murmuring on the chord of my instrument
> (P 27).

One may classify in this category also the numerous verses in which Dard tells that he is only an echo, although stonehearted people will not even cast back the echo of his words to him. The idea of the chain in prison which gives a strange sound (an image invented by some of his predecessors in the Indian Style) occurs likewise several times; and so does his self-portrait as the bell of the caravan (U 121), again very popular with Sufi-minded poets.

As much as Dard talks about the problems of theology and the relation between poetry and religion, he never mentions those poems which have made his name immortal, e.g., the small collection of little more than a thousand Urdu lines. In these verses which look extremely fragile he has introduced into Urdu, the vocabulary of traditional Sufism and Persian poetry with such an ease that one barely senses the deep mystical meaning of his lines. He became the undisputed master of mystical Urdu poetry, and is probably the only poet who has achieved a complete blending of mysticism and verse. His poems are short, often composed in short meters, too, and their imagery, though following traditional love-lyrics, reflects the loneliness of the great mystic: he complains that nobody listens to his words, and everybody talks about his own grief. What a strange life:

> Is this a heart, o Lord, or else a house for guests?
> Sometimes there lodges grief, sometimes there lodges rest.
> (U 5)

Are human beings not like footprints on water (U 42), or their lives like a footprint on the way towards non-existence? (A 207). Or is this whole created world anything but a Fata Morgana—dust which looks like water (P 15, 38), the pearls of which disappear again from one's hand. And still he feels that he is a footprint of someone greater, lying in the dust in order to show people the right path, as he explains in highflown terminology a lovely Persian quatrain, which is almost verbatim repeated in Urdu. Then again, he sees himself as a wet eyelash or a cut-off vine; at night, he feels dark like the evening, at dawn he has a torn shirt like the morning, and is as flighty as the passing wave of the morning breeze. And the hand of heaven turns him even after death 'like sand in an hourglass' (P 59).[7] He strives to discover the one Divine beauty under the manifold manifestations, whether he sees the world as a dream, a fountain reflecting the sun (U 61), or a shadow play, or, most charmingly, as a bottle containing a fairy.[8] Dard's central idea, e.g., that the divine light is hidden behind the gross material bodies, makes him particularly fond of this image, which was often found in Rumi's verse and then, again, in Indo-Persian lyrics. For him, it is more than a poetical game; for his heart is fragile like glass:

> *I keep in my heart your picture*
> *just as a fairy is kept in the bottle* (P 134).

Love opens the eye of vision until the lover understands that:

> *in every stone is glass,*
> *in every glass-bottle a fairy* (U 111).

Deeper and deeper layers of understanding are unveiled until he perceives the Divine beauty whose subtlety, *laṭāfat*, is hidden in the coarseness, *kathāfat*, of created things (P 70). And thus he carries over the image into his prose to point to his favorite idea:

> As much as the Divine Most Holy Essence is higher than every pure and impure rank of the contingent existing beings, yet every stone of material creatureliness is, like the bottle of individuation, a place of manifestation for the fairy of divine fineness (D 339).

Only when the glass-bottle is broken, the fairy can be duly recognized: to be broken, *shikast*, is one of the central terms in Naqshbandi poetry. Thus, the traditional image of the soulbird which

---

[7] The hourglass must have become fashionable shortly before 1600; Ibrahim Adilshah of Bijapur mentions it in one of his poems, as did the court poets of the Jihangir period. A famous painting by Bichitr shows Emperor Jihangir sitting on something like a hourglass-like throne; it is dated 1625 (cf. Ettinghausen, Paintings of the Sultans and Emperors of India, plate 14). The image occurs very frequently in Bedil's poetry, and Andalib admonishes his reader:

Be sober like the sand of the hour glass,
and go ahead in counting your days (NA I 438)

[8] The image of the 'fairy in the bottle' was very common with the Indo-Persian poets of the 17th century; Shah Gulshan asks his beloved to look in the mirror: then she would have the fairy and the bottle (= glass) together. (Ikram, *Armaghān-i Pāk*, p. 281). In Bedil's Diwan (*Kulliyāt* I), the image occurs on pp. 71, 100, 114, 147, 259, 260.

breaks his cage, or 'breaks' the colors of his wings, occurs often in Dard's verse.

He also ponders the unsolvable contrast in the garden of this world, that rosegarden which he has described time and again in sweet and fragrant words. But 'why does the dew weep while the rose is smiling?' (U 45). Is this not the story of his own life?

Our meeting is like that
of the dew-drop and the rose—
All the smiling is from you,
all the weeping is from us (A 276).

For, as he says elsewhere:

Like dew, for a moment into the weeping eye,
have we come for the sake of seeing (P 130).

Dard had a considerable number of disciples. Most important among them are Qiyamuddin Qa 'im Chandpuri (d. 1795) who was considered to be one of the best *ghazal*-writers in 18th century Urdu literature, and also produced a biographical handbook on Urdu writing poets. Besides, Thana 'ullah Khan Firaq belonged to Dard's circle; his uncle, the poet Hidayat, had likewise been instructed by Dard. Muhammad Ismail Tapish (d. after 1814) migrated to Lucknow where he attached himself to the sons of Shah Alam II. Mushafi was happy to have met Dard several times before migrating to Oudh. There are also some Hindu poets who joined the circle of the 'sincere Muhammadan' Dard. And the Hindu Lachmi Narayan Shafiq expresses the hope that Dard might pass through his town, 'for to meet such people is something like worship.' Small wonder that Dard's son Alam (d. after 1807) was also a poet in his own right. Most remarkable, however, are the achievements of his younger brother Mir Athar, whose *Mathnawi Khwab u khayal*, Dream and Phantasy, is a most intriguing love story which has been regarded as the sublimation of a deep personal experience the vanity of which the young poet realized thanks to his brother Mir Dard (as prologue and epilogue explain).

Only toward the end of his life we find a few sentences that give a clue to his growing fame, although he complains (N 64) that nobody really knew him as he is, so that everybody 'runs in the arena of his own opinion concerning me.' He regards the

fame which comes in old age as 'the sound of the drum of departure;' yet, in a fit of pride he cannot help mentioning that already

> from my early youth the Phoenix of my fame spread its wings over
> the four directions ... (N 147).

In A 311, that means: after 1193/1779, Dard confesses, apparently with some pleasure:

> Though I, a person sitting in the corner and choosing solitude, have
> never set my foot outside my house and am absolutely not inclined to
> show and spectacle; yet, by Divine grace, a large number of people
> have made the sweet remembrance of my words the sweetmeat of
> their assemblies, and due to their good opinion they do not look at
> the faults of me who consists completely of shortcomings.

Still later, towards the end of his life, he boasts and complains of
his success as a writer in one and the same sentence:

> After becoming the everyday talk of élite and ordinary people and
> becoming famous in the world, I have become for myself a strange
> pain; I have become a headache (cf. P 54).
> I wrote surprising acceptable things and fell on the tongues of men
> and gave the reins of free will off my hands. May God make me say
> whatever He wants and in a way that pleases Him—I do not claim to
> be a poet nor do I pretend to be a master (S 237).

A few lines later he sighs that:

> The bird of my individuation has fallen into the snare of fame, and as
> much as he longs for complete annihilation, he cannot help saying
> 'Perhaps that God's will even after my death will keep this perishable
> being fettered in the cage of existence some more time—as long as it is
> decreed—by means of his name ...' (S 239).

But these sentences with their strange blending of pride, hope
for fame and an uncouth feeling that a mystic should not gain
fame as a poet, are the only remarks Dard himself makes about
his poetical art. Compared to the very scare information about
his poetical activity we find many more allusions to his mystical
experiences which were the only 'real' thing in life for him.

From the day Mir Dard succeeded his father he had been
deeply involved in writing books for guidance and in teaching
people, so that toward the end of his life he could proudly attest:

> We with confused state have never and from nobody hidden the mode
> of love and serene purity in our heart, and not a single secret of the

> secrets of the Path and religion is left which we had not written down, and we did not keep quiet in the assemblies that tongue of resplendent explanation of the candle of the assembly, and we have delineated the complete rules of the lofty Muhammadan Path. Thus, all our inward and outward states are manifest from our discoursing and writing ... (D 336)

Although he sometimes modestly claims not to be a typical ascetic, yet the burden of directing people toward the right path has been given to him,

> Since for God, talent is not a condition, but for the talent, His gift is the condition (A 186).

His attitude seems at times simple and unpretentious, his high self-esteem notwithstanding; the dangerous mode of *tashayyukh*, i.e., to behave like a self-made mystical leader which he blames often in others, is, as he asserts, not found in him (S 244). But apparently he, too, had to suffer from envious colleagues (A 335); yet he felt that he lived under the constant protection of his *Nāṣir* (helper) and knows the 'scorpion-natured hypocrites' too well to be worried by their behavior. And in one of his last notes (S 255) he praises God who has led him and put him on the seat of conveying the message and spiritual directorship which he has adorned with clearest explanation and finest description. But he considers himself

> not a Sufi that I may open the door of Sufism, and not a molla that I should show debate and disputation. I am a pure Muhammadan, and I am intoxicated by the 'pure wine' (Sura 76/21). And from me, the intoxicated one, you must hear the Tale of the Beloved, and from Dard the madman you must listen to the Lamentation of the Nightingale, for the Lamentation of the Nightingale is in the world because of the pain, and pain (Dard) because of the Lamentation of the Nightingale (N 50).

> *The Sufi by his Sufism became absolutely pure,*
> *The molla blackened the page with mentioning grammar,*
> *We, whose heart has gone, o Dard, have read our lesson*
> *In the school of love from the Lament of the Nightingale.*

Mir Dard put down his ideas first in the *'Ilm ul-kitāb* which was intended as a commentary for the *Wāridāt* which he had offered to his father. Their number is 111:—110 is the numerical value of the name Ali, his ancestor, and the odd number is added 'since God is an odd number and loves odd number' (K 97). There is no logical sequence in these *Wāridāt*—they have appeared without outward reason from God (cf. K 91); but when these unbound words from the Well Preserved Tablet came down into the temporal and spatial fetters of pronunciation and writing they became separated and

> reached from their spiritual subtlety (*laṭāfat*) the material coarseness (*kathāfat*) of writing.

Therefore he had to put them into an order of earlier and later verses. Dard's brother Mir Muhammad Athar had urged him to collect the *Wāridāt* and to explain them, and just as the voluminous *Nāla-yi ʿAndalīb* grew out of a story told in three nights, the 111 *wāridāt* developed into the 648 big pages of the *ʿIlm ul-kitāb* (called by some admirers 'the greatest ocean of Sufism'). Dard meditated on its contents for a long time, and he wrote it down almost 12 years after his father's death, when he was about fifty lunar years old (K 473).

The *ʿIlm ul-kitāb* is a strange book: 'Since in the seal of the hearts of the lovers the name of their beloved is engraved,' each of its chapters (after a long introduction to the whole work) begins with the invocation '*Yā Nāṣir*,' alluding to his father's name, but of course, also reminding the reader of God's name *an-Nāṣir*

> so that everybody who reads the books and *risālas* and compositions and writings should first see this famous name, and everywhere in the book of our actions this blessed name is written, and all the sins and rebellions of us, the sinners, become wiped out and forgiven through the spiritual power of his name (S 17).

An-Nāṣir is further a surname of both the Prophet and of Ali, and the prophet's daughter Fatima, Ali's wife, was likewise called *an-Nāṣira* (K 95), so that Dard could exhaust almost every possible meaning of this blessed word. Muhammad Nasir himself had, as Firaq tells, suggested that every member of his house should bear a name connected with '*Nāṣir*' for the sake of blessing; thus, even the servants were called *Nāṣir Qulī* or *Nāṣir Bakhsh*. It was believed that by this sacred name the members of the family would always remain victorious and successful; every letter which began with the formula *Huwa an-Nāṣir*, 'He is the Victorious' was supposed to yield a positive result for the writer (F 92).

After the *basmala*, the name of the chapter is given, relying upon some Quranic words: then an Arabic introduction explains the inner meaning of this title and—at least sometimes—the broad outlines of the chapter. Its main part is usually in Persian, often highly technical, and full of terms of logic and other sciences; it also occurs that a whole chapter is composed exclusively in Arabic, such as N. 85 'About the Appearance of the Names and Qualities and the Concealment of the Essence.' Eventually one reaches a quatrain, e.g., one of those *wāridāt* which form the essence of the chapter, further a text in rhymed prose, interrupted by numerous long comments. A *fāida* usually closes the chapter. The length of a *wārid*, plus explanations, varies from 2 to 10 pages. The Western reader will certainly enjoy the original *wāridāt*; their long winded commentaries in sometimes abstruse formulations are less enjoyable. Dard discusses in them all the stages and stations of mystical life, and sometimes includes interesting information about his own life; he ends with a praise of love, which means for him primarily love of his father-*shaikh*, and love of the Prophet. The contents of the *'Ilm ul-kitāb* show that Mir Dard was well versed in the traditional Sufi and non-Sufi literature. He quotes the commentary of Zamakhshari, confronting his interpretation of the Light-Verse (Sura 24/35) with that of Imam Ghazzali (the only theologian whom his father, too, mentions by name;) he cites Taftazani and Ashʿari, the Theology of Aristotle, the commentaries of Ibn Arabi, Abdur Razzaq Kashi and Qaisari; among the Sufis the Naqshbandiyya from Baha ʾuddin Naqshband to Ubaidullah Ahrar and Ahmad Sirhindi is, of course, well represented; but there are also quotations from Bayezid Bistami, the *sulṭān al-ʿārifīn* (K 300), whose negative theology had a certain attraction for the Central Asian and Naqshbandi mystics (contrary to al-Hallaj whom Dard despises thoroughly). Besides Ghazzali, his model-writer from the Baghdadian school, Abu Talib Makki (d. 990), is mentioned; among the poets Hafiz, Jami, and especially Maulana Rumi are cited—the latter mystic is often quoted in Andalib's *Nāla*, too. The number of quotations, though, diminishes in the course of time.

Dard's aim is to support each and every of his theological thoughts by quotations from the Quran and the Prophetic traditions; for what can not be found in these sources is for him non-existent. It is natural that he, like all mystics, had a predilection for certain Quranic verses and *hadith*. The central Quranic word of his theology is also the favorite verse of earlier Sufis. 'Whithersoever ye turn there is the Face of God' (Sura 2/109). The introduction as well as many details of the *'Ilm ul-kitāb* show that Dard was a thinker in the Hanafi Ash'ari tradition—his *'aqīda* (p. 72 f.) fits exactly into the well-known type of orthodox Muslim creeds with its belief in the reality of corporal resurrection, the possibility of the vision of God in the other world, the idea that faith can neither increase nor decrease by works, that *īmān* and *islām* are one and the same, that man is higher than the angels, etc. He follows also the nominalist way of the Ash'arite school by declaring that good is what God has declared to be good. The long *'aqīda* in the introduction is followed by a discussion of the differences between *hamd*, 'praise,' *shukr*, 'thank,' and *madh*, 'praising'; he then turns to one of his favorite topics about the Divine names and their manifestation in creation and finally proves that the names of the Prophet, *Muhammad* and *Ahmad*, show his close connection with God since the root *hmd* can be used only in relation with God.

The reader is taken by surprise when Mir Dard turns towards the end of his deliberations (No. 110) to the subject of love, a topic so dear to generations of mystics who sung of their intoxicating love in immortal verses, after losing themselves completely in the joy of suffering through love. Dard who used the word love, *mahabba*, not very frequently in his book offers us in this chapter a short *mathnawī* of 30 verses in the meter *hazaj* which begin with a chain of anaphors, repeating *mahabba* 19 times; and thus is very similar to the *mathnawī Daryā-yi 'ishq* by his friend Mir Taqi Mir. But the difference in content is revealing: Mir sings of the endless power of love as revealed in the sufferings of a loving couple, and follows the model of mystical love songs closely. Dard, on the other hand, describes love as an ocean; when this sea billows the stream of the power of faith and the current of the relation of creed begins to sweep away reason and intellect like straw and casts all doubts and unnecessary thoughts on the shore, so that obedience of God, the Prophet, and the *imāms* alone remain in the heart. That means, love is for him nothing but a state somewhat more comprehensive than faith; the definition of love as 'obedience,' typical of the early orthodox stance, is maintained. Then, after a longish description of love, which conforms in its poetical expression to normal Sufi poetry and is made 'orthodox' only by Dard's commentaries, he turns, *via* a short homage to the Prophet, to his father, a turn which is introduced by the hemistich 'Love is the helper (*nāsir*) of the lovers' and followed in the 19th verse by an allusion to Shah Gulshan, 'Love is the spring for the *rosegarden* of the heart' (p. 641). The meditation ends again in a prayer in which the mystic claims:

> This is the song of the nightingale, not pain,

and asks for spiritual help for himself and his brother through his father, for

> though my book (of actions) is absolutely black like the tresses of the beloved, I am a madman, fettered by the chain of love of my friend (i.e., Andalib (p. 644)).

The final paragraph of the *'Ilm ul-kitāb* (p. 648) is typical of Dard's theology—the book ends with a quatrain in honor of the Prophet:

> That holy essence is present in every moment
> And looks everywhere on the state of the inhabitants of the world.
> My hand is at the skirt of the Prophet and his family—
> In both worlds is Muhammad the Helper (*Nāsir*).

> I mean: the holy essence and the purified spirit of the most eminent Repository of Guidance, the Shelter of Prophethood, whose firm religion is living and standing till doomsday, is in every moment and every wink with us, the Muhammadans, in a presence without how, and alive in spiritual life, and the state of the whole world and its inhabitants is clear and evident for him. And as he in the time of his corporal life inspite of being in this world explained the good things of the other world and eyewitnessed the world of *barzakh* and resurrection, just so, inspite of having left this perishable world and having entered the world of spirits he is conversant with the state of this world and is all the time present and viewing and preserving and helping (*nāsir*).

> And I, who is the smallest of the Muhammadans, put the hand of my seeking favor at the skirt of the intercession of the Intercessor of the sinners and his pure family, and I have such a love for the Prophet and his family on my carpet, and the same pure essence of Muhammad is our helper in both worlds.

> And the elegance of the word *Muḥammad Nāsir* which occurs in the

quatrain is not hidden from understanding; for it is both a hint to the just mentioned meaning and at the same time the blessed name of the 'Qibla of both worlds' and 'Ka'ba of both existences,' the veritable *sayyid* and most right *imām*, the helper of the nation and the religion, the prince of the Muhammadans, Khwaja Muhammad Nasir Muhammadi ...

It is indeed a fine pun on the name of his father who is here, as in a number of similar cases, brought into such a close union with the Prophet that the reader is confused as to whom the reference belongs.

After finishing this magnum opus, Mir Dard composed the book which is, besides his Urdu *dīwān*, best known—the *Nāla-yi dard*, 'Lamentation of Pain.' Its name is, of course, modelled after the *Nāla-yi 'Andalīb*. Shortly afterwards followed the *Ah-i sard*, 'The cold sigh': both expressions occur already towards the end of the *'Ilm ul-kitāb* when the author writes about this book

> though like a cold sigh and a lamentation full of pain you should not read it superficially and you should know that these few words are full of many meanings ... (K 586).

Dard explains the compositions of his *Nāla* with the fact that he, who constantly walks on the street of 'Who knows God talks much' and only rarely turns the reins of useless explanation towards the corner of silence according to the word 'Who knows God becomes silent' had composed his important book and considered it finished;

> but still, after the completion of that book scattered words trickled down on the confused heart, and involuntarily and necessarily the tremulous hand moved to jot them down and made nothing but my own poems enter this *risāla*.

His brother Athar collected the words, and thus

> the drops which came down from the cloud of Divine mercy were brought together (N 2).

Mir Athar invented also an elegant chronogram for the beginning of the *Nāla-yi dard* which yields the date 1190/1776 (N 3).

Dard felt that his *Nāla*, which we would classify as a kind of spiritual diary, was a most effective means for guiding people the right way, and thinks that

> those hearts in which my complaint has no result are certainly harder than a mountain or even more obstinate, for when one complains in a

mountain range, at least an echo comes from that side—now in those stonehearted people, if it has not even that much influence that a first echo comes up or a teardrop rains from the eye of their insight, then they are naturally worse than mountains ... And if I should utter such lamentations in a mountainous place every hill would become torn to pieces from its influence ... O woe to you, you have put the cotton of 'They have ears and do not hear with them' into your ears and keep the veil of 'They have hearts and do not think with them' on the face of your intellect that you do not listen to my lamentations with the ear of your heart! (N 244).

Mir Dard composed the *Nāla* and the following three books according to the same principle: each book contains 341 short paragraphs called by names corresponding to the general title. Thus the *Nāla-yi dard* has 341 *nāla* 'lamentations' the *Ah-i sard* comprises 341 *ah*, 'sighs,' the *Dard-i dil*, 341 *dard*, 'pains,' and the *Sham ᶜ-i mahfil*, 341 *nūr*, 'light.' The number 341 was chosen because it is the numerical value of the word *Nāsir*, so that Dard's mystical connection with his father and guide is once more established.

After Mir Dard had finished his 'Lamentation,' when he had

drawn the hand from writing, and the steed of his pen, which was hot-racing and wanted to run about more, became disappointed and had no more hope for continuing his race—but as in the veil of every despair there is hope hidden,

a rain of continuous inspirations suddenly reached his heart, and he started writing again, according to the Quranic verse 'The sea would be empty before the words of my Lord come to an end.' (Sura 18/109). His faithful brother again found the chronogramm for the *Ah-i sard* which gives the year 1193/1779. Dard himself regarded the two first *risālas* as one book and probably had hoped to write the *Ah* while still involved in the *Nāla*, for there are some hints to the expression *Ah-i sard*. Although, as he complains, the copyists and writers of his time do not like to write long books he urges them to keep the two short books in one binding and not to separate them from each other (p. 71-72). Indeed, they are very similar, consisting of short sighs, some prayers, aphorisms which allude to peculiarities of the mystical path in lovely, though complicated Persian style; in short, they are a kind of devotional book interspersed with verse. The depth of Dard's religious feeling is palpable, and the reader who has

struggled his way through the *Ilm ul-kitāb* feels happy in the
more emotional atmosphere of these two books of which the
Ah-i sard seems to me even more perfect as a work of art. Dard,
this stern defender of the difference of *ʿabd*, the human servant,
and *rabb*, the Divine Lord; who so often has attacked the representatives of *sukr*, 'intoxication' appears in these later works
more mellowed, and softened by the fire of Divine love. He now
uses sometimes the symbolism of the lover and beloved, and even
speaks of his own 'intoxication.' But again, in the *Ah*, the author
complains of those with hard hearts whose cold thoughts are not
impressed by his sighs, though many people want to note them
down and relate them to their friends (A 180). He admits that
these books are not 'so far from the understanding of common
people' (A 147) as the *ʿIlm ul-kitāb*.

When the composition of the second book was finished the
same thing happened as before: the mystical writer found that
the rain of Divine inspiration did not cease, and that

> as much as my elementary form became weaker, yet my power of
> speech did not become weaker (A 332, cf. A 339, D p. 135).

Thus he began to note down his two last books at the same time
as the chronogramm shows in 1195/1781. But he finished *Dard-i
dil* slightly before completing *Shamʿ-i mahfil*. He considered
those four *risālas* to be a complete introduction into his thought,

> which should keep away everybody from the four sides of greed and
> passion and bring into view the four sides of the manifestation of
> 'Whithersoever ye turn there is the Face of God' (Sura 2/109) and make
> man sit squatted (Persian 'squared') on the four pillars of content-
> ment and firm constancy and make him independent of everything
> besides God (D 194).

This way of playing with numerals reminds the reader of Nasir
Andalib's way of describing the six formulae of faith as 'protec-
tions for the six directions of the world' which are crowned by
the prayer for the Prophet. The last two *risālas* are less attractive
than the first two; the sentences become more involved, the paragraphs longer and more tedious. The *Dard-i dil* contains a comparatively great number of prayers and heart-felt complaints, further meditations on old age and death; *Shamʿ-i mahfil* is, as its
name indicates, meant for the edification of the assembly of
readers and listeners. Now and then the unusual way of applying

highly poetical images to very abstract contents puzzles the reader more than is the case in earlier treatises. It seems that Dard noted down his warmer and more personal feelings in *Dard-i dil* while keeping the more didactic passages for *Sham ʿ -i maḥfil*. He finished the latter book in the beginning of 1199/the last days of 1784. He had just reached the age of 66 lunar years and died shortly afterwards—strangely enough, his *Wāridāt*, too, had been completed a few days before his father passed away at the age of 66 lunar years. The date is indicated by a chronogramm by 'his brother in this world and the next, and work-companion in the inward and outward' (S 341).

Dard's Persian *Dīwān* was collected from the poetry scattered in his prose work, and is not an independent book.

All of Dard's books give some interesting insights into his mystical life, but only a few words are devoted to the world and what is in it. This is all the more surprising as the time after Nasir Andalib's death was characterized by major events in the political field. During the period in which the *Four Risālas* were composed, e.g., between 1770 and 1785, many changes took place in Delhi. In January 1772, Shah Alam II returned to Delhi, and being a good poet in his own right, with the penname *Aftāb*, 'Sun,' he used to attend some of the meetings in Dard's house. His main advisor, the Persian born Najaf Khan, who was on good terms with the British, died in 1782. Then, the Mahratta chief Sindhia maneuvered to seize control of the court, supported by Warren Hastings. The Rohillas had proved, again, a source of unrest, after the increasing ambitions of the British and the Nawwabs of Oudh had resulted in the death of their gifted leader Hafiz Rahmat Khan in 1774. The young Rohilla Ghulam Qadir thought of revenge; he became *amīr ul-umarā ʿ* in 1787. One year later he blinded Shah Alam II and was in turn cruelly put to death by Sindhia's troops. The poor king continued to rule under the protection of the British until he died in 1806—a blind 'Sun,' whose sad fate Dard dit not live to see.

MYSTICAL THEOLOGY

Mir Dard's extremely close connection with his father led him to develop one of his most surprising mystical theories. Since the Middle Ages, *fanā ʾ fi ʾsh-shaikh*, annihilation in and identification with the mystical leader, was considered necessary in the orders. As moderate a mystic as Ghazzali had stressed the importance of complete surrender to the *shaikh* so that the *murīd* would be like the corpse in the hand of the washerman; the great Persian mystical poets like Attar and Rumi had touched the same chord. Dard underlines the importance of the *pīr* more than his predecessors:

> God's custom is to bring spiritual bounty from the living to the living.

and even Uwais al-Qarani, known as 'Sufi without *shaikh*, was, according to him, spiritually connected with the Prophet and received his initiation into the path through him; for initiation is the basis for successful progress in the *tarīqa*.[9] Direct illumination is impossible—either it happens after the initiation or the mystic, after his first experience, seeks a master to guide him further (K 638).

> The *shaikh* is in his group like the prophet in his people (K 60)

as he says with a *hadīth*, and the office of *shaikh* is vicegerency of the prophecy, and thus not available to every saint (K 451). From *fanā ' fi 'sh-shaikh* the adept should reach *fanā ' fi 'r-rasūl*, 'annihilation in the Prophet,' and eventually *fanā ' fi Allāh*, 'annihilation in God'—a state which had been during the first centuries of Islamic mysticism, the only goal of the wayfarer. The 'threefold annihilation' is an upward movement which leads the disciples to higher experiences of reality and culminates, according to most classical doctrines (at least with those who prefer mystical sobriety to mystical intoxication) in *baqā ' billāh*, 'remaining in God.' *Baqā '* is, however, also the first stage on the way down, for, as Mir Dard formulates it:

> *Fanā '* in God is directed toward God, and *baqā '* in God is directed toward creation, and one calls the most perfect wayfarer him who comes down more than others, and then again gets firmly established in the *baqā '* in the Prophet, and he who is on this descendant rank is called higher and more lofty than he who is still in ascent, for the end is the return to the beginning ... (K 115). [10]

---

[9] About the importance of initiation cf. Meier, 'Vom Wesen der islamischen Mystik', p. 16.

[10] Cf. the quotation of the Naqshbandi master Abdur Rahim Fedai Efendi: 'Our lowest way is the ascent from creation towards God, our highest way is the descent from God to creation' in H. L. Şuşud, *Islam tasavvufunda Hacegân hanedani*, p. 161.

But, and here a new interpretation begins, higher than he who has reached *baqā'* in the Prophet is he who has found *baqā'* in the *shaikh*, for he has completed the whole circle.

> This (is the) terminating rank which God Almighty has kept for the pure Muhammadans whereas the others with all their power cannot be honored by it. Most of those with weak faith who are without love—in the thought that they consider themselves as annihilated in God and in the Prophet—say about these most perfect mystics who find the intense love of the mystical leader and the utter-most degree of veneration of the *pīr*, that they be still in the rank of *fanā' fī'sh-shaikh* and strongly bound by this relation ... But we have surpassed this rank! (K 116)

And he attests that he,

> the lowest of the Muhammadans, has been created for the sake of venerating his *pīr*, and for the relation of faith. Thus, everybody who venerates the *pīr* and has faith is my soul and the beloved of my heart (N 117).

I think we can not blame those mystics who would not acknowledge the new spiritual rank of *baqā' fī'sh-shaikh* which Mir Dard defended, for this was born out of his own personal experience in his relation to his father, a relation which nobody else could possibly imitate or experience.

It is the follower of the Muhammadan Path who is exclusively blessed with his experience. And this *tarīqa Muhammadiyya* is, indeed, the center of Dard's preaching and life. In his view, *kalām*, philosophy and mystical knowledge are merely servants of the *tarīqa Muhammadiyya*, which is higher and subtler than anything else (K 157). For—as Dard says, with an allusion to the classical tripartition *sharī'a-tarīqa-haqīqa*, the *haqīqa Muhammadiyya* (the pre-eternal reality of Muhammad as the first individuation) is higher than all the other individuations; therefore, the *sharī'a Muhammadiyya* superseded every other law, and the *tarīqa Muhammadiyya* is, logically, the best and most comprehensive path leading to salvation (K 64; cf. 376, 380). To be sure, a number of religious leaders in the later eighteenth and early nineteenth centuries—like the Idrisiya-Sanusiyya affiliations in North Africa and especially Ahmad Brelwi in India, who derived his attitude from Dard's school—had called their *tarīqas* 'Muhammadiyya,' and the veneration of the Prophet was their central aim; however, it will be difficult to find a statement like Dard's words:

Humanity consists of Muhammadanism,

so that someone who is not a 'Muhammadan' remains outside the fold of the faithful; he is, so to speak, not a human being at all, but intrinsically worse than an animal, as is proved by the Quranic word 'They are like beasts' (Sura 7/178) (K 432).

The 'sincere Muhammadan' will be qualified by the qualifications of the four caliphs, as Dard's father says (Na I, 430, 435), and the Prophet himself grants his companions, friends and disciples all the degrees of the stages of proximity, like the 'proximity to the perfections of Prophethood,' of vicegerency, of wisdom, etc., according to the degree of their annihilation in him, their association with him, their dependence upon him, etc. (NA II, 335).

But how to become a 'sincere Muhammadan' and thus reach salvation? Dard, following his father's fundamentalism, sees in the ṭariqa Muhammadiyya nothing but the perfect reliance upon the Quran and Prophetic tradition. He stresses, thus, the importance of the five pillars of faith; among them, prayer and fasting are, as for most mystics, central.

Throughout his work, Mir Dard made many allusions to the classical ways of education of the adept in the Naqshbandi tradition. There are, of course, differences in the mystical ways: some schools begin with the education of the lower soul—the 'greater holy war' (K 533); others with the purification of the heart; but since the mystical path is considered a cyclical movement, either way is useful (K 534). The disciple has to know that

Evil is what the religious law declares as evil (K 432)

and that 'this world is the seed-bed for the other world' as Maulana Rumi's favorite ḥadīth claims (K 526):

Each of our actions is like a rose or a thorn which we plant for ourselves (K 98).

Eating, drinking, dressing are subject to detailed rules (K 521ff.; cf. the classical handbooks on Sufi education). Perfect trust in God, tawakkul, is basic for the disciple, but if he experiences mental discomfort during his attempt to rely absolutely upon

God's gifts, he had better earn his livelihood and follow the Prophet's advice:

> Bind your camel's knees notwithstanding your trust in God (K 241, 243).

Dard knows the importance of *qabḍ*, the state of constraint, since

> the stronger the compression the larger the expansion (*basṭ*). (K 124)

Former masters had regarded the complete surrender to God in the state of *qabḍ* as preferable to the joyful expansion of the self in *basṭ*. Over and over again patience is recommended:

> Complaint and lament are calamities, patience and constancy are blessings and.causes of salvation (K 552).

As for the dichotomy of the states of *ṣabr*, patience, and *shukr*, gratitude, so often discussed by the early Sufis, Dard links them exclusively with their primary cause, not with the world:

> The sincere Muhammadans keep the antimony of 'The sight did not rove' (Sura 53/17) before their eyes and do not care so much for the benefits and afflictions of this world as to connect their gratitude and patience with them (K 346).

One of the requirements of the path, especially among the Naqshbandis, is *ṣoḥbat*, the conversation with the master, which guarantees not only a perpetual control of the disciple's progress but the constant flow of spiritual energy from the *shaikh* to the *murīd*. For according to the *hadīth*, 'Religion consists in giving good advice.' In rare cases the perusal of the master's books can be substituted for oral *ṣoḥbat* (K 499; cf. 431).

> The result of the whole 'journey,' and devotions and recollections is that the heart becomes free from all besides God, and is made ready for constant presence and vision, so that it keeps in its hand the thread of patience in affliction through contentment with fate, (the thread) of enduring distasteful events, and that of the strength to refrain from carnal desires (K 307).

On the path different kinds of revelation (*kashf*) can be experienced. (1) *kashf kaunī*, as the result of asceticism, pious actions and purification of the lower soul; it becomes manifest in dreams and clairvoyance (2) *kashf ilāhī*, a fruit of constant worship and polishing of the heart, which results in the knowledge of the world of spirits and cardiognosy. (3) *kashf ʿaqlī*, which can be reached by polishing the moral faculties, and can be experienced by the philosophers as well. (4) *kashf īmānī* is the fruit of perfect faith, after man's acquiring proximity to the perfections of prophethood; then he is blessed by direct divine addresses; he talks with the angels, meets the spirits of the prophets, sees the Night of Might and the blessings of Ramadan in human form in the *ʿālam al-mithāl* ... (K 443). [11]

Miracles will occur to the wayfarer; they are real and true, but

miracles are the menstruation of men (K 449),

for the friends of a king will never divulge the secrets he entrusts to them. Dervishdom does not consist of astrology and geomancy (K 447), but many of the contemporary *shaikhs* are nothing but 'religious shopkeepers' (K 445).

Dard often attacks those who remain in the state of *sukr*, intoxication; overwhelmed by their mystical states, they

sing tunes which ought not to be sung (K 284)

for as the *sharīʿa* prohibits 'real' wine, thus the *ṭarīqa* forbids the 'spiritual wine,' e.g., the divulgence of the subtleties of mystical union (K 183). In the state of *sukr* the mystic experiences not a complete annihilation but only the *qurb an-nawāfil* (K 250) which is expressed in the famous *ḥadīth*:

> ... My servant doth not cease to draw nigh unto Me by voluntary works of devotion (*nawāfil*) until I love him, and when I love him, I am his ear, so that he hears by Me, and his eye, so that he sees by Me, and his tongue, so that he speaks by Me, and his hand, so that he takes by Me.

Much higher is the state reached by the *qurb al-farāʾiḍ*, the proximity of the legally prescribed actions, for this is the state of the Prophet, which is higher than that of the saints (NA I 272).

This statement is closely connected with Dard's attitude toward the adherents of the theory of *waḥdat al-wujūd* who usually speak of the *qurb al-nawāfil*. [12] According to his interpretation,

---

[11] About the various degrees of illumination cf. R. A. Nicholson, 'Studies in Islamic Mysticism', ch. II; about the *ʿālam al-mithāl*: Fazlur Rahman, Dream, imagination, and *ʿālam al-mithāl*, in Grunebaum-Caillois, The Dream and Human Society.

[12] A good analysis of Mir Dard's theology is found in the hitherto unpublished thesis by J. G. J. ter Haar, 'De visie van Shah Wali Allah al-Dihlawi op de wahdat

they imagine to have direct access to Reality, and overwhelmed by their idea that there is only one reality, they go so far as to interpret even the Quran according to their insight and rely, on the whole, too much upon their intellects, while the followers of the *wahdat ash-shuhūd* closely follow the revelation and wander on the path of faith, allowing the intellect only a secondary role. The intellectualist approach of many interpreters of Ibn Arabi and his doctrine is indeed a problem for the historian of Sufism even in our day.

On the other hand, Dard accuses in harsh words the broad masses who repeat the idea that 'Everything is He'—every little Yogi has the mouth full of these ideas, and here lies the major danger: everyone who talks about *wahdat al-wujūd* without having reached the experience (which is, in itself, legitimate) is a heretic. For it is extremely dangerous (as he points out in *Wārid* 28, which deals with the various forms of mystical *tauhīd*) to see God as *kullī tabīʿ ī*, a 'natural Universal' which is manifest in the creatures. In this chapter, as often in various chapters of his books, Dard emphasizes the good Naqshbandi formula *Hama az ōst*, 'Everything is from Him,' and his favorite image, that of the mirror, fits well into his interpretation of the Divine transcendence, for if the world is regarded as a mirror which reflects God's beauty, then it is clear that mirror and reflected beauty are two separate things, and that the mirror gains its value only by its capacity of reflecting true beauty, while its back side is black and, so to speak, non-existent (an image used in almost the same formulation by Maulana Rumi). Dard carefully elaborates his point, not denying that the followers of *wahdat al-wujūd* may have some truth in their subjective experience, but, as he says in an interesting comparison, the followers of the *wahdat ash-shuhūd* are like the physicians who follow the Greek medical system, and usually help people, or at least do not harm them, whereas the other group is comparable to Indian physicians who may be able to heal a man immediately but also to kill him quickly—as most of them do indeed, as he sarcastically adds (K 183 f.).

Yet, even the differences between the two types of *tauhīd*

---

al-wujud en de wahdat al-shuhud en een tweetal reacties hierop', Leiden 1974. I am grateful to Professor J. M. S. Baljon that he sent me a copy of the relevant pages.

point merely to a higher reality: neither *wujūd* nor *shuhūd* are Quranic terms, and the only goal which the faithful should try to reach is the *tauhīd-i muhammadī*, as preached in the *tarīqa Muhammadiyya*.

Dard knows from experience that the 'children of the Path' usually go through a period of intoxication when they reach 'adolescence,' i.e., the middle stages of the path, and then they want to talk without restraint about love and union; but when they mature, i.e., come down in the circle of the path, they become moderate, and in old age, when the circle is completed, they prefer silence (K 127).

Dard often speaks of the cyclic movement of the mystic:

> *Commencement and determination are one in our circle,*
> *We are the line of the compasses—our end is our beginning.*
> (P 27)

This movement is connected, in his theological view, with the figure of the *shaikh*, not, as we would imagine, with a return to the primordial source of life in God.

In his theories of ascent and descent Dard does not explicitly describe—as his father and many others had done—the 'journey towards God' as man's ascension to the rank of that divine name which is his Lord, *rabb* (NA I: 271), since every creature is *marbūb*, the passive correlation of one of the active divine names (the Prophet Muhammad being the *marbūb* of the name Allah, K 110).[13] Dard discusses God's Most Beautiful Names in a longish chapter (K 196ff.); he first explains, in Arabic, their essence, then, in Persian, their relation to the creation, for:

> It is the light of the Names which illuminates creation (P 76)

and the 100 Names are comparable to the hundred petals of a centifolia, which form one flower, as Andalib had said in a lovely verse (NA I 260). God, best described as Light (Sura 24/35) reveals this light in various degrees in the creation; it becomes visible first in the Prophet (K 111; D 203), and

> one must see the divine Beauty in the Mustafian (= Muhammad's) mirror.

---

[13] About the problem of *rabb-marbūb* see H. Corbin, 'Creative Imagination', p. 120 ff.

Hence the rays of the divine names enter the world, and are made manifest in man, who is the stage for the manifestation of the names and attributes (K 464), the microcosm reflecting the divine attributes (K 139), so that Dard can proudly address God:

Whatever we have heard of Thee, we have seen in man (U 28).

Such claims lead him in his poetry sometimes to expressions which we would expect rather from faithful followers of the theory of Unity of Being. He not only claims, as did hundreds of poets in Turkisch, Persian, Urdu, Sindhi, and Panjabi that:

In the garden of the World
we are rose, and we are thorn,
where there is a friend, it's us,
where a rival: it is us (U 56),

but reaches what seems like unihibited subjectivism in verses like this:

The rose of the world withered due to our withering;
The heart of mankind froze due to our freezing;
We were the cause of the consideration of the world—
The world became nothing due to our dying (P 77).

For it is the heart of man in which God dwells rather than in heaven or eath (A 302), as Dard says, quoting a well-known *ḥadīth qudsī*; it is man who is

the seal of the degree of creation, for after him no species has come into existence and he is the sealing of the hand of Omnipotence, for God Most Exalted has said 'I created him with both my hands.' (Sura 38/77) He is, so to speak, the divine seal which has been put on the page of contingency, and the Greatest Name of God has become radiant from the bezel of his forehead. The *alif* of his stature points to God's unity, and the *tughrā* of his composition, e.g., the absolute comprehensive picture of his eyes, is a *hā* with two eyes which indicates divine ipseity (*huwiyya*). His mouth is the door of the treasure of divine mysteries which is open at the time of speaking, and he has a face which everywhere holds the mirror of the face of God (Sura 2/109), and he has an eyebrow for which the word 'We honoured the children of Adam' (Sura 17/72) is valid... (K 422). For, if he reaches the experience of unity he resembles himself an *alif*, with the numerical value 1, and is taken out of the numbers connected with imagined multiplicity (K 561).

In fact,

> *Although Adam had not wings*
> *He has reached a place that was not destined even for angels*
> (U 9).

It is this high rank of man which enables him to ascend through the stages of prophets toward the proximity of Muhammad, and thus towards the *ḥaqīqa Muḥammadiyya*, the first principle of individuation. Dard has experienced this way which is not uncommon among Sufis. (I remember a conversation of some people in Istanbul who explained that Pir X and Pir Y could not get along well 'since this one is on the stage of Moses and that one on the stage of Khidr').

Mir Dard first discusses the problem of vicegerency, *khilāfat*. According to him, real vicegerency of the Prophet is conditioned by proximity of time—the time of the *khulafā' ar-rāshidūn* was finished, as Muhammad had predicted, thirty years after his death, when Ali was murdered in 661. However, for the saints such a proximity of time is not necessary. He himself is the first and true vicegerent of his father, the Prince of the Muhammadans, who was both by his descendance as true *sayyid* and his experience closest to the Prophet. His own title First of the Muhammadans points both to the proximity in time and in space, and to him the Prophetic *hadīth* can be applied: 'He is the first who believed in me and the first who will be resurrected on Doomsday with me.' Then he writes in Arabic, as always when he conveys his deepest secrets:

> And He made him his closest friend (*ṣafī*) and his vicegerent on earth and the first vicegerent by virtue of the Adamic sanctity; (Sura 2/31) and God saved him from the ruses of the lower self and the Satan, and made him His friend (*nājī*) by virtue of the Noahic sanctity;
> and God softened the heart of the unfeeling before him and sent to him people of melodies by virtue of the Davidic sanctity;
> and He made him ruler of the kingdom of his body and his nature, by a manifest power, by virtue of the Solomonic sanctity;
> and God made him a friend (*khalīl*) and extinguished the fire of wrath in his nature so that it became 'cool and peaceful' (Sura 21/70) by virtue of the Abrahamic sanctity;
> and God made die the natural passions and slaughtered his lower soul and made him pure from the worldly concern, and he became completely cut off from this world and what is in it, and God honored him with a mighty slaughtering (Sura 37/108) in front of his mild father,

and his father put the knife on his throat in one of the states of being drawn near to God in the beginning of his way, with the intention of slaughtering him for God, and God accepted him well, and thus he is really one who has been slaughtered by God and remained safe in the outward form, as his father gave him the good tiding 'Who has not seen a dead person wandering around on earth may look at this son of mine who lives through me and through me he moves;' and in this state he gained the Ishmaelian sanctity.

And God beautified his creation and character and made him loved by Himself and accepted by His beloved (Muhammad) and attracted the hearts to Him and cast love for him into the heart of his father—a most intense love—and he taught him the interpretations by virtue of the Josephian sanctity (Sura 12/45f);

and God talked to him in inspirational words when he called him 'Verily I am God, put off the shoes' (Sura 20/12) of the relations with both worlds from the foot of your ascent and throw away from the hand of your knowledge the stick with which you lean on things besides Me, for you are in the holy valley' (by virtue of) the Mosaic sanctity

... And God made him one of His complete words and breathed into him from His spirit (Sura 15/29; 38/72), and he became a spirit from Him (Sura 4/169) by virtue of the Jesuic sanctity.

And God honored him with that perfect comprehensiveness which is the end of the perfections by virtue of the Muhammadan sanctity, and he became according to 'Follow me, then God will make you loved by His beloved' and he was veiled in the veil of pure Muhammadanism and annihilated in the Prophet, and no name and trace remained with him, and God manifested upon him His name The Comprising (*jāmiᶜ*) and helped him with angelic support.

And he knows through Gabrielic help without mediation of sciences written in books, and he eats with Michaelian help without outward secondary causes, and he breathes through Israfilian breath and loosens the parts of his body and collects them every time, and he sleeps and awakes every day and is drawn toward death every time by Azrailian attraction. God created him as a complete person in respect to reason, lower soul, spirit and body, and as a place of manifestation of all His names and the manifestations of His attributes, and as He made him His vicegerent on earth in general on humanity generally, did he also make him the vicegerent of his vicegerent on the carpet of specialization, especially for completing His bounty upon him in general and in special, and for perfecting his religion in summary and in detail, and He approved for him of Islam outwardly and inwardly, (cf. Sura 5/5) and made him sit on the throne of vicegerency of his father, as heritage and in realization, and on the seat of the followers of His prophet by attestation and Divine success from God. And he inclined on his invented throne called *al-miᶜyar*, and 'Ornament of the prayer-niche and the pulpit,' and put on his God-be-

stowed crown and lifted his Muhammadan banner and called the faithful with special invitation to the pure Muhammadanism, and returned
to His prophet and was united to His friend thanks to the attraction
of his Lord to whom everything returns. (IK 504 f.)

This description contains a large number of allusions to the
qualities of the Quranic prophets who stand for the various
psychological qualities of man, which are perfectly integrated in
the Prophet Muhammad: Adam is the vicegerent of God, Noah,
of course, is connected with the salvation from the dangers of the
flood. David—the alleged author of the Psalms—is, in Islamic tradition, gifted with unusual musical powers which manifest themselves in Dard in his fondness of music and the constant visits of
masters of music to his house. But David is also the prophet
endowed with the capacity of softening iron and making it into
coats of mail, just as Dard was able to soften the hearts of the
worldly. Solomon is the ruler over man and spirits. Abraham,
thrown by Nimrud into the blazing fire, found the pyre cool like
a garden, and becomes, thus, the model of happiness in suffering,
or, as in Dard's case, an image for the sublimation of the fire of
wrath and lower qualities. Ishmael, not Isaac, is the proposed
offering according to the Quran; but we do not know to which
event in his youth Dard alludes in this passage. Did his father, in
a state of mystical rapture, act like Abraham and was willing to
sacrifice his most beloved son at the beginning of the Muhammadan Path? Does it refer to the sufferings which young Dard
experienced when his father had his first visions? Or is this a kind
of initiation-act which is reminiscent of the initiation in many a
primitive society, and especially in Shamanism? Or is it only the
experience Dard had while his father was graced with the vision
of Imam Hasan? In any case, something unusual must have happened, when the boy was still very young.

But it seems typical of later hagiography that Firaq, in his
account of his ancestor's mystical experiences, skips this detail of
the 'Ismailian sanctity' from his integral translation of the passage (F 124). Joseph is, in poetical and mystical imagery, not
only the model of perfect beauty but also, as in Dard's passage,
the prophet who could interpret dreams.

Dard mentions here only a certain number of great prophets,
not all of those who are mentioned in the Quran, and then, in the
most important book on prophetology, Ibn Arabi's *fuṣūṣ al-ḥikam*

as representatives of the different relations of the Divine with the sphere of humanity. One may be tempted to connect this description with that given by Muhammad Nasir (NA I 243, 259 and II 652 f.) who—though not completely logical,—connects seven or nine attributes of God with the great prophets as it is not rare in later Sufism: Adam manifests the Divine Will or—in the larger chain which he considers typical of the *tarīqa Muhammadiyya*—Creativity; Jesus, Life; Abraham, Knowledge; Noah, Power; David, Hearing; Jacob, Seeing; and Muhammad, Existence, i.e., the most comprehensive attribute (which is the hallmark of the *tarīqa Muhammadiyya*, as Nasir held). All these degrees should be traversed by the mystics. However, Dard's list is more comprehensive and varied, and only in a few cases conforms to the list of his father.

Strange are his relations with the four great archangels, [14] and the passage that his limbs were loosened and put together every day reminds us, once more, of shamanistic practices. [15] A number of Muslim saints in India had the ability of dissolving their limbs so that spectators sometimes were horrified by this sight. When Dard mentions the 'God-bestowed' (*wahbī*) crown one is reminded of Ahmad Sirhindi's *qayyūmiyya* doctrine according to which the *qayyūm* is granted a special quality which is *mauhūb* and distinguishes him from the other beings. However, it is difficult to discern where the throne and the crown belong which the mystic had received from the Lord and which made him the real representative of Him and His prophet on earth—although here influences of the *qayyūmiyya* doctrine seem to be close at hand. As to the 'Muhammadan banner' it plays an important role in the symbolism of his father's book, where it is described as a kind of lance; 'When some brave hero takes it in his hand, and a number of people with sword and shield surround him, he can alone and

---

[14] Michael is the angel in whose hands is, *inter alia*, the nourishment of living beings; this quality of his is alluded to by the masters of Persian mystical poetry, such as Sanā ʾi, Attar, and Rumi, and was mentioned still by nineteenth century poets like Ghalib in Delhi. Cf. M. Horten, Die religiöse Gedankenwelt des Volkes im Islam, p. 62.

[15] Shaman tales contain numerous examples of the loosening of the limbs during initiation. There are also some examples from Muslim saints, mainly in India, thus Pir Chhata in Sind: 'Somebody saw (during the *dhikr*) that the limbs of this love-slain man fell apart, and each of them with a separate tongue proclaimed the name of God' (M. Aʿzam Thattawi, *Tuhfat at-tāhirīn*, p. 159); cf. Dara Shikoh, *Sakīnat al-auliyā* p. 207.

on his own, gain victory over them' (NA I 322, cf. 834, II 868).

We have another interesting document about Mir Dard's mystical life in K 61 ff. He has (K 402) asserted that the things which were unveiled to him and which God made understand him, are beyond the state of the venerable Shaikh Ibn Arabi 'who is the leader and the fountain-head of the Sufis ...' and whose terminology he uses to a large extent in spite of his aversion to the dangerous *wujūdiyya*-theories and his repeated claims that he is neither a Sufi nor a molla, but simply a 'pure Muhammadan.' His account about his visions is revealing in supporting his claim to have reached an extremely high mystical stage (though members of the *mujaddidī* school often claimed, and still claim, that they have passed the delusive state of *waḥdat al-wujūd* and have reached the much superior state of *waḥdat ash-shuhūd*). Dard's experience is of a slightly different kind. He begins in Arabic, for God talked to him, and such an audition is possible only in the language of the Quran:

> He spoke to me: O Vicegerent of God and o Sign (*āya*) of God, verily I have witnessed your state of servantship (*ᶜubūdiyya*); now you witness my Divinity, for you are My servant and he whom I have accepted and whom My prophet has accepted.
>
> I said: O Lord, I witness, that there is no God but Thou, and I witness that Thou are a witness over all things. O my God and object of my worship, and there is no goal for me besides Thee! I am the family-member of Thy beloved and part of Thy Nightingale.
>
> And He said: O ᶜAbdallah, o who knows God (*ᶜārif billāh*), verily I have made you a place of manifestation comprising all My manifestations, so bring now My signs to all my creatures. And I have called you the Utmost Sum Total (*jamᶜ*) and the Muhammadan Sum Total, and who obeys you obeys God and the Prophet.
>
> I said: O Lord, I accept all Thy orders and call the people to Thy religion and Thy Islam; so lead them to me and to my father so that I may lead them to Thee and to Thy prophet, and Thou guidest whom Thou willst.
>
> He said: O you to whom have come the *wāridāt*, o Source of the signs, verily We have made you a sign for people so that perhaps they become guided, but most of the people do not know.
>
> I said: O Lord, Thou knowest what is in me and I do not know what is in Thee—if thou punishest them—they are Thy servants, and if thou forgivest them—Thou art the Wise.
>
> And He said: Say: If Reality were more than that which was unveiled to me, then God would verily have unveiled it to me, for He, Most High, has completed for me my religion and perfected for me His

favor and agreed for me Islam as religion, and if the veil would be opened I would not gain more certitude—verily my Lord possesses mighty bounty. (cf. P. 8).

After this report of his vision in which he was invested as the true successor of the Prophet, Mir Dard goes on speaking of the names which God had bestowed upon him. We know that some Muslim mystics in early times used different names for themselves—one of the most confusing chapters in the biography of the martyr mystic al-Hallaj was (at least for his family and his enemies), the fact that he called himself differently in every country, and letters were addressed to him accordingly. Later mystics were graced with the knowledge of their heavenly names which were different from their normal names—Najmuddin Kubra is an outstanding example of this experience. Dard who had dwelt quite a while on his proper names *Khwāja Mīr* and *Dard*, gives, in this paragraph, a strange combination of his 'real' names. His longish discussion of the Divine Names is closely connected with this subject: for the Divine names are the vehicle through which God can be recognized in the world and thus he, who knows his own names knows those of God, according to the *hadīth* 'Who knows himself knows the Lord;' for the divine names become manifested in different human beings. Dard, like many mystics before him, has understood the Quranic story that 'God taught Adam the names' (Sura 2/32) as a symbol for 'investing him with his Divine attributes.'

> The name and mark which is Khwaja Mir Dard is only my relative name which was fixed, not my essential name; for in the essential name there must not be the consideration of one who considers it and the putting of one who puts it (on somebody). And it must not disappear when the person disappears.
> And I have got many of these attributal and relative names, namely: Light of the Helper - Son of the imām - Lamentation of the Nightingale—Pain of the friend—Pain with result (Dard with his younger brother, Athar)—Secret of the father—Rosegarden of Reality—Nightingale of the path—Sign of God—He who knows God—the Great Khwaja—My I (*man-i man*)—the Place upon which the inspirations have come down (*mūrid alwāridāt*)—Who has been supported by support—the Master of *tauhīd*—Spirit of the world—Behind the Behind—Pure Muhammadan—First of the Muhammadans—Guide of the Helper—Proof of the Helper—Essence of the Helper—Adornment of the Helper—Unseparable part—Adjoining to the One—and other names which can not be counted ...

For He taught Adam all the names, that means He made man the
place of manifestation for all His names and cast the light of His
perfections into this mirror. But according to the custom of the Lord
I shall show before you 99 names which point to my all comprehen-
sive human reality, and at some time I have been elected with them:
Light (*nūr*) - Manifestation (*zuhūr*) - Knowing - Known - Summarizing
- Separating - Comprehending - Collected - Outward - Inward - Witness
- Witnessed - Hearing - Heard - With Beauty - With only little tremen-
dous Majesty - Intended - Existent - Non-existent - Imagined - Seeker -
Sought - Lover - Beloved - Speaking - Seeing - Slave - Living - Guiding -
Unique - Disciple - Feeling - Perceptible - Gifted with reason - Intelli-
gible - Source of divine signs - Compriser of attributes - Noble from
two sides - Happy in both worlds - Repentant - Going - Pure - Without
Fear - Patient - Grateful - Trusting in God - Guaranteeing - Merciful -
He upon whom mercy is bestowed - He who is forgiven - Kind - Wise -
Faithful - Muslim - Dear to the hearts - Leader - Independent - Mean-
ingful - Truth - Absolute - Fettered - Supported - Named - Enigma -
Magnet - Who is without cheating - Most complete manifestation place
- Greatest part - Reality of realities - Well wisher of the creatures -
Divine melody - Instrument of awareness - Loving heart - Sincere
servant - Absolute certitude - Clear explanation - Man of good quali-
ties - Companion on the path - With straight character - Without needs
- Billowing ocean - Speech without tongue - Tongue without speech -
Friendly heart - Soul - Saint - Rich - Poor - Prince - Eternal - Guided -
Heir - Vicegerent of God - Drawn near - Refined - Acting - Compre-
hensive - Sent - Lord of the Prayer mat. And my essential name is in
Persian the word *man*, 'I', and in Arabic the word *anā*, 'I' ... (K 62).

This concept 'I' is common to every language and to every-
body and through it the one Divine existence manifests itself—
Andalib had argued in exactly the same way, only adding the
Urdu pronouns (NA I 245).

Dard's 99 names—as well as his attributive names— are psycho-
logically highly interesting. They are put together apparently
partly according to reasons of harmony, for many of them
rhyme. Arabic and Persian expressions alternate without fixed
rules, and one is surprised to find a large number of names which
are used, otherwise, only for God himself—from Light, which is
the central concept of Divine existence in Dard's theology, to
Behind the Behind, one of the favorite expressions of Sufis to
denote the ineffable Divine existence.

Dard does not develop further theories from this unveiling of
his own divinely bestowed names, and only once, in a later sentence (N 306) he alludes to these 99 names and stresses the com-

bination *pāk-bībāk*, 'pure, fearless,' which helps him to live according to the Quranic word 'They do not fear the blame of a blaming one' (Sura 5/59). This peculiar set of names gives him the strength to speak whatever is in his heart, so 'that no shopkeeper-shai<u>kh</u> could explain the reality with this correctness, not any contemptible ecstatic could utter words of such truthfulness.'

The idea of surrounding a human being with a large number of honorific names is definitely inherited from his father who has, in the *Nāla-yi ʿAndalīb*, invented long chains of titles for his heroes (NA I 84, II 123) and heroines (NA II 127) and even negative attributes for the evil forces (NA I 290). In Dard's case they may also point to the problems that puzzled him for his childhood to his last day: the search for identity. [16]

THE ASCETIC AND 'THE WORLD'.

Dard's spiritual diaries, as we may call his *Four Risālas*, only rarely speak of the afflictions which his hometown had to undergo almost every year. His friend Mir compared Delhi to a colorful picture-book full of miniatures, which are now faded; Dard, in turn, said in a quatrain with clever puns, written according to the sequence of the book shortly after 1190/1776:

> *Delhi, which time has now devastated:*
> *Tears are flowing now instead of its river.*
> *This town had been like the face of the lovely,*
> *And its suburbs like the down of the beloved ones!*

The blessed town of Delhi, in which is the burial garden of the 'Qibla of the Worlds' and which God may keep cultivated until resurrection was a wonderful rosegarden, but has now been trampled down by the autumn of events of time. It had lovely rivulets and trees and in-

---

[16] The problem is very well summed up by Merlin Swartz in his article, 'The Position of Jews in Arab Lands', in: Reflections on the Middle East Crisis, ed. H. Mason, p. 30: 'A man's name was viewed as participating in the very essence of his person and, as such revealed something of the essential character of his being. This meant, in effect, that a man's name was bound up in the most intimate way with the question of his identity.' R. Kipling's 'Kim' contains also a fine remark about the importance of the name (ch. 11). The *dhikr* of the Divine Names, mentioned NA II 108, meant for Dard to 'acquire the Divine names' (K 217), as it was said *takhallaqu bi-akhlāq Allāh*, Acquire the qualities of God, a remark which may help to understand his own 99 names.

habited places of people of all kinds, and has now become the plunder
of the blow of fate. It was in every respect of the surface of earth
alike to the face of the moonlike beloved and charming like the freshness of the mole (pun on *sabzī*, 'greenery' and 'freshness'). O God,
keep it from all the afflictions and calamities and make it a safe place
and nourish its people from fruits and grant that those who enter it be
safe. (N 104).

Though he alludes once to 'the sphere which goes awry and the
froward time and the different events which they produce'
(D 154) he maintains that those who have found themselves close
to God are steadfast in their behavior; but it seems that he, too,
was troubled by the unlucky inhabitants of the town who sought
shelter and help with him. The relevant sentence may have been
written about 1196/1782 when the whole of Delhi territory was
afflicted by a famine which 'swept away something like a third to
a half of the rural population'. May we perhaps date to this
period his strange Persian quatrain about the swarms of thronging
locusts which, however, disappear because they have no true
leader? (P 94). Dard complains that the confused thoughts of the
sons of time make him pensive, perplexed and grieved, and that
'from all the four sides strange strange whirlstorms of dust of
their minds' rise:

> From four sides the dust of hearts rose so much
> That it brought me, while still alive, under the dust.

He prays that God may preserve the unhappy population and not
allow foreign armies to enter the town, and keep the inhabitants
free from affliction and pillage and from difficulties in earning
their lives, and preserve them from thinking that

one has to go here, or to go there ... What behoves them is to follow
the path of God and the Muhammadan path, so that they may pluck
the roses of inner blessings from the rosegarden of their company and
listen to the lamentation of the Nightingale and understand his books.

To realize this ideal was probably difficult for the poverty
stricken, hungry and helpless inhabitants of Delhi!

However, Dard's preoccupation with the people was not only
theoretical although he never entered practical politics as did
Shah Waliullah. Late in his work (D 270) he once more speaks of
the destructions and how people sought shelter and tells that he,
for about a year, used to spend all day, from before the morning

prayer till after the night prayer, at his father's tomb, without taking with him any friend or child; in the evening the friends would gather and would drag home 'that bewildered person of the valley of faith' but early in the morning he turned again to the sacred place where he offered his prayer, hoping for help from *an-Nāṣir*, The Helper. A quatrain describes this state—his father's tomb is the threshold from which he does not want to get separated.

These visits were the only interruption of his daily routine. He tells that he constantly lived in the *bait al-maʿmūr* of his Pir, i.e., in his paternal *dargāh*, and never went out but to visit his father's tomb, for:

> it has been said 'Who is in one place is everywhere, and who is everywhere is nowhere' (A 312).

Yet these are only a few scattered remarks. In general, the afflictions that came over Dehli did not disturb him too much; they rather proved to him that real life is found only in the Divine Presence:

> Why should I go out? It means just a loss of time, for everywhere there is nothing apparent but annihilation in annihilation and at every place the lustre of 'Everything is perishing but God's Face' (Sura 28/88) becomes visible. And I melt every moment like ice from the vision of the sun of Reality and destroy in every wink my personification which is bound by supposition: not a sound of a chord lifts the head of desire from the shirt of my heart, and not a harmony raises the flame of sound from the harp of my heart. There is no suitability in body and soul, and no capacity in the marrow of my bones, and the most strange rosegarden of 'I recognized my Lord through the vitiation of my intentions' blossomed, and everywhere the twig of 'There is nothing sought but God' sprouts (D 33).

Indeed, why should he go out? In true Naqshbandi fashion (which is a development of earlier mystical theories) Dard tried to practice *safar dar waṭan*, 'journey in one's home,' one of the eight principles on the Path. He himself has explained this term (K 468): it means, first, that the wayfarer leaves his lower and bad qualities, reaches works of obedience, and acquires praiseworthy qualities in his interior journey. This results in the mystic's return to God and his constant raising through the various ranks of existence, and eventually leads him to the place of Unity, where his true homeland is. This is the technical aspect of *safar dar waṭan*, but Dard, like many of the 17th and 18th century poets in India uses the term also as a poetical device. Combined with another important aspect of Naqshbandi training, the *khalwat dar anjuman*, 'seclusion in the multitude,' he analyses this constant interplay of journey and being at home:

> *Existence is travelling, non-existence is home,*
> *the heart is solitude, and the eye multitude* (U 127).

The sky, too, is constantly caught in 'travel in its home' (P 11, U 8), and so is the candle when it melts, travelling toward annihilation (P 124). If one sees it correctly, travelling is home, and home is travelling (P 14, cf. P 24, 35), until the seeker has reached a state of selflessness where there is

> *no thought of a journey,*
> *no reminiscence of home* (U 54).

Here, in this world, the mystic experiences exile and prison: Dard speaks of the *qaid-i firang*, 'European prison,' an expression that had become popular after the first attacks by the Portuguese on Indian harbors in the mid-16th century. Nasir Andalib had frequently used this word and since the Europeans were connected, in some strange way of poetical thinking, with colorful paintings, Dard connects the multicolored show of this world with a European prison into which the soul-birds have fallen, bewitched by the lovely hues and shapes (S 61). And thus, he strove to liberate his soul-bird from the dazzling outward world and travel back home, to the colorless source of colors.

As little as Mir Dard speaks about the terrible events in the political life in Delhi during the third quarter of the 18th century, as silent is he about other facts of daily life. What did he think about family life, women and children? Once he admonishes men in a longish sermon (K 523) not to overdress, 'for outward decoration is a sign of inward depravity,' and, he continues:

> This is the sake of women. These creatures with weak intellect which God has created for this occupation have nothing but this work on their carpet, and if they do not adorn themselves what should they do and what would happen, and as long as they do not show themselves nicely to their husband, how could that work which is necessary for begetting and procreation be done frequently and nicely, and how would the human race appear?

Was this traditional Islamic view the real opinion of a man who spoke with such deep love of his venerable, pious mother? Even more: his father had spoken with high regard of the pious and God-seeking women who entered the Muhammadan Path and will gain their reward already in this world (NA II 344), and had praised the *mu 'mināt*—the believing women:

> What shall I say about the pious women? For some of them have progressed so far that they have surpassed many men in learning and mystical knowledge and love and charity ...

He was sure that they, too, will be blessed with the vision of God in the other world (NA I 832), an idea not generally accepted by Muslim theologians. Of course, Muhammad Nasir, too, held that the wife should regard her husband as the representative of the Lord, according to the Prophetic tradition: 'If it were permissable to prostrate before anyone but God, I would say that the wives should prostrate before their husbands' (NA I 578)—a *hadīth* which reminds us rather of Hindu ideals of marriage where the husband is, in fact, the representative of Divine power. Muhammad Nasir even uses the idea of man being the manifestation of the different Divine names and qualities in an allegory: the virgin recognizes, in the moment of consummation of marriage, in her husband the qualities of Tremendous Majesty (*jalāl*) instead of those of Mercy (*jamāl*) to which she was used before; but the husband explains to her that this seeming cruelty of his by piercing her body is only the sign of highest love by which she reaches 'naked union' (NA I 560).

As for Dard himself, his prejorative remark about women was, like some other paragraphs of the *'Ilm ul-kitāb*, probably merely theoretical, for in later time in his life (N 70) he all of a sudden exclaims in the midst of mystical discussion:

> I love my wife and family very very dearly and am very much captured in the love of wife and children. God knows whether this comes from the animal powers, or is due to human modes, or is only a sensual love, or barely the appearance of the Lordship of Mercifulness—in any case, my friend is he who loves them. For today or tomorrow it will happen that I lift my foot from here and entrust them to the Real Protector and Helper; who but the merciful God will love them after me?

Of course, he puts his love of his family into a wider frame; just as the Prophet said 'Fatima is part of me,' thus they are part of him, since love of the family of the Prophet is a duty for every believer, it includes his own family (being true sayyids) too—every blessing uttered for Muhammad and his family works also upon his family.

This 'family' also comprises particularly the fourth caliph, Ali ibn abi Talib, 'the unveiler of the pre-eternal knowledge, the one acquainted with hidden and open mysteries' who is, according to his own statement, the dot beneath the letter *b* of the *basmala*:

> All mysteries of the Divine speech are in the Glorious Quran, and all the mysteries of the Quran are in the *Sūrat al-Fātiha*, and all mysteries of the *Fātiha* are in the formula *Bismillāh*, and all the mysteries of the *Basmala* are in the *b* of *Bismillāh*, and all the mysteries of the *b* are in the dot beneath the *b*, and I am this dot beneath the *b* (K 75).

This high place of Ali leads Dard at a later point to meditate about the veneration of the 'Shah of Najaf,' whose love is necessary for every 'true Muhammadan':

> If you have the pearl of Aden in your hand but do not bring the richness of the heart into your hand, nothing but empty-handedness will be your gain, and if you have the pearl of Najaf in your palm, and do not engrave the love of the Shah of Najaf in your heart, then there is nothing for you but rubbing the palms of regret (S 212).

Love of the family is one of the outstanding features in Mir Dard's personality. If one remembers the harsh words of some early Sufis against the fetters of family life, the love of family and children, or reads how leaders of the Chishtiyya order in India were notorious for the disinterest in their families one understands that Mir Dard's attitude is by no means typical of a Sufi. Time and again he mentions he beloved brother, Athar, and his relation with his own son, Mir Muhammad Diya un-Nasir, reflects in a certain way his own relation to his father Andalib (K 639/540):

> O ignorant and veiled man—the tenderness of the father which is lavishly spent upon the son is a manifestation of the kindness of His lordliness, for in this form the Lord of Lords nourishes His slave, and casts love from Himself into the heart of the father, so that he may love his son and show high ambition in nourishing and educating him. Further, to follow him—I mean the father—and to obey the sire who is the place of manifestation of the names 'Creator' and 'Lord' is essentially the same as to obey Him ... just as he who obeys the Prophet

obeys God; for the Prophet is the spiritual father, and that is why his pure wives are called the mothers of the faithful, and the father is the vicegerent of the Prophet, ... especially when the father is a sincere Muhammadan and also a spiritual guide, for thanks to the grace of God a rotten and unworthy son never comes to such an excellent father. O God, forgive me and my parents and be merciful to them since they have educated me when I was little ...

Dard continues his meditation about the relation of father and son until he concludes that a special relation of love exists between them—the father is, for the son, the manifestation of Divine mercy, and the son is, for the father, a Divine gift (wahb),

and the tenderness and education which we have seen from our elders towards ourselves should be executed upon our little ones, and we should not make faults in polishing and instructing them and should spread the shade of mildness on their head, but not so much that they become spoiled and useless ... (K 556).

Dard had three children—at least, the names of his three surviving children are given as Alam, Barati Begum, and Zinat un-Nisa Begum. Mir Alam, who lived for a long time in Bengal, became leader of the convent after his uncle Athar. His son, Mir Muhammad Bakhsh died during his father's lifetime; a daughter, Amani Begum, had a daughter Umda Begum, who, in turn had a daughter Shams un-Nisa Begum. Her son, Nasir Nadhir with the pen-name Firaq, is the author of the *Maikhana-yi Dard*, the only comprehensive description of Dard and his family. As to Barati Begum, she died without issue; Zinat un-Nisa was the mother of the poet Muhammad Nasir Ranj (d. 1845), one of whose daughters was married to the poet Momin Khan Momin (d. 1851) who, besides writing charming love poetry has also praised and encouraged the followers of the *tariqa Muhammadiyya* under Ahmad of Bareilly and Ismail Shahid in their struggle against the Sikh.

Dard sees his family first and foremost as the family of 'pure Muhammadans' and thus he tells:

Just as the lamentation of the venerable Nightingale completely includes the meaning Pain, 'Dard,' and pain becomes generated and results from it, thus *dard*, 'pain' comprises the meaning of 'result', *athar*, and result comes from pain, and thus my dear brother is in this respect my associate, and we are two brothers both in form and in reality—in form because we are from one mother and father, and in reality because we are on one path and knowledge. In short, when the time of mercy came and Divine mercy became effervescent, I took all my children and the family of the Qibla of Both Worlds under my protection and made them enter the rank of a sincere Muhammadan, and made them pass before the eyes of his Excellency and this High Person accepted them with the view of grace, and I brought all my family and children and the relatives of the Qibla of Both Worlds according to their different ranks and took them till resurrection under his protection and brought them to his Eminency, and he sponsored them under his fold and brought them in the presence of the most holy Prophet, and he took all of them in the fold of his intercession and brought them in the palace of Divine proximity and wanted intercession for them. From there it was (divinely) directed: 'They have been honored by Sincere Muhammadanism and belong with their faith and their confidence into the group of Our servants who have been brought near and upon We have mercy and forgive them ...' (K 418).

And at present, the author asserts, a number of friends and disciples who have studied his and his father's books have come, and he has brought them into the Divine presence and considered them his own family according to the prophetic tradition 'Who walks on my way these are my family.'

It is, in a certain way, consoling to see that in the following paragraph Dard explains at length the possibility that even those elect ones, nay, even he, himself are still weak creatures and liable to sinning.

It may be mentioned at random that the family tradition counts even some jinns among Mir Dard's disciples, who had been converted by his son Alam in far-away Bengal and then stayed in his house (F 143).

OLD AGE

Life passed from station to station:

Childhood passed, and then youth was reached;
Now comes old age—do not be negligent.
As much as you are on your own place like the thread of
the rosary,
The stations pass on the way like beads (R 116).

Dard's last books contain numerous allusions to his age (he was in his late fifties when he began to compose the *Nāla*). Now

the time for return to the Lord has come, and it is better to retire
from people and to consider the world a hut of sorrows in repentance
and penitence (N 33).

Somewhat later he thinks that he now better 'should keep the
flame of the tongue silent' (A 201). This image can be better
understood when one thinks of the general poetical idea that old
age resembles the morning. As for the candle, it has to be extinguished at dawn. This morning is welcome to him, for it brings
peace of the heart, which makes the day radiant.

> But I have spent the night of youth also mostly awake and have never
> rested like immersed on a bed of negligence, and even though I have
> slumbered a trifle I became soon awake again and opened the eye of
> understanding-a-warning and looked towards the state of old age ...
> and spent my whole life in waiting for death (D 309).

We find a great number of verses with this imagery in Dard's
Persian and Urdu lyrics and he has commented upon this imagery
in a long-winded paragraph (K 276); the morning, bearing the
shirt of the night is like the poet's breast out of which the heart
comes sun-like (U 122); but the longer the more he sees in the
whiteness of dawn a reminder of the shroud (P 11, 53).

Happy that he has left behind him that night of youth, he
enjoys the fact that with the decline of animal powers and the
perfection of human qualities, man loses sensuous appetites and
resembles more the angels (D 180). These thoughts moved him,
in his 62nd year, when he began to write down Sham ᶜ -i mahfil;
for at this age there is no time for long hope (tūl-i amal) (Intr. cf.
P 35). What should one do at this age?

> Now one should make the eye weep like the dew-drop and expect the
> rise of the sun of the smaller resurrection, and not slumber in the
> sleep of negligence like narcissus-buds ... (S 86).

Essentially he seems to enjoy his age though

> age which brings damage has made me very lean, but the help of my
> Pir had put light into my cup so that I can light the candle of guidance
> from this light and do not burn from the grief of weakness of old age,
> and I do not turn too much toward the repair of my body and do not
> spend much thinking in caring for it; but I estimate well the handful
> of bones which I have as morsel for the mouth of the grave, and do
> absolutely not open the door of caring for the body, and do not fall
> into the snare of thinking how to get fatter ... (S 170).

The danger of spoiling his 'material body which is God's she-camel' (Sura 7/71) (S 261) was certainly far from the mystical poet about whose ascetic practices his biographers tell amazing things. Besides, the economic and political situation in Delhi in the 1780's was certainly not such that a man could easily enjoy life and get fatter.

After all, contentment was the major quality of the ascetically minded mystics from the very beginning of Sufi history; and Dard says, with a slight attempt to joke, and using the comparison, eye = goblet, which frequently recurs in early Urdu poetry:

Here, you have to be content with two goblets,
It is the house of the eye, not a house of drunkenness.
(U 65).

Mir Dard is reported to have rigorously kept his fast, until the 'fingernail of the crescent' opens the closed mouth of the fasting servant (P 91/92); he even added to the prescribed ways of fasting, as modern leaders of the Naqshbandiyya, too, ascribe great importance to rigid fasting, though otherwise this order does not begin the instruction with 'breaking the lower self' of the novice but rather with purifying and educating his heart. Firaq, as several others, mentions a certain kind of fasting, called *dīrh fāqa*, which consisted of abstaining from food and drinking for 21 nights and days (F 121); other aspects of Dard's fasting are likewise mentioned. We are inclined to sympathize with the complaint of his little daughter when a plate, dreamt of for days, was carried away by the father to feed the guests in the mosque instead of his family ... To what extent these stories are historically true, is difficult to prove: they conform to the traditional ascetic ideal but must contain at least some truth.

Mir Dard proudly speaks of his poverty (*faqr*). When he confronts general poverty and poverty of the elite, the latter is for him, as for Attar, an equivalent of *fanā*, 'annihilation,' and permanent remaining in God, and is 'a rank among the ranks of proximity':

And praised be God who made me one of the poor who are exclusively kept in God's way, and made 'poverty my pride' so that I became independent of everything besides Him, and made the Divine Greatness (*kibriyā*) my cloak and Grandeur my veil, and veiled me in the light of His tremendous Majesty from the views, and showed me to the eyes by

the appearance of His mercy and honored me with the robe of honor
of the subsistence of truth in God ... And I am under the domes of His
wealth and Greatness, and nobody but He and His prophet
knows me by my countenance since I am the poor of His door and the
beggar for mercy from Him, and my Lord did not allow me to go to
the doors of the princes and the sultan, and I belong to the 'benchers'
(ahl-i suffa) of poverty which was the pride of our Prophet ... I belong
to his family which God has purified. God is the friend of the faithful
and it is He who made me one of the sayyids and sent upon me
blessings and opened my breast and put off me my burden which
pressed my back and uplifted my memory so that I found ease in the
very pressure, and together with outward pressure I found inward ease
in every state (K 605) [the whole paragraph is in Arabic].

That means, he is closest to his ancestor, the Prophet, because of
the high rank of poverty which brings him under the protection
of God—

> *From the fountainhead of poverty*
> *drank the date-palm of my richness* (P 6).

He compares his poverty to a wilderness:

Praise be to God that this wretched madman until now has nicely
traversed the endless deserts of poverty and never nourished the beasts
of animal imaginations in the corner of his free mind—may God make
him reach by virtue of His grace the end of this sacred valley ...
(N 82).

But *faqr* is not only the state of which the Prophet was proud;
Ali ibn Abi Talib is likewise credited with having written the line:

We are satisfied with the lot of the mighty among us;
We have knowledge, and the ignorant have money.
For money disappears soon,
But knowledge remains and does not finish.

His poverty is not bankruptcy (U 90) but rather the kingdom of
absolute peace of mind; when one longs no more for the king's
crown nor for the beggar's cap. It is told that he, in his youth,
asked Muhammad Shah, the ruler, not to disturb him by his visits
(F 121) though he later did not mind the presence of Shah
Alam II in his musical sessions. Still, he sings proudly:

> *Kings are never mentioned, Dard, in our meetings;*
> *Only sometimes Ibrahim Adham has been mentioned!*
> (U 15).

For he, the prince of Balkh, gave up the throne for the happiness of perfect poverty. In a charming verse Dard sings:

> *On the throne of rulership sits everyone, o Dard,*
> *Who gives his throne to the wind, like Solomon* (P 13).

The greatest evil is *ḥirṣ*, 'greed', a word which occurs often in Dard's later prose and his poetry. He admonishes his disciples to forget everything in recollecting God

> so that the spider of negligence does not weave the warp and woof of the thought of expecting livelihood in your mind, and the fly of greed never sits on the gracious table of inward collection (*jam*ᶜ*iyat*) (D 200).

Greed, as much as wealth and power which result from it make man stonehearted—Dard had more than enough opportunities to watch the greed of the politicians who struggled in Delhi with every kind of intrigue, hatred, and meanness. He reverses the classical image of the rain drop which gains its real value by becoming a pearl:

> *Whosoever becomes mighty and rich, his heart becomes hard—*
> *Every drop which became a pearl gets a stone-heart* (P 34).

He was free from this kind of greed, but free also from the greed which caused most of his contemporary poets to leave Delhi for a safer place where they could better sell their poetry. He had been waiting for death throughout his life,

> and I thought every sound which I heard to be the lament of mourning for myself, and considered every door which I saw the gate of my own grave. What shall I say how I brought the night of my youth to an end with sleeplessness until this day, and how I passed it with awareness so that I sometimes put my ear on the sound of the feet of the coming of my beloved and sometimes opened the door of my heart to 'Truth came and falsehood was destroyed' (Sura 17/83) (D 309).

In this expectation he had spent his youth until he was blessed with the overwhelming vision of Divine reality in which he, then, lived throughout his ripe age.

But the question 'Who am I?' which had made him cry in his childhood never ceased puzzling him, though on a higher level of mystical embarrassment:

Drowned in the sea of pure bewilderment the shore of which is in-
visible, and so much lost in the ocean of the vision of the Absolute
Being that I can not see a trace from my own partial existence, it is
impossible that I should come to myself—and how could I reach, then,
God? (N 271, cf. N 136).

His poetry touches the same chord and sometimes reaches expressions which we would rather expect in a modern 'poet of the
Ego' than in a mystic who is supposed to lose his self in constant
contemplation, if not union, of God:

If the shaikh makes me reach God, what does it matter?
Oh, I offer myself to him who brings me to myself! (P 11)

For, as he says in another verse:

We are unaware of our own manifestation in this garden:
The narcissus does not see its own spring with its own eye
(P 45).

In all his ecstatic moments and his search for an answer he
could never find

the answer to the question 'Who am I? and how and where shall I die
and how and why did I live till now?' And I see the gnosis and interior
knowledge of all the human beings beneath this greatest amazement
of mine—for they have woven the warp and woof of imagination for
themselves; and I find the peace and quietude of the individualities of
my race beneath this highest bewilderment of mine, for they have
found consolation with their own thoughts of reckoning and supposi-
tion. From the Eternal Help (i.e., Abdul Qadir Gilani) the word 'My
foot is on the neck of every saint' appeared perhaps in the effer-
vescence of such a state, and from the beloved of the Most Exalted,
Shah Naqshband, the phrase 'Whatever was seen and known is all
otherness and must be denied with the word No' probably came on
his lips in the moment of such an unveiling—in any case, until the
breaking of resurrection this very light of the sun of 'I have a time
with God' sheds its rays on the heart of his pure family, and the grace
of this pure Muhammadan gives light to this group (N 63).

Again, the highest vision and complete detachment from this
world is granted especially to members of the family of the Prophet—both Gilani and Naqshband were *sayyids*, and the Prophetic tradition 'I have a time with God to which even Gabriel has
no access' is the central truth: for in this experience the closest
possible approximation of man and God has been expressed, an

approximation which can be inherited (as he thinks, exclusively)
by the Prophet's offspring.

Nevertheless, the question of his own existence is repeated
again and again:

> Though a world sings the fame of me, the lost one, and people come
> and look at me according to their thoughts, but ... the door of self-
> knowledge does absolutely not yet open, and it was not yet found
> who I am and for what all this longing of mine is. And still stranger is,
> that in spite of not knowing (myself) I always remain in the torture of
> my self. Then it was understood that the figure of my existence sits
> like a bezel with the name of somebody else, and the dream of my
> selfhood sees, like velvet, the thought of others, and I am just like a
> seal with my mind dug up from my side, and like velvet, my whole
> body is standing hair, top to bottom wounded by existence. [17] God
> may keep me safe from the evil in both worlds and leave not the
> burden of the suspicion of my existence in my head ... (S 120).

The image of the bezel is very frequent in mystical poetry
(certainly not without allusions to Ibn Arabi's *Fuṣūṣ al-ḥikam*,
'Bezels of Wisdom'). [18] The heart of the saint is often compared
to a ringstone on which the Divine names and attributes are
engraved. 'All my faults become perfectly correct like a sealring'
(P 144), but it behooves man to get away once the impression of
this seal is left in the world (P 84), e.g., when his outward form
disappears, which points to the engraved name of God (P 56), for
the bezel has no selfishness (*khūdī*) (P 7, cf. P 147). Dard once
sees his attributive names engraved on the seal of his own existence, and becomes confused as to his real being all the more as
he is 'black-faced' (e.g., disgraced) like a sealing—ring
(K 505)—who is he, and where does he stand in front of the
Divine Reality? Although everybody knows him, and although he
is capable of explaining so many things to his disciples, he has
not found himself—'like a mirror, completely drowned in the
perspiration of confusion' (N 205).

Dard's famous Urdu verse:

> *The states of the two worlds are clear to my heart—*
> *Till now I have not understood what I am ...* (U 49)

---

[17]   In Persian, the velvet is considered to be sleeping, when it is soft and no hair
stands up; the image of the velvet whose hair stands up and which is, so to speak,
awake in confusion or horror, became very fashionable in 17th and 18th century
Indo-Muslim literature, mainly in Bedil's work.

[18]   More bezels: P 118, 146, U 96, 139; as image of transitoriness P 101: the kings
of the world are compared to sealstones which have now been lifted.

reflects the same attitude, and may have been written at the same time when he sighs (N 326):

> As much as I came to know God, I did not become selfknowing, and though I reached God I did not reach myself; for to know God is the same as to acknowledge the inability of knowing oneself ...

The reason for this seeming contradiction is that selfknowledge belongs only to God, namely the knowledge of the Essence itself. Such a knowledge, however, is impossible for the contingent being which lives and exists only through Divine grace. Classical Sufism had already held that the right to say 'I' belongs only to God; Dard, like many mystics, expands this idea, and yet tries to find the secret of his own existence which is non-real as far as it is contingent and not necessary, and is real as far as it is endowed by God with existence and forms the mirror of and the manifestation-place for the Divine Names. Thus the question 'Who am I?' can never be solved properly. Dard strictly denies the possibility of essential union of man and God, which would mean that man is part of God. Man is created in time and can never become God even though all Divine names are manifested through him. This is the idea which he defends against the *wujūdi-* mystics. Sometimes, though, his argumentation passes the limits of logical expression.

In the last phase of his life he once more sighs:

> Woe, where shall I seek my lost heart and which side should I go to follow it, and whom shall I ask what is good for it, and how can I become 'one with heart' (*ṣāhib-i dil*)? For my melancholy heart has, in thinking of the Essence which is the 'Behind the Behind,' gone so far from itself and has hidden itself so much from my dull view that no information about its going reaches this imaginary individuation—and how could it reach anybody else? And the sound of its feet does not reach the ear of me, the unknown—and how less could others hear it? But then I understood that according to the fact that everything which falls into a salt mine becomes salt, this consumed one has reached the degree of absence, attaining slowly the place which he has reached, and concealed itself from my outwardly-seeing eye in the veil of concealment and got lost in the very place where it ran around. And 'everything perishes save His Face' (Sura 28/88) (D 161).

The lost heart, so common in the mystical poetry, is completely submerged in the world of the Unseen, the Divine essence, perhaps, as some Naqshbandis would say, in the '*adam*,' the 'positive Not-Being,' i.e., the divine 'beyond Allah.' The image of the salt mine is found as early as in Attar's poetry and in Rumi's *Math-nawī* for the state of *fanā*ʾ and spiritual regeneration, as Rumi says:

> When a dead ass falls into a salt mine,
> He puts ass-ness and the state of death aside (M II 1344).

Dard's constant preoccupation with death and annihilation—so typical of classical Sufism—resulted in his high evaluation of a common custom in popular Islam, e.g., visiting of tombs, since 'tombs are so to speak the footprint of those who have gone the way of annihilation' (A 162).

In his ʿ*aqīda*, Dard faithfully defends the reality of the escha-tological instrumentarium, although the only goal for the mystic is eternal life in the contemplation of the Divine Light. However, it is a sign of love that people should visit the tombs of their deceased family members, and recite there the *fātiḥa* and other efficient prayers so that God may also grant them a good end thanks to this good deed. For such a visit is an atonement for sins, and people may become more thoughtful about their own end: big people would become more tender and gracious toward the small, and the small would understand that their happiness lies in serving the great people (A 247). The faithful should also look after the tombs and keep them well and urge others to visit the tombs of the great, i.e., of the pious and saints, and they should gather to remember the anniversary of their death. Only those without insight do not consider such visits necessary or do not find spiritual happiness and bliss in such an act, for

> they do not see any difference between stone and brick, or between Kaʿba and church.

How could they, then, hope to find the intercession of those whom they have neglected? (S 117)

> *The one who has no living heart*
> *Does not come to our tomb* ... (P 39)

he says in one of his poems, and the mutual relation of the living and the dead is expressed in the lines:

> *You must pass by the tomb of us, the strangers—*
> *As long as we were alive, we passed through your street*
> (p 46).

Often he had mentioned, in his poems, life as a sleep, a dream, according to the Prophetic tradition 'Human beings are asleep, and when they die they awake'. Every manifestation in this world, so full of grief, seemed to him the longer the more like a passing dream the interpretation of which can be found only in the other world. He complains that numberless beautiful figures have gone under the dust, which thus has turned into a treasure-house of beauty, but every handful of dust was once a heart (P 96)—an idea which was certainly not new in Islamic poetry, but has, in its Urdu expression, influenced Ghalib's famous ghazal with the rhyme-word *hogā 'iñ*, 'have been'. Now it becomes time for him to go, since 'all friends have gone to sleep' (U 93). And he expressed this feeling in his most famous line:

> *Woe, ignorant man, at the time*
> *of death this truth will be proved:*
> *A dream was, whatever we saw,*
> *whatever we heard, was a tale* (U 2) [19]

A dream—but for north western India it was such a nightmare that even the hope for the morning-light of eternity at the end of this night was no longer expressed in verses full of hope, as Rumi had done long ago in triumphant joy. Dard rather believed in his father's verse:

> *The stories of love are long, very long—*
> *Where is the sleep of non-existence?* (NA II 718).

To be sure, our poet had reached a state where he saw unity in the conflicting manifestations of the One and where the rose became the perfect paradox:

> *Joy and grief have only one shape in this world:*
> *You may call the rose open-hearted (with joy), or broken-*
> *hearted ...* (U 41),

But even the feeling that his own fame was growing was only the cause for a short sigh for Dard: he knew that man, listening today to tales, will fall asleep soon, and become a tale himself (P 137).

---

[19]   The combination of 'sleep' and 'tale' goed back to 12th century Persian poetry, and was a favorite topos in Indo-Muslim poetry: children are put to sleep by telling them tales.

Thus he finished his last aphorisms and was taken out of this perishable world on January 11, 1785, at the age of sixtysix lunar years—that means, exactly at the age his father had reached. He considered the promised time of his death a spiritual grace, since 66 is the numerical value of the word 'Allah.' He was buried close to his father in the place near the Turkoman Gate in Delhi, called the *Baghiche-yi Mīr Dard*, and what he says about the saints who have been blessed with living, radiant hearts, can well be said about him:

> The lustre of the star of happiness of those with enlightened mind never accepts dimness, and the luminousness of the luminary of the fortune of those with living hearts becomes not dark, even after their death. Even if the destroying Time does not light a candle at the tomb of those great men, still, every morning and evening, or rather permanently, a confidence burns in the grief of those pure people. God Almighty is always their companion and friend in the tomb, and the independent heart of their friends is the candle of their grave. To die and to live is the same for those whose lower soul is annihilated, and eternal duration is the fate of those who have left themselves. During their life they had dug out their hearts from themselves, and after death are they living and steadfast in the life of eternally remaining in God. (S 80).

CHAPTER THREE

DARD AND THE ART OF SPEECH[1]

Speech is the candle of the assembly of being, and silence is the splendor of the banquet of worship of God. Make this candle radiant in the presence of those endowed with insight, and add to this splendor in the company of those who do good works. And he who combines both is very successful ... (N 61).

Thus says Mir Dard about a dilemma which the mystics of Islam summarized during the Middle Ages in two well known sentences. 'He who knows God becomes silent' (= 'his tongue becomes short') and 'He who knows God becomes talkative' (= 'his tongue becomes long'). In the last bewilderment of union, or in the amazement of him who recognizes himself as the mirror of the radiant and ineffable Divine beauty, speech is no longer possible, and the mystic remains 'breathless with adoration' or 'drowned in the sweat of bewilderment like a mirror' without opening his mouth. On the other hand, the experience which has overwhelmed him for a while, is so fascinating that he feels compelled to convey it to others. But since the Divine Reality cannot be properly expressed in words and symbols, the mystic, out of necessity, tries to form new words, and attempts at circumscribing his experiences in repetitive sentences, in long chains of anaphora, in endless variations of the one central theme—that of loving union. If he should belong to the category of those who prefer mystical sobriety to mystical intoxication, he will surely strive to express his experiences in such a form that the adepts of the path may understand, that means, he will compose treatises of advice and exhortation.

However, the problem remains: how do mysticism (and, we may add, religious experience in general) and poetry go together? Is it possible to combine them, or is such a combination illicit in the eyes of both mystics and poets?

The mystic, during his highest experience, must be silent; the

---

[1] A German version of this chapter was published in the 'Festgabe deutscher Iranisten zur 2500-Jahrfeier Irans'; the English text, however, does not follow the German exactly.

poet, in his turn, must live in the society—even though this society be, as mostly for an Oriental poet, the environment of feudal circles, of kings and wealthy *amīrs*, who could pay for his praise, or pay off his satires. Even if the poet built an imaginative world of his own around himself, he was as much a member of the society as any artisan and craftsman, and poetry was indeed —as in our Middle Ages—considered an art and profession which could be studied like anything else. Suffice it to look at the oft-quoted passages from the handbooks of medieval Islamic poetry in which the poet is instructed how to learn by heart many thousand verses of classical and contemporary poetry, and how to study not only metrics, prosody and the art of versification but also a number of other arts and sciences, from astrology (to cast his master's horoscope in ingenious verses) to medicine (to congratulate him in proper terms when he took the 'bath of recovering.').[2] The ideal in the Islamic society was the *poeta doctus*, not the spontaneous poet who speaks out whatever is in his heart. In this respect, Persian, Turkish and Urdu poets can be compared to the contemporaries of the Mughal court poets, the learned English Metaphysical Poets.

However, the problem of how to combine religion and poetry was discussed in the Islamic environment not from the viewpoint of the mystic, but rather from the viewpoint of the defender of prophetic inspiration and divinely revealed law. The Quran clearly attests that Muhammad was not a poet—the word 'poet' taken here in the pre-Islamic meaning of somebody endowed with a special spiritual power, possessed by a *jinn* or *shaiṭān* whose supernatural insinuations made the 'poet' almost synonymous with 'soothsayer' and 'magician', hence a sought-after arbitrary in tribal feuds. Muhammad certainly was not a poet even though the Quran was revealed in the form of rhymed prose which the ancient soothsayers sometimes used. The revelation he received was contrary to what the poets intended, and Sura 26 contains an attack against the pagan poets who rove through every valley and do not act in accordance to their words. For Muhammad, however, and for his faithful followers, the 'word' as heard in the Quran, was the most holy revelation of God in time and space, so

---

[2] The best introduction into these problems is still Nizami Arudi's *Chahār Maqāla*, ed. and transl. by E. G. Browne.

much so that it was defined by later theologians as being co-eternal with God. Harry Wolfson has coined the poignant term 'inlibration' for the Islamic revelation 'in the book' as contrasting with the Christian 'incarnation' 'in the flesh'. From the Prophet's experience the high veneration of the Quranic word, and, at the same time, the aversion to the misuse of words for irreverent, irreligious and sensual purposes can be understood. Later Islamic scholars who studied the art of poetics discussed in detail the different sayings of the Prophet and often quoted his—alleged? —verdict against the poets: 'If somebody's belly were filled with pus until it bursts it would be better for him than that it were filled with poetry.' Did he not say that poetry is the *nafth ash-shaitān*, 'what Satan has spit out?' Poetry in the 'pagan' sense had no room in the Islamic orthodoxy; for its contents were mostly concerned with things prohibited by the Divine Law, i.e., with wine and with free love, be it of girls or of boys. Of course, the poets might recur to the Quran and defend their use of lascivious topics by quoting Sura 26/227: 'They do say what they do not do.' Still, the odium of something illicit remained with their works. Later theoreticians developed subtle theories about truth and lie in poetry—did not one of the authorities say that the most beautiful poem is that which is most untrue (*akdhab*)?[3]

Perhaps the best definition of Muhammad's role as a prophet and the orthodox Islamic view as contrasting with the art of the poets has been brought forth by Goethe in the *Noten und Abhandlungen zum West-Oestlichen Divan* where he writes about the difference between prophet and poet:

> Beide sind von einem Gott ergriffen und befeuert, der Poet aber vergeudet die ihm verliehene Gabe im Genuss, um Genuss hervorzubringen, Ehre durch das Hervorgebrachte zu erlangen, allenfalls ein bequemes Leben ... Der Prophet hingegen sieht nur auf einen einzigen bestimmten Zweck; solchen zu erlangen, bedient er sich der einfachsten Mittel. Irgendeine Lehre will er verkünden und, wie um eine Standarte, durch sie und um sie die Völker versammeln. Hierzu bedarf es nur, dass die Welt glaube! Er muss also eintönig werden und bleiben, denn das Mannigfaltige glaubt man nicht, man erkennt es ...

---

[3] For the whole question see W. Heinrichs, 'Arabische Dichtung und griechische Poetik'; J. Ch. Bürgel, 'Lüge und Wahrheit in der arabischen Dichtung'; and H. Ritter, 'Hat die religiöse Orthodoxie einen Einfluss auf die Dekadenz des Islam ausgeübt?'

Muhammad disliked the traditional poetry; but he used the service of Hassan ibn Thabit to whom we owe the first praise-poem in honor of the Prophet, a category which grew during the later centuries in all parts of the Muslim world. Still, religious poetry proper never developed in orthodox circles. It appears only among the mystics who felt free to use the whole treasure of metaphors and comparisons which the profane poets had invented. For them, everything could become a symbol of the eternal Truth, or be regarded as a reflection of the everlasting Beauty. Later, the non-mystic poets in turn took over the mystics' style of speech and thus the charming Persian lyrics with their puzzling double entendres, full of subtleties, came into existence.

It seems as if the Muslim mystics, particularly in the Persian speaking area, did not give much thought to the problem of how to express their experiences and feelings in poetical form. On the contrary, their output in poetry is much larger than that of most non-mystical writers. The old saying about the complete silence of him who has reached God was applied by many of them not so much to the poetical expressions of their experiences but rather to the so-called *shaṭḥiyāt*, theopathic expressions which some of the great Sufis had uttered in the state of ecstasy, proclaiming their union with God in open words. These mystics (as later generations held) had not yet reached the perfect state of union; they were still in the position of asserting their own existence by such strange words as 'I am the Absolute Truth' or 'Glory be to me'—but 'when the water boils it becomes silent'[4] and 'when the torrent reaches the sea it no longer roars.' However, to sing about one's experiences in poetry, or to write them down for the benefit of the disciples was not understood as contradicting the proverbial silence of the Men of God. Thus, the Spanish-born mystic Ibn Arabi (d. 1240) left more than 300 works which still await detailed study; among the Persians Fariduddin Attar (d. 1220), with his Biographies of the Saints, his lyrics, and his numerous mystical epics is even surpassed in spiritual fertility by Maulana Jalaluddin Rumi, whose didactic *Mathnawī* comprises ca. 26000 couplets, while his lyrical *Dīwān* consists of more than 30000 distichs. How often did Maulana

---

[4] Thus Janullah Rizwi, in Sadarangani, Persian Poets of Sind, p. 180 f.

Rumi address himself at the end of a poem 'Be quiet!' How often did he repeat that the experience of divine love can be expressed only in metaphorical form—and still, in spite of all these caveats, he never tired of encircling the Divine beauty with ever fresh metaphors and allegories taken from all aspects of nature and human life.

Dard himself says once—but directed rather to the bookish scholar, than to all too talkative mystics:

> *O you who have spoiled your whole life in disputation—*
> *One point of silence is (like) hundred kinds of books!*
> (P 82).

Not only the orthodox but also some members of the 'sober' fraternities looked with a certain displeasure upon the endless repetitions by mystical poets on the story of Love and Beauty, upon their expressions of longing, pain, melting, and intoxication, and were inclined to think that an advanced mystic should not talk that much.

Mir Dard has taken his stand in this question. More than many other pious Muslims, he is a great lover and defender of the art of speaking and writing. Thus he solves the problem according to his personal theological insight:

> 'Who knows God, becomes silent':—What is meant by this word is not, that those saints who do not bring forth on their tongues a single word of the realities and gnostic problems and who have not a single book of their own composition or writing should have gained a special proximity to the Divine Essence, and that those saints whom God has granted the healing speech and whom He has made 'possessor of a book' have got as their share only the proximity of the Attributes. God forbid! The rank of such 'men of heart' who are, like the prophets, 'possessors of a book' is higher ...;

for they are able to explain the Divine Realities, to teach the differences of the Divine Names and Attributes as far as human beings can understand it (K 577).

'Uninformed people' think that only the immature Sufis talk too much and open their lips to show the Divine mysteries, whereas those 'with mature brains' are silent. This is, however, according to Dard's opinion, not correct; for those who are spiritually enlightened are always prone to explain their experiences with the purpose of guiding people the right path (D 241).

Dard is one of the Muslims who have explicitly stated the importance of the Word. Although every Muslim believes in the Divine origin of the Quranic word, and admits that the worlds came into existence by the Divine order *Kun* 'Be' not many among the mystics have expressed this essential faith in the Word as primary Divine revelation and highest possible manifestation of Divine power in the world as indefatigably as did Dard. Through the word everything becomes existent and visible,

> the mirror of the word shows the face of the speaker of the word, and the looking-glass of speech opens the veil from the beauty of the orator. Nay, if the foot of speech were not there, nothing would appear to anybody. The cause for the existence of everything is the word 'Be' and all the Divine orders have reached the ear through the mediation of the word of God and the Prophet ... (S 157).

Thus, he considers the *amānat*, the trust which God offered to the heaven and the mountains and which was, eventually, accepted by man (Sura 33/72) to be the word and the faculty of speech, not, as many mystics did, as love, or as the capacity of choosing between good and evil, nor, as Iqbal held, as the possibility of individuation:

> Speech is a Divine trust which He has especially granted His vicegerent (K 518).

Was not man, God's vicegerent on earth, called the *haiwān nāṭiq*, the animal endowed with speech, the *zoon logikon*?

Just as the creation reflects the beauty of the Creator who has brought it into existence by this very word 'Be', thus the audible word in its differentiations directs the auditor towards the speaker: the Quran makes the faithful understand the infinite greatness and wisdom of the Lord, and human speech indicates the character of the speaker;

> Speech is the scent of man and the odor of the speaker (K 517).

There is also a less poetical image, namely the comparison of speech to the vial by which the physician can immediately diagnosticize the illness of the patient (K 132). Exactly as two persons become acquainted with each other by speaking and exchanging their names (S 157), thus speech wipes the verdigris from the mirror of the mind (K 518) and makes it clear so that it can reflect the character of the speaker. When one hears a man speak, one sees his character with the eye of one's heart, for:

> the colorfulness of the word is an indication to the colorfulness of the nature of the speaker (D 225).
> The word is the mirror of the beauty of him who speaks it (S 31),

and the listener

> may pluck the rose of the vision of the speaker from the color of the word.

Just as children preserve the qualities of their ancestors, books preserve the memory of those who have written them, and others are inspired by them—Dard uses this example in connection with his father's *Nāla-yi ʿAndalīb* and his own books which were, so to speak, derived from his father's masterpiece (D 255). To read somebody's books is like keeping company with him, and the understanding people see the color of the word and the different degrees with the eye of their heart, so that hearing, reading, and spiritual seeing is almost the same: the expression 'color of speech' and similar metaphors in which hearing and seeing are interchangeable occurs frequently in the poetry of the 17th century India. The expression 'seeing the color of speech' gives a new aspect to images such as 'candle of the tongue,' 'flame of the tongue,' (P 64), or 'candle of speech.' Dard has often compared 'the word of those with pure hearts' to 'the candle of this bed-chamber' (i.e., the dark world which is the place of slumber, N 272) or to the 'candle of the banquet of Divine love' (292). Thus, the title of his last treatise, *Shamʿ-i mahfil*, 'Candle of the Assembly,' alludes to his own function as the speaker who illuminates the circle of adepts with his radiant words.[5]

> *The honor of him who has got a tongue is the word—*
> *the silent candle is dishonored* (lit. 'black-faced,' P 33).

But the mystic-poet, too, experiences the dilemma of silence and speech:

---

[5] One should not forget that the term *shamʿ-i mahfil* is used in one of the most famous poems in honor of the Prophet, the ghazal *namīdānam kujā būdam* which is wrongly attributed to Amir Khusrau. There, the term occurs in the final line, and an Indo-Muslim reader will usually remember the combination *Muhammad shamʿ-i mahfil būd* ... when reading this expression.

We are all tongues from head to feet, like candles,
But where would it be possible to talk?

And when the Beloved appears in the dark night, the 'tongue of
the candle' becomes without wish and word, (U 15).

'To possess a book' means for Mir Dard, good Muslim as he is,
the highest rank of a prophet or a saint. One should never forget
that it was Islam that brought into existence the distinction of
book-religion and religion without scripture—a distinction which
still forms an important category in the history of religions. The
reverence for the written word is deeply rooted in the mind of
the Muslims from the days of the Prophet; out of this reverence
the art of calligraphy developed and became one of the distin-
guishing features of Islamic culture. To be sure, some of the
mystics thought that the first stage to reach the Divine realities
was 'to break the inkpots and to throw away the books'; but that
was only a natural reaction against the hairsplitting bookishness
of some of the lawyer divines and scholastic theologians. Abu
Hanifa and Shafiᶜi, the leaders of the two greatest legal schools,
are often ridiculed by the mystics (starting with Sanaᶜi
(d. 1131)), as much as the philosophers who do not know the
experience of love. The illiterate mystical lover who looks at the
Creator and knows only the *alif* and who is contrasted with
those who study theology and law (cf. p. 208 ff) is a recurring
figure in Islamic poetry.

Mir Dard was well aware of the uninspiring character of many
of the theological, philosophical, and even mystical books which
were studied in 18th century India; commentaries and supercom-
mentaries, extracts and new commentaries were composed for
the classical works, without adding anything new to the old contents. He describes (with a number of puns) what he considers to
be a real 'book' in *Wārid* No. 99 with the title: 'About the useful-
ness of good books' (K 591).

> Not every prophet is 'possessor of a book', and in the group of those
> who are sent not every messenger can open the lock of this door.
> Now, how could every saint have the suitability for carrying the bur-
> den of this special trust, and when could every blockhead stand the
> arrival of spiritual graces? 'If we had sent it on a mountain it would
> have split' (Sura 59/21). The compositions (*muʾallafāt*) of most of
> the saints and gnostics who have collected books and treatises and call
> them their 'original books' (*muṣannafāt*) are such only by name,

which is used metaphorically; and the note-books of many of the scholars and virtuous people which they have put together and which they imagine to be original books are completely compositions that are devoid of the meaning of Reality; and the writings of the philosophers and rationalists which later generations of their followers have written and which they consider as their original works are completely copied from the problems and rules of the previous generations which are (only) put into different expression. Now—what is, then, original work and where does it appear in our time? The leaders of those who have reached Reality from among the above mentioned factions have written in some places in their books some fresh points and new elegant sentences, and for that reason the drum of their role as assertor of the truth and fine expert has sounded loudly, and the voice of their fame has reached the ear of everybody who has ears to hear ...

A book which is filled from the beginning to end with problems according to 'No ear has heard' and an original work which is completely full with gnostic problems according to 'It did not come into the heart of a human being' cannot be completed unless the Holy Ghost (i.e., Gabriel) helps, and (then) a perfect application of 'Verily He has sent it down on your heart' will be reached with God's permission. 'Original work' (*tasnif*) is the expression for this kind of book which has been mentioned, namely, that neither the way of its expressions should be like the expressions of other books, so that a compilation (*ta 'lif*) be possible, nor the putting of its problems similar to the problems of others, so that a doubt about its being copied arise. It must be completely in a special manner, and should contain new and high problems and fresh and charming terminology, and should be confirmed by Quranic verses and *hadith* and revelations and proofs, and should cause the strengthening of the faith and motivate the sharpening of creed, and be reason for the wellfare in this life and prosperity in the next. In fact, such an original book is a fine good work to which no other good work can be compared.

Mir Dard, repeating this idea several times, held that on Doomsday, the ink of the writers of such noble books will be equal to the blood of the martyrs; he relies here upon a *hadith* which was often quoted in the Middle Ages in order to highlight the importance of studies and writing. He repeats it once more when speaking of the inspired writers (A 222) who only write down what God makes rain into their hearts,—a remark which shows that the kind of ideal book mentioned here should be written under inspiration and is not produced by the efforts of human intellect. That is a central point to which he returns frequently.

Dard continues his sermon about books with the statement that not only the pure religion of Islam is grounded in a book, but that all the theological and philosophical schools likewise need books, and in every science it is just the most perfect people who have written valid textbooks, 'and the reward for this work is great ...'. Even more:

> and the writers and those who copy the books full of blessings and the readers and those who look into them are also comprised in the blessing and take part in the heavenly reward

which is allotted to the martyr-like authors (K 591).

To speak words of guidance and to write books—that was, in Dard's opinion, the noblest occupation of the wise—*sohbat*, spiritual conversation between master and disciple, and its fixation in writing belong to the most important aspects of the Naqshbandi tradition. Books are, for Dard, spiritual children,

> and a gnostic without a book is like a man without children, and a work which is absurdly unconnected, is like a child with a bad character (K 592).

Thus, later in his life, he thanks God who has granted him satisfactory offspring both externally and spiritually. His words sometimes remind the reader of John Donne's comparison of man and book, in his *Devotions*,[6] though in the opposite way:

> The time that a word remains is, like the life of him who has written the word, called a pawn of death, and the last end of the word and of him who has said it, is annihilation in annihilation. Then, the like of books which for a long time appear on the page of destiny is like a great person for whom death lies in ambush during long years; and the like of books which are just now composed and the drum of whose fame becomes a bit louder is like young people whom God may make reach old age or who may die young. And the like of pages and treatises whose authors are always under the burden of pregnancy with them though those compositions have not yet come out of the womb of namelessness—those are like babes who, if they remain safe from smallpocks and other diseases, will perhaps reach the time of a weak youth. But this hope is only their (the author's) supposition, for eventually all of them have to die. And since those strong ones do not last the rest will also not last, and how would it be possible for these weak ones without head and tail to remain? In any case, nobody would approve of death for his own child, but wishes that it live up to its natural life-span. Otherwise, the choice belongs to God, and everyone who has a child is entangled in these circumstances. God may give him a capable and worthy child, and not such a mischief may be

---

[6] *Devotions upon emergent occasions* Nr. XVII.

generated as becomes mostly the cause for dishonoring the father. And thanks to God that He Almighty, Who, just as He has granted this rebellious servant fortunate external children, has given him also spiritual children, namely the inventions of this lowest servant, all with deep meaning (N 308).

Dard speaks also of the old truth that the sayings and the faith of a person must not necessarily be alike; his first poems still show, as he confesses, restlessness and inclination towards all-embracing (pantheistic) mysticism; nevertheless, evil drunkenness and *shathiyāt* have never come upon his tongue ... (K 400).

He is well aware of the limits of poetry, and he who boasted of having never composed anything worldly:

I have not been drowned and consumed myself in this work with careful observances, and have never praised or satirized anybody, and have not said anything according to the order of a person ... (K 91)

says, in a later period of his life:

Poetry is not such a perfection that a human being should make it his profession and be proud of it, but it is one of the human skills, under the condition that it is not conditioned by searching gifts and running about from place to place, and that one does not utter panegyrics and satires for the sake of worldly reward, for then it is a sort of beggary and implies greed and meanness of the lower soul ... (N 28).

But still, poetry is a high art, and in one of his last aphorisms, Dard cannot help blaming those who are not acquainted with its beauty:

To consider the art of poetry something easy grows from ignorance, and it is easy not to think of any perfection out of not-understanding and ignorance; for either the ascetics without experience of Reality out of their foolishness regard those 'disciples of the Merciful' as 'too much talking,' or the ignorant scholars, out of the pride of their own book-reading, count these mirror holders of 'He taught him speech' as nonsense-talkers. Then, for whom would poetry appear and from whose mouth would a tasteful word come into existence? It needs much strong and concrete relation with the Inventor, the Bounteous Bestower, so that a harmonious and charming speech emerge from the tongue. Not every animal, unaquainted with speaking, finds this inner meaning from speech, and not every man-shaped being, who is far from humanity, can carry the burden of this trust (S 327).

Still, Dard is not always certain about his own activities in the field of poetry. As much as he is sure of the inspired character of

most if it, he confesses in his later years that he sometimes turns
to saying poetry and feels uneasy when doing so, yet continues in
it, though ashamed,

> in the hope without motive that perhaps in some blossoming ground
> the sprouts of fresh poetry may grow with the watering of such a
> weeping without result, and that somebody may smell the rose of its
> strange meaning (—one of those who understand the meaning and have
> the faculty of smelling—) so that his heart may begin to tremble and
> he utter a prayer for forgiveness for this sinner (D 310).

We may guess that he alludes here to the poetical instruction
which he gave throughout his life to a large number of Urdu
poets, instructions, which were quite far from 'inspired' poetry,
but certainly 'planted the sprout of poetry' into the hearts of his
disciples.

Apparently, some people did not understand the real meaning
of the song of Dard who was 'the nightingale in the rose garden
of inner meaning;' they wanted to prove that there were some
objectionable topics in his poems. Therefore, he had to declare
once more that he was not a 'poet' and rather followed the
Divine word of 'We did not teach him poetry' (Sura 36/69)
(D 138). Even modern critics have tried to interpret two thirds of
Dard's Urdu poetry as profane, and considered him 'first a man,
then a theologian.'[7] This seems absurd to somebody who has
gone through his whole work and sees how Dard sings when love
and Divine grace urge him to sing. He therefore underlines that
the reader should understand that

> God has created everybody for some work, and ... every individual of
> the human race is distinguished by a specialization, and every human
> being has got a special order. I was made for the things which are
> connected with me, and the binding of love was cast into my breast
> without hatred, and I was granted, like the candle, the tongue of clear
> speech ... (D 288).[8]

Constant weeping, singing, and lamenting, that is his occupation,
and he jots down whatever comes into his heart.

> *Are these your poems, Dard, or lamentations,*
> *which tear the heart this way?* (U 58).

---

[7] Thus M. Sadiq, History of Urdu Literature, p. 103.

[8] Dard underlines this question of everyone's 'special occupation' by quoting the
famous *hadith* 'The evildoer is condemned already in his mother's womb ...', s.
A. J. Wensinck, Concordance, s.v. *šaqī*.

Strangely enough, he does not lack the self praise so typical of Oriental poets, and claims that he has

> from the beginning of youth until the time of ripe age uttered words in hundred colors and pierced numberless pearls of inner meaning in every moment with the thread of his breath ... (D 115).

And he confesses, with a charming smile:

> I have a strange heart: whatever comes into it is brought immediately upon the tongue, and it does absolutely not care for the fitting and the unfitting ...

Dard himself wonders whether he is brimful of madness, which would mean that he is lower than an animal, or is most close to the Divine Protector, which would mean, that he belongs to the chosen ones about whom God has said 'They do not fear the blame of a blaming one' (Sura 5/59). And so it is left to his colleagues to decide whether they consider him nothing but a crazy poet or believe, as the companions of the Prophet did, that 'our companion is not mad' (Sura 81/22) (N 71).

This allusion to the Prophet is typical of his way of reasoning—the combination of his perfect identification with his father-shaikh, his close relationship with the Prophet in his quality of being 'the first of the Muhammadans' and the fact that he is a true sayyid, sometimes leads him to rather daring comparisons and claims.

He once confesses without hesitation:

> The sweet words which I write are a table of delicacies which I choose for the tasteful, and the sad lamentations which I bring forth from the scratching of my pen are heart-enchanting songs which I sing for the longing, so that perhaps the desiring become successful and the doors of their hearts open, and all those my sad lamentations are for the sake of showing the way to the erring, and every access of my lamentation is a cause for the access of others (N 216).

His duty is, and that he repeats over and over again, to touch the souls of men with his songs, to melt their hearts with alchemy of Divine Love, as he says in an Urdu verse:

> *Do not be proud of the elixir, o moon-like one!*
> *Better than alchemy is it, to melt a heart.* (U 4)

He aims at leading them along the path of love, the path of the true and sincere Muhammadans. For a poem, new and full of love, is also not less than a pathetic sigh, and a harmonious word and nice contents have, of course, a way into the hearts (A 290).

But, as he sighs in a sweet and easy flowing Urdu line, only God knows whether 'my complaints will have result or not ...'. 'I weep and I make weep' (A 279, D 245)—that is his profession, and tears are his capital:

That tear which has come out from my heart—
Each drop is not less than a piece of diamant.

He is like the candle, not only as the radiant light of the assembly but also in his constant melting from the fire of love, weeping with his eyes widely open (P 29), and the reed of his pen is changed under the flow of inspiration, into a complaining reed-flute—a reminiscence of the immortal introductory poem of Jalaluddin Rumi's *Mathnawī*, the 'Song of the Reed,' which has furnished innumerable poets with symbols (A 224). But it is only those who have an eye to see with whom such a candle can speak—it is silent for those with blind hearts (P 16). By shining for them, the candle Dard has become an affliction and consuming pain for himself (P 10). But that means that he needs no longer candles for his meetings: he brings the burnt scars of his heart (U 71) which will unfold into fireworks, as Ghalib would say a century later. As to the image of the candle it became even more fitting when old age drew near. For age, which should bring silence and tranquility into the longing heart, is often compared in Indo-Persian poetry to the morning, the whiteness of the hair reminding the poet of the white light of dawn. As the whole life is like night or like a dream, death brings the morning-splendor of eternity (cf. D 88). Thus Dard sighs in a Persian quatrain:

How long do you make long your tongue like the candle?
It is better to be silent, for the morning drew near!

For the candle is extinguished when the radiant morning sun appears (P 101).

In the beginning of his last treatise, Dard once more describes his own state as a poet who witnesses the Divine Beauty, using the imagery of the garden which he—'son of Nightingale'—preferred. Like the pen with cut-off tongue, has he revealed many mysteries, and has brought numberless obscure problems 'from the contingency of the wombs into the bridal seat of manifestations,' for

> in the rosegarden of 'Be and it was' the garden adorning 'He created man' (Sura 55/2) made—through the irrigation of 'He taught him clear speech' (Sura 55/3),—the lily of my individuation ten-tongued by the growing of the ten senses and caressed the twigs of my hands and feet, or rather leaf by leaf of every limb, by lifting up the charge of 'God who made speak everything made us speak' ... It made this waxing body of mine completely like the bush of Moses, singing the tune (*maqām*) of *tauhīd*, and from every root of my hair it made grow an index-finger for beckoning to the direction of the One Real; and the art of existentialisation has made me directing toward the existence of the Artist, and has made manifest from me, the perfectly ignorant one, without words all the mysteries of His complete words ... (S 3).

In short, each limb, each hair of his is a witness of God's creative power and God's Unity (cf. P 63)—the expression for index-finger is *angusht-i shahādat*, containing the expression *shahādat*, 'profession of faith;' 'tune of *tauhīd*' contains a pun on *maqām*, which means not only 'tune' but likewise 'mystical station.' Thus, not only his words, but his whole state, *ḥāl*, speaks of God and witnesses His Unity.

> *Like the candle, each limb of mine has been transformed into a tongue* (P 41).

Shortly before his death, when the treatise *Dard-i dil* was just completed, Dard says in a revealing phrase:

> In this person a strange action is going on; for when I want to write anything of the things that come into my heart, a bewilderment of the Essence and Majesty and an incredible overpowering appears, so that the tongue of the pen becomes bound and the hand of writing remains back; but when I sit idly and quietly the endless rain of Divine realities and gnostic problems, fresh and obscure, rains from the cloud of mercy upon my heart according to 'What no ear has heard,' and the beauty of many unveilings connected with the last degree of the veil of the Unseen according to 'What no eye has seen' becomes visible, and God knows what kind of use from this order of His can be expected ... (D 341).

He summarizes here an experience which most mystics and a number of poets share, e.g., the feeling that their words are not produced by themselves but rather dictated by a higher power, and that they are only vessels for special revelations. Dard has alluded to the inspired character of his work several times, but this passage is particularly interesting since it shows his perfect passivity in receiving the message. This kind of inspired writing is not rare in Islamic mysticism: it is said that the greatest Arabic writing mystical poet, Ibn al-Farid (d. 1235), composed his highly sophisticated poetry in the state of 'absence,' but probably the most famous example is that of his younger contemporary Maulana Rumi who turned into a poet after the loss of his mystical beloved Shamsaddin Tabrizi, and whose *Mathnawī* contains a number of interesting instances where he admits that only the vision of the beloved (in that case, Husamuddin Chelebi) could inspire him to write poetry:

> *I think of rhymes, but my beloved says:*
> *Don't think of anything but of my face* ... (M I 1727).

Rumi has well explained the difference between the inspired poet and the imitator: one experiences Reality and is comparable, in his sweet words, to David, the master of music in Islamic mythology, the words of the other are barely an echo, and nothing worth listening to (M II 493 f.).

Mir Dard has often felt that he is only an instrument in the hand of the great Writer; however, such an instrument is necessary to make the Divine words seen and heard in the world of created beings:

> What am I, and what is my speech? These words have come into putting down by accident, and are mostly a case for disappointment. I who is an imagined and relative being—what am I, and who am I in counting the individations without end? This act is a cooperation between Lord and servant, for the Lord who is a necessary individuation is in the rank of the writer, and the servant who is a contingent individuation is in the role of the pen, and neither from the pen alone comes a picture into existence, nor does it appear from the writer alone—
>> If He were not and we were not,
>> Whatever is would, then, be not,

as he closes with a line taken from Ibn Arabi's *Fuṣūṣ al-ḥikam*.[9] For according to his theories, poetical inspiration is one of the aspects of the famous Divine saying, 'I was a hidden treasure and

---

[9] *Fuṣūṣ al-ḥikam*, ed. A. A. Affifi, Cairo 1954, *faṣṣ* XV, p. 143.

wanted to be known' (K 98). Just as God created the whole
world in order to manifest His names and attributes in the mirror
of the different levels of creation, He can also use man as a pen
which writes down His eternal words which never end—Dard
often cites the Quranic word 'If the sea were ink ...' (Sura
18/109) to support his view that the Divine revelations will never
be terminated. The speech of 'those with living hearts' translates,
so to speak, Divine speech into human words; 'their fingers are
the tongue of the pen of the Divine hand,' and 'the hand of
Divine Omnipotence comes out of their sleeves' when they note
down their inspirations (N 201).

Dard often repeats this comparison of men with the pen, a
comparison which was used before him by many mystics and
poets, reminding the pious reader of the well known Prophetic
saying that man is between two fingers of the Merciful who turns
him wherever He wants.

The uncontrollable experience of inspiration is the reason why
Dard's compositions are without any visible outward order—both
the *Wāridāt* and the Lamentations came without intention,

> so that even sometimes poems came in inversed order and earlier
> paragraphs contain the ends of a *ghazal*, or vice versa (N 337).

Why should he, then, take any preparations for making his verses
or his words more elaborate, or think of the rules of versification?

> *I am unlettered, but I have a heart, from whose emanation*
> *of grace*
> *In the world every letter of mine is a book* (P 65).

And:

> *I am not a poet that I should sketch the picture of talking,*

he admits in a Persian *rubāʿī*. That means, his art is contrary to
the normal artistic ideal of most Persian writing poets, which is
'to carve the statue out of the stone,' or 'to see the dance of the
unshaped idols already in the rock,' as Ghalib puts it (though this
very image is found in Dard's Urdu poetry too (U 47)), and then
to offer the reader a perfect work of art in which even the finest
details are hammered out and embellished. In classical Persian
imagery the stone-carver Farhad was shown chiselling the picture

of his beloved Shirin out of the rock, and not in vain did the
poets compare their art to that of the 'Mountain-digger' Farhad:
they painfully dig their way and carve their pictures 'with their
eyelashes' as the *topos* says. Dard, however, experiences a spontaneous flow of words and images. It is almost the same feeling as
expressed by Jalaluddin Rumi who, with a little joke, writes in
one of his *ghazals* that the '*mufta ʿilun mufta ʿilun mufta ʿilun,*'
i.e., the forms of Arabo-Persian prosody, 'killed him.' This kind
of 'inspired' or 'automatic' writing is still found among the Muslim mystics; I personally have witnessed how Turkish mystics
were granted *wāridāt* or *doghush*, 'born things,' which overcame
them without their own knowledge. [10] It is, however, natural that
the forms and the contents of these inspired poems should vary
according to the spiritual rank and the educational and cultural
background of the mystic concerned: when an 'inspired' blacksmith from Adana expressed his 'born things' in popular meters
with the vocabulary that is used since centuries in Anatolia by
the wandering minstrels of Divine love, Mir Dard's inspired
poems and prose-pieces bear everywhere the stamp of his highly
sophisticated education and his deep-rooted knowledge of classical Persian poetry (which he also wrote, sometimes, without inspiration).

The fact that inspirations are granted according to the spiritual
preparation of the mystic or poet, is well expressed by Dard in
his *Wārid* No. 16, 'Inspired word about the expression of topics
concerning God's Unity in poetical metaphors' (K 148 f.). Here,
the author first defines poetry and poetical expression, and the
magical quality of poetry; but only the Prophet could speak in
highly rhetoric style without being a poet, for had he been a
'poet' nobody would have believed his message. But in spite of
the Quranic verdict in Sura 26 and some unfriendly *hadith*
(which Dard, however, does not mention) Muhammad himself
listened to poetry, and both his wife ʿAʾisha and his beloved
daughter Fatima are related to have said some verses. Dard thinks
that the *hadith* 'The Holy Ghost (= Gabriel) helps him' has been
uttered in describing the faithful poet, and his theory that the
true poet is helped by the angel of inspiration relies upon it. It is

[10]   For the problem see A. Schimmel, Yunus Emre, Numen VIII 1, 1961

a fact that quite a few mystical poets in Islamic literature have alluded to inspiration by Gabriel or his Persian counterpart Sarosh. Dard writes:

> Further, for the saints of God who do not claim that prophetic inspiration (*waḥy*) comes down on them it does not matter to say poems; on the contrary, it is an excellent human perfection, and those are the 'disciples of the Merciful.'

The 'disciples of the Merciful,' as he loves to call the inspired poets, are according to his own definition, 'those who are annihilated in the whirlpool of annihilation in God' (A 222) and do not talk from themselves. He admits that there is an important difference between the divinely inspired words of the saints and the poetically inspired words of the ordinary poets though some of the works of the saints show also a rare combination of both inspirational and poetical quality. But the inspirations vary according to the degree of sanctity—those who live still in the 'proximity of sainthood' are in a somewhat shadelike state, whereas those who have reached the 'proximity of prophetic perfections' are blessed with inspirations without mediation of any visible means; but the inspirations of those who have attained to the 'Pure Muhammadiyya' are beyond the seeing and understanding even of the aforementioned groups of saints, and 'as long as you do not know (this state) ...'

> But at least the inspiration of saints with knowledge and practice in poetry will be more true and better by degrees than the inspirations of unscholarly and unpoetical saints both as for their meaning and their expression, and this Divine speech 'without how' will thus be colored by the colors of the vessel in which the inspiration is made apparent ... (K 149).

This last metaphor, that the color of the vessel determines the color of the fluid contained in it, has been used from the early days of Muslim mysticism to distinguish the various degrees of inspiration, or of unitive experience. But the passage shows also how proud Dard was of his high education and art, and how little he thought of the numerous mystics of low birth who lived all around the country and attracted people with their simple songs.

To be sure, not a single word of the real saints and gnostics is 'devoid of a subtle relation of outward and inward form and meaning,' but—and here we will agree with Dard—these saints often try to write poems only for the sake of instruction, and such products are 'mostly deprived of charm and poetical measure and form, etc. ...'

> They have only shown that peculiar problem and question in symmetrical form. And when this problem becomes explained in short and summarized due the fetters of meter, it is useful because it is easy to remember and to memorize, but it has nothing in common with poetry but rhyme and meter ... (K 288).

Dard alludes here to the popular way of composing long rhyming pieces about the miracles of the prophets, the details of faith and religious law, and about more or less abstruse problems of mystical theology for the sake of instruction, just as a number of rhymed treatises on logic and Arabic grammar have served through centuries for the instruction of students. Most of them are, in fact, extremely boring, and poetical instructions about the details of the mystical path, in whatever language they may be written, can only rarely be considered to be enchanting poetry. But even in our century the poetical form was chosen by some thinkers for their message because it made it easier for the audience to remember the contents thus conveyed. Dard is perfectly right with his criticism, and he probably thinks also of many of the uniform repetitions of certain mystical phrases which occur again and again especially in later Persian literature. But he does not accept the pure artists either and continues:

> The poems which come from the master poets who are not acquainted with the Reality and which show purely perfection of poetical technique—those are mostly completely made of metaphors and are bare of any reality, (they are) only exaggerations and lies ...

For both groups, but even more for the pure poets, the Quranic dictum about those 'who say what they do not do' is valid, and it seems not without inner reason that Dard comes back to the statement about such a discrepancy several times: the acts of the saints go farther than their poetical expression, and the way of the poets does not conform to their sayings (A 53); the gnostics are advised to act as true confessors of Unity by practising unison of word and deed so that they do not 'scratch the heart with the fingernail of "Why do they say what they do not do" ' (A 51, cf. 292).

Only those who combine both graces—Divine inspiration and the gift of poetical saying—and are supported by the Holy Ghost (as he stresses once more) can be called the real 'disciples of the Merciful' and their speech

> is so comprehensive that the people of outward sense and metaphors become enamoured and absorbed by its charme and measure and confess their own inability as to (imitating) its outward form, and the masters of Reality and the gnostics confirm and verify the mysteries of those and take their spiritual bounty and share from them. And it is this kind of poems that is meant by the word 'Verily there is wisdom in poetry,' and it is such a speech and manifestation which is the object of the saying 'Verily there is magic in speech' (K 289).

That is why Dard addresses his colleagues in a Persian quatrain:

> *As much as you become incomparable in asceticism*
> *Or drive your mount in knowledge and virtue,*
> *Do not look with contempt toward the poets,*
> *But read 'Verily there is some wisdom in poetry.'* (P 141).

In fact, nobody can imitate the poetry and words of those divinely inspired masters, and 'the flag "Bring a Sura like it" (Sura 2/21) appears at every place, where such a word is recited ...' This is, indeed, a rather daring comparison of inspired poetry with the words of the Holy Quran! (D 5).

How could dry scholars understand this mystery of 'knowledge from Us' (Sura 18/65)? Dard does not hesitate to apply to the scholars and to the pure artists in the field of poetry the Quranic word that they are 'like the donkey who carries books' (Sura 62/5) though he politely omits the 'donkey' from the well-known quotation. Meaningless books, full of errors and sins, that is what those people offer to their readers:

> As for the scholars full of technique and the poets mighty of words who decorate their expressions and try their dispositions—that is
> - something which becomes possible by carrying a load of '... who carries books' and opens for the foot of man the way of 'In every valley do they err' (Sura 26/226) ...' (D 5).

Only the inspired saints bring knowledge directly from God and thus illuminate the assembly of the faithful—'but nobody can see them as it behoves' (D 5).

It is clear that Dard with such words alludes to his own situation—he, the mystic and poet, had probably to suffer from the dislike of the dry scholars of his age and perhaps also from some of his colleagues in the Naqshbandi order. That is why he felt

compelled to defend himself by drawing the line between the
two types of poetry so sharply:

> One is that of sensual passion which appears with the intention of
> becoming famous and the wish that one's memory should remain alive
> even after one's death, and similar other worldly intentions, like the
> word of the poets and the scholars. And God has denied that such a
> kind of speech should be attributed to His Prophet by saying, 'He
> does not speak from passion, and it is not the word of a poet.' (Sura
> 53/4; 69/41). The other kind is without human power and strength,
> only by inspiration (*ilqā'*) of the Merciful ... (D 3).

The first group follow their worldly aims, may they be hidden
behind so-called scholarly purposes, and work hard in embel-
lishing their speech and writing, whereas a divinely inspired word
pours out without human effort and will last forever.

Dard, the 'story-singing nightingale of the rose-garden of inven-
tion' (A 93), was sure that his works, at least the largest part of
them, belonged to the second category, and he never tired of
speaking of his inspirations. However, towards the end of his life,
the idea of a certain fame which he had acquired during his
lifetime and which, as he hoped, would also continue after his
death, can be sensed behind some of his most modest words. His
mystical theories do not explain his way of teaching poetry, and
we must suppose that, in this field, he followed exactly the classical methods of instructing the disciples in the rules of poetry and
correcting their verses—as he smilingly says in an Urdu *ghazal*
that 'it would be possible to write another *ghazal* if you can
change the rhyme-word'—and then continues with the next *ghazal* with a slight variation of the rhyme. In his house the theoretical foundations of Urdu poetry were established in the mid
18th century. But Dard is far away from the early period of
Islam, when orthodox Zahirites wrote books on worldly, though
chaste love—such as Da'ud az-Zahiri's (d. 909) famous *Kitāb az-
zahra*, and Ibn Hazm's (d. 1046) *Tauq al-hamāma*, 'The Dove's
Necklace', or when orthodox Hanbalites scholars did not mind
studying and interpreting the *Maqāmāt al-Harīrī*, this most witty
collection of 'short stories' in highly sophisticated rhyming prose.
Dard, however, never mentions the 'worldly' side of his poetical
activity which is considered, by modern critics, perhaps the most
important aspect of his life.

In this capacity, too, he must have had the feeling of giving his friends guidance, for whatever he wrote, he considered as a help for his contemporaries, opening their hearts and showing them the right path. He considered his own productions, especially the *'Ilm ul-kitāb*, to be only second to the revealed books; e.g., the Divine word of the Quran, the inspired words of the Prophet, and the guide-book of his father Andalib. That is why he can address his disciples in the later part of the *'Ilm ul-kitāb* with a solemn Arabic formula filled with Quranic words:

> God has been kind to you by giving you this book—so take it with its strengths and memorize what is in it, perhaps you will believe. God made all the other books of the mystical path and Sufism and ethics unnecessary for you by its signs (*āyāt*), and completed your religion and perfected for you His grace and made Islam your religion and made rise upon you, when you read it, the sun of sincere Muhammadanism raising on the highest horizon, a sun which never sets ... (K 543).

CHAPTER FOUR

DARD AND THE PROBLEM OF PRAYER

Lex orandi lex credendi—this saying is valid for Muslims as much as for the faithful in other religions. Few documents in the spiritual history of Islam are as revealing as are the various kinds of prayers which were uttered by the great mystics and theologians or noted down by poets and gnostics in the course of more than a millenium. Prayers attributed to the Prophet and his companions were collected in many a pious book as a model for every Muslim; Ghazzali's *Ihyā ʿulūm ad-dīn* is a very typical instance. Prayers, uttered by the first generations in Islam show how the faithful trembled with fear of the Last Judgment or ended on a note of hope and trust in God's unending mercy and forgiveness. In the mid-8th century we find the simple, almost 'evangelical' prayers of the Persian preacher Yahya ibn Muʿadh who expressed his unshakable hope in the Divine grace in short, pithy sentences full of love. At the same time, his elder contemporary in Egypt, the great mystic and, as is said, magician, Dhu ʾn-Nun listened to the prayers of everything created and translated them into words of hymnic beauty and psalm-like power. Slightly later, Hallaj's prayers reveal a longing of the soul which is almost beyond expression in logical words. In later times, Islamic literature shows an almost infinite variety of poetical prayers which form the introductory parts of most Persian, Turkish and Urdu epics; mystics and non-mystical poets alike composed high-sounding hymns in which they tried to describe God's Unity and the mysteries of His creative work in ever new metaphors and ever more far fetched images. There are also the meditations of the gnostics, or such prayers as combine astrological and alchemistic vocabulary with the expression of hope in God's power. It is as though the poets and mystics were weaving a colorful brocade of words with the intention to please God and to show His greatness to the world. But one should not forget the short sighs born out of despair, as they are sometimes put by mystical poets into the mouths of lunatics and demented people: they dare to doubt the wisdom of God's creation and speak out feelings which the mentally sound Muslim would never have allowed to trespass his lips. But even these prayers full of strife and agony, as we find them mainly in Attar's poetry and in the Turkish Bektashi tradition, usually end in man's submission to God's inscrutable will.[1] Maulana Rumi—contrary to the more critical and pessimistic Attar—always refers the rebelling worshipper back to the unexplicable way in which God shows his love just by *not* answering every prayer. It was also Rumi who expressed most perfectly the philosophy of the *oratio infusa*, known in Islam since long ago. He coined the poetical formulation of the truth that man is not able to pray unless God puts the wish for prayer into his heart; nay, that man's prayer is in itself God's answer.[2] One may also think of similar, though more theosophically tinged ideas in Ibn Arabi's theories: H. Corbin has ingeniously analyzed his image of the 'prayer of the heliotrope'. Islamic literature is replete with prayer poems in simple words, invented by mystic bards in the Anatolian plains or nomads in the highlands of Afghanistan; and we listen to the loving sighs of the mystics who longed for union and prayed that the 'I' which still veiled their eternal beloved might be lifted in 'naked union', or in the vision of the pre-eternal Divine Light. And numerous unknown poets translated the hope of the masses in Muhammad's intercession at Doomsday into unsophisticated folk songs, voicing the never ending cry for forgiveness of sins and strong trust in God and His messenger.

It can be said without exaggeration that every mode of Islamic thought and feeling has been expressed in the form of prayers; and it is easy to discern the different types of prayer which have been classified by F. Heiler as 'prophetic' and 'mystical', although these types are rarely found in complete purity.

The same rich differentiation of prayer-life can be witnessed in the prayers of Mir Dard as found in his *Four Risāla*, or at the end of some chapters in the *'Ilm ul-kitāb*. In the latter case, though, the formal Arabic style, following the model of traditional prayers as related by Ghazzali and other theologians, is prevalent. But besides his highly artistic prayers in florid Persian and those in poignant classical Arabic, one should not overlook the small Urdu poems in which Dard expresses his love and hope, and

---

[1] Cf. H. Ritter, 'Muslim Mystics' Strife with God', Oriens V.
[2] Cf. A. Schimmel, 'Maulānā Rūmī's Story on Prayer', in: Yādnāma Jan Rypka.

ponders the secret of the relation between necessary and contingent existence in simple and unsophisticated words:

> *The reason for want (*iftiqār*) is our contingency—*
> We *may be or not be—but* Thy *Being is necessary* (U 2).

The forms of address in Dard's prayers vary from the frequently used 'O my God!' (*ilāhī*) to expressions like 'Absolute Existence!'; the Most Beautiful Names of God, like Merciful, Forgiving, Giver etc. occur as well as poetical words 'Sun of the Sky of Lordliness' and 'Cupbearer of the goblet of the Grace of Existence' (A 119); God as 'Coverer of faults' stands beside the 'Sacred Valley of Absolute Existence' (A 123) or 'Spring of the Rosegarden of Divine transcendence (*tanzīh*)' (A 192). Yet the simple *ilāhī* or *khudāwandā*, 'O Lord!' are much important in the whole picture of his prayer-life as it reveals itself particularly in the *Risālas*.

Dard sometimes deals with problems of prayer in general. One of the rules for the 'Pure Muhammadans' as set by his father, was to pray the five ritual prayers in the company of the faithful. Nasir Andalib had likewise dwelt in extenso upon the rules for purity, and had gone into such detail that his son did not need repeat these facts in his writings. He alludes now and then to his fondness of nightly prayer—being recommended in the Quran, though not a binding duty on the believers, the nightly prayer (*tahajjud*) was always cherished by the mystics who found here the opportunity of conversing with the Divine beloved in the solitude of the night. Some of the finest prayers of early Sufis have been uttered in connection with the night-vigils.

> O my God, if Thou wouldst show at daytime such acts of proximity and closeness as Thou producest thanks to Thy accepted messenger at night during the *tahajjud*-prayer, it would not be far from Thy kindness towards Thy servants (A 186).

Thus says Mir Dard, and he sighs also that every night he hopes to spend all night in prayers, and by remaining awake

> we beat the head every evening on the stone of striving that we may grasp the end of the tresses of the charming beloved 'Remaining awake' with the hand of success (D 232).

Still, he complains that often he was overcome by human weakness and vexed by a problem that had troubled the minds of many pious before him, e.g., whether or not it is allowed to pray at all. He solves the problem thus:

> To ask nothing from God and not to pray is a zeal which is out of place but which occurs sometimes with the noble because they suspect that they have understood the Truth in their way; but it is not fitting for the rank of servantship (A 92).

That means, that it is a proof of mental haughtiness to give up prayer, and that would be incompatible with the highest rank man can reach, that of the faithful 'servant of God' ('abd). Did not God promise men that He would answer their prayers? (Sura 40/62). Yet, it is likewise not right to ask God without shame for everything, as do the immature, who imagine that all their prayers would be accepted by God.

> But the most perfect are free from both ways and are without will in praying and not-praying ...

This, however, is a state which the 'people like animals' (Sura 7/178) do not understand. It is wrong, says Dard, to recite the *fātiha* for worldly purposes; when reciting this prayer with uplifted hands one should do it without any hope for an answer or being granted a wish (S 220).

The involuntary prayers of the true saints are described by Dard in his usual poetic language. When reading such passages, though, one should remember that the comparison of the leaves of the plane-tree to human hands is almost as old as Persian lyrical poetry, and that the metaphor of 'praying leaves' is also not rare in Indo-Persian poetry:

> The hand of prayer of the gnostics is, like the leaves of the plane-tree, turning the leaves of the booklet of choicelessness whose object is not, to grasp the skirt of the rose of wish. It is just following the blowing of the wind of destiny; whatever kind it moves them they are moved. And the high ambition (*himmat*) of the saints is, like the stature of the naked free cypress, freedom from the garments of every borrowing, for he does not think of getting the happiness of anything claimed. He is thus content with the contentment of the Omnipotent, and wherever He turns him, he turns, and those great people do not open the door of wish from their own side and do not afflict the hands of their supportlessness with the movement of any desire ... (S 118).

That means: Prayer is sometimes given, a Divine grant, not a human activity. Dard follows here the traditional mystic view, so beautifully expressed by Rumi and others. Yet, the 'wind of

Divine activity' has moved him into the most divergent directions of prayer, and every form, from the simple prayer for forgiveness to high contemplation, is found in his works. It should be noted that the number of prayers for forgiveness, in which he recurs upon God's eternal grace, are more frequently found than contemplative and philosophical prayers. Here, the orthodox traditional Islamic view of man as the 'servant before God' shows itself in practical theology: their goal is not union, as for the 'intoxicated' mystics, but forgiveness and, at the most, vision of eternal beauty.

One should not forget in this connection that for the mystics the central act of worship was *dhikr*, the constant recollection of God. Mir Dard had learned the theoretical foundations of *dhikr* from his father, and followed his practice in the Naqshbandi tradition.

In his theories, one of the most important aspects of religious life for the Sincere Muhammadan is to recite the Divine names every morning and evening, to meditate upon their meanings, and, in case of need, invoke the name which is fitting for that peculiar occasion (K 201).[3] However, Dard never ceases to emphasize that all the manifold names point to the Divine unity (K 217). As he says in an Arabic quatrain:

> *God manifested Himself by the appearance of the Names,*
> *Him do we find by the presence of the Names,*
> *Just as the moon is illuminated by the sun,*
> *Thus creation is lit by the light of the Names* (P 76).

But meditation of the Divine names is not the only method of *dhikr* taught by Dard (cf. K 161 ff.). Constant *dhikr* is for him the very center of religious life (cf. K 624 f.), the safest way that leads to presence or vision.

> And when one says *lā ilāha illā Allāh*, There is no deity save God, one should think in one's heart *lā maᶜbūda illā Allāh*, There is no object of worship save Him, and *lā maqṣūda illā Allāh*, There is no object of desire save Him (K 624).

Once he even goes so far as to attest that

---

[3] Cf. R. A. Nicholson, 'Studies in Islamic Mysticism', p. 93 ff. A good introduction into the use of Divine Names is Ibn Ataᵓ Allah, *Miftāḥ al-falāḥ wa miṣbāḥ al-arwāḥ*.

the innermost of the innermost is *la maujūda illā Allāh*, There is
nothing existent save God (K 132),

a formulation which brings him very close to the utterances of
the representatives of *wahdat al-wujūd*, whom he otherwise attacked so mercilessly.

Faithful to the Naqshbandi tradition Dard teaches the *dhikr* of
the five *latā 'if* (K 112), the spiritual centers of man, and develops his theories about this technique in *Wārid* No. 110 (K 637) in
a detailed Arabic description. He discerns the *dhikr qalbī*, located
in the heart, at the left side of the breast, pronounced in love and
longing, the *dhikr rūhī*, performed at the right side of the breast
in quietude and tranquillity, the *dhikr sirrī*, pronounced in in-
timacy, close to the left side of the breast, the *dhikr khafawī*,
performed close to the right corner of the breast and connected
with absence and extinction of the self, and the *dhikr akhfawī*, in
the center of the breast, which is the sign of annihilation and
consummation. The *dhikr* is, then, extended to the brain in perfect contentment (*dhikr nafsī*, connected with the *nafs qaddīsa*,
the sanctified soul) and eventually permeates the whole being
(*haqīqa insāniyya*), body and soul, when man reaches perfect
recollectedness and peace—this is the *dhikr sultānī*. The source of
dhikr is love (K 637); but, as Dard stated elsewhere (K 132) constant practice is required to attain the highest stage of *dhikr*,
which is a medicine for the soul—the physician, too, does not
learn from books but has to practice his art. (Medical terminology is often applied to the mystics' psychological progress in
Sufi literature, and the image of the Beloved or mystical master
as a physician is almost as old as Sufi literature).

Since Dard had learned methods of meditation from his father,
Andalib's most interesting description of *dhikr* and meditation is
worth quoting in connection with Dard's own approach:

(The adept) sees the blessed figure of the word *Allāh* in the color of
light written on the tablet of his heart and the mirror of his imagination ... Then he will understand himself opposite this form or beneath
it or at its right or left side, and he should strive to bring himself
toward this light ... And whenever he finds himself in the middle of
the rank of *alif* and *lām*, he must proceed and take his place between
the two *lāms*, and then walk from there, and bring himself between
the *lām* and the *hā*; and with high ambition he leaves this place too
and sees himself in the middle of the ringlet of the *hā*. At the begin-

ning of his journey will he find his head in this ringlet, but eventually he will find that his whole self has found repose in this house and will find God as the Surrounding, and himself as the surrounded one (NA I 270).[4]

This is a perfect interpretation of the highest goal of the Naqsh-bandi mystic, e.g., to be surrounded by the eternal Light but not lost in it, just as the pearl is in the ocean and yet distinct from it. This is the station of true confession of Unity as it is practiced by the Sincere Muhammadans:

> immersion in the contemplation of God along with preservation of the stages of servantship (K 609).

But such a submersion cannot be reached save by Divine Grace (K 311).

Dard inherited the inclination towards light-mysticism, as it is expressed in the idea of being surrounded by the light of the *h*, from his father who extended the imagery, in harmony with the great mystics, to the Prophet, the first manifestation of the Divine Light:

> Oh you whose light is the *basmala* of the Quran of appearance,
> Your body is all light, and your cheek the *Sūrat an-Nūr*.
> Here you are the leader of the people, there the intercessor—
> O place of the manifestation of the Names 'Guiding' and 'Forgiver'!
> (NA II 104).

He remained faithful to the idea that God should be best described as Light, this Quaranic description being much more fitting than strange pseudo-philosophical expressions which have no foundation in the Quran and the tradition. Thus, a long prayer is addressed to God, the Light of Heaven and earth (Sura 24/35), revealed first, dawn-like, in the light of Muhammad; every one of the contingent beings participates in the spiritual bounty of this light according to its capacity (D 203)—he himself, as he often asserts, has thus become 'the candle of the assembly of those with heart': does he not call people to God with burned soul, melting heart, and weeping? (S 129). And where should be darkness in the world, since 'God is the Light of Heaven and earth?' (P 83). It is only logical that the last word

---

[4] About the importance of the letter *h* cf. F. Meier, 'Vom Wesen der islamischen Mystik', p. 30, Anm. 15 and 17.

that is noted down in his books is the Arabic prayer for light which was transmitted from the Prophet and elaborated by Ghazzali and many other mystical writers. A few days before his death he wrote:

> O God, make in my heart a light and in my soul a light and on my tongue a light and in my sight a light, and in my hearing a light, and at my right a light, and at my left a light, and make behind me a light and before me a light and above me a light and beneath me a light, and in my nerves a light and in my flesh a light and in my blood a light and in my hair a light and in my skin a light and give me light and strengthen my light and make me light (S 341).

All mystics have emphasized that the most important aspect of _dhikr_, and in fact of every prayer, is the 'presence of the heart'. That is why Dard, too, sighs:

> O my God, we with negligent heart: when we outwardly practice loud _dhikr_ with our tongues, what is the use if the door of presence and vision in the interior does not open? And we with ignorant nature, when we measure out the way of realities and gnostic problems by talking, it is all useless, for it brings no injury to the wall of our existence (e.g., it does not break our existence). Had we once remembered Thee as it behooves, we would have forgotten ourselves completely, and if one time we had brought Thy pure name upon our tongues as it is worthy, we would have thrown the burden of the suspicion of selfhood from the shoulder of our knowledge. O Thou Singer of 'Everything is passing but His Face' (Sura 28/88), and Who begins the song of 'He is the First and the Last ...'! (Sura 57/3) (D 229).

Sometimes Dard notes down a kind of prayers the most perfect examples of which are found, in Islamic mysticism, in the prayers of Yahya ibn Muʿadh (d. ca. 872), who juxtaposed the greatness and power of God and the unimportance of the lowly servant, and yet appealed in unfading trust to the inexhaustible treasure of mercy of the Merciful. Dard, though in a more sophisticated style, sighs too:

> O my God, if Thy mercy and forgiveness ask for excuses, then what does sin matter? And if Thy justice and independence bar the way, then even the face of obedience is black (A 156).

When Yahya ibn Muʿadh prays:

> O God, you know that I do not deserve Paradise and have no strength to endure Hell—now the matter is left to Thy Grace,[5]

---

[5] Attar, _Tadhkirat al-auliyā_ I 310.

then Dard varies the same theme:

> O my God, man is not a fiery creature that Thou should cast him in
> the fire, and he is not an airy (or: sensual) being that Thou should put
> him into the icy storm of hell! Man is a creature of dust in perfect
> lowliness—now, what wilst Thou do with a handful of dust other than
> forgive? (D 191).

In one of the longer prayers where Dard expresses his hope for
the Prophet's intercession and the satisfaction of his father, he
continues his introducing remarks with a long chain of rhyming
sentences (rhyme—*if*):

> I have an elegant heart so that I do not come out of the obligation of
> elegance, and as companion I have got a lower soul whom I cannot
> withstand; and I have a weak body which has no power for asceticism
> and worship; and I have a lean soul which always rains laziness and
> leisure. Now, what comes from such an idle servant, and what appears
> from the hand of me, the confused one? If Thou showest grace, and if
> Thou orderest with justice, then only the sincerity and the supplica-
> tion of the heart is sufficient, and all those accomplishments of fasting
> and ritual prayer are also enough booty. I mean: do not look on this
> thinking: 'It ought to be like this or that', but rather see what comes
> from whom, and accept my easy worship more than the hard asce-
> ticism of others, and regard my state with the eye of kindness. If
> Thou askest everyone about obedience, say:
>> I have brought Khwaja Mir Dard into the state of servantship
>> (N 123).

As he does in this highly involved prayer, Dard likes the formula
'If Thou would do this or that, it would not be far from Thy
mercy—Thy kindness—Thy favor ...', thus reminding God of his
kindness on previous occasions. His prayers usually comprise his
family and the group of the Sincere Muhammadans:

> Just as Thou givest our daily bread to use in this world, although we
> are useless people, thus it is not far from Thy forgiveness to make
> enter us, the Muhammadans, into Paradise without reckoning (D 112).

Right worship is the central action of the pious, and therefore
Dard is sure that:

> If something can be done by words, then is in my hand the flag of
> praise for God's kindness under which is everything that exists; and
> when it is supported by actions, then the Prophetic tradition 'We did
> not worship Thee according to the right worship, as it behoves Thee'

asks for forgiveness, and the glad tidings of 'Verily God forgives all the sins' (Sura 39/54) is refuge in refuge—and Thou art the Forgiving, the Merciful (N 129).

And he speaks of his constant crying in repentance:

In the hope that it may wash off there the book of my actions,
I have made white (e.g., blind) my black eye by weeping (P 13, cf. U 17).

The best consolation for the faithful is that God had promised: 'I am with the thought of my servant', i.e., I behave as my servant thinks of Me; and since man tends to imagine God as merciful He will certainly not disappoint him. This Divine promise, which also forms one of the foundation stones in the concept of *tawak-kul*, 'trust in God', is for Dard 'the goblet which intoxicates the worshipper every moment' (D 316). Therefore, he calls upon the strong and powerful God to remind Him of His promise:

In view of his creatureliness every servant, imperfect or perfect, learn-ed or ignorant, is alike in the court of the grandeur of Thy Creator-ship, and the human picture which is the comprehensive place of manifestations, has the worthiness of all manifestations. But I ... wish that Thou mayest show for this worthless creature the act of 'I act as My servant thinks of Me' ... (D 26).

There are many Quranic verses and Prophetic traditions upon which the pious Muslim can rely in his hope for forgiveness. God has said in the Quran 'Do not despair of God's grace' (Sura 39/54) (A 233), and has spoken of the change of evil actions into good ones (D 316, D 10). One should not forget, however, that Dard has commented upon this very Divine promise (Sura 11/116) in a long paragraph in *'Ilm ul-kitāb* in order to show that it does not encourage man to sinning, but rather means a sublimation of human actions. Nevertheless, his own hope for forgiveness relies heavily upon this Quranic saying:

As much as I have a useless heart,
A crooked understanding and a very ignorant nature—
With that much of God's mercy without reason
I have the hope of being accepted in Thy palace (P 118).

But it seems that the center of his hope is the intercession of the Prophet; though not to be derived clearly from the Quran, this idea had found its expression very early in the traditions, and became the center of general Muslim piety:

> *O Lord, whatever nuisance I work and speak: Forgive!*
> *I am carrying a load of sins and say: Forgive!*
> *Since I have an intercessor like Muhammad for Doomsday—*
> *I bring a hundred bunches of sins and say: Forgive!* (P 112).

In Dard's case, the problem of intercession becomes slightly complicated because he usually adds the hope for his father's help to the normal expressions about intercession: he takes refuge not only in the Prophet but also in the 'Prince of the Muhammadans' (A 233) and hopes that God will not leave him with blackened face in the presence of the lightful personality of his father, whose grace and help is implored (D 10). As much as Dard trusts in God's absolute forgiveness as much does he repeat his relation with his father—

> As much as we have brought forth faults, yet we are those who believe in Thy Nightingale! (N 131).

This faith gave him strength to pray not only for himself but likewise for the members of his family and his order as Noah saved his family during the flood (for the image of the ark, with Muhammad as the pilot, well symbolizes the Islamic community, *umma*, on its journey towards eternity):

> I helpless Muhammadan, who every time brings forth a whole flood from weeping in repenting my sins hand over my heart only into the hand of Thy forgiveness and acceptance and the intercession of Thy Prophet, and I take all the sincere Muhammadans with me in Thy protection and the grace of my helper (*Nāsir*), and Thou art with me in every state anow and in the future (D 303).

Dard, as all mystics, was aware of the constant tension between Divine *jamāl* and *jalāl*, the Fascinans and the Tremendum as the two revealed aspects of the Perfection of the Deity, a tension which is witnessed in the sun whose heat is both life-giving and life-destroying: Rumi's famous warning to his friend Husamuddin who wanted to know more about the Sun of Tabriz (*Math.*, I 130) come as much to mind as Arjuna's vision of Krishna whose real being is consuming fire. Dard follows the established path of adoration when he addresses the 'sun of the Sky of Uniqueness':

> As much as Thy perfect beauty enlightens all the existing beings with the light of 'My mercy comprises everything', as much burns Thy majestic Majesty all the existent beings with the fire of 'Everything is vanishing save His Face' (Sura 28/88) (A 338).

This can lead him to formulations which sound like those of the *wujūdī*-mystics whom he disliked so deeply:

> *If one says that He is both the Guiding (*hādī*) and He Who leads astray, (*Muḍill*)*
> *then all are on the way, and no one is erring (*gumrāh*)*
> (U 51).

Considering that Mir Dard lived through the darkest time in the history of his beloved hometown Delhi, we understand that he, at times, asked the meaning of God's acting like that with the Muslims; but he always came back to acknowledge:

> Many strange wisdoms are visible in every of Thy actions (D 121).

As he says in a prayer in the midst of destruction:

> O Who brings into existence everything good and ugly, and who polishes the mirror of every stone and clay ...
> Thou didst not create anything futile and didst not look at anything of absurdity, which fact is revealed by the Quranic word: 'We did not create you in vain ...' (Sura 23/117).

It is strange to see that Dard remained, in a certain way, untouched by the catastrophes and sufferings around him. Not long before he noted down his conviction of God's unquestionable wisdom, he had spoken to God about the problem of whether he would be worthy of Divine grace, and had expressed his certitude that he was to remain aloof from worldly concerns:

> I know by certainty that Thou wilst not make me grieved about the sorrow of this world (D 62).

This feeling strengthens his hope that he will also be saved in the other world in spite of his sins. But he goes farther and dreams of being completely rescued from the burden of existence:

> *When I am alive, I am sullied by the thought of the body,*
> *When I am dead, Paradise and Hell are my home-land.*
> *O Lord, tell me, swearing by Thy Pure Name:*
> *How can I cast the burden of Existence from my shoulders?* (P 119).

Mir Dard expresses in many of his prayers the hope for vision, for his highest goal is the contemplation of the Divine Light. The Quranic word 'Whithersoever ye turn your faces, there is the Face of God' (Sura 2/109) is the focal point of his theology and, hence, of his prayer-life. It does not involve a pantheistic view of all-embracing unity, but rather the feeling that God becomes visible and palpable through His creation which attests to His greatness and beauty. That is why he asks God time and again to lift the veil which still covers His traces here and there, and to grant him a seeing eye which discovers His beauty in the creation, and a hearing ear to listen to His voice in every sound (D 13). He implores the Lord to cast off the veil (burqa‘) of 'Sights do not reach Him' (Sura 6/103), and tells him that he ought not answer the true Muhammadans' prayers by 'Thou shalt not see Me' as he did with Moses (Sura 7/139) but rather give these followers of His Prophet the rank of 'And he saw what he saw', an allusion to Muhammad's vision as described in Sura 53 (D 29, cf. D. 117). Traditional Sufi formulations are built into his prayers, such as the oft repeated statement of 'I did not see anything but I saw God before it and with it and in it and behind it', which he poetically describes as the rank of one who sits 'squatting (Persian: squared) on the four cushions' of such a vision (S 29); seated thus comfortably in permanent contemplation he asks for the cup of the attraction of Divine proximity. He may also describe the waxing stronger of the inward sight as 'eye-glasses' which enhance the power of the outward eyes (A 32)—poets before him had regarded the 'mirror of the knee', on which the meditating Sufi puts his head, as 'eye-glasses for the eyes of the heart'.[6] This hope for vision is expressed both in his poetry and his prose:

> We, absorbed by Thy Beauty-cum-Perfection do not see anything but Thy manifest signs in all the horizons ... When there is the light of faith it sells the blandishment of the manifestation of Thy face, and when there is the darkness of infidelity it is wearing black from the shade of Thy tresses (A 96),

---

[6] The image of the eyeglasses occurs, as far as I can see, first in Urfi's (d. 1591) poetry, (Kulliyāt, Mathn. p. 469). That coincides with the time when eyeglasses were first represented in Indian miniatures. The image became very popular in the 17th and 18th centuries; Dard uses it in some of his verses and in A,32, A 231 and S 123 in longish deliberations. Cf. also Shah Abdul Latif's use of the word, p. 208.

as he sings in the traditional imagery of Persian poetry to express the various manifestations of God in the colorful play of day and night, of faith and infidelity, of Beauty and Wrath.

> *Whether madrasa or monastery, whether Ka῾ ba or idol-temple:*
> *They were all guest-houses, but you are the owner of the house* (U 2).

But still, the 'long tresses' of phenomena make it difficult for the heart that is entangled by their charm to reach the truth hidden beneath them. And taking over the old image of the narcissus as the seeing eye, Dard describes those with insight as narcissus sitting on a stem that is empty from selfhood (D 244).

God, the 'bestower of bounty of existence and cupbearer of the grace of being' is asked to help man,

> for the goblet of our individuation is thirsty for the wine of 'Remaining in God' (A 119).
> For all the determined existences in the whole world have drunk a sip from the mode of the Existence of the Absolute Being ... and the goblet of the individuation of everything created is filled with the wine of the vision of the Creator, and the glass of individualization of everything made is full with the liquor of the manifestation of the Maker (A 113).

Even Dard, who usually dislikes the imagery of intoxication, because it belongs to a lower level of experience, cannot help using the traditional images of wine and cup-bearer to explain that the creatures are like glasses, gaining their true character only by the wine that is contained in them (D 175).

We should not take such utterances at surface value and understand them as expressions of pantheistic views. That becomes clear from another prayer, when Dard tries to find a *via media* between the two theories the adherents of which fought with each other during his life-time:

> O God, the confession of Unity of Being is a kind of bad behaviour (*bi-adabi*), and the open show of Unity of Vision is a crooked discourse—the best speech is the word: 'There is no God but God' (D 223).

Here, as often, does he show an aversion to the technical terminology as used by his elder compatriot Shah Waliullah and many others. The True Muhammadan should not use such terms but

rather go back to the Quranic assertion of God's unity; that is
sufficient for salvation. Dard was very much against pantheists,
self-styled Sufis, and other people whom he considered dangerous for the fabric of Islamic religious life; yet, he claims that he
nourishes no hatred against anyone:

> O my God, I who thinks good, have never cast the arrow of evil prayer
> (e.g., curse) towards an enemy and I do not open my lips but for
> wellwishing for the creatures of God, and the bird of the arrow of my
> prayer does not fly in the air (or: wish) to shed anybody's blood; my
> request is only that the kingbird of happiness, e.g., of being accepted
> by Thee, may open its wings upon me and that Thou keepest me safe
> in both worlds, and that Thou placest the eye of Mercifulness towards
> me, through the Holy Prophet and my beloved mystical master, upon
> him and his family blessings and peace (A 160).

The longing language of Divine love is used in these prayers not
too often since love, as we saw in ʿIlm ul-kitāb, was usually
interpreted as 'love of God through love of the Prophet and the
mystical guide'. Still, Dard knew of the power of love, which he
saw revealed in the fact that even stones contain sparks and have,
thus, 'a burnt liver' (U 148). Love is 'a great affliction' indeed
(U 111):

> Man Thou createdst for the pain of love—
> Thou hast Thy angels for obedience! (U 63).

But only towards the end of his life, in Dard-i dil, the mystic
turns more frequently to that love-symbolism which he otherwise
tried to avoid in his prose, rather preferring expressions like
'sweetnesses of companionship' (ladhdhat-i maʿiyyat) (A 321).
In these prayers from the early 1780's, God appears to him as the
real goal of search and the 'ascertained' (taḥqīqī) beloved the fire
of whose love

> melts the grape of the heart and makes it a strange wine in the ban-
> quet of those who have taste and longing (D 330).

This is one of the few instances where Dard uses the word mastī,
'intoxication', for the God-given state of the mystic; but in the
same prayer he soon returns to quasi-philosophical terminology.
In another prayer he asks for an eye which should be

> the flask for the wine of pain of love, just as the heart should be a
> bottle for the wine of grief of intimacy (D 175).

Here, we shall have to place Urdu verses like this:

I am drunk—what orders the pīr *of the magi me to do?*
Shall I kiss the vat's foot, or the hand of the jar? (U 72).

He addresses his 'absolute Beloved' (D 163), who has sent down the human spirit from the holy place of proximity into corporal grossity and sensual desires. But more than in this kind of poetical prayers is he interested in the fate of the lovers who have given their souls in the way of God by realizing the Muhammadan Path: God may grant them the rank of martyrs, for though they may not have attained this high rank outwardly, yet they die every moment inwardly in the way of annihilation in God (D 84). The idea of the 'martyrs of love', which had inspired so many poets and mystics in the Islamic world, is connected here, once more, with the favorite Prophetic tradition 'Die before ye die': both point to the way of annihilation in God, an experience which the followers of the Muhammadan Path can realize better than anyone else. Examples like this show that Dard's whole imagery consists more or less of the images inherited from his predecessors in Persian poetry. His prayers, too, are permeated by combinations of traditional images, which are, however, often twisted in the way typical of the Indian Style in poetry and applied in surprising turns to the Sincere Muhammadans. Just as Dard represents himself often under the symbol of the 'candle of speech', he repeatedly speaks of the fire by which God consumes him (a logical outcome of his light-mysticism, but also an image that occurs frequently in Indo-Persian poetry):

God has cast a strange lightning of love into the harvest of my existence, and has put a strange fire of intuitive knowledge of myself into the ashes of my individuation. (A 241).

This lightning flashes the moment man recognizes Unity:

My eye-opening was the house-destroying lightning
Which burnt the furniture of my imagined existence (P 28).

The complaint of being burnt is worded differently in another prayer. While the images of the 'bird whose nest is destroyed by the lightning' or the 'harvest burnt by the lightning' belong to the favorite images of the Indo-Persian school, the metaphor of moth and candle goes back to Hallaj's *Kitāb aṭ-ṭawāsīn* and has furnished innumerable poets with touching phrases until it reached Europe, there to form the centre of Goethe's *Selige Sehnsucht* in the *West-Östlicher Divan*. Dard utters a prayer filled with comparisons (candle = bone, moth's wing = paper) which sound somewhat weird to us, but are common in his poetry:

> If Thy real love casts the lot of me, the weak one, then this must be from the bones of the candle, and if Thy ascertained love accomplishes something in the writing of the horoscope of me, the one with broken wings, the paper must be from the moth's wings ... (D 238).

Is not the lover in love

> *ritually slaughtered, a moth, and a ball—*
> *having given his life, burnt, and with turning head?* (P 85).

Dard also uses the imagery of weaving, well known to the poets of Muslim countries, to allude to the contrast between God's essence, his attributes, and the creatures, and we are reminded of the numerous examples in history of religions when the pious describe the starry sky or the sunlight as God's visible garment, or speak of the robe of His mercy which covers His ineffable essence and enables man to grasp 'the hem of his loving-kindness'.

> Just as the nakedness of negation of relations and attributions was specialized for the beautiful stature of Thy Unique Essence thus the dressing of the garments of dignities and reverences has become a sealing for the lovely figure of Thy High Essence; and every limited being has the warp and woof of its own existence from the thread of the generosity of Thy Absolute Existence ... (A 299).

Muslim mystics had used the image of the shadow-play for a long time: suffice it to mention Attar's tragic story of the Turkish puppet-player in his *Ushturnāma*, or the description of man's life as a shadow-play by his younger contemporary in Egypt, Umar ibn al-Farid. To members of a culture where the shadow-play was one of the few possibilities of 'dramatical' entertainment the image offered itself, and was popular with Turkish mystical writers as much as with those in Muslim India. Therefore, Dard addresses God, the eternal Light around whom the world is spread like a lampshade (P 43):

> Like to a lamp of the shadow-play where the world of spirits, or the world of imagination (ʿ *ālam-i miṯẖāl*) play round in the heart of the

perfect gnostics, and the world of Unseen becomes unveiled to them in even this world of visibility—: O Thou who makes everything high and low: as much as this servant made of dust does not lift his head from the dusty earth and cannot fly towards the angelic heaven, yet Thy limitless grace has made manifest all the marvels and subtleties of the higher world in this very place in his interior mirror, and the angels and spirits are permanently assembled in the completely united banquet of such pure people, and all the ranks of Hahut and Lahut and Divine Majesty become visible in the looking glass of the heart of those of holy nature (A 191).

Is not man's existence itself the shade, veiling the lamp?

We ourselves were the veil before our friend's face—
We opened our eyes, and no veil was left (U 18).

For 'the light of the eye is a shirt for Yusuf' (P 24, 53).

Sometimes Dard gets caught in his own poetical language and daydreams of the mystery of Absoluteness and limitation as it offered itself to him every moment. He knows: he can address God as the 'Sacred Valley of Absolute Existence', but how to describe this valley?

The sand dunes of the imagined contingent existences bring forth waves in this desert and fetter the feet of everything existent with the chains of limitations (A 123).

The wayfarer has to traverse this desert in the hope of reaching the pure Essence which lies behind the shifting dunes, but the desert of Absoluteness is grasped every moment anew in the snare of unexpected limitations, and never shows itself to the thirsty pilgrim. Yet, even the dunes at least point to the reality that is hidden behind them, and thus become the *Khiżr-i rāh*, the mystical guide (U 102), as Dard says with an image taken from Abu Talib Kalim.[7]

Besides this powerful image of God as the depth of the desert stands another description which is more in tune with the traditional poetical idiom: God, 'making everyone with wounded heart like a smiling rose' (A 316) is addressed as the 'spring of the rose garden of Divine transcendence (*tanzīh*) whose unqualified

---

[7] Kalim, *Dīwān, ghazal* Nr. 1. Out of the great number of verses which mention the *rēg-i rawān*, the shifting sand-dunes, Bedils comparison of the dunes with a throbbing heart in the desert, excited in the hope to see the beloved, (*Kulliyāt* I 14) should be singled out for its beauty.

manifestations give color to the palm trees in the roseparterre of
anthropomorphism (*tashbīh*)'; he is therefore asked to

> unveil the face of 'Whithersoever ye turn there is the Face of God'
> (Sura 2/109) so that we may see at every side nothing but the appear-
> ance of Thy existence in the world, and in every form pluck nothing
> but the rose of vision in this rose-bed (A 192).

The constant tension between the hope to reach God's innermost
essence by going behind the treacherous desert of manifestations,
and the wish to recognize Him in every thing created is typical of
Dard's meditations, and is also reflected in his poetry.

Sometimes, the mystic uses strange stylistic devices to make
his prayers more attractive, or at least less traditional. Thus
shortly before his death he imitates an official letter with all the
intricacies of protocol and high-flown phrases in rhyming prose:

> To the Excellency of lofty honorific names, the Refuge of the crea-
> tures, the Highness, Lord of lords, exalted be His power and general
> be His favor,
> from the pre-eternal and eternal poor servant Khwaja Mir Muhammad,
> after the presentation of servantship and lowliness, which are the
> distinctive marks of slaves with creed and the work of the Muslim
> servants, be it submitted:
> O God, since everybody writes something to everybody, and brings
> forth letters and stories, and the people of transactions write and
> recite to each other, and bring words and speech on the tongue of the
> pen (—that means that the employees write also petitions to the
> rulers, and the servants sketch petitions to their masters, and the
> lovers write letters and messages to their beloved ones, and the seekers
> send messages and greetings to those whom they seek—):
> therefore this meanest servant from among Thy free creatures, who
> knows nobody but Thee, and has nothing to do with anybody brings
> all he has said and written specially to the place of Thy most lightful
> view, and brings all he says and does specially in the meltingplace of
> the ear of Thy acceptance and requests: O real King of both worlds
> and Master of this world and the other, o my Beloved, o Sought by
> soul and body, o Who cherishes His servant, Without need, and Skill-
> ful Master without companion: what comes from this weak and in-
> capable slave but inability and disappointment, and what behoves a
> lean servant without soul but crying for help and showing of pov-
> erty? And what is opened by the hand of helplessness of him with
> miserable state but the door of blame and shame? And what appears
> from him who is shade-like fallen on this dark earth and has left the
> reins off his hand but confusion and incapability of servantship? Nec-
> essary is this: that this miserable dervish puts this into a petition, and
> possible is this: that this nothing without existence makes clear the

real state of his (mind)—more, o Lord, would be to transgress the limit
of etiquette! (S 330).

In his Persian prayers, Dard sometimes seems to be completely
carried away by the plays of words as they are poured forth in
admiration. The endless praise of God's never ending bounty, and
the feeling that not even the smallest atom would have existence
without God's creative power leads him at times to such long and
complicated sentences that one can barely follow their grammatical and theological threads. His Arabic prayers, as they are usually scattered through *'Ilm ul-kitāb*, are in general more traditional; they develop out of inherited prayer formulas and are
connected with Quranic verses. More frequently than in the Persian prayers, where Dard the poet is sometimes stronger than
Dard the theologian, we find prayers for forgiveness for his family (see S 314); others may point to Dard's role and his high rank
as the interpreter of the Book and the leader of 'Sincere Muhammadans'. In such cases, they often contain a number of God's
Most Beautiful Names, or conversations between God and His
servant. A typical example belongs to his later days: he reminds
God of His promise when He once addressed him:

'O My servant, I have created you with my hand and blessed be the
Lord, the best of creators!' And I said: 'O Lord, I do not doubt that I
am Thy servant and Thy creature; so forgive him whom Thou has
created with Thy hand, even if I have rebelled against Thee, verily
Thou art the Forgiver the Merciful!' And He said: 'By My mercy, I
forgive you, and again forgive you and again forgive you and who
follows you and who follows those who follow you until the Day of
Resurrection, and I am the Forgiver, the Mild!' And I said: 'Praise be
to God the Beautiful, and from the Beautiful One comes nothing but
Beauty ...' (S 249).

Besides such expressions of spiritual pride one finds little sighs in
which Dard appears as the broken, modest seeker, content with
just touching the Beloved's feet:

We have no desire to be angels and reach heaven—
This is the heart's wish: to reach Thy feet! (U 69)

For:

If we not see Thee in Thy manifestation,
It is alike whether we see the world or not. (U 17).

But his meditations always turn back to his heart, that house of God, which is separate from the world and filled with the light of God's presence.

> *What difference is of wounds and roses,*
> *if there's no fragrance in the rose?*
> *What has a heart to do, what knows it*
> *if Thou not dwellst inmidst the heart?* (U 70).

He experiences his breast as the Sinai of never ending manifestations of the Divine Light and Fire, and continues:

> O God of the world, all the manifestations of Thy most beautiful names are manifest in man according to 'He taught Adam the names' (Sura 2/32), and, O Creator of Heaven and earth, without doubt Thy place is according to the word '(Heaven and earth do not contain me, but) the heart of my faithful servant contains me' (A 302).

This experience of God as the *dulcis hospes animae* who enters the broken heart of man secretly, consoles him also at times when he is overwhelmed by the Quranic word 'The sights do not reach Him' (Sura 6/103), and:

> the fact that Thou canst not be seen constantly adds to our longing and love (A 229).

It is a long way until the mystic can discover the Divine Beloved 'closer than his jugular vein' (Sura 50/16), and Dard has sighed:

> *All life I listened but from far to Him,*
> *In dreamtimes only I embraced Him,*
> *Now, since I have become a mirror clear:*
> *He sees Himself in me, I don't see Him!* (P 78)

Once he has reached this state by polishing his heart in constant meditation and recollection of the Divine names, he discovers God in his heart and everywhere. Seeing and not-seeing becomes alike, and the mystery of the shifting sand dunes is solved. Like the Sufi in Maulana Rumi's story, he finds the garden in himself, and needs not to look at the created gardens anymore. Everything is in himself, for God is there:

> *We better close our ears and eyes to all,*
> *for Thou hast made us ear all, and all eye.* (P 4).

Secretly the beloved comes, for why should the mystic prostrate himself at the door of the house of his heart unless He be dwelling there? Dard alludes to this last mystery of loving union, of illumination by the Divine Light, in a touching prayer:

> O God, we who have been sitting so much in quietude in our own house and have never come out from our own door, and have cut off the warp and woof of lust and pleasure with the dagger of trust in God, and are not inclined towards the people of the world—perhaps Thou hast come through the door and hast honored this poor house without bringing me out of my own door?
>
> Perhaps thou hast come through my door,
> that my head lies on my threshold? (N 228).

SHAH ABDUL LATIF OF BHIT

(1689-1752)

CHAPTER FIVE

SHAH ABDUL LATIF'S LIFE AND TEACHING

Shah Abdul Latif is buried in a beautiful mausoleum in Bhit Shah near Hala, north east of Hyderabad/Sind. His shrine, crowned by a graceful minaret, was erected by the Kalhoro prince Ghulam Shah Kalhoro in 1765; it is covered with blue and white tiles as are typical of Hala district; they show flower motifs, and the pillars at the corners seem to grow out of large tulips. Although not outstanding as a work of architecture the building and the adjacent graveyard impress the visitor by their peculiar charm. The ceiling of the entrance hall shows the traditional workmanship of this area: between the wooden framework small brownish-olive-yellowish rectangular tiles are set in, a style found in many saints' tombs in Sind. To accomodate at least part of the innumerable visitors who flock to Bhit Shah in the days of the ʿurs, when the memory of the mystic's death is celebrated in the month of Safar, a guest house has recently been built. A cultural center is being developed. Every Thursday evening, till late at night, the few dervishes who still continue the tradition of Shah Abdul Latif sing his poetry inside the compound of the mausoleum.

Contrary to Mir Dard, Shah Latif did not leave any notes about his life or the development of his mystical theories; besides a few dry facts we know about him merely some legends of more or less authentic character. But his poetry is enough to make us acquainted with his personality. This man from a sayyid and Sufi family ingeniously wove together the various strands of Islamic mystical thought and indigenous Sindhi poetry. One hundred twenty five years ago, young Richard Burton wrote in his book 'Sind, and the Races that inhabit the Valley of the Indus:'

> Shah Bhitai ... had the disadvantage of contending against a barbarous dialect, and composing for an unimaginative people. His ornaments of verse are chiefly alliterations, puns, and jingling of words. He displays his learning by allusions to the literature of Arabia and Persia, and not unfrequently indulges in quotation. His compositions are all upon subjects familiar to the people, strained to convey a strange idea. As

might be expected, he is more homely and common-place than Ibn
Fariz or Hafiz; at the same time, he is more practical, and some
portions of his writings display an appreciation of domestic happiness
scarcely to be expected from one of his order.

Hence his poetry is the delight of all that can understand it. The
learned praise it for its beauty, and are fond of hearing it recited to the
sound of the guitar. Even the unlearned generally know select portions by heart, and take the trouble to become acquainted with their
meaning.[1]

At the same time, the German missionary Ernest Trumpp was
working in Karachi to learn Sindhi and published in the 1860's
several studies about Shah Latif, culminating in his edition of
Shāh jō Risālō (Leipzig 1866), the first print of the famous collection of poetry, which comprises more than 1200 pages in the
manuscript at his disposal. In his remarks about Shah Abdul Latif
and the topics of his poems Trumpp, completely devoted to the
sober study of grammatical forms and, besides, a strictly anti-
mystically minded protestant minister harshly attacked the
mystical contents of the *Risālō*; but even he had to admit that
the persevering reader will find many verses which amply repay
him for the difficult labor of going through the whole text. Indeed, the style of the *Risālō* is extremely difficult and offers
problems even to those whose mother tongue is the complicated
and melodious Sindhi.[2] But while Mir Dard's comprehensive
prose and poetry was never made available to a Western audience,
Shah Abdul Latif attracted a considerable number of scholars—
Indians, Pakistanis, and Westerners—who studied his poetry and
offered its contents to the English reading public. Lilaram Watanmal's 'Shah Abdul Latif,' issued in 1889, is still valuable for
interesting remarks about Shah Latif's life and for its useful vocabulary. Most research, however, was carried out in Sindhi. Even
after partition, both the Sindhi Hindus in India and the Sindhi
Muslims in Pakistan continued their work, which resulted in a
number of editions and analyses, such as Motilal Jotwani's welcome study of Shah Latif's poetical technique in his recent book

---

[1]   R. Burton, 'Sind and the races ...,' p. 203.

[2]   I have to acknowledge the help of many Sindhi friends whose interpretations,
though, sometimes differed considerably. Besides, Dr. N.A. Baloch, Hyderabad, the
authority on Sindhi folklore; Dr. Motilal Jotwani, Delhi; and Mr. Ghulam Rabbani
Agro, Hyderabad have answered a number of questions. Still, I do not claim that all
enigmas are solved, and other translators may as well reach different conclusions.

on Shah Abdul Latif. The most comprehensive study in English is that by T. H. Sorley, 'Shah Abdul Latif of Bhit,' which appeared first in 1940 and offers not only a good survey of the *Risālō* but also a detailed picture of the social and political setting in 18th century Sind; it contains fine, though rather free translations of major parts of the *Risālō*. Sorley, however, was not a trained Islamicist; some of his usually correct statements must be verified and deepened in the light of history of religions by taking into consideration the development of mystical thought and poetry in Islam. A partial translation in English verse of the *Risālō* was offered by Mrs. Elsa Qazi, who captured well the form and spirit of the work. Besides, an almost limitless amount of speeches, articles, booklets, and devotional literature was published, mainly in Sindhi, so that one of the leading Pakistani scholars, himself a great admirer of Shah Abdul Latif, could sigh:

> Shah was the crown of the Sufis, Shah was a folk poet, Shah was the master of *ragas*, Shah was a patriot, Shah was a congressman, Shah was a Muslim Leaguer, Shah was Rumi, Shah was Goethe, Shah has produced Hir, Shah has made alive Marui—in short, Shah is the medicine for every illness, Shah is the remedy for every pain. That means, the same thing that has been done to Ghalib and Iqbal we have done to Shah Sahib.[3]

Indeed, there is always the danger that great poetry will be interpreted by every reader according to his own feelings, and also according to certain opportunist or even political tendencies; and since contradictions cannot be excluded in the verse of a great poet, let alone a religious, or mystically minded, poet, everyone finds in him what he has sought. This is all the more true since Shah Abdul Latif has once called his verses *āyāt*, 'divine signs,' hence comparable to Quranic verses:

> *What you consider to be verses, those are* āyāts (Sohṇī VI 25).

Shāh jō Risālō is, as Sorley has correctly remarked, 'a web of many strands.'[4] They reach from the poet's thorough knowledge of the Quran, of the Prophetic tradition and of Persian mystical poetry, particularly that of Jalaluddin Rumi, to the folksongs of Indian villages. A few Hindu traditions are also preserved, for

---

[3] H. Rashdi, '*Shāh kāfia jō mūjid na āhe*,' in: *Mehran jūn maujūn*, p. 218.
[4] Sorley, 'Shah Abdul Latif', p. 236.

some of the stories which form the basis of the mystical interpretations are of Hindu origin. One may also admit of some Balochi influence, understandable in the light of historical events; but there was certainly no relation with Urdu poetry which was just emerging in northern India during Shah's lifetime. Similarities in structure and imagery with Panjabi mystical folk poetry, which reached its apex with Bullhe Shah during exactly the same period, are, of course, conspicuous. Many later Sindhi Sufi poets, mainly those of Baloch origin, used also the northern dialect of Sindhi, Siraiki, which forms the transition to Panjabi; thus, the imagery of both, or rather all three, linguistic areas is very closely related, as is to be expected from the inhabitants of predominatly rural provinces.

Shah Abdul Latif's *Risālō* consists (in the excellent Bombay edition) of thirty chapters, *Sur*, which deal with different topics.[5] Each of them is named according to the musical mode in which it is sung, and which points to the contents. Each *Sur* has a number of chapters, consisting of irregular numbers of verses in Indian meters; each chapter closes with a *wā 'ī*, that is, a longer poem with one main line which is repeated, in singing, after every line of the poem.[6] Many *Surs* rely upon well-known folk tales, as is the case in the Panjab, too. Some of these stories have a historical basis and can be dated back to the 14th and 15th centuries; those belong to Shah's favorite topics. Without entering into a detailed description of the stories, which were known to everyone, Shah singles out some particularly impressive moments to develop his teachings about suffering and love so that even very worldly heroes and heroines are transformed completely into symbols of the Godseeking soul.

The sequence of the *Surs* is, according to the Bombay edition, as follows:

Kalyān, a purely mystical song, begins with a deep felt hymni-

---

[5] The sequence of the Hyderabad edition, 1974, is as follows: Kalyān - Jaman - Khanbhāt - Sarirāg - Samūndī - Sohnī - Sārang - Kēdārū - Abrī - Maʾ dhūrī - Dēsī - Kōhyārī - Ḥusainī - Sōrathī - Bērāg Hindī - Hīr - Barvō Sindhī - Mūmal Rāṇō - Khāhōṛī - Rāmakalī - Ripa - Līlā - Bilāwal - Dahar - Kapā ʾiti - Pirbhāī - Ghatū - Shīh Kēdārū - Asā - Mārū ʾi - Dhanasarī - Pūrab - Kāmōd - Karā ʾil - Dhūl Māru'i - Tīh akhari Sassu ʾi. Some of the chapters are not found in the other editions.

[6] The poetical form is reminiscent of many of Kabir's poems, and of the poetry of the *Adi Granth*. A number of ragas used in the *Risālō* are also used in the *Adi Granth* (see E. Trumpp's introduction to his translation).

cal praise of God, the One, who manifests Himself under different forms. But to reach Him, the seeker has to undergo much tribulation, and the following parts contain a detailed description of various ways of suffering in the path of God and of enjoying the afflictions. These ideas are continued in *Sur Yaman Kalyāṇ*, musically a derivation from the first Sur, and like it belonging to the evening *rāgs*, which are supposed to give the heart peace. In both *Surs* the traditional Sufi ideals are explained (see Ch. VI).

Sur Khanbhāt is a night melody, so that the allusions to moon and stars as weak reflections of the friend's loveliness are most fitting. It deals with the journey of the camel toward the most beautiful and radiant beloved, and contains lively remarks about the restive camel's habits, typical for a poet who lived in a camel breeding society: the camel is, of course, the symbol of the lower soul which has to be tamed and driven towards the beloved, be it the Prophet, or God Himself; there, it will no longer stick to thorns and thistles in which it indulges on the road, but will enjoy the green garden of paradise.

The following two *Surs*, *Sarīrāg* (an afternoon *rāg*) and *Sāmūndī*, are connected with the dangers of seafaring: in the ocean of this world the boat has to be guided by the ever-aware pilot, the true mystical guide, or by the Prophet himself. The fragile boat 'man' requires sails made of sincerity and right action, and the cargo should be prayers (Sr. VI 11) so that it may reach safely Port Aden, which name points both to the Arabian city and the paradisical 'gardens of Eden.' The various stages of sailing to Ceylon are described—a true 'passage to more than India'—from which the lucky merchants may return with pearls and spices. But, alas! today only a few faithful dealers in jewels are found, and most of them offer cheap beads instead of precious pearls. The events are seen through the eyes of the lonely, desperate wife whose husband had gone out into the dangerous sea to perform the journey of the soul through the raving waves of this world in the hope of heavenly reward; her complaints, partly utilizing the vocabulary of the Sassui-circle, are very amorous and sweet. The melody of *Sāmūndī* is an indigenous Sindhi folk song.

The topic of the sea, or river, with its whirlpools and sandbanks forms also the center of the next *Sur*, which bears the name of *Sohnī*, 'the Beautiful,' 'who died swimming.' This is a

tragic love story which reverts the classical motif of Hero and
Leander: here, the heroine Sohni, unhappily married to a man
whom she despises, swims every night to the island where her
beloved Mehar grazes the buffalos. One night her sister-in-law
replaces the jar, which she uses as sort of a swimming vest, by a
vessel of unbaked clay, and she dies in the whirling waves. Shah
begins the story in the most dramatic moment, when the young
woman cries out for help in the cold river, attacked by croco-
diles. The whole chapter is merely an extension of this dreadful
and yet hoped for moment, when the vessel of her body breaks
and she, faithful to her pre-eternal love-covenant with Mehar, will
be forever united with the friend through death.

Sohni is one of the favorite folk tales in both Sind and the
Panjab.[7] But even more famous is the story which Shah Latif has
made the subject of the following five *Surs* and which is alluded
to in many other verses of the *Risālō*. It is the intriguing story of
Sassui (*Abrī*, 'the weak one,' *Maᶜdhūrī*, 'the helpless one,' *Dēsī*,
'the native one,' *Kōhyārī*, 'the mountaineer,' and *Ḥusainī*, in the
tragic melody of the dirges in Muharram). Sassui, a beautiful girl,
was found by a washerman in Bhambhore, who adopted her. The
fame of her beauty spread widely, and eventually even Punhun,
the Baloch prince of Kech, decided to see her. At the end of
numerous complicated adventures he stayed with Sassui, but his
relatives came one night, made the couple drunk, and carried
away Punhun on their speedy camels, while the young woman
was fast asleep. Shah's chapters deal with her search for the
beloved: following the tracks of Punhun's camels, she runs in
despair through desert and forests where blue snakes and other
frightening creatures live (Abrī II 9):—snakes are here, as in traditional religious imagery, symbols of the devil from which, as
Shah says elsewhere, the peacock-like Yogis keep aloof, or
rather, kill it (Karāyil II). Even the wild animals and trees and
birds begin to share her grief and cry with her. Eventually she
perishes on the road. This tragic story becomes for Shah the
parable of the seeker on the mystical path who undergoes all
kinds of tribulations in the quest of God whom he will find, at

---

[7]   R. Burton has given the contents of most of the Sindhi folktales in his book on
Sind; recently, the most famous tales with their variants have been published by the
Sindhi Adabi Board, Hyderabad. There are also some 19th century English translations
available.

the end of the road, in his own heart, and Sassui, roaming in the wilderness and talking to the beasts, becomes something like a feminine counterpart of the Arabic Majnun who, demented by his longing for Laila, is taken by the mystics of the Persian and Turkish tradition as the paragon of the true lover: he, too, experiences his unity with Laila when he is almost dying after years of yearning in the desert.

The following *Sur* has again a traditional story as its background, e.g., that of *Lilā Chanēsar*, which can be dated back to the time of Jam Chanesar, one of the Summa rulers in 14th century Sind. It has often been retold in Sindhi and Persian. Chanesar's wife, the spoiled and pleasure-loving Lila, is enticed by another woman by a necklace worth 900,000 rupees to allow the former owner of the necklace to spend one night with Chanesar. Furious that he had been 'sold' Chanesar divorces Lila, and she has to undergo a long process of purification until she is once more acceptable in her husband's presence. Shah tells only her suffering and pining, and describes how the queen has to become a slave in order to be accepted by the Lord. Another folktale of similar character is that of *Mūmal Rānō* which forms the basis of the following *Sur*; it originated in Lower Sind some time in the 15th century, and tells the adventures of Mumal, a beautiful and dangerous, courtesanlike woman, and her lover Rano. Rano, wrongly assuming that she has cheated him one night, leaves her alone. Eventually, after a long period of waiting, the loving woman is purified and united with the beloved, whose light she knows and recognizes everywhere.

Sur Mārui goes back to a historical event in the 14th century; the home of the heroine is located in Thar desert, where the mighty Omar of Omarkot kidnapped her. But the lovely maiden refuses to become the nobleman's wife, as much as he tortures her, and eventually is sent back to her beloved village to which she had remained faithful even under the heaviest pressures.

As I have come here, thus I will go to them. (Mār. VI I)

Sur Kāmōd relies upon another historical event. It is the famous tale of Prince Jam Tamachi's falling in love with the charming fishermaid Nuri (15th century). Nuri makes the prince happy by her perfect surrender and obedience which causes him to raise her above all the other queens: she is the *nafs muṭma 'inna*, 'the soul at peace' (Sura 89/27), returning to her Lord. *Kāmōḍ* is one of the most peaceful *Surs*, to be sung at the time of early afternoon, when one dozes on a big Sindhi swinging bed. It is the only *Sur* that sings of fulfilled love and happiness, not of burning love and hopeless search.

The very short *Sur Ghātū* takes up once more the theme of the world or *nafs* under the image of the dangerous, merciless sea with its monsters which swallow the fishermen, and the Sindhi reader will remember the story of brave Morirro who slayed the whale that had killed his six brothers.

> *The fishermen got deep into the whirlpool and killed the shark of desire.*
> *Now their eyes beam with joy.* (I 15)

But there is also much realism in the description of the dangerous current in the coastal area near Karachi between Clifton and Manorha.

Sur Sōraṭhi, edited and translated first by E. Trumpp, is built upon a Hindu tale from Girnar, Gujrat, according to which King Diyaj offered his head to the minstrel who had enchanted him by his music. Trumpp has retold the complicated and most abstruse details of this story not sparing with sarcastic remarks. At the end of his introduction he concludes:

> It is barely necessary to say a word about this black aspect of Indian life, which can find certain consolation only in individual extinction. Those local tales are for us important in so far as we learn from them something about Indian thinking and life style at a time when there are barely any historical reports available. The outlines which this tale offers us are indeed melancholy enough and show us Hinduism in its complete decomposition and deepest moral decline; it is a picture of crime and absolute obtusity, nothing else. We can very well recognize from the Muslim elaboration of an originally Hindu tale how much even the strong monotheistic deism of Islam has become modified and corrupted in Sind, as in other parts of India, by its contact with Hinduism. Suicide, for instance, which is contrary to the ideals of Islam, is called here 'an enjoyable action' ... We have already alluded to the fact that in Abdul Latif's hands this whole tale has got a Sufic tinge and will be understood in that way. The bard who plays on the heart's harp, is the *murshid* who enthralls the heart so much and fills it with such great longing for its origin that it sacrifices everything (though after much opposition and hard struggle with the material body which always drags it down into the sensual world) and at last

even gives up the individual life in order to revel in endless nothing-
ness, being freed from the fetters of matter. The language abounds in
grotesque images the meaning of which is more than doubtful even to
the natives; on the other hand, there is no lack of many empty alliterations, as is the case in all Sufi compositions; the thread of thought is
at times long winded and agressive, and the intellectual poverty of
modern Indian poetry is covered by an idle jingle of words.[8]

Part of Trumpp's criticism, however, is born from the fact that
his manuscript of the *Risālō* was hopelessly confused so that the
sequence of events is without any logical order. Nevertheless,
even the unprejudiced reader will have some difficulties in appre-
ciating the description of the generous ruler who offers his head
to a bard who, in the full original story, was destined to kill him
according to his horoscope; but for Shah, selfsurrender at the
bidding of the mystical beloved, and the heavenly quality of
music is the central theme of this *Sur.*

From the world of Hindu legend the poet returns to Islamic
subjects in the following two *Surs: Kēdaro*, an old mourning
melody, is devoted to the martyrs of Kerbela who were slain,
lead by the Prophet's grandson Husain, on 10 Muharram (10 Oc-
tober) 680 by the forces of the Omayyads. *Sur Sārang*, the rain-
song, ingeniously blends the traditional Indian imagery of waiting
for rain with the veneration of the Prophet. (See pp. 256 ff).

Sur Āsā belongs to the sweetest chapters of the *Risālō*; it is
filled with mystical wisdom and poetical imagery, but does not
rely as much on folk tradition as some other *Surs*, whereas *Sur
Ripa*, a short song, describes in impressive images the longing of
the lonely wife for her husband.

Sur Khāhōrī is written in praise of the Yogis who walk from
the village of Ganji Takar near present-day Hyderabad to the
sacred mountain Hinglaj (an ancient Shiva sanctuary in Balochistan) and suffer every possible discomfort. They are further described in detail in the long-winded chapters of *Sur Rāmakalī*,
which constitutes for the historian of religion one of the most
interesting parts of the *Risālō* (see pp. 219 ff.) Inserted between the
two songs in praise of the Yogis as 'perfect men' is *Sur Barvō
Sindhī*, written to a lovely evening tune, which expresses the
deep veneration of the poet for his beautiful and mysterious,

---

[8]   E. Trumpp, Sorathi. ZDMG 17/1863.

powerful and mild, divine lord, utilizing, toward the end, again the theme of Sassui.

A topic which is not rarely found in the poetry of Sind and the Panjab is the spinning of cotton, one of the most important occupations of women. This is the theme of *Kāpā ʾitī*, which name points to traditional folk melodies sung by the womenfolk while spinning. Here, the connection between the spinning woman and the soul which is busy with the constant recollection of God is obvious; and the Quranic imagery of God as the merchant who buys man's soul is extended to the idea that the cotton thread, e.g., the heart, has to be refined and prepared with utmost care so that the spinning soul will not be rejected by the merchant.[9]

In *Sur Pūrab*, 'East', the poet describes the feelings of the loving woman who sends out the crow to find out how her beloved is; the crow, *kāng*, is the typical messenger bird in Sind, as was the pigeon in high Persian poetry, and its importance has often been underlined in Sindhi folk songs and mystical poetry. But out of this first touching verse Shah turns once more to the Yogis and warns them not to make false pretenses in yogidom. The theme of the soul-bird—of which the crow is a variation—is taken up in extenso in *Sur Karā ʾil*, the song of the swan who is admonished not to fly and dive with the other, unclean birds, but continue to feed on pearls.

In the following Sur, *Pirbhātī*, 'Early Morning', man's soul is seen as a wandering minstrel who is kindly treated by the ruler of Las Bela, the representative of the Almighty Lord. *Sur Ḍahar* gives in its first chapter a fine description of the dried-up tree, a common sight in the valley of the ever shifting Indus and its tributaries, but also a sight which leads the poet to a praise of the Prophet's kindness in the second part while the Sassui imagery is utilized toward the end. *Sur Bilāwal* (I, II) contains a number of historical allusions to the powerful rulers of Sind who in the end appear to be symbols of Muhammad's grace and munificence. A little joke about Shah Latif's friend and servant forms the last chapter of this *Sur*; he, though 'stinking', 'a glutton', 'ugly,'—to mention only a few of his epithets—becomes purified in the rose-water-like company of the master. *Sur Bilāwal* is probably the

---

[9] For the spinning motif in Panjabi cf. L. Ramakrishna, 'Panjabi Sufi Poets,' p. XVII.

most difficult one to appreciate for a non-Sindhi reader.

Shah Abdul Latif's poetry is the first apex of a long literary development, the beginnings of which we cannot properly distinguish. Sind, as other countries, had, and still has, a big treasure of folk poetry, ballads, and working songs; folk tales are located in the different parts of the country, be it the hill slopes of Balochistan, the desert region of Thar Parkar, the fertile plains that were watered by the Indus, or the shifting creeks near the Indus mouth. It seems that in Sind, as in other parts of the Muslim world, the Sufis are responsible for the development of the spoken language into a literary one. The first verses we know in Sindhi were composed by those mystics who migrated from their homeland to Burhanpur in Central India, and are reported to have used little verses in their mother tongue during the sessions of mystical concerts when music and dancing were in full swing. That was shortly after 1530. At the same time, the first known major poet of Sind wrote mystical verses out of which seven are still extant. It is the mystically inclined Qazi Qadan of Sehwan (d. 1551), a follower of the Mahdi of Jaunpur (d. 1505) whose success in the Lower Indus Valley had been remarkable and whose thoughts were apparently transmitted to Akbar through his literary friends Abu 'l-Fazl and Faizi, the sons of the Mahdi's follower, Muhammad Nagori. [10] Qazi Qadan's poetry has all the ingredients of later Sufi verse: the lines are short and express mystical hints in a dense grammatical construction. His verse:

Lōkān sarf^u nahw^u, mūñ mutali^{c} ^{u} supriñ^a
(Leave the people with grammar and syntax, I contemplate the Beloved),

has become almost proverbial and is echoed throughout the centuries in poetical variations. Qazi Qadan's tradition was continued in the country; Shah Abdul Latif's great-grandfather Shah Abdul Karim of Bulrri (1536-1623) is the most important figure in the next century; in his Persian malfūzāt 93 verses in Sindhi are preserved, which contain all the ingredients of later mystical poetry. [11] He seems to be the first one to use allusions to Sindhi folk tales in his verses, thus to Sassui:

---

[10]   A.S. Bazmee Ansari, 'Sayyid Muhammad Jawnpuri and his Movement,' gives a good introduction.

[11]   Motilal Jotwani, 'Shah Abdul Karim,' New Delhi 1970, discusses form and contents of his poetry.

> *Nobody ever took with himself*
> *two things at once from Bhambhore,*
> *Yearning for the beloved,*
> *and attachment with one's world.* [12]

Shah Latif has inserted some of his ancestor's lines into his own poetry. Tender lines speak of the swan that dives for pearls, but sketch also miniature pictures of village life:

> *Like a jar poised on woman-water-carrier,*
> *and a bird on the water,*
> *Our beloved in the same way*
> *has been close to our soul.* [13]

After a number of minor poets a step forward in the development of Sufi poetry was made by Miyan Shah ʿInat from Nasrpur, a Sufi of the Qadiri order which was introduced in the Indus Valley in the late 15th century. He died in the beginning of the 18th century. His poetry, which foreshadows Shah Abdul Latif's verse, was the first to be arranged in 19 *Surs*, and was therefore called a *Risālō*.

All these poems are extremely difficult to disentangle due to the density of the language, which allows of most complicated and not always very transparent combinations of grammatical forms. Alone the fact that the unique beloved is often referred to as 'the friends' or other plural constructions, makes a proper translation difficult, although we may think of the Persian use of *īshān* 'they' as honorific title for a mystic, especially in the Central Asian Naqshbandi tradition.

Shah Abdul Latif's *Risālō* is no exception. Some of its verses almost defy literal translation, all the more since the poet was very fond of alliterations (very much to Trumpp's dismay!) and sometimes changed the form of words according to the exigencies of a more poetical style and also to the harmonious flow of the music, for the *Risālō* is meant to be sung, not to be theologically and grammatically dissected. One should never forget that his poetry, as that of his predecessors, grew out of folk songs; and folk poetry, particularly that sung by women, has a peculiar style, using many terms of endearment which are otherwise rarely

---

[12]   Jotwani, l.c. Nr. XVII.
[13]   id. Nr. XIII.

found. Thus the beautiful closing verses (*wāʾī*) in *Sur Mārui I*, which the homesick girl sings, are in their approach reminiscent of some bridal songs which the recently married woman sings when she longs for her paternal home and misses the care of her parents and playmates. [14]

> My heart is in the village ... Could I go home! ... Could I die in Malir ...!

Shah Latif loves to show his heroines as they tenderly address their beloved in terms of endearment, Punhun becomes *Punhal*, *Kōhyārī*, 'mountaineer,' *Kōhyārial* (Abrī IX 12), just as Arabic mystical poets such as Ibn al-Farid had a predilection for diminutives. The Sindhi girls call the messenger bird *kāngal*, or *kāngrrō* ('dear little crow'), and Shah Latif in general, largely uses the diminutive ending *-rrō, -rrī* as formative element to express the true feminine way of speaking. Now and then we meet strange forms for originally Arabic or Persian words; thus *jihāj* (Sar. I 12) for *jihāz*, 'ship,' a pronunciation still typical of the Sind-Gujrat and Panjabi area, where *j* and *z* are often interchanged. Arabic broken plurals are treated like Sindhi singulars; the rhyme follows, as in the works of his contemporaries, the actual pronunciation, not the Arabic writing system;[15] words can be changed for the sake of rhyme. Some chapters contain a whole repertoire of Arabic expressions, often strangely mixed with Sindhi verbal constructions,[16] and we even find a surprising allusion to Arabic grammatical terminology to explain the interplay of 'proximity' and 'being broken.'[17] Charming wrong etymologies, as are a peculiarity of popular Sufi poets, are also found; thus, when the sailing boat, *ghurāb*, is connected with *gharīb*, 'foreign, forlorn,' or the word for darkness, tenebrae, *andhōkār*, is spelled *hindūkār*: a reminiscence of the equation Hindu- = black, which

---

[14] Cf. A. Schimmel, 'Hochzeitslieder der Frauen im Industal', an article based on Dr. N.A. Baloch's edition of the *Gghīch* in Sindhi.

[15] For instance *ṭuyūran, wuhūshan* (Abrī I 11), ʿ*abath* rhymes with *habas, jawāb* is made *jabāb* to rhyme with *kabāb* (Kal. III 6), in Kam. I *mahram* and *mahrūm* are confused.

[16] Thus in Kōh. I, where Arabic forms like *qum* 'rise', *ijlis* 'sit down' and others are found.

[17] *Kasarati ahē qurba mē, idghām mē iʿrāb* (Sohn. I *wāʾī*): In approximation there is multiplicity, in doubling a consonant by *tashdīd*, inflection.

occurs so frequently in Persian and Turkish traditional poetry (Abrī II 10). [18] Now and then, other languages are mentioned:

> They carry Punhun, speaking Balochi (Dēsī II 9),

where 'Balochi' is the language of the foreign invaders, incomprehensible to the poor Sindhi woman.

One who has learned Persian is addressed in *Asā IV 23*. Pre-Islamic ideas are natural in literature that draws upon Hindu tales; thus Sassui is sometimes called a *bānbhan* (Abrī I 10), a 'Brahmin girl,' or is praised because she is becoming a yogini (Abrī III 10); the heroines also speak of the funeral pyre (thus Sām. I 8)

On the whole, the vocabulary of *Shāh jō Risālō* is pure Sindhi and contains numerous technical terms from seafaring, fishing, milking, churning, spinning and hunting, in short, from all those professions which were common in the country. It is fascinating to watch how Shah Abdul Latif succeeds in blending this popular tradition with that of Islamic mysticism.

There are many allusions to the Quran and the Prophet (see Ch. VII), but one can agree with Sorley that 'it would have been sufficient for the author of the *Risālō* to be acquainted with Maulana Jalaluddin Rumi's *Mathnawī* alone.' [19] Indeed, Rumi's influence on the Indo-Pakistani subcontinent cannot be over-rated. The poet-saint of Panipat, Bu ʿAli Qalandar (d. 1327), is related to have met Maulana Rumi; his *mathnawīs* clearly show traces of Rumi's work. [20] As early as in the 15th century, 'the holy brahmin recited the *Mathnawī*' in East Bengal. [21] Commentaries of the *Mathnawī* are available not only in numerous Persian works composed during the Muslim rule (even illustrated copies of this 'Quran in the Persian tongue' were produced during the sultanate period in Delhi), [22] but also in numerous indigenous idioms; the work was partly or in full translated into many native languages. Rumi's style of writing deeply influenced the poetry

---

[18]   Cf. A. Schimmel, 'Turk and Hindu', in IV. Levi della Vida Conference, 1975, for the motif of the 'black' Hindu.

[19]   A. Schimmel, *Mevlâna Rumi'nin Şark ve Garp'ta tesirleri*; the problem will be discussed in detail in my forthcoming book on Rumi (Persian Heritage Series).

[20]   Bu Ali Qalandar of Panipat (d. 1327) is supposed to have visited Konya; his Persian *mathnawīs* show clear traces of his being acquainted with Rumi's *Mathnawī*; see H.S. Tafhimi, Bu Ali Qalandar, Ph. D. thesis, Karachi 1975.

[21]   Enamul Haq, 'Muslim Bengali Literature,' p. 42.

[22]   In the National Museum Delhi, seven miniatures, ms. 48.6/15.

in these tongues, and his *Mathnawī* was known to the broad masses as much as it was loved and recited at the Mughal court in Delhi, and served the Kalhoro prince to gain back the sympathies of Shah Abdul Latif. Not only Dara Shikoh, the mystically minded heir apparent of the Mughal Empire largely relied upon Rumi's poetry in his own writings; his brother Aurangzeb, too, used to shed tears when listening to a touching performance of *Mathnawī* recitation. In Sind there were many pious who, by their recitation of the *Mathnawī*, 'kept the marketplace of union warm', and Rumi's work was quoted by stern Naqshbandis as much as by members of the more emotional orders.

In several verses of *Shāh jō Risālō* the reader is immediately reminded of Rumi's sayings, particularly in *Sur Yaman Kalyāṇ* V (see p. 206 f.). The poet speaks of the reedflute, known from the first verses of the *Mathnawī*, to explain Sassui's longing, when she cries in separation from Punhun just as the flute complains, longing for home for her reedbed:

> *The cut-off [flute] wails and the [half-]killed woman cries—*
> *That one remembers having been [one with] the tree, this*
> *one longs for her beloved.* (Maᶜ ḏẖ. VI 19)

Ever clearer is another verse:

> *As grass and straw, being cut, complain,*
> *suddenly the sigh of the pain of the beloved comes* (BS I 2)

Sūr Āsā (III) contains an allusion to the story of the blind and the elephant which, though popular long before Rumi, has gained special fame thanks to his version in the *Mathnawī*: [23] the outwardly blind cannot grasp reality in its wholeness; they touch only small parts of the whole elephant, while those who are inwardly blind, that means: who have closed their eyes to the world and what is in it, will find the source of unity. When the poet says that finally no 'I' is left in the castle of the Kechis who, being Punhun's people, represent The Beloved, one sees the connection with Rumi's tale about the lover and the beloved: when

---

[23] *Mathnawī* III 1259 ff., taken over by Bu Ali Qalandar in his *mathnawi* I, cf. Tafhimi, i.c. 325 f. See F. Meier, 'Zur Geschichte der Legende von den Blinden und dem Elefanten,' in: Das Problem der Natur im esoterischen Monismus des Islams, Eranos-Jahrbuch 14/1946, p. 174

the lover, after maturing in the fire of separation, is finally allowed to enter the house of his friend, for he has left his I, and

> there is no room for two I in this small house. [24]

The most touching, for most unexpected, quotation is that in
Sassui's story (Abrī I 8), where one of the deepest lines from the
Mathnawī (Vol. I 1741) is translated in simple Sindhi:

> *Not only the thirsty seek the water,*
> *the water as well seeks the thirsty.*

To be sure, the idea of the mutual longing of God, the fountain-
head of grace, and the soul that yearns for this source of love,
was known to the muslim mystics long before Rumi; the Quranic
word 'He loves them and they love Him' (Sura 5/59) could easily
be taken as proof for the truth that God's love precedes man's
love. It formed the basis of great mystical poetry until Shah Latif
applied it to his heroine who almost died from thirst in the desert
hills. How would she undergo these tribulations if not the beloved were longing for her and attracting her until union is
achieved?

One may ask to what extent Shah Abdul Latif's musical imagery was influenced by Rumi. The expression that all veins have
become a *rabāb* (Kal. III 6, Ripa I 21) on which pain and grief
play their tunes, is not rare in traditional Sufi poetry. But once
perfection is reached, 'their veins play the melody of He is One'
(Asā IV 47). The overwhelming power of music is best represented in *Sur Sōraṭhi*: a cruel Hindu story is transformed into a
praise of the heavenly harmony for which the soul leaves everything on earth.

> *With your fiddle's bow*
> *you have cut my heart at night* (Sōr. IV 3).

The same idea occurs in *Rāmakalī* (I 19ff), where the poet praises
the fiddles of the Yogis, those 'golden instruments' by which
man is induced into a wonderful state of mind. Even the *murlī*,
the snake charmer's instrument, is mentioned in this connection;
this wind instrument can indeed produce strange effects by its
heart-rending sound. The skillful application of the various classical Indian tunes and Sindhi folk melodies to the contents of the

---

[24]   *Mathnawī* I 3056-64.

Risālō is remarkable. Once Shah alludes to his technique of blending his topics: Sassui says that 'the Husainian mode' should be sung for her, which is the melody used for *marthiyas* for the martyrs of Kerbela (Hus. VI 10): thus he connects here the martyress of love with the Prophet's suffering family, for in their afflictions, too, Divine Love manifested itself.

Shah Abdul Latif follows the traditional imagery of Sufi poetry by devoting one of his Surs, *Karā 'il*, to the swan. Bird symbolism was common in the Islamic world since long; the time-honored image of the rose and the nightingale became almost a catchword to denote the character of Persian poetry. The soul as a bird is an age old symbol in many early religious traditions in East and West. Sanā'i of Ghazna (d. ca. 1131) ingeniously interpreted the 'Litany of the birds' in one of his great Persian *qaṣīdas*,[25] half a century before his Khorassanian compatriot 'Attar produced the masterpiece of this symbolism with his *Manṭiq uṭ-ṭair*, The Bird's Conversation. He tells the journey of the birds who eventually, after passing through the seven valleys, discover that they themselves, being *sī murgh*, 'thirty birds,' are the *Sīmurgh*, the King of Birds; the purified soul recognizes at the end of the road her essential unity with the Divine. Shah Latif may have inherited his bird imagery from his Muslim precursors; he could also, as he indeed did, go back to the Indian legends of the swan, or wild goose, who dives only into the clearest water in order to find a pearl, while herons, cranes, and other water-fowl are content with the dirty water the world offers them, an image often used by Kabir. *Sur Karā'il* uses this idea to admonish the seeker's soul to imitate the noble bird's example and not to follow the lower birds.

> *When, meditating, you have looked only once towards the swans,*
> *You will never again make friendship with the cranes* (Kar. I 12).

Rumi had expressed similar ideas in the context of nightingale and raven, falcon and crow respectively: the nightingale longs for the eternal rose garden, the falcon for his master's fist, while raven and crows are bound to the hibernal world of the material

---

[25]   Sanā'i, *Dīwān*, p. 30-35.

senses. The imagery of the swan must have been popular in Sind
for a long time, for Abdul Karim uses it more than a century
before his descendant Latif:

> *A swan feeds on pearls,*
>   *he dives deep down,*
> *He who plays in the shallows,*
>   *is only an ordinary bird.* [26]

At the end of the same *Sur*, Shah Latif introduces another allegory known from the Indian tradition, e.g., that of the black bee
which becomes enamoured by the blue lotus. The miracle of true
love is that the bee in the sky and the flower on the water are
united by its attraction.

As much as Shah Latif is a faithful follower of the Sufi tradition, his poetry would certainly not have attracted the Sindhi
speaking people for more than two centuries, had he only dwelt
upon highly mystical topics, and offered them the kind of pious
high-falutin that not a few among the mystical writers used to
prepare. In his use of everyday imagery he is, in a certain way,
comparable to Maulana Jalaluddin, who, too, could be inspired
to fly to celestial heights of mystical love poetry by almost everything in the world, be it the kitten-like white buds in spring or a
rag-dealer who buys old outworn shoes; the colorful but dead
pictures in the bath house or the behavior of naughty little children who refuse to go to school. Like Rumi, though on a smaller
scale, Shah Latif enjoys to describe everyday sceneries and offers
in his verse a vivid picture of the conditions of the Sind countryside during the early 18th century. We admire Lila, the elegant
and spoiled lady, on her swinging bed (these colorful, laquer-
work beds are still a specialty of Sind); drums and kettle-drums
are beaten at her door. We watch the wife of the seafaring merchant who binds pieces of cloth on sacred trees and pours fragrant otto and oil on the waves of the Indus to secure her husband's safe return (Sam. V 2): still in our day the trees near
Sindhi shrines are decorated with many pieces of cloth, preferably red, in the shape of little flags or tiny cradles, which are
attached there for the sake of a vow, as it is usual almost everywhere in the Islamic world.

---

[26]   Jotwani, 'Shah Abul Karim,' p. 13; see also Ch. Vaudeville, 'Kabir', esp. Nr. 10,
p. 206, and Nr. 18, p. 256; J. Parsram, Sufis, p. 171

Shah Latif alludes to the custom of cutting off the nose of shameless people and describes a person without any shame by saying:

> *When you have a hundred thousand noses,*
> *what is the use in cutting one of them?* (Mum. VIII 25),

That means the person is so wicked that he, or she, cannot even be properly punished. Then, again, we find picturesque descriptions of scenes and persons; such as of the wandering Yogi:

> *Yesterday we met a Kapari, a begging Babu,*
> *a Swami with a shawl around his head, a beautiful rosary,*
> *seeing and showing, with wounded heart there came a*
> faqīr.

> *Yesterday we met a Kapari, a radiant moon* (māh-i munīr),
> *Awakening inspiration and pain of separation came the*
> faqīr, *the Yogi* ..

> *Yesterday we met a Kapari, a Babu, dust-colored,*
> *a green shawl over his shoulders, a Swami with a golden*
> *rosary* ... (Mum. I 1, 2, 4).

Mumal herself, the heroine whose beauty has completely bewitched the poor Babu, is described as wearing 'dresses like roses, and shawls on their heads like fresh betel leaves' (Mum. III 1-2); her hair is perfumed with jasmine oil, her body with ambra; so that even the bees are intoxicated when she washes her hair. One almost sees the glittering of her and her girl friends' silver and gold ornaments.—There are touching flash lights which reveal more of real life than long descriptions, thus the remark about the way the poor inhabitants of the Thar (whose coarse, red woolen blankets are so much better than silk and velvet, Mar. III 1 ff)[27] will feast when the imprisoned Marui will return: 'All will drink milk!' (Mar. IV 2). Only when one has seen the Thar covered with green after copious rains one can appreciate Marui's description of her village and the various grains and berries which are found, then, in the desert region (Mar. IX VII) The helpless young woman, who shivers in the northern wind because she has

---

[27] Mitthi in the Thar desert is still famous for the handwoven and hand-dyed fabrics, in which a dark red and brown are most conspicuous; the area produces also beautiful flat-woven rugs.

no proper quilt is seen very realistically, as much as she is converted into a symbol of the soul. Other, more elaborate pictures,
are those in *Sur Sārang* which describe in detail the activities in
the countryside when the rainy season begins.

Shah Latif is also well aware of dramatic effects. Not only that
he usually begins his chapters with a heart rending outcry of the
heroine at the most crucial point of her life; he also gives poignant descriptions of the mental state of these women: the blood
that drops from Sassui's eyes has soiled her spinning-wheel and
distaff (Ḥus. II 11). The desolate young woman is shown as she
runs through the desert while the sun sets behind the thorn
bushes and trees (Ḥus. I 8-11), a scene which can be appreciated
by those who know the glowing evenings at the western border
of Sind, when all of a sudden, darkness overtakes the wayfarer,
and nothing is left but the sounds of a few animals. But the
suffering of the lovers seems to be necessary for the continuation
of life:

> *In the lover's heart clouds, in the eyes raindrops* (Ripa I 17).

Maulana Rumi often used this image to express the hope that
his weeping might awake the flowers of grace in his friend's
heart. Shah Latif is more practical:

> *By weeping have I given color to the poor trees* (Ripa II 3)

He does not express the hope for supernatural events, but simply
thinks of the dried-up trees which may be refreshed by the abun-
dant rain of tears (as they will be quickened by the rain of grace,
so vividly described in other *Surs*).—Shah uses also an image
known to the Indo-Persian poets for a long time:

> *What you see at dawn, that is no dew, o man!*
> *You see the tears which the night has shed seeing man's*
> *sorrows.* (Ḍh. III 16).

It becomes fresh in his verse because he connects the dew—in the
Persian tradition generally regarded as 'tears of the nightingales'—
with the theme of the lonely woman.

Sur Ripa contains some particularly interesting descriptions of
the lover's activities: (II 8.9.): the lover's heart is so mixed with
the thought of the friend as water rushing down from a watermill
is mixed with the earth; and the seeker moves the thought 'How

can I reach my friend' in his mind like a boatsman wriggling with his boat around in the water (one can still see this kind of flat boat on the Indus). In the same *Sur* (II 13-15) Shah Latif uses the potter's kiln as a model for the lover's correct behavior: burning all day he is not supposed to show any signs of heat or smoke in order not to divulge his secret; for the vessel can be baked only when the flames are covered. Silence is the prerequisite for maturity. One century later, Ghalib in Delhi would sing, alluding to Abraham's fate in the blazing pyre:

> *It is said that Abraham did not burn in the pyre—*
> *Look, how I can burn without flames and sparks!* [28]

The expression that love, or the beloved, causes the fire of a hot bath (*hamām*) to burn in the soul, belongs to this group of images (Abrī VI 1, Rām. I 2); the bath-imagery is also frequent in Maulana Rumi's poetry. The idea to make a thief the ideal master for the lovers is not quite original either, but it is still impressive: to lie awake all night, to be silent and stealthily reach one's goal: is that not the way the lover should behave in order to grasp the precious pearl of union? The moment a sound is uttered, union will become impossible.

When Shah Abdul Latif resembles Rumi in the use of everyday images he also resembles him to a certain extent in his way of shifting his images. The reader of Rumi's *Mathnawī* is often surprised to find the same figure representing now a positive, now a negative aspect, and sometimes tales end quite differently from what logic would expect. Shah Abdul Latif is not free from such defects either, if they can be called 'defects' in the sense of classical poetry. The introduction of the image of the oyster which patiently waits for the drop of April rain that will grow in her into a pearl is certainly no 'logical' in the description of an inhabitant of the Thar desert (Mār. V 14-16), as much as the image is fitting for Marui's general attitude and was used by poets like Kabir, too, in praising the faithful young wife who waits for the blessed raindrop [29]. Likewise, a reader not acquainted with Sindhi folk poetry will be surprised to find allusions to letter writing in Marui's sighs:

---

[28] Ghalib, *Ghazaliyāt-i Fārsī*, Nr. 78.
[29] Cf. Vaudeville, 'Kabir', esp. Nr. XXIV verse 1 and 9, 212, 214.

*The ink (e.g., the tears of blood) is in my hand, bring some
paper!
The tears do not allow me to write as they fall on the pen*
(Mâr. II 4)

But this topic, imitating a standard topos of high poetry, is general among the Sindhis, so that most of the girls who never
learned how a pen looks or knew even a single letter always
complain that they do not receive letters from their friends, or
want to write toward their families. This topic occurs also often
in wedding songs. The invocations of the crow who serves as
messenger instead of the 'classical' pigeon is, then, elaborated
most charmingly: the longing girl promised the crow even to
wind gold around its feathers provided the bird gives her some
news from her beloved (Pūr. I 8).

Strange changes of the acting and suffering subject are also
found in some places, thus in *Mūmal Rāṇō* which is, on the
whole, one of the most picturesque chapters of the *Risālō*. In the
beginning, Rano's longing is kindled by the Babu, so that he
decides to hurry to the palace of Kak, as the *wā'ī* dramatically
describes. The description of beautiful Mumal, with her hatchet-
like eyes and arrow-like eyelashes, who, Turandot-like, kills so
many longing strangers that the tombs of her sacrifices form a
whole graveyard outside Kak, (Mūm. II 2) is completely in harmony with the usual description of the 'cruel beloved', so often
extolled in Persian and Turkish poetry, and also described in
many of Shah's own verses. But after the introductory chapter
the scene changes, and Mumal, deserted by Rano, who misunder-
stood a joke of hers, turns into the complaining soul who sees in
Rano the ideal leader, the representative of God, and eventually
it is she who finds Rano and Kak and the palaces in her own soul,
expressing, then, the final happiness of identification of lover
and beloved in a touching song. A modern reader would expect
that Rano would need purification after his mistake. But it is
always the woman who has to suffer. And thus, Mumal had to be
fitted into Shah Abdul Latif's general imagery, which means, that
she had to represent the searching soul.

This leads us to the most outstanding characteristics of Shah's
poetry: in his work we find a symbolism which, alien to the
traditional Arabo-Persian mystical love poetry, is taken from the

Indian tradition. In the poetical language of early Sufis of the Arabic speaking world, such as Dhu 'n-Nun and Hallaj, there is no trace of worldly love. Later, in the finest poems of the Arabic mystical tradition, e.g., those by Ibn al-Farid (d. 1235), but also in the charming *Tarjumān al ashwāq* of his contemporary, the Magister Magnus of theosophical mysticism, Ibn ʿArabi (d. 1240) the language shows the soul as a man who longs for the divine beauty as revealed most perfectly in woman; hence these poets use the names of traditional heroines of pre-Islamic poetry, such as Salma or Hind to point to the Divine Beloved. In the Persian tradition, on the other hand, the two lovers are generally imagined as male; the allusions to the fresh 'green' down of the young moon-like friend and similar features leave no doubt about the sex of the beloved object. One feminine figure, that of Zulaikha in her longing and pining for Joseph, appears in the Persian and Turkish tradition, where Joseph becomes the paragon of charm and manifestation of Divine Beauty, and Potiphar's lustful wife, purified by unceasing repentance, is transformed into a longing mystical soul who eventually reaches the beloved. In the Indian tradition, however, the soul is always represented as a seeking female, and the beloved, or husband, represents God; the seeker-poet identifies himself with the *virahiṇī*, the longing young wife, of the folk-songs. [30] This imagery is not only found in Hindu mythology and legends, but permeates likewise the Muslim poetry in the native languages, beginning from early Ismaili poetry in Sind and Gujrat to the first examples of mystical Urdu writings in the 15th and 16th centuries in Southern India, and it became the central topic of Sindhi and Panjabi folk mysticism. As we saw (p. 89) even a highly sophisticated 18th century mystic like Nasir Muhammad Andalib used the tradition that it is almost women's duty to prostrate themselves before their husbands, a tradition which modern Sindhi interpreters of the *Risālō* also quote with great delight. To understand this symbolism better we may remember that in early ascetic Sufism the lower soul, *nafs*, is usually seen if not as an animal then as a woman; since the noun '*nafs*' is feminine, this equation was easy, and belongs to the favorite images even in high Persian poetry. But this crude symbolism is refined in the Indian tradition, of which Shah Abdul Latif's poems offer a perfect example.

---

[30]   id. p. 146.

His male heroes are of noble origin: Punhun is a Baloch knight, while Sassui is only a washerman's (adopted) daughter. He is used to musk, she is stained with soap (Dēsī IV 15). Rano is a Rajput, member of the warrior class, who is attracted by the courtesan Mumal; Tamachi is the ruler of Sind who elects a fisher-maid as his consort. Even Mehar, who temporarily serves as a buffalo keeper, is of higher social standing than Sohni, the potter's daughter. In a few places the heroines feel like being burned on the funeral pyre after losing their beloved. The lot of the deserted woman is touchingly described in various chapters of the *Risālō*, most beautifully in *Sur Ḍahar*, where the author's prayer to the Prophet, who covers the sins of his people in his limitless kindness, leads to the sorrows of the woman who, aware of her sins, implores the help of her heavenly husband—the *nafs* is shown on her way to purification:

> *Make some turn, o husband, to the hut of me, the lonely one,*
> *Darling, covering me, sweetheart, under your hem!* (Ḍah. III 1)

But the young woman is told by the poet that she will certainly not find her husband by sleeping, or by turning to others;

> *To turn to others and fight with the husband,*
> *is like leaving the wheat and gathering empty husks* (Ḍah. III 7).

The soul that turns towards objects of worship besides God will never be saved—the One Beloved is necessary for her salvation. God is the *sattār*, The Covering, who covers the lonely woman with his grace, provided she repents and implores him.

Breaking the appetites of the *nafs* is the seeker's duty. Even the *grande dames* of the folk tales, Lila and Mumal, have to be converted into humble slaves: Lila is called *maˀ dhūrī*, 'helpless' (Lila I 1), and thus equated with Sassui, who often sings of her wish to become a humble slave-girl

> whose hair tufts are in the hand of the Balochis (Kōhy. III 10),

a servant-maid

> who would love to put the dust of their feet on her limbs (Dēsī III 9).

If these ladies can at all obtain the forgiveness of the Lord then
only through patience and by crushing their pride and their
haughtiness, typical manifestations of the untamed *nafs*; they
have to remain constantly awake remembering their beloved—as
the Sufi has to spend his nights in the *dhikr* (recollection) of
God. The model case of an ideal woman in her sublimated state
as *nafs muṭma᾽inna*, 'Soul at peace' (Sura 89/27) is Nuri, the
fisher maid (*mōhānī*), who admits time and again that she, belonging to the low *gandrī* caste, was full of faults before Jam
Tamachi took her into his castle. The Mohana traditionally belonged to the lowest social strata in Sind, and their women were
noted for beauty and not too strict morals. The story of *Nuri
Tamachi* as told in *Kāmōḍ* may contain a reminiscence of the
Indian tale of the Princess with the fish-smell, [31] but it can also
be explained in the Sufi tradition as an inverted form of the
oft-used Persian theme of *Shāh ū gadā*, 'King and Beggar', or, on
a higher and even historical level, of Mahmud and Ayaz. [32] Just
as the warrior king and conqueror of Northwest India, Mahmud
of Ghazna, was completely enchanted by the obedience and
loving veneration of his Turkish officer Ayaz so that he became
'the slave of his slave,' thus Tamachi enjoys Nuri's modesty and
obedience. There is not a trace of coquetry (*nāz*) in Nuri; she is
all *niyāz* 'petitioning,' (a word, which, by the way, is often used in
the *Maḥmūd Ayāz* story for the sake of its fitting rhyme). En-
thralled by her softness, the Lord covers her and all those who belong to her with unending kindness:

> *Whether Kinjhar lake, whether Byzantium—it is full of
> graces* (in᾽ āmī) (Kām. I 16).

Nowhere else in the *Risālō* is the character of the king as representative of God expressed as clearly as in *Kāmōḍ*, where the
Quranic words about Allah are applied to him, whose throne is
kibriyā, 'Divine Grandeur.' What a miracle that this wonderful
king covers with his grace an insignificant, low caste girl like

---

[31]   M. Eliade, 'Die Religionen und das Heilige', p. 242
[32]   For the whole problem cf. H. Ritter, 'Das Meer der Seele'; the topic King and
Beggar, prominent in Ahmad Ghazzali's *Sawānih*, has been discussed by H. Ethé, 'König und Derwisch, Romantisch-mystisches Epos vom Scheich Hilali', 1870, and the
tradition of Mahmud Ayaz in the early period by *Gertrud Spies*, 'Mahmud von Ghazna
bei Farid ud' din Attar', 1959.

Nuri! The quintessence of this story, and essentially of all the stories in the *Risālō*, is this: O heart, be obedient, realize the relation ʿ*abd - rabb*, 'slave and Lord'; then you will be called to enjoy complete peace in the loving embrace of the divine beloved (Rumi would say 'like the falcon who, after long digressions, eventually turns home to the Sultan's fist and rubs his head at the master's breast'). [33]

There is no end to the sighs of deserted women, of the outcries of lonely souls, in *Shāh jō Risālō*. They feel the nails (*mikh, mik*) of love in their hearts which fix them to their beloved, and call out:

> *If you should come once, remembering me, o beloved, I would spread under your feet my eyelashes, and lay my hair on the ground,*
> *O beloved, I shall spend all my life in seeking* (BS I 6).

There is no end to true love, because there is no end to the beauty of the Beloved, as already Dhu 'n-Nūn and later Abu Hamid Ghazzali had stated.

> *His dream-image has intoxicated my mind* (BS I 21).

His beauty is alike to the green garment of the soil (Ripa II 7); when he walks out of his house earth and heaven are delighted, and the houris stand in silent admiration and confusion 'in full etiquette' (BS II 6, cf. Ḥus. II wā 'ī). One may detect here an allusion to the Prophetic tradition 'Verily God is beautiful and loves beauty,' a favorite hadith with the Sufis, which may also be intended when Marui, after months of imprisonment in Omar's castle, complains that she has lost her beauty and dares not go back to the Marus, who are so beautiful that only the lovely ones are acceptable in their presence (Mar. V 1-10): the soul sullied by the dirt and dust of this world, has to undergo thorough purification before she is allowed to return into the presence of the eternally beautiful Lord.

The topic of *khwāb-i ghaflat*, 'sleep of negligence,' is central in Shah's poetry. Not only Sassui has to undergo punishment because of her sleep, the lonely wives in *Ḍahar III* and *Ripa II* likewise complain, or are scolded by the poet, that they have lost their husbands because they stretched out their feet in their beds.

---

[33] *Dīwān-i Kabīr* ed. Furuzanfar Nr. 1353, Mathnawī II 1131 ff.

Had Sassui not slept comfortably, how would the Balochis have carried away her beloved? But the same warning can be applied to the seafaring merchants as well (Sar. III 20); every moment of slumber can cause damage to the boat. And will there not be enough lonely nights in the grave? Why then, spend the few nights of life in sleep instead of enjoying the friend's sweet discourse (Dah. III 17)? This constant admonition to remain awake is derived from the classical Sufi tradition: the mystic is called to remain awake and to remember the Lord, by performing the nightly prayers or constant *dhikr*, as it was Sufi custom from the very beginning of Islamic mystical life. The nightly vigils were always considered a great boon for the lovers, for in these lonely hours they could continue spiritual conversations with the divine Beloved, dialogues, which cannot be properly translated into human words.

Is there any meaning in staying in one's shabby hut or in the deserted village? No, the soul has to leave this world, and has to enter the *tariqa*, the Path, to perform the pilgrimage, as it has been described by so many mystical poets in East and West, be they Attar in his *Mantiq ut-tair*, or J. Bunyan in his *Pilgrim's Progress*. [34] When Sassui bursts out into the words:

I will put fire in Bhambhore! (Ḥus. IV, *wā 'ī*),

she expresses in a fitting symbol her wish to forget completely her worldly attachments. Bhambhore, where the beloved had once appeared to her, is of no use without him: the world can serve, for a short while, as the place of Divine manifestations, but once the soul is deprived of this vision due to her own laziness and heedlessness, it is impossible to find the beloved in this place; one has to cut off all worldly relations and joys and to enter the narrow road that leads into the wilderness. Only those who are completely naked, and do not carry any burden with them, can cross the mountains and reach Kech (Maʿ dh. II 8). Indeed, the major part of *Shāh jō Risālō* consists of a praise of the path, and of the never ending travelling of the lovers. The Sindhi poet stands here in the line of Attar's successors—similar to the birds in *Mantiq ut-tair*, Sassui crosses deserts, mountains and valleys:

---

[34] The subject of the mystical journey is central to almost all traditions; cf. the relevant passages in E. Underhill, 'Mysticism', and every study on phenomenology of religion.

To travel after Punhun, that is my happiness (Ma^c <u>dh</u>. III 1);

and the seeker who was enchanted by the Yogis, the true saints, tries to follow them to the inaccessible heights of Mount Hinglaj. The heart is restless like a camel (Ripa I 14); *Sur Khanbhāt* is a perfect description of the journey of the soul toward the Friend. Shah Abdul Latif dramatically describes the attempts to bring the stubborn camel-soul on the right path, and to make him move faster by reminding him of his noble pedigree and promising him golden reins and fine trappings; but the ignorant creature prefers to graze on saltish desert plants instead of eating the sandalwood by which the impatient rider tries to cajole him. But eventually the camel, reaching the garden of the Friend, becomes precious, and is, again, a representative of the soul at peace (Sura 89/27). This is a common image in mystical poetry; Maulana Rumi has written dozens of charming verses in which he represents the human soul by a camel, preferably an intoxicated camel, which is so enchanted by the friend's beauty, or his sweet song that he does not even feel the burden of duties on his back. Likewise, the restive horse is a typical image of the soul on her way towards God, [35] and Shah even introduces the Persian *khar*, 'donkey' for the *nafs*, the lower instincts (Līlā I 6), a word that is used more than any other term in Persian to denote the dirty 'flesh.'

The soul is supposed to undergo the afflictions on the road in perfect patience. But there are moments when Shah Latif seems to forget the goal of the journey, namely, union with the beloved, and becomes lost in the quest for quest's sake:

I will seek, I will seek, I will not find—!

Thus says Sassui, in the moment of most painful journeying, and the poet uses exactly the same expression when he speaks of his search for the Yogis who, thus, become a counterpart of the Balochis: both are symbols for the Perfect Man through whose whole being radiates the perfection of the eternal beloved (Hus. VI, 3-4, Rām. I. 18). For while the beloved is only 'in the eyes' in the moment of union, he occupies the whole heart and mind during separation and is, hence, even more 'real' than in union

---

[35] For the topos cf. A. Schimmel, 'Nur ein störrisches Pferd', in: Ex Orbe Religionum, Leiden 1972.

(Ḥus. V 12). With such words, Shah Abdul Latif is close to a feeling that was expressed, time and again, by the great representatives of 'personal mysticism' who knew the secret of:

The endless torment
of love unfulfilled,
the greater torment
of love fulfilled,

as T. S. Eliot has put it, and as Muhammad Iqbal, following Ghazzali's interpretation of infinite longing, has proclaimed in our day in the Indo-Muslim world. In the moment of union, there remains nothing but a 'Thou' without distinction, or the Divine 'I' without any trace of the human 'I', while love can be felt and experienced only as long as the search e.g., the feeling of duality continues. This search, however, usually leads to the discovery that it is useless to pass through outward roads, to overcome outward distances: the path leads through the forests of the soul (Abri III 12), into man's own heart.

Go with the heart toward the beloved, do not cut distance with the feet,
Do not ask for the way in the hills, come spiritually, o Sassui! (Abri III 12)

When finally the tree 'Existence' is cut, then union is possible, and according to the Prophetic saying 'Who knows himself knows his Lord' the seeker will find, eventually, his beloved in himself, 'radiant as the moon,' as Rumi experienced it at the end of his search for his lost friend Shams-i Tabrizi.

Shah Abdul Latif knows that all the adventures his heroines have to undergo are destined from pre-eternity, as he often says with allusions to the God's creative act and word (see p. 243). The goal of the lover is, in true Sufi tradition, to go back to the moment before God spoke his first word, to the time when man was as he was before he was, before the pre-eternal unity was split into a Divine 'I' and a human 'Thou'. [36] Sound and echo, which came into existence by God's address to the souls, point to that duality behind which the longing soul wants to return (Kal. I 19   ). The human 'I', that means the claim of independent per-

---

[36]   A fine analysis of this attitude in R.C. Zaehner, 'Hindu and Muslim Mysticism', p. 135 ff.

sonal existence, is the true enemy of man, for, as the Sufis for-
mulated as early as in the 8th century, 'Only God has the right to
say 'I'.' [37] The seeker is mislead by the misbehavior of the Ego
that behaves as though it were an independent reality, an act
which almost amounts to *shirk*, associationism, e.g., to see part-
ners, secondary deities, besides the One God. But even this
gravest sin can be forgiven, as Shah contests, with God's Quranic
promise (Kôhy. III *wā 'ī*).

There are innumerable ways to purify the soul so that it returns
to the beautiful Lord in complete purity. Not all souls are as
heroic as Marui, who endured the imprisonment in Omar's colorful castle, the symbol of the world with its temptations; that is
why she, after spending her days and nights in weeping, and
refusing to accept any of the ruler's blandishments, was granted
return to her eternal abode, the pasture ground of the shepherds
in Malir, which in its simplicity contrasts so strongly with the
world that is decked out fair.

It is the duty of the mystical guide, as representative of the
Prophet, and finally of God, to help the soul in this process of
purification. For 'without the beloved, Sohni is unclean,' and his
company is for her like a ritual bath that takes away impurity
(*najāsat*) from a woman (Sohni. Mut. 2,3). We know from
classical Sufism that the Pir's methods were often harsh and even
cruel, particularly for those who were used to a more tender way
of education. Shah Latif therefore compares the mystical beloved
in the context of the circle of Sassui the washerwoman to the
washerman who mistreats the laundry with his stick (BS II
11), a sight well known to every inhabitant of India and Pakistan, but also not far from Jalaluddin Rumi's description of the
beloved as a bleacher who deals with the laundry. The mystical
beloved can also be a dyer, who first casts the dirty soul into a
decolorization chemical to clean it from spots of sin and colors
of attachment, and then puts it into the vat with the true color
(Kôhy. IV 10) in order to give it, as Rumi says in a similar
image, [38] the *ṣibghat Allāh* (Sura 2/132), the 'coloring of God'.
Or the master is a blacksmith who puts the iron ore into the
furnace to melt and purify it, then mistreats it with a hammer,

---

[37] See P. Nwyia, 'Exegèse coranique et langage mystique', p. 249 about al-Khar-
raz.

[38] *Mathnawī* II 1345.

bellows, and cold water until it becomes fine and useful steel (YK I 17). Only after such a procedure the same master can join the seeker's soul with that of the beloved, just as the blacksmith joins two links of a chain together so that they can never be separated again (BS II 5). The beloved may also be compared to the elixir by whose touch iron is transformed into gold (Pirbh. I 25). The *nafs ammāra*, which incites to evil (Sura 12/53), e.g., man's lower instincts which call to laziness, pride, haughtiness, or greed (as in Lila's case when she 'sold' her husband for a diamond necklace) has to be broken: *shikast*, 'being broken' is one of the most important terms in later Sufism. Sohni experiences this 'being broken' when the vessel dissolves in the middle of the torrent and she is drowned: the symbolization of the body as 'a jar of unbaked clay, taken with one on a journey' is common to the Indian tradition. [39] Shah's account of Sohni's story is almost an exact exteriorization of what Maulana Rumi had described in one of his most ecstatic ghazals, [40] singing of the 'wave of *alast*' which shatters the vessel of the body and destroys it so that it is eventually united with the ocean (Sohṇ. V 11). All of Shah's heroines are told that:

> The lover was joined to her by pain,
> the sweetheart was not joined to her by pleasure (Abri VIII 14),

and that the only thing that is required on the long way towards the beloved is suffering. Hence the imagery of the physician: the beloved both gives the pain and cures it (YK I 1ff), for only he who has wounded the heart can heal and restore it. The Yogis are models of this behavior, which seems so contrary to every human wish: for them, hunger is a feast, just as for ordinary people fastbreaking is the feast par excellence, and what others would call illness and pain is joy for them:

> What is pain itself, that is the peace of the soul (Kal. III 6).

Sometimes one feels like reading a Sindhi translation of Shah's contemporary, the Christian mystic G. Tersteegen's (1697-1769) hymn 'Kommt, Kinder, lasst uns gehen ...' in which the Path is described so beautifully:

---

[39]   Cf. Vaudeville, 'Kabir', Nr. 15, p. 239.

[40]   *Diwān-i Kabīr* Nr. 463.

Geht's der Natur entgegen,
so geht's gerad und fein!
Die Fleisch und Sinnen pflegen
noch schlechte Pilger sein.
Verlasst die Kreatur
und was euch sonst will binden;
lasst gar euch selbst dahinten:
es geht durchs Sterben nur.

or some other poets of German 18th century Pietism who sang about the marvellous results of suffering which 'collects the senses ... and is like angels' guardianship ...', asking 'Suffering, who is worthy of you?' Indeed, it would not be difficult to bring close parallels to Shah's 'path of suffering,' as it had been developed by the Sufis in Hallaj's succession, from Christian hymns about the *imitatio Christi* in meekness and glad acceptance of pain.

In Shah Latif's poetry, however, this emphasis on suffering leads to most cruel descriptions of the fate of the lover, faithful to the tradition of Indo-Persian mystical and profane poetry. In *Kalyān*, the most purely 'mystical' song in the *Risālō*, the initiate is told to roast his flesh over the skewer (II 10). The knife with which the beloved cuts his throat should be blunt so that he feels the friend's hand a bit longer (II 12)—an idea often repeated by the court poets of India during the 17th and 18th centuries, who indulged in descriptions of this kind, as remained very much alive even during the 19th century in Ghalib's Urdu verse. The beloved kills poor Sassui 'like a little goat' (Kōhy. IV 9), and her designation as *qarībānī*, 'the near one', may well be intended as a pun on *qurbānī*, 'a sacrifice,' for all lovers are sacrificed like animals slaughtered at the festival of pilgrimage. A very naturalistic feeling of the importance of shedding blood in order to make the divine Lord and beloved happy permeates this poetry—: again, who would not think of the *Blut-und-Wunden* poetry of the Christian Church, if one does not prefer to turn to sacrifices at Indian temples and shrines? Shah Latif therefore does not hesitate to describe how limbs and heads are being cooked in a kettle (Kal. II 26); one is reminded of Rumi's verse that the beloved is a butcher dealing in lovers' hearts and livers,[41] not to mention the

---

[41]   id. Nr. 1600.—A typical example of this attitude is a Persian quatrain, attri-

innumerable verses in Persian and Turkish poetry where the hearts and livers of wretched lovers become roast-meat (*kabāb*).

The imagery of corporeal pain is particularly strong in the Sassui circle:

> *When the wild beasts eat my flesh,*
> *then my bones go to the friends* (Dēsī I 26).

She wishes that the crows of Kech, where her beloved dwells, may pluck and eat her flesh (Abrī X wā 'ī), or else, that the dogs of Kech should eat her (Maᶜ dh. I 1), an image which leads the poet to the idea of the soul-dog. But the lover has other wishes, too, in order to suffer even more. In ecstatic longing the woman calls out:

> *I will take my heart out so that the crow eats it before the friend,*
> *so that he says 'Who is the sacrifice,'* qurbānī? (Pūr. I 12).

Many of these sighs of burning passion remind the reader immediately of the legends of Husain ibn Mansur al-Hallaj who said, when speaking of God 'Kindness is from Him, but suffering is He Himself.' Indeed, we may assume that the image of Hallaj, who had wandered through the Indus Valley in 905, has impressed the poets of this part of the Islamic world even more than elsewhere. [42] His name and fame as the martyr of love was known all over the Muslim countries, particularly in the countries with Persian tradition, where the word 'Mansur' has become a cypher for the claim of having attained union. Did he not ecstatically say: *Anā 'l-ḥaqq*, 'I am the absolute Truth'? But this word (which was not, as legend has it, an enthusiastic cry but the quintessence of his thinking and feeling) made him also the model case of the lover who divulged the secret of love and therefore had to be

---

buted to Sarmad, one of the Sufis of 'Hallajian succession'; it is, however, much older.

> In the kitchen of love they slaughter only the good ones,
> They do not kill those with lean qualities and bad character.
> If you are a sincere lover, dont be scared by being killed;
> Everyone who is not killed there is a dead body.

It is typical that this very verse has been quoted by Qani, *Maqālāt ash-shuᶜ arā*, p. 35, in connection with the martyr-mystic Shah Inayat of Jhok.

[42]   L. Massignon, 'La Passion d'al-Husayn ibn Mansour al-Hallaj', 2 vols., 1922; cf. A. Schimmel, 'al-Halladsch, Märtyrer der Gottesliebe', Köln 1969, and the same, 'The Martyr-Mystic al-Hallaj in Sindhi Folk-Poetry', Numen IX.

punished. Shah Abdul Latif is only one of the numerous poets in Sind and the Panjab who have alluded to his sayings and, even more, to his suffering: wherever in this poetry the gallows are mentioned, we can see the shadow of Hallaj, for whom the gallows were the final station on his way to the divine beloved. The gallows are, as Shah Latif says (Kal. II 6 sequ.), the bridal bed for the lover,[43] the place where he can enjoy union with the beloved, as Sindhi folk poetry still sings in touching variations of the same theme; hence, the wayfarer is called to 'climb on the gallows tree a hundred times a day.' Sassui, the roaming lover, belongs to the same group of initiates who are asked to sacrifice themselves:

> You will climb upon the trees, becoming food for the vultures—
> Sassui has climbed on the gallows (Maʿ dh. VII 11).

The arena of love (mahabbata jō maidānu), one of Shah Latif's favorite expressions, is the place where the seekers can prove their spiritual maturity:

> In the arena of love do not think of the head—
> Climb on the beloved's gallows that you may become healed;
> Love is a dragon; those who have been devoured know that! (Kal. II 17,15. sequ.).

Hallaj's word anā ʾl-haqq, usually interpreted by Muslim poets to mean 'I am God', in a pantheistic sense, was the motto for thousands of ecstatic mystics throughout the centuries; it occurs also in Shāh jō Risālō. But contrary to his younger contemporary, the enthusiastic hymnodist Sachal Sarmast, and later Sindhi folk bards Shah only covertly alludes to the famous saying:

> Water earth stream—one cry;
> Tree bush: one call: 'I am the Truth!
> The whole country is filled with Mansurs—
> how many of them wilst Thou have executed (Sohnī IX 1-2)?

---

[43] In a Sindhi folksong I once heard the expression lāū lagan for Hallaj's death on the gallows; that means: the moment when bride and bridegroom hit seven times each others' head. The same term occurs in Kal. II 16 for the lover who should be as lovingly close as a bride to those in whose hand is a knife.

The last line of this verse has become almost proverbial and prefigures numerous verses in Sachal's poems when he goes on specifying the names in the long lines of martyrs who have been slain by their Divine beloved. Shah Latif is more careful and less outspoken in his allusions when he continues his musings with stating the essential Unity of Being in a traditional image:

All the waves here:
a hundred thousand dresses,
but the water is one (Sohnī IX 3).

And it is this unity which Sohni realizes in her final annihilation in the river. Only once more a statement similar to that in the Sohni story is repeated, this time in connection with Sassui:

Everything is Thou—
why doest thou give the sentence [to death]? (Abrī V 1).

It may be mentioned at random that the symbolism of Moth and Candle, mentioned in the *Risālō* only once or twice, though a standard topos in classical Persian poetry, goes back to Hallaj. But also the description of the unlucky lover, which was used by Hallaj to depict Satan's sad fate and was then applied by later generations to himself, is found in an almost verbatim translation in *Asā IV 38-39*:

God cast him into the ocean, the hands tied—
And said to him: Beware lest you become wet! [44]

The predicament of Satan who was called to prostrate himself before Adam and yet knew that he had to obey God's eternal order that nobody but He should be worshipped, is expressed here in a simple and poignant image. In fact, the Hallajian image of Iblis was taken up by Shah Latif (see p. 210). Even more pertinent to the general mystical symbolism of the *Risālō* and its emphasis on sacrifice is Shibli's dream about Hallaj's death in which God proclaimed that He, or His beauty, would be the bloodmoney for those martyred on the Path: Sassui is consoled with these words (Abrī XI 6, Ḥus. IX 20 f). The fate of the martyr mystic of Bagdad becomes a model for Shah's heroines who pray, as he did, that God might take away the 'I' that stands as a veil between the lover and the beloved.

---

[44]   Ibn Khallikan, *Wafayāt al-aʿyān*, ed. M. de Slane, p. 227.

Even the eyes are a veil, for they are *majāzī*, 'metaphorical',
while God, the Eternal Beauty, can be seen only with the 'true'
eye of the soul: only *haqīqī* eyes can see *haqīqat*, Reality and
Divine truth (Asā III 1). We may think in this connection of the
Turkish expression *gözünden kiskanmak*, 'to be jealous of one's
own eyes' which expresses well the attitude of the lover who
feels that even the eyes which see the beloved are still an unnecessary medium between the heart and the friend, an idea taken
over from Persian love-mysticism of the Ahmad Ghazzali
school. [45]

When the poet once threatens his eyes which see anything
besides the friend by telling them that he would tear them out to
feed to the crows with them (Asā II 1-4), he probably thinks of
the Quranic word 'Whithersoever ye turn, there is the Face of
God' (Sura 2/109), which was one of Dard's favorite verses, too.
Those who are blind, e.g., whose spiritual eyes have not yet been
opened, see only forms and small details; they

> feel with their hands and do not see with true eyes (Asā III 31),

as he says in the story of the blind and the elephant (Asā III
26 ff); but the leaders, endowed with insight (*basīrat*) see the
elephant in reality, *fi'l-haqīqat*. But there is another blindness
as well: when Shah Latif advises his followers to 'become blind'
in order to see the vision of the beloved (Abrī XI, Ripa I 25) one
is reminded not only of the underlying story in the *Mathnawī* but
likewise of Rumi's story of the Sufi (it was originally Rabiᶜa
al-Adawiyya) who, lost in meditation, did not look at the gardens
in spring, for 'the garden and flowers are inside:' [46]

> *Black night, white day—this is the light of the attributes—:*
> *where there is the Friend's presence, there is no color nor*
> *form* (Khāh. III 15).

This is the axis around which Shah Latif's poetry moves as much
as does Dard's mystical system. He, therefore, uses also the old
maxim of Sufism, that one should make one's heart a mirror in
order to see the friend in it (Sohnī VII 12); but while the mirror

---

[45]   The 15th chapter of Ahmad Ghazzali's *Sawānih* deals with this problem, which
became central in later love lyrics.

[46]   *Mathnawī* IV 1359 ff. The story goes back to Attar's *Tadhkirat al-auliyā* and is
found also in his *Musibatnāma*.

imagery is frequent in traditional Persian mystical poetry, and belongs to Dard's central symbols, it was apparently less popular in a rural environment.

All the way through the chapters of the *Risālō* the importance of the mystical leader is implicitly understood. In many cases it will be difficult to decide whether the beloved represents God, the Prophet, or the Pir. Only in a few places the mystical guide is mentioned overtly as a *conditio sine qua non* for the seeker, and in *Sarīrāg* he assumes the figure of the pilot who leads the boat safely through the ocean of this world so that its precious cargo cannot be plundered. However, as much as the necessity of the Pir is understood, Shah Latif never indulges in deliberations about his veneration or the duties of the initiate towards him: only in poetical allusions he introduces his listeners to the mysteries of the Path.

What, then, is the message he wants to convey? Is it only a clever play with inherited forms, the skilful use of traditional songs and tales as vehicles for generally accepted ideas in the Sufi tradition? He certainly did not call his listeners to rebellion against the outward forces, or to the formation of a closely knit mystical community. His mysticism is individualistic, and has as its center only one story: that of the return of the loving soul to her Lord.

Shah Abdul Latif dwells particularly on one aspect of this age-old story, e.g., the transformation and sublimation of the lower soul, the *nafs ammāra*, into the higher soul, *muṭma 'inna*. All his heroines undergo this process. Lila, the proud and worldly grande dame suffers in the process of repentance: her *nafs* becomes *lawwāma*, 'blaming,' (Sura 75/2); until she is completely broken so that she may be accepted once more in the presence of her husband. Mumal, the bewitching and self-conscious lady, experiences for the first time the pangs of love, and after long days and nights of weeping she eventually realizes Rano's constant presence: everything is covered by the moonlike radiance of his beauty. To her final experience, as to that of many of the heroines, the Quranic word 'There are signs on earth, and in yourselves—do you not see? (Sura 51/21) can be applied. Marui is the immaculate soul in the worldly prison; cut off from her primordial home, she sings out her longing like the reedflute that is cut off the reedbed, and is reunited with her beloved because she had remained faithful to the pre-eternal covenant of love; she is, in a certain way, a spiritual sister of Nuri [who has already reached the station of the 'soul at peace', after leaving her lowly background]. Sohni knows of the power of love which makes everything easy:

> *The stream fast, the canals strong—*
> *where love is, there is the current weak* (Sohn. I 1)

Thus, she crosses the ocean of the world and will be united with Mehar in the eternal ocean of Unity, once her vessel is broken. But Shah's favorite heroine, almost his *alter ego*, is Sassui, who burns in constant searching between the fire of separation and the fire of the desert (Hus. II 1), and whose 'dowry are the stones of Mount Pabb' (Hus. X 27).

> *The first and the last is to walk to my beloved* (Abrī I 1).

Sassui is certainly the most dramatic figure in the *Risālō*. It is in her story that Shah Latif reaches the culmination of his mystical teaching: having 'drunk the cup of thirst' she experiences that the water, too, longs for the thirsty; she recognizes Punhun's followers even in the angel of death, and at the end of her road, she begins to sing out her pain:

> *Oh voice in the desert, as though it were a wild goose:*
> *A call from the water's depth—*
> *it is the 'Ah' of Love ...*
>
> *Oh voice in the desert, like a fiddle's melody:*
> *It is the song of love—only ordinary people thought*
> *it to be a woman's voice* (Maᶜdh. VII 21, 22).

The voice of love: the loving woman has been transformed completely into love. She has thus achieved the highest mystical experience, to which H. Corbin points in his analysis of Ruzbihan Baqli's work, [47] namely, the transformation of the lover not only into the beloved, but into the principle of love, which embraces everything. In this simple looking verse one feels more than anywhere else the true depth of Shah's own experience. Seen under this aspect of the soul's transformation into love, every suffering on the Path becomes easy and even Mount Pabb cannot show its

---

[47]   Baqli, *Sharh-i shathiyāt*, ed. H. Corbin, para. 57.

strength before Sassui who, forgetting her body like gazelles, and flying like an eagle, goes to the beloved (Desi V). The process of purification, painful as it may be in the first moment, becomes a constant joy for the lover who is sure that he will be united, one day, with the eternal source of life and that means, for him, of love.

CHAPTER SIX

SUFIS AND YOGIS IN SHAH ABDUL LATIF'S POETRY

The whole *Risālō* can be regarded as a poetical expression of
the secrets of the Path; yet, in a number of places Shah Latif has
mentioned certain pre-requisites, or dangers, for the wayfarer
more extensively than in others, and he has even devoted a few
Surs completely to the description of the true men of God, be
they Sufis or Yogis. However, he has never tried to systematize
his thoughts, or to put before his listeners a complete introduction to Sufi doctrines of this or that school of thought. None of
the great *ṭarīqas* is mentioned, nor any of the sanctuaries to
which the inhabitants of Sind flocked at many occasions. The
careful observer will, nevertheless, discover a sufficient number
of remarks that help him to form an idea of Shah Abdul Latif's
way to guide the novice on the Path until he, or she, may have
reached the state of perfection. As in classical Sufism, the absolutely basic attitude for everyone who wants to enter the Path is
ikhlāṣ, sincerity, (BS III 4), as he says in *Sur Asā*:

> *According to the face you are Khalil (Abraham), in the*
> *interior you are Adhar, (Abraham's idol-worshipping fa-*
> *ther).*
> *Do not claim health; you are sick now,*
> *There is no name for hypocrisy, where there is the sublime*
> *Lord;*
> *In the face you are a Muslim, but little in the heart!*
> *In union with the Lord there is no allusion to duality.*
> *O God, says Abdul Latif, please make the way of life*
> *correct!* (Asā III wā 'ī).

And he takes up this remark about the double-faced hypocrite
in the next chapter of the same *Sur*:

> *That is not a kind of faith* (īmān), *as you call yourself one*
> *who utters the profession of faith'* (kalima-gō),
> *There is treachery in your heart, associationism, and Satan:*
> *In the face a Muslim, you are an Adhar in your interior.*

You are a liar in infidelity—don't call yourself an infidel:
You are not at all a Hindu, the brahmin's thread does not fit
you,
The caste-mark is for those, who are true in their paganism
(Asā IV 14, 15).

That means, whether Muslim or Hindu, monotheist or idol worshipper, man has to be sincere and not to make claims to sanctity
which he cannot realize. For it is easy to claim love with one's
tongue: the proof has to be given by undertaking the difficult
way towards the beloved (BS III 3). Besides this central attitude
of perfect sincerity so often praised in classical Sufi sayings, the
novice should always act with *adab*, correct behavior towards
everybody (Hus. IV 4). *Adab*, as we saw in Dard's biography, was
considered the *conditio sine qua non* both on the mystical path,
and in everyday life.

It is said that Shah Latif was an *uwaisī* mystic, e.g., that he had
no formal spiritual master, and hence did not belong to any of
the acknowledged chains of initiation. Yet, he quotes with ap-
proval an Arabic saying about the necessity of the mystical
guide: 'Who walks on the Path without shaikh?' (Dēsī II 3) and
continues his instructions to Sassui with the famous Sufi saying:
'Who has no shaikh, his shaikh is Satan' (id. II 4). We saw earlier
that the methods of the mystical guide are described in some
places with quite drastic images.

Whosoever enters the path should know the different ranges in
the spiritual journey. Shah mentions them several times, though
not always in proper order: they are the *sharīʿa*, the divine law,
the *ṭarīqa*, the mystical path, *ḥaqīqa*, the divine Truth, and/or
maʿrifa, gnosis or intuitive knowledge which stands, for Shah
Abdul Latif, either above *ḥaqīqat* or replaces it (Rām. V 14, Kal.
I 24, Sohnī III 10 only three stages).

Make the ṭarīqa your support, recognize the sharīʿa,
make the heart acquainted with the ḥaqīqa, know the place
of maʿrifa (Asā IV 40).

Maʿrifa, intuitive knowledge of God, is once called the pearl
(Sar. II 7), which the divers in the ocean of the world strive to
find.

The seeker who enters the path—as did Sassui—has to follow
exact rules: he has to leave greed (Sōr. I 6), the greatest danger

for the soul, which should become poor and humble. *Tauba*,
repentance, is the means by which to cross the ocean of life (Sar.
II 5). In this process, be it seen as the taming of the camel *'nafs'*
(as in *Khanbhāt*), as the Greater Holy War, or as the journey to
the safe port, as in the songs of the seafarers, constant wakefulness is required, but also *tawakkul*, 'trust in God', a central quality of the Sufi, which embraces many utterances of complete self
surrender into the will of God, and hope for his help, as described particularly in *Sarīrāg* and *Sohnī* (VII 9)

> *Turn over all actions to the Glorious*, subhān,
> *Realize complete surrender, having removed grief and*
> *thought*,
> *(Then) the Almighty will produce, by His grace, what you*
> *need* (Sarīr. II 2.)

Patience, too, is essential, as Shah proves with Quranic and Prophetic words (cf. Dēsī IV 5, Ripa I 23). But patience, *sabr*,
should not be a one-sided attitude of the soul; its correlative is
shukr, gratitude (Abrī X 9 f.). As much as Shah tells his heroines
to practice patience under the afflictions of love as much does he
teach them to reach the stage of contentment, *ridā*, and of gratitude. For:

> *All is sweet that comes from the Beloved's side—*
> *It is never bitter if you taste it with care* (Kal. III 11)

Some of his *wā'ī*s express this gratitude in beautiful words, such
as in the story of Sohni:

> *Who lives at the door of the Giver with gratitude—*
> *there is no limit to the praise which I would make for the*
> *beloved* (lāl) (Sohnī Mut. *wā'ī* 6)—

This is most probably an allusion to the Prophetic tradition 'I
cannot reckon up Thy praise' which was quoted by many mystics
to show that they were incapable of praising God's mercy suffi-
ciently since even the Prophet could not properly speak out the
due words of praise and laud.

Shah Latif knows also the varying and shifting states of the
traveller's heart, and explains to the lover that both *qabd* and
bast, 'constraint' and 'extention,' grief and joy, come from God
(BS. I 18) and belong together (like the movement of breathing,

or the systole and diastole of the heart, as traditional Sufi imagery would add).

All the wayfarers have to learn that the path is so difficult, the mountains so steep, that they cannot take without them anything that burdens their mind. Complete severing of relations, *qaṭʿ at-taʿalluq*, that is what the Yogis in *Rāmakalī* and the hero of *Sur Sōraṭhi* experience (Rām. II 5, VII 19, Sōr. III 16), and what Sassui learns in the desert. They 'burn the jungle of worldly desires' (Khah. III 9), and 'cut the tree Existence' (Abrī XI 4). In every moment the seeker should feel like a sacrifice and must be ready to sacrifice everything: *ḥāl qurbān māl qurbān*, both mystical state and worldly possessions have to be given up (Mūm. V 16). One has first to give up the world, then the otherworld by no longer caring for the joys of Paradise or fearing Hell fire, and eventually even to give up the 'giving up,' *tark at-tark*; that means, that the perfected Sufi does no longer think of what he is leaving behind, but is completely turned towards God, and his will is surrendered into the will of God (Asā IV 4). And after 'dying before death' he may reach the goal of the mystics, *fanā*, annihilation in God (Asā I 17, Kēd. VI 12, Rām. II 6).

Then, he recognizes the essential unity behind the outward forms of existence, and understands that the waves are many, but the essence of water is one.

> *From unity came multiplicity, multiplicity is all union;*
> *Reality is one: do not be mistaken!*
>
> *He is 'Mighty is His Greatness', (jalāl) He is all Beauty (jamāl),*
> *He is the image of the beloved, He is perfection of loveliness (kamāl)*
> *He Himself becomes master and disciple, He is all imagination,*
> *And through Him the state of all things becomes known.*
>
> *He is this, and He is that, He is God, and He is death,*
> *He the Beloved, He the breath, He the enemy, and He the helper.* (Kal. I 15, 16, 18).

His essential Perfection shows itself in the interplay of Majesty and Beauty, of Wrath and Kindness, of Fire and Light. The primordial unity was divided into call and echo at the moment of

creation, but the annihilated mystic goes back and finds this
unity again, and can say with an application of the Quranic word
'Whithersoever ye turn, there is the Face of God' (Sura 2/109):

> *There is a castle with a thousand doors,*
> *with windows beyond all counting,*
> *Wherever I turn my eyes, there I see the Lord* (Kal. I 20).

Did not Mir Dard sing in a Persian quatrain:

> *When your heart sees Reality,*
> *Then every atom of creation is a window of His house*
> (P 83)?

In this state, where the Sufi has lost his self, even the ritual
prayer is no longer required, nay, has become impossible (Asa I
11, 12), as Hallaj had exclaimed in one of his verses:

> When the 'young man' (e.g., true lover) attains to the perfection of
> generosity
> and becomes confused from union with the beloved by intoxication
> Then he witnesses truly what passion makes witness him:
> That the ritual prayer of the lovers is infidelity.[1]

For those who have reached this stage, even sleep is worship;
they live in unity, proclaim unity with all limbs, and although
their eyes seem asleep their hearts are awake (Asā IV 40 f.) as the
Prophet experienced.

> *Those, whose body is a rosary, the soul a bead of the rosary,*
> *the heart a tanboura—*
> *They play on the strings of the secret of unity:*
> *'He is One, has no companion'—thus they sing—*
> *For those sleep is fitting, slumber is worship for them.*

But to reach this state, a long and painful way is necessary.
The Yogis, says Shah Latif, are no companions for weak people;
they belong to the spiritual élite whose ways are much too high
for the ordinary believers, who would never be able to undergo
the hardships of the path. After all, only those in whose pre-eternal fate such a love is written will enter the desert, or dare swim
in the dangerous river: 'The Sufi's cap must have been sewn in
pre-eternity,' says Attar once, and Shah Latif is of the same
opinion.

---

[1] Hallaj, *Dīwān*, muq. Nr. 20.

The only more technical description of some Sufi terms, namely of the stages of Divine manifestations, is found in *Sur Rāmakalī*, the important chapter which also (the only time in the *Risālō*!) contains the expression ʿ*adam*, 'not-being,' a word often used by the mystics to denote the 'abyss of the Godhead,' the innermost depth of the unqualified divine life as it was from eternity to eternity.

Although allusions to the Path permeate the whole *Risālō*, we may single out three *Surs* in which Shah Latif dwells more than in others upon the requirements of the soul's journey, and which contain a comparatively greater number of mystical technical terms. These *Surs* are *Yaman Kalyāṇ*, which deals with the ideal Sufi, and *Rāmakalī*, where the Yogis are praised as the perfect models of the sanctified man, further *Khāhōrī*, in which the theme of the Yogis is once more elaborated. An analysis of the two main *Surs* will show how the mystic of Bhit interpreted the quest of the true seeker, and with which traditions he supported his theories. We should, however, not forget that the language of both chapters, as of the other parts of the *Risālō*, sometimes poses serious problems to the interpreter because of its density, and because sometimes the poet seems to sacrifice grammatical clarity for the sake of an elegant rhyme or alliteration, and we may not be mistaken to see at least in some of his verses examples of that paradoxical language by which mystics all over the world tried to hide their ideas rather than reveal them, or attempted at awakening a non-rational understanding of the Truth in their listeners' minds. But the picture of the Man of God, as it emerges from his sketchy verses, is impressive enough, and explains many of the images used in the other chapters.

Sur Yaman Kalyāṇ is a derivation from *Kalyāṇ*, and should be sung in the evening; it is meant to bring peace to the soul. *Yaman* means, as the commentator states, 'allusion, symbol,' and indeed has Shah Latif put many symbolical expressions, *ishārāt*, into this very *Sur*. Its analysis offers the following picture:[2]

I, (1-20, *wā ʾī*.)
    1-4 *You the beloved, you the physician, you the medicine for pain!*

---

[2] Cf. A. Schimmel, 'Šāh ʿAbdul Laṭīf's Beschreibung des wahren Sufi', in: Festschrift Fritz Meier, where a great number of footnotes and comparisons are given.

> *Sir, in the mind there are kinds of sufferings, Lord,*
> *heal! o master! the ill ones!*

This is the topic of the first chapter of this *Sur*, and in a terminology well known to the Sufis Shah Abdul Latif describes that the beloved is both lover and physician, whose 'sweet words' can cure those with 'destroyed heart,' an idea also expressed in other parts of the *Risālō* (thus Abrī IV *wā'ī*). Compared to him, the physicians of this world have nothing to offer, and if their medicines have any effect at all, then only thanks to his order. But while the earthly physicians try to heal the lover by means of drugs and powders, the beloved tears open his wounds time and again. Thus the lover cries out:

> 6.   *Hit, beloved! Lift the hand, don't take it down, be*
> *kind!*
> *O my friend, I may die from my wound so that I may*
> *gain honor!*

The beloved is asked to take out his arrow from the quiver, and wherever this arrow hits there the help of the physicians is of no avail. Only the word of the friend can cure the smarting lover.

This meditation about wounds and suffering, about nightly weeping and the recollection of the friend extends over 19 verses; in the last verse before the *wā'ī*, the poet makes one of his heroines describe the true lover:

> *O dear mother, I do not trust those who shed tears; having*
> *brought water into their eyes, they show them to the*
> *world—*
> *Those who think of the beloved do neither cry nor do they*
> *speak.*

Silence is recommended throughout the *Risālō*: to divulge the secret would be the major sin which makes true union impossible.

In Chapter II, (1-19, *wā'ī*,), this motif is ever more elaborated. Only the view of the beloved is medicine for sick people. But abstinence is also required; the stupid people who follow the appetites of their lower selves can not be cured.

> 8.   *If you want to meet the friend, then learn from the*
> *thieves, whose festival is to be awake—no rest all night:*

searching around they have come, uttering no word,
they have ascended the gallows, they do not explain
anything ...

The lovers will reach the vision of the beloved through nightly
vigils, staying awake in silence in order to gain the hidden treasure and even if they were killed by the knife, would not divulge
their goal.

In this last line, the allusion to Hallaj's death on the gallows is
clear; for he was executed, as legend has it, for openly proclaiming the secret of loving union. The motif of the thief is found
already in the poems of Shah Latif's ancestor, Shah Abdul
Karim. It may be that a story told by Attar has influenced this
imagery: in the *Tadhkirat al-Auliyā*ʾ he says about Junaid of
Bagdad, in the *Muṣibatnāma*, however, about Shibli, that he
kissed the feet of a thief who had been hanged, for this man was
perfect in his profession and had to pay for his perfection with
his life.[3] That, we may conclude, is the ideal of the true lover as
well.

> 10. *Whilst the physicians were seated, the friend entering*
>   *came to my door*
>   *The pain went far off with the coming of my wonder-*
>   *ful (friend).*

And the lover cries out:

> 13. *O physician! Do not give pulverized medicaments!*
>   *May I not become better!*
>   *My beloved may arrive, and help me one day!*

This topic is carried over into the *wāʾī*, too. Not to be healed
is preferable, for only when the pain becomes intolerable, the
physician will appear. One century later, Ghalib sang in Delhi:

When pain transgresses the limits, it becomes medicine.[4]

The third chapter (1-27, *wāʾī*) begins with a cry, for the fire
of love burns the lover—
Come and see face to face, if you do not believe! His liver,
kidney and intestines are roasting on the skewer, an image that

---

[3]   Attar, *Tadhkirat al-auliyā*ʾ II 18; *Muṣibatnāma* 9/2.
[4]   Ghalib, *Urdu Diwān, radīf ho-jānā.*

leads again to that of the arrow, which pierces the flesh (v. 7 contains the different names of the arrow) and can not be taken out.

> 9.   *Ask the moth about the news of their burning; who, being alive, put their existence in the fire, whose livers—the spears of love have touched them!*

The motif of moth and candle (9-13), based on Hallaj's short but poignant allegory in the *Kitāb aṭ-ṭawāsīn*, is taken up here, but is less elaborate than in comparable Persian or Turkish mystical poetry. (14.) In fact, the moths enjoy themselves in burning and become like lovely flowers, (15) but they should be silent lest ignorant people cause separation between them and the beloved.

This imagery of fire, very popular in Persian, and especially in 18th century Indo-Persian poetry, leads Shah Abdul Latif to the image of the blacksmith's fire (17 f.): the mystical guide is the blacksmith who knows the qualities of the raw ore and works upon it until he transforms it into valuable steel. Likewise, the spiritual guide cleans his disciple from rust, puts him into the fire of suffering so that he matures, hardens him with cold water, and eventually polishes him until he reaches, as Ghalib would say, the degree of *alif-i ṣaiqal*, a highly brilliant quality which is cleverly connected, by the later poet, with the letter *alif*, the cypher of God's unity.[5] Shah Abdul Latif, however, does not enter into such subtle speculations. He uses the symbol of the blacksmith in two more places, once, very similar to this verse, in *Rāmakalī* (see p. 227), although it is not very common in traditional imagery. One may add to these examples that Marui is praised because her perseverance has melted the chains in her prison (Mār. XI). As for the motif of the iron in fire, it goes back to the classical Sufi tradition, as it was known before in Christian mystical theology from at least the writings of Origines onward. In the Persian tradition, the best known relevant passage is that in Rumi's *Mathnawī*, where the poet describes the experience of mystical union with the tale of the log of iron in the fire: eventually, the iron calls out 'I am the fire!', although its essence is still different from, and can never be the same as fire—that is how Maulana explains the secret of Hallaj's *Anā'l-ḥaqq*.[6] The *wāᵓī*, then, de-

---

[5]   Ghalib *Kulliyāt*, IV Nr. 8; *Urdu Dīwān radīf samājhā.*

[6]   *Mathnawī* II 1347; E. Underhill, 'Mysticism,' p. 421 for Christian use of the

scribes the arrival of the beloved who quickens the thirsty by making them drink from the depth of the sea (of grace) and takes away illness from the sick.

Chapter IV (1-23, *wā 'ī*) continues the imagery of the last *wā 'ī*, e.g., that of drinking and intoxication.

> 2.   *One goblet—two persons: love does not do thus!*
> *They put away duality, when the dagger of love ar-*
> *rives.*

Poets may put different goblets before the drinkers, but not so the true lovers (the Persian quotation *bar khīz, badih, sāqī*, 'Get up, cupbearer, and give' may be intended to point to traditional Persian poetry, perhaps to Hafiz).

> 4.   *Where there are ten millions of murderers, there turn*
> *your eyes,*
> *Poison is sought by those who do not care for life.*

The true guides put poison into the cup and make it circulate: may we think of a variation of Hallaj's famous quatrain *nadīmī*, in which he combines the motif of the cupbearer with that of the executioner?[7] The perfect mystical guide is the wine-seller who has poison-like wine, an expression that occurs almost verbatim in Kabir's mystical poetry. It should be remembered that the *kalāl* or wine-distiller is considered, in parts of Indo-Pakistan, a member of the most despised caste. Here, he is called *muki*, from the Persian *mugh*, 'magian,' e.g., Zoroastrian, the general term for the 'old man of the tavern' in classical Persian poetry. Shah Latif complains that today there is lack of true wine-bibbers who would be ready to offer their heads for the wine (of union) and wait for the moment that the dagger or the saw will be put on their heads. This latter verse is likely to contain an allusion to Zakariya who, according to Islamic legends, was killed when he sought refuge in a hollow tree which was, then, sawed at the order of his enemy, the Jewish king; he becomes one of the 'martyrs of love' in Sindhi folk-poetry. The topic of 'giving away

---

image from Origines to Jacob Boehme. See also Dara Shikoh, in: L. Massignon et Cl. Huart, 'Les entretiens de Lahore', in: JA Oct.-Dec. 1926, p. 325–Kabir, too, uses the image of the blacksmith for the true Guru, see Vaudeville, 'Kabir,' Nr. 1 p. 159.

[7]   Hallaj, *Diwān*, muq. Nr. 37.

one's head' is further elaborated in *Sur Sōrathi.* A verse similar to
Shah's saying is already found in Shah Abdul Karim's poetry.[8]

> 23. *You cannot learn a good counsel from the wine seller—*
>   *Pass the night weeping, distilling liquor.*

That means, the true lover should transform his tears into precious wine; for much weeping will gain him the love of his friend.
The *wā'ī* is a happy song of gratitude for the beloved who was
kind enough to come to see the lover.

V. 1.

> 1. *Safe Sufis have become those who have retired from*
>   *the manifold (*ak*thar*),*
>   *not forgetting the play of those who play the love-*
>   *game, counselling with the beloved, intoxication*
>   *(*rindī*) has made them reach.*

Mystical union can be reached only by giving up worldly relations; the state of intoxication, caused by the wine mentioned in
the previous chapter, can bring man closer to God to talk to him
without words. *Rindī* is the state of the advanced mystic, a word
very frequently used in the poetry of Hafiz and his followers.

> 2. *The Sufi is in all, like the breath of life in the veins,*[9]
>   *Those who do not utter a little word as they think of*
>   *the last breath (e.g., practice* dhikr; *thus the com-*
>   *mentary)*
>   *It is sin for him if he should make anything open.*

It seems that the meaning is this: just as the *dhikr* *khafī*, the
silent recollection, runs through the veins in every breathing of
the mystic, thus the Sufi himself, completely transformed into
recollection, is hidden in the world and yet keeps it alive. Simi-
larly are the Yogis described (Khāh. I 1), that 'they seek the
magnificent Lord with *khafī*,' e.g., silent *dhikr*, and have trans-
gressed the station of *lā-makān*,' where there is no place.'

> 3. *Grieved by giving, content by not-giving they have be-*
>   *come,*

---

[8] Jotwani, 'Shah Abdul Karim,' Nr. XXXVI; the image is also found several times
in Kabir's verse.
[9] Jotwani translates 'ether' instead of 'breath of life'.

Sufis they have become because they do not carry any-
thing with them.

The perfect Sufi is the *faqir*, who has attained in his complete
needlessness, the state of *rida*, contentment. One may think also
in this connection of the equation *faqr*, poverty, and *fana*, annihilation, which found its most daring expression in the word
al-faqr idha tamma huwa Allah, 'When poverty becomes completed it is Allah,' a saying which was repeated from the days of
Attar everywhere in the Eastern Muslim world. [10] It plays on the
contrast between God, the Eternally Rich and Self-Sufficient,
and man, the poor, destitute slave. Once man has reached the
state of perfect poverty, giving up whatever he has and whatever
he is, including the last trace of self-will, he is annihilated in and
united with the everlasting richness of God (cf. Sura 35/16).

4. *The Sufi is 'without religious form;' nobody has under-*
    stood him;
    He struggles deep in his interior, his foot has no trace,
    For him who has enmity with him, he has become a
    helper.

'Without religious form:' the text has *la-kufi*. This expression is
found in a similar context in the poetry of Shah Latif's younger
contemporary, the militant Naqshbandi Sufi Abdur Rahim Girhori who says about the perfect mystics (by him, as often by
Shah, called *Kapari*, e.g., Yogi, a special group of Sanyasin), that
'they have gone away from *kufi* and their relation is with the *la*,'
that means, with the negation of everything save God. The editor
explains the expression as *farqo*, 'distinction, separation;' but it
really means 'kufic' and is, as such, the epithet of Abu Hanifa of
Kufa, the founder of the Hanafi law school (d. 767) which was,
and still is, prevalent in Indo-Pakistan. Hujwiri praised Abu Hanifa the Kufian, [11] and in Sana 'i's (d. ca. 1131) *Hadiqat al-haqiqat*
the *Kufi* is often confronted with the *Sufi*. Since in Sufi poetry
from the days of Sana 'i onward, both Abu Hanifa and ash-
Shafi'i, the founders of legal schools, have become paragons of

---

[10] For the history of this word see Schimmel, 'Mystical Dimensions,' p. 123; it is
known to Rumi and Jami as well as to Bedil, and both Qadiriyya and Naqshbandiyya
mystics have used it.
[11] Hujwiri, *Kashf al-mahjub*, transl. R.A. Nicholson, p. 93 ff.

dry legalism and are contrasted with the true lover, the term *lā-kūfī* meant probably first 'not belonging to Abu Hanifa's *madhhab*' and was then used to designate some one without affiliation to a particular religious rite. For the lover, the differences of the legal schools are completely unimportant. [12] We assume that out of this logic the Trumpp edition of *Shāh jō Risālō* adds here:

> *If you have read* Kanz Qudūrī Kāfiya *and understand all of them,*
> *It is as though a lame ant, fallen into a pit, would regard the sky.* [13]

This verse is almost proverbial. Sindhi and Panjabi mystical poets have regarded the three books mentioned in its first line as symbols of useless bookishness: *Kanz al-ᶜummāl* by the Indian scholar Ali al-Muttaqi al-Hindi (d. 1567) is the widely used, practical collection of Prophetic traditions; *Qudūrī* is the handbook of Hanafi law known after its author, the Iraqi jurist Ahmad al-Quduri (d. 1037), and the *Kāfiya* is the grammatical poem by the Spanish-born Ibn Mālik (d. 1274) according to which children in Indian madrasas were instructed in Arabic. All the three are required by those who seek ᶜ*ilm*, outward knowledge, but this kind of knowledge, as indeed all studying, is not required in the way of love. It was probably Shah Latif's ancestor Abdul Karim who invented this type of poetry, which became very popular in later times. Thus, Sachal Sarmast (d. 1826) says more than once:

> Intoxication came from the wine of this Mansur-dom,
> *Kanz* and *Qudūrī* became annihilated!

The true lover, 'Mansur' Hallaj is confronted with the representatives of the theological establishment, a favorite topic of many Sindhi and Siraiki poems. Sachal's spiritual heir, Bedil of Rohri, sings therefore:

> The ordinary men read *Kanz Qudūrī*,
> the lovers wisdom from God (ᶜ*ilm ladunnī*, Sura 18/65).

---

[12] The term occurs in the *Ḥadīqat al-ḥaqīqa I* 132, III 274, 278, VII 494, 496, VIII 578.

[13] The Hyderabad edition has this verse, with a long line of similar verses, at the end of *Yaman Kalyān*, v. 41-44.

As for the lame ant which wants to climb on a hair to the moon, it is known to Attar as a symbol of utter helplessness.

5. *The Sufi has cleaned and washed off the pages of existence,*
   Then he has been granted during his life the vision of the friend.

The Urdu translation says that he has made his body a mirror, which is a classical formulation; for only the heart that is completely polished and is not stained by the rust of worldly attachments can reflect the beauty of God already in this life. But the text has clearly, 'leaf, page,' *waraq*, and that fits into a group of images which were widely used by the Persian writing poets of the Subcontinent. Since oriental ink is solvable in water, the washing off of a page, or a slate of wood as used in school, is a very common image; many poets have claimed that their tears will wash off the black letters from the book of their sins and thus gain them God's forgiveness (cf. p. 135). Shah Abdul Latif, too, thinks that Sassui, in a moment of weakness, wants to wash off the word 'Separation' from the tablet of fate (Ḥus. VIII 8).

6. *You wish to be called Sufi! To the Sufis (something) like this is not fitting,*
   Cut the headgear, take and cast it in fire!

The Sufi cap, often mentioned as the distinctive mark of the mystic, and varying in shape and color according to the affiliation of the Sufi, was quite early regarded by the advanced mystic with some mistrust: as early a mystical poet as Yunus Emre in Turkey (d. 1321) attacks the would-be Sufi who is proud of his cap, and long before him one finds Hujwiri's biting remarks about those who make their patched frocks almost an object of worship. [14] In Shah's verse, too, the cap appears as a sign of self-confidence, perhaps even of hypocrisy. Such a cap should be thrown away, for not he is a Sufi who feels secure in his peculiar dress, but he who proceeds 'naked' on the path of love, without any possessions but thirsting for union through annihilation, as the following verse proves.

---

[14] Cf. Hujwiri, l.c. p. 48 and 56 about the *khirqa*; *Yunus Emre Divani* Nr. CLXVIII, LVII.

> 7. *If you put a cap on your neck, then become a real*
>   *Sufi: Reaching the goblet of poison, drink the full*
>   *glass,*
>   *The place (of honor) will be of those, who have*
>   *reached the (mystical) state.*

'Place' may be meant here as 'place of honor,' but the combination with the term *ḥāl*, 'mystical state' makes it also possible to
understand the word as a translation of *maqām*, 'mystical station'; that would be an exact parallel to the use in *Rām. V 14*,
the most detailed description of the Path.

> 8. *Put up in the body the secret tent of the Powerful. Open-*
>   *ly* (jalī) *make run with the tongue all day [the* dhikr].
>   *With thought seek in the Quran the Greatest Name [of*
>   *God], Coming to any other door, do not try to find this*
>   *high priced pearl.*

The contrast of *jalī* and *khafī*, hidden and open, in line 1 and 2
points to the various kinds of recollection: God, present in every
breath, is everywhere, and His name should be manifest by constant recollection with the tongue. *Dhikr* and *fikr*, meditation
and thinking, are juxtaposed: may be that both of them together
will help the Sufi to find the Greatest Name of God, which is
contained in the Quran. For, as the Sufis repeatedly said: 'One
hour of thinking is better than 70 years of worship.' This pearl
cannot be found by other means. The high priced pearl is probably, parallel to similar expressions in the *Risālō*, the pearl of
ma ͨrifa, of immediate and intuitive experience of God, which
can be attained by constant recollection. In the work of the great
Suhrawardi leader of Sind in the 17th century, Makhdum Nuh of
Hala, the *dhikr* itself is called a high priced pearl. [15]

The motif of the pearl offers itself easily to the writers of
traditional mystical poetry; it is the one precious pearl of the
Gospel. Shah Abdul Latif has used the pearl-theme twice, in *Sur
Sārang* (IS 30), and most beautifully in *Sur Māru ᵓī* (X 13-16),
where the faithful girl is compared to an oyster that sits silently
in the salty ocean, waiting in patience for the drop of April rain
that will develop into a jewel in her heart. For Maru ᵇi waits,

---

[15] The motif of the 'precious pearl' is elaborated by A. Bausani, 'Storia della
letteratura neo-persiana', p. 260.

fasting and weeping, for a sign of love from her primordial beloved and despises the multicolored ocean in which she has to
live for a certain period. The image of the divine grace as rain, so
common in oriental poetry (s. p. 256) fits exactly into this setting.

9.   *The word turns confused in egotism.*
      The self has no knowledge (or: does not know itself),
      A magician has spread out a spell.

The world is a phantasmagory: We may think of the Indian concept of *māyā*, but even an orthodox Naqshbandi mystic in Sind,
like Girhori, quotes the Arabic saying *ad-dunyā sihr*, 'The world
is magic.' Every created being is caught in egotism, but nobody
knows the true nature of the self. To know one's self, however,
could be the way of salvation because it can prove the perishable
nature of creation and thus lead man to recognize Him who has
created this whole colorful and deceiving picture. To know one's
self means also, to know one's Lord, as the Prophetic tradition
says. Once the unity of the innermost soul and the Lord is recognized, the pictures of the world are no longer tempting—they are
no more real than the pictures on the turning shadow screen.

But how to reach the One, who is hidden behind the multitude, constituting the source of beauty, power and perfection?

Shah Latif gives his answer in a series of verses in which he
refers to Rumi, the great model of mystical thought. That seems,
at least in the light of Shah's sources, the easiest explanation of
the following sequence of verses, all of which contain the word
Rumi. Lilaram Watanmal. however, sees in these verses allusions
to the content of the story of the Chinese and the Rumi painters
as told in the *Mathnawi*.[16] That would make, again, perfect
sense, for while the Chinese painters in this tale decorated their
walls with incredibly beautiful forms and colors, the Rumi painters just polished the marble wall, and when the curtain was lifted,
their white, polished wall reflected the multitude of colorful
Chinese pictures: the polished heart reflects the various colors
which are caused by the breaking of the One Divine colorless

---

[16]   L. Watanmal, Life of Shah Abdul Latif, p. 58. The story occurs in the *Mathnawi* I 3467 ff., but is found in Nizami as well, although in different form.

light in creation. This ambiguity lends a peculiar charm to the following verses. [17]

10. *Searching is the multitude the source of beauty—*
    This is Rumi's religious conviction.
    Who has seen the grazing place does not talk any more.

11. *Searching is the multitude the source of beauty—*
    this is Rumi's thought;
    Man is here from where? you do not see the spell made up.

12. *Searching is the multitude the source of beauty,*
    has Rumi said.
    When you lift the veil, direct vision (mushāhadō) will happen through it.

13. *Searching is the multitude the source of beauty,*
    this is Rumi's meeting place;
    first to lose one's self, then to see the Beloved.

The second line is a quotation from Shah Abdul Karim who then continues:

The beloved is not separated from you, turn only your face inside. [18]

This expression—God as the beloved who is not contained by heaven and earth but dwells in the seeker's innermost heart—is commonplace in mystical poetry, and has inspired poets in Turkey, Iran, and the Subcontinent to some of their tenderest verses: we may mention here particularly Niyazi Misri in 17th century Turkey and Sachal Sarmast in 18th century Sind.

14. *Searching is the multitude the source of beauty,*
    this is Rumi's (message of) tranquility;
    Those who have seen the Truth never talk anything.

Truth, *sat*, is the equivalent of Arabic *ḥaqq*, a word that leads once more to the Hallajian imagery; for he, claiming that he was the Truth, talked too much and had to be executed.

---

[17] It should be remembered, that the Hyderabad edition has a different reading of the initial part of each verse, which caused Dr. N.A. Baloch's interpretation in his article 'Shah Abdul Latif and Rumi', 1973
[18] Jotwani, 'Shah Abdul Karim' Nr. XIX

> 15. *Searching is the multitude the source of beauty,*
>   *this is Rumi's room.*
>   *When the door of separation is broken, the vision*
>   *happens through it.*

The word *ōtāq*, 'sitting room,' often occurs in Shah's poetry. This word of Turkish origin is always used in the *Risālō* to describe the Divine presence: it is Punhun's place in the Sassui circle, Mehar's place in the Sohni tale, and is also the high hall where the Yogis meet and inspire those who have come to listen to their songs (Rām. IX 3-13) as it is now the part of the compound where honored male guests are received by the host. The word was in use already before Shah Latif; it is found in Mian Inat's verse as well, and points to the Turkish influence that was prevalent in Sind from 1520 onward, when the Turkish dynasty of the Arghun, descending from Afghanistan, overcame the last indigenous Sindhi rulers; they themselves were followed by the Turkish family of the Tarkhan under whom Sind fell to the Mughal Empire. The connection of the word *ōtāq* with the dwelling place of the ruler is spiritualized in Shah Abdul Latif's verse, but expresses well his idea of God as the King and Lord par excellence.

> 16. *Externally adulterers (*zānī*), in thinking they have*
>   *become annihilated,*
>   *those, in whose body is the arrow of instruction,*
>   *They have recited in their hearts the divine (*haqqānī*)*
>   *letter.*

The Sufi may look a criminal in his outward appearance (we may think of the practices of the *malāmatiyya* who deliberately drew people's blame upon themselves); but inwardly he is completely annihilated by constant meditation and recitation (*daur*) of the Quran. The motif of the arrow, mentioned in Chapter III, is taken up in a different context. Here, the arrow is the letter *alif*, which reminds the poet by its straight shape, of this weapon. The image is not new; already Amir Khusrau in the late 13th century Delhi had used it, and panegyrists like Anwari and Watwat had seen their masters' enemies 'crooked like a *dāl* due to the *alif*-like arrows' of the king. Turkish poetry knows the combination as well, as Fuzuli says in the 16th century:

> When your arrow was dipped in blood in the weeping eye, you would
> have thought that it was an *alif*, written in blood.

The Sufis have constantly dwelt upon the relation of the isolated letter *alif*, which has the numerical value One, with God; and as much as it could be taken as representing God's unity and transcendence as much could it point to the slender beloved's graceful stature. Many legends tell that a saint was illiterate and knew only the *alif*: that is said about the Turkish folk poet Yunus Emre, the Panjabi poet Bullhe Shah, and our Abdul Latif as well. A few examples from the Pakistani regional languages suffice to show how generally accepted the image was:

> Who has studied the *alif*, needs not read the chapter *b* (Sultan Bahu, d. 1694 in the Panjab).
>
> The mollas have made me read lessons, they have not reached beyond the *alif* (Bullhe Shah).
>
> The mollas read again and again from thousands of books,
> but when the true religion is [a man's] study, then the letter *alif* is enough (Khushhal Khan Khatak, the Pathan warrior, d. 1689).

In *Sur Rāmakalī*, Shah Abdul Latif speaks, as we shall presently see, of the homeless Yogis again in connection with the *alif*. He also uses, in a somewhat surprising image, the word 'the eyeglasses of *alif*' (ᶜ*ainak*), through which man should look in order to find unity (Asā IV 13): the eye-glass was, as we mentioned in discussing Dard's poetry, a favorite image of Indo-Muslim poets from the late 16th century onward, when the first miniatures represent learned people wearing eye-glasses. The positive evaluation of the eye-glass in Shah's verse contradicts the use of this image in the work of his younger compatriot Muhammad Zaman Lanwari, who explained outward science as an eye-glass that stands between the eye and the goal of seeing.

In Shah Abdul Latif's poetry the *alif* is connected, as becomes clear from the following lines not only with the word *Allāh* but with the first letter of the word *alastu* 'Am I not your Lord' as well.

> 17. *Those who read the repetition of aches, the lesson of pain,*
> *In their hands the tablet of thought, they study* (muṭā-liᶜ) *silently;*

> *Those who read the page in which they see the beloved.*

The use of *mutāli͑* immediately leads back to Qazi Qadan's famous verse:

Leave the people with their grammar, I study the beloved,

and the same 16th century mystic has used the motif of reading the Divine letter in another of his seven extant Sindhi verses:

Whatever I have read I read it again and again, this very letter (e.g., the *alif*).

And Sultan Bahu in the Panjab uses exactly the same expression in his Golden Alphabet when he speaks of studying, *mutāli͑* , the first letter.

> 18. *Forgotten have I the lesson! I do not remember the first line!*
> *Until today, alas! this page has never been studied.*

We may understand these lines as an allusion to Adam's forgetfulness as mentioned in Sura 20/115, to which the poet has pointed also in a different connection (Sār. II wā ʾī). Did man not forget that he once, before creation, had promised God to acknowledge Him as the only Lord till Doomsday?

> 19. *I have studied that page of union.*
> *In which thou art, only thou, no other sound for as much as a moment.*
> 20. *Those who do not think of the line in whose beginning is an* alif,
> *Wrongly they look at other pages for the sake of the Beloved.*

The line is *alastu bi-rabbikum* (Sura 7/171). Those who do not remember the primordial covenant between God and man will never find the Lord, for He cannot be found on the pages of created, non-eternal existence. The only way to find Him is to return to the moment before the separation which is first attested in the *alast*-experience.

> 21. *Those who have thought of the line in whose beginning there is an* alif,

> *'There is no goal is both worlds' [but God]—thus they*
> *desire.*
> *Winding paths they have sought and found, have*
> *become content with the Merciful.*

'Difficult winding paths' follows the commentary and the
Urdu translation; the grammatical construction is not clear. In
any case the connection with the difficult roads traversed by
both Sassui and the Yogis is understood. The knowledge that
there is no other goal in the world but God (the Arabic text of
this oft-quoted maxim is given) makes the seekers happy; they
know that the way leads from the *alif* of *alastu* to the *alif* of
Allāh, and the most dangerous roads do not offer them any
difficulty; they wander in full harmony with the Divine decree.

> 22. *Those who have become content with the Merciful,*
> *seek and find difficult paths,*
> *The congratulations of union have come to them.*

Perfect contentment, *riḍā*, is a prerequisite for the unitive
experience which cannot be attained as long as there is still a
single trace of self-will.

> 23. *Having read the letter, o miserable one, from where*
> *will you become a judge?*
> *You are confused and are selfish—do not come there*
> *like that!*
> *Ask the taste of this sip from Azazil.*

A man who expects to reach high offices and worldly dignity
by reading the letter of unity is as mistaken as he who hopes for
spiritual gain while still bound to the letters of worldly books. He
is selfish, and does not understand how to walk in the path of
love. Only Azazil, that is Satan, can inform him about the secret
of the profession of unity and of disinterested love.

> 24. *Lover is Azazil, all the others are liars,*
> *By the way of love the accursed one was honored.*

Lāl, 'red' seems to be a translation of the Persian *surkh-rū*,
'red-faced' e.g., honored, if it is not taken as 'beloved.' Shah
Abdul Latif here takes up the satanology of Hallaj as expressed in
his *Kitāb at-ṭawāsīn*: Satan, 'more monotheist than God

Himself,'[19] refused to fall down before the created Adam, faithful to God's order to prostrate one's self only before Him. Satan was cursed because of his outward disobedience which involved, however, his inward loving obedience. The predicament of the archangel who was condemned for his rebellion which, according to Hallaj, was meant 'to declare God Holy'[20] has moved some Islamic mystics to touching songs: Sana'i has interpreted Satan's lament in most beautiful verses;[21] and for Ahmad Ghazzali Satan is the prototype of the lover who suffers damnation and separation willingly because God looks upon him, and who wears his damnation like a robe of honor. It seems that Attar's relevant verses in the *Mantiq ut-tair*[22] were known in Muslim India, and I am inclined to interpret Shah Latif's verse:

> *Take the knife, cut the limbs, behave correctly, do not be stingy,*
> *I will understand your friendliness when you look, beloved!* (BS II 2)

as pertaining to the same satanology: the beloved is called to mistreat the lover, and to add to his afflictions, which are welcome as long as he looks at him (the hunter looks at the target which his arrow has to pierce).

To be sure, most interpreters have seen in Satan's refusal to fall down before Adam an act of onesightedness, of calculating intellect which could not recognize the spark of Divine Love in Adam; still, the Hallajian theories lived under the surface and now and then appeared in ecstatic expressions like that of Sarmad, of our Shah Latif, or his younger compatriot, Sachal Sarmast, until they were once more brought into a fascinating system by Muhammad Iqbal. It should not be overlooked, though, that there are also negative descriptions of Satan in Shah's poetry (see Asā IV 16, 17), which conform to the general Muslim attitude.

---

[19] H. Ritter, Das Meer der Seele, p. 538 Anm. 6. A typical expression of this feeling is Sarmad's verse:
> Go, learn the art of service from Satan,
> chose one qibla and do not prostrate yourself before anyone else!

(*Ikram, Armaghān-i pāk* p. 238). For the bibliography on 'mystical satanology' cf. Schimmel, 'Mystical Dimensions', p. 193 f.

[20] Hallaj, *Diwān*, muq. Nr. 28-29.

[21] Sana'i, *Diwān*, p. 871.

[22] Attar, *Mantiq ut-tair*, p. 217.

25. *When I had read for myself the preceding lesson,*
     First I recognized myself, the treasure of the self,
     Where gnosis in the beginning had made the soul
     lightful[?]
     The page was turned back, and I met the moment of
     union.

The lesson of *alast* leads the mystic to recognize his innermost
self (again, the tradition 'Who knows himself, knows his Lord'),
and thus to reach the primordial state of union once more. Here,
the version of the famous tradition which I found in a
19th century manuscript of Sindhi mystical poetry would find its
place: 'Who knows himself through *fanā*, 'annihilation,' knows
his Lord through *baqā*, 'remaining in him.'[23] This elegant
formulation may have been common among the Sindhi Sufis.

26. *Those who do not understand much when one letter is*
     left out,
     What shall be done to them after they have been made
     hear the whole speech?

Those who cling to single letters and do not understand the
allusions without letters cannot be illuminated, even though the
Sufi reads and re-reads to them the whole sermon of unity.

27. *They have read it over and again, but it has not become*
     mature in their hearts,
     Sins rain from them, when they turn over more
     pages.

Those who have not reached true understanding accumulate
more sins the more they read learned books; Sufism is 'to clean
the heart and not, to blacken the face of paper', as was said in
early times. This aversion to bookish learning, which seems
typical of a mystic from a rural background, was, however, also
wellknown among poets who were themselves prolific writers:
even Mir Dard says:

From the time that I am reading the lesson of *tauhīd*,
How many books do I read in every letter! (U 143).

[23] I saw this version in a manuscript of Miskin Laghari in the possession of
Nawwab Hajj Noor Ali Laghari, Tajpur, Sind.

It is also common in the mystical tradition outside, or besides, Islam in India: Kabir's poetry offers fine examples of the same imagery when he sings: [24]

> Kabir, give up studying,
>   throw your books away,
> Search among the fifty-two letters
>   and concentrate on *rā* and *ma* ...
> Reading book after book the whole world died,
>   and none ever became learned.
> He who can decipher just a syllable of 'Love'
>   is the true Pandit.

The true Yogis, therefore, have turned over all pages and closed the books (Khāh. II 2), because they have found 'the page of Union', *wiṣāl* (Rām. II 10) and no outward letter can blacken any more the book of their actions which will be brought forth at the Day of Judgment.

> 28. *Read, o read the lesson of this pain!*
>   *O, put a* mīm *into the soul, an* alif *before it;*
>   *Move this melody in your heart, says Latif.*

The *mīm* is the letter of Muhammad, and its numerical value of forty points, according to later Sufi theories, to the forty stages between man and God. Panjabi and Sindhi Sufis were particularly fond of this imagery which is connected with the famous *hadīth* qudsī 'I am Ahmad without m = *Ahad*, One' (see p. 260) Thus, Sultan Bahu teaches in his Golden Alphabet:

> True salvation belongs to those who put a *mīm* to the alif!

Mian Shah Inat, too, uses this symbolism, and Shah Abdul Latif himself mentions the combination *alif-mīm* several times (Pūrab II, wā'ī; Sohṇ. III 9). The Hindu interpreters of the *Risālō* have tended to see in this combination of letters an allusion to the sacred syllable OM; but this seems too far fetched, and has no parallels in Shah Latif's poetry, although an anecdote relates that Latif's ancestor, Shah Abdul Karim, was taught 'the one crooked word', e.g., OM, by an ascetic in Ahmadabad.

> 29. *Read the letter alif, forget the whole page;*
>   *Purify your interior—how many pages will you read?*

---

[24]   Vaudeville, 'Kabir', Nr. 33, p. 308.

The study of many books is useless, for only one thing is necessary for man's salvation, and that is the knowledge of Allah. As Attar says:

> To make the heart white is better than to make paper black,

and according to Molla Jami (d. 1492), the Sufi should strive to lift the veils, not, to collect books. Shah Inat, too, offers a formulation which prefigures Shah Abdul Latif's verse.

> 30. *Whenever you turn over the page, then you have seen sin—*
> *What shall be done with a speech in which the beloved does not dwell?*

This is a variant of verse 27; the study of texts adds to the sin of worldliness, for the Beloved is manifest already in the very first letter, *alif*. It is somewhat surprising that Shah Latif, in this connection, does not mention the necessity of a mystical guide who alone could teach the initiate how to read this letter of divinity. Long before him, Yunus Emre in Turkey had said:

> When you read the black from the white for a thousand years
> it does not lead to anything, unless you go to a perfect guide.

> 31. *Oh scribe, as you write, joining the* lām *with the* alif,
> *Thus, our beloved rests in our soul.*

'Joining *lām* with *alif* they write nicely letters,' thus says the Sindhi version of *Lailā Majnūn*. The connection of these two letters was a symbol for the closest possible union, so much so that *lām-alif* could even be called a single letter in an alleged *ḥadīth*, on which a sober scholar like Qalqashandi in 15th century Egypt still relies. The *lām-alif* is sometimes used to denote the quick succession of events, but usually represents the lovers in embrace (thus already in early Arabic literature). Rumi speaks of the '*alif*'s being annihilated in the *lām*,' and an Indo-Persian poet of the 17th century cleverly develops this idea in a verse:

> The *lām* of my figure became an *lām-alif* (e.g., *lā*, 'no') with the *alif* of your stature,
> that means that my existence became annihilated (*lā*, 'no') in union with you. [25]

---

[25] For the imagery of lam-alif, and of letters in general, cf. Schimmel, 'Mystical Dimensions', p. 419 ff.

32. *Why do you raze out the paper, and waste ink?*
    Seek information from there, from where the letters
    are being prepared.

Since letters and words come from Allah, neither paper nor ink nor intellectual excercises are required to reach true illumination.

33. *Just as forty times forty days [seclusion] [is precious]*
    Thus is the vision of the Friend.
    What kind of addition, oh scribe, have you made on
    the pages?
    When you turn the page twenty times, it is still the
    same letter.

Only by loving meditation in the seclusion the Beloved can be found, not by intellectual efforts. Or else: the vision of the Beloved is as precious as forty times forty days of seclusion, which are required for the adept. This interpretation would lead logically to the next verse:

34. *The body a mosque, the mind a cell, have I made forty*
    (days' seclusion)
    Why not (rather) worship the One all the eight watches
    (24 hours)?
    Then you recognize yourself that He is everywhere in
    front of you.

The image of the body as a mosque is repeated in the description of the Yogis;[26] and the lover is called to find the Lord through unceasing worship, until he discovers, as the last verse says in somewhat enigmatic terms, that no place is empty of the manifestation of the One, although the ignorant do not realize that.

35. *Everywhere in front of you; no place is empty of Him.*
    Those who are separated from Him—how should one
    not call them cowards?
    The Beloved (muḥib) is in my soul, I ignorant person
    recognized (that).

---

[26] Cf. also A. Schimmel, 'Islam und Hinduismus', in: Das grosse Gespräch der Religionen, Terra Nova 2, p. 103 ff.

The first *wā'ī* of this chapter speaks, once more, of suffering through love, the second one teaches the lover wakefulness, for the days of youth will pass soon.

VI (1-19, *wā'ī*).

1-2. The beloved is a heroic knight like David, the lover a poor wretched weakling. The Beloved annihilates him cruelly under the hooves of his horse. 3-6. He is also comparable to Cain; in his eyes are sharp arrows with which he tears to pieces those who sacrifice themselves; one single arrow would be sufficient to kill the lover.

The imagery is derived from the classical image of the beloved as a cruel Turkish warrior, often intoxicated, and never seen without his war implements. Such descriptions of the beloved 'Turk' are a topos in medieval Persian poetry, and occur in the Subcontinent from the days of Amir Khusrau, who indulged in poetical addresses to the cruel but lovable 'drunken Turk.' Although Shah Latif usually depicts the beloved with bow and arrow, he also sees him once coming 'with a gun in the armpit' (Dah. IV 18), and the appearance of both images side by side reminds the visitor of Sind of the pictorial representations of heroes on the tombstones in the Chaukandi tombs near Karachi, where the Balochi warrior is sometimes shown with horse and arrow, but once or twice also with a gun. These tombstones, which seem to date back to Shah Abdul Latif's period, thus illustrate his poetical imagery, as they also contain fine carvings of women's jewelry, reminiscent of Lila's precious *naulakha*-necklace.

It was easy to utilize this 'feudal' imagery in mystical context, since the suffering of the lover is the central topic of Sufi poetry in the Indo-Persian and Turkish tradition. Attar, to mention only one example, expresses several times the wish to possess a hundred lives so that he might be able to offer each of them to the friend's arrow, and Shah Latif does not tire of showing his listeners the friend's majestic beauty:

> *His eyes are sharp swords, and his eyebrows, similar to black humble-bees, are spears* (BS II 9).

Did not already Hallaj tell the beloved:

I became all hearts, which ask thee to wound them? [27]

7. The lover has to make his breast a shield without anger; and
13-18 begin each with the line:

In the arena of love, lover, become a target!

But he also may address the beloved:

10. *Putting the arrow on the bow, Lord, do not hit me,*
Thou art in me—thou mayest not hit thyself!

A very similar verse is found in Kabir's poetry. 15 ff. the poet
claims that love is a dragon,

18. *(last line) that is known to those who are swallowed by*
it.

One should go back, with this image, to Ruzbihan Baqli's
description of love as a lion or to Maulana Rumi's comparison of
love with a 'wild black lion.'

17. Whosoever has put his feet in the arena of love has already
given his head to the gallows, as the poet says with a clear
reference to Hallaj; for

19. *Love is not a game that boys could play it.*

The duty of the lovers is to give up hope and to enter the
battlefield: in this praise of the 'martyrs of love' the connection
with the heroes of Kerbela can be easily made. Did not the
Prophet say 'Who loves and remains chaste and dies, dies as a
martyr?'

The *wā'ī* reminds the *faqīr* of his duty to stay awake at night,
remembering the Lord. This theme of *dhikr*, recollection, is
taken up in VII (1-14, *wā'ī*).

1. The lovers do not forget God for a moment. They lose the
breath of life, if they should utter a sigh. 3. As long as the lover
does not weep day and night at the friend's door he will not be
accepted in his presence, and (4) as long as there is still a single
drop of blood in his body he cannot claim to really love. 7.
Loving (*sikaṇa*) and gallows (*sūrī*) begin with the same letter. The
lover must therefore not hide himself, but rather throw himself
in the courtyard of the beloved and not leave his door. Who

---

[27]   Hallaj, *Dīwān*, muq. Nr. 36.

wants to learn love should learn it in the company of those who have true knowledge of love.

Verse 9-14 contains the invitations:

> Lovers, come and sit at the road; the door; the store; the lane, the way of the beloved.

Then they will become honored (*surkhrū*) (12). This last idea harks back to formulations given by Rabi'a al-Adawiyya and other early Sufis who taught that 'love is to stay at the door of the beloved even when one is driven away.' In later times, however, most mystics would rather praise the lover who prefers the separation wanted by the friend to the proximity wanted by himself, because this latter wish still implies self-will, and hence 'otherness.'

The *wā'ī* takes up the gallows' theme once more. Having ascended the gallows, the lovers flee from anything else; and the intelligent become completely confused and cannot solve this enigma.

As usual, this theme is carried over to the next chapter, VIII (1-24, *wā'ī*). The physician does not come unless it is necessary, e.g., before the patient is really painstrucken. This conforms to the traditional Sufi view, expressed by Attar and others: 'There is no remedy unless you have got pain.'

> 3. *Those who have climbed on the gallows, have reached health—*
> *It is a sweet affliction for the lovers.*

4. The beloved acts as is written on the Well Preserved Tablet, and

> 5. *When He Himself gives you to drink,*
> *then you would like to be a camel to drink,*

that means, to be able to swallow an immense amount of water, Ordinary people cannot understand the gold-like secret of love. Whatever comes from the beloved is wisdom.

13. 'God is with the patient,' thus spoke God (Sura 8/67). Patience is like musk. When one is blamed one should not answer. This path is recommended in order to become a trusted friend at all doors. Those who beat their souls in silence and make it into wax are gold.

21. All day to put the face on the knees according to the etiquette and to remain in solitude—these are the qualities of the true lovers. (The position for meditation is to put the head on the knees).

> 24. *Put into your interior a* muftī *(i.e., keep your conscience awake),*
> *so that you do not need the Qadi.*

This advice seems to go back to a *hadīth* 'Ask your heart for a legal decision,' to which also a verse in *Rāmakalī* (VII 4) is related.

The *wā'ī* emphasizes the search for the right company: one should look for those beautiful friends with whom one finds happiness.

> *At the door of my friends will be some longing [people] like me o my girl-friends,*
> *The dust of the friends' foot is collyrium for the eyes.*

The importance of right company belongs to the central teachings of Sufism: just as the dog of the Seven Sleepers became sanctified because he faithfully kept company with his saintly masters, and just as cheap material can acquire the scent of musk and ambra when it remains long enough close to these perfumes, thus the human soul can be sanctified in the company of the spiritually advanced.

This last chapter contains a great number of traditional advices for the Sufi: to be silent, patient, content, in constant meditation, following the prescribed etiquette in order to subdue the *nafs*: that is how he should behave day and night.

The ideal of the mystical seeker is even clearer described in *Sur Rāmakalī*, where the Yogis are praised as the perfected human beings. Shah Abdul Latif had spent some time—probably three years—in the company of wandering Yogis, and it is said that he visited with them many of the places mentioned in the *Risālō*. That may or may not be true—but the deep impression which the Yogis left in his heart cannot be denied. Yet only once he alludes to the ascetic practices of these saints, who, by virtue of their *tapas* 'burnt Jonagarh' (Kar. II 9). We may, however, assume that the frequent remarks about 'burning' are connected with this experience of 'spiritual fire', thus the impressive description of their burning the forest of the lower instincts which, thus, is turned into a waste desert (Khāh. III 9 f.).

The first chapter of *Sur Rāmakalī* consists of 41 verses, the last lines of which repeat with hammering intensity:

> *I cannot live without them!*

The Yogis are called by different names: *Sāmī (swāmī)*, *Werāgī*, *Kaparī*, but also *Nāng*, 'naked', or simply *Bābū*. Their description conforms very much to the one given by Charlotte Vaudeville of the *Nāth Yogis*, called also *Jogis* in Kabir's poetry where they, though worshippers of Shiva, the *nāth* par excellence, (cf. Rām. XI 55), appear as the true monotheists; their 'slit ears' and matted hairs are mentioned by Shah Latif as well.[28] For Shah, they are *nūrī* and *nārī* (1), lightful and fiery, thus representing the two aspects of God, the eternal Beauty as revealed in light, and His Majesty and wrath, which becomes visible in the fire. The Yogis, he complains, have left the place where they used to sit, after turning the seeker's heart into a bath-house fire (2) and producing a true doomsday for him by leaving him alone. They have taken the way eastward (8).

Here, one of the recurring themes of the *Risālō* is touched. East is, for Shah, the eternal spiritual homeland, which is alluded to also in the very name of *Sur Pūrab*, 'East'. He follows the old spiritual tradition of the *Ex Oriente lux*-type. In Islam it was particularly Shihabuddin Suhrawardi Maqtul, the *shaikh ul-ishrāq*, master of the philosophy of Illumination (exec. 1191) who poetically described the eternal home of the soul in the East. Captured in the Western Exile, *al-ghurbat al-gharbiyya*, the soul has to return to her Eastern homeland on long and difficult roads in order to find salvation. As much as Suhrawardi's philosophy was known among the Indo-Muslim intellectuals there may have been other sources to Shah Latif's imagery as well, for Kabir, the weaver-mystic of the 15th century, speaks likewise of the mysterious East, and mentions the 'Eastern language,' which may be a hint at the secret language of the mystics.[29] This symbolism, common to the inhabitants of Europe and Western Asia, was taken over in the West by the Rosicrucians and later by the German romantic poets: the *Morgenland*, the spiritual East

---

[28]   Vaudeville, 'Kabir', p. 85 ff.
[29]   id., Nr. 18 p. 257.

was their home where they meant to find the key for eternal wisdom and happiness.

Shah Latif has used this symbolism rather frequently, and even though Mount Hinglaj, the 'spiritual goal' is geographically located west of Sind in the Las Bela region, his Yogis' journey was still 'towards the East' (cf. Pūrb. I *wā ʾī*).

> *They are on the road, wandering eastward,*
> *Sacrificing this house they put their tents further ahead.*
> (Pūr. II 8).

These are the true seekers, not those who cut or slit their ears for the sake of show. Those are the true lovers, as Shah Latif says in *Rāmakalī* I, who have touched *lāhūt*, the dwelling place of divinity, and have become *lāhūtī* themselves (as often in Khah. I): The fact that Lahut is also the name of a famous cave with stalactites in Balochistan, adds to the charme of this imagery. Reaching Lahut, they have become rubies, *yāqūt* (7); they produce no words, *qāl*, but only mystical state, *hāl*. Latif tells that the caravan of the Swamis has come to Qalat (23), and from there takes the way to Hinglaj (28 ff). But such a journey is possible only for those who have given up their self, *khūdī*, and do not carry the load of egotism with them (25, 26). They have reached the highest possible stage on the path, e.g., *tark at-tark*, 'giving up even the giving-up' (39).

Separated from them, Shah Abdul Latif expresses his longing with the same words as he has put in Sassui's mouth:

> *I will seek, I will seek and not find* (Rām. I 18),

and the cross connection with the Sassui circle is all the more logical as the *wā ʾīs* of *Rāmakalī* also are put into the mouth of a longing female. How much Shah Latif has islamized his Yogis becomes clear from verse 32, where he praises the Shiva-followers 'whose leader is Ali.' Such an expression reminds the reader of the way Ismaili *ginans* place Ali into the framework of Hindu mythology by declaring him to be the tenth *avatār* of Vishnu. [30]

The most outstanding feature of Chapter I is the emphasis laid on the musical activities of the Yogis. Their whistles are all gold, and the listener is killed by the fiddle (19), or even by the 'knife

---

[30] G. Khakee, 'The Dasa Avatar of the Ismaili Satpanthi of Indo Pakistan', Harvard', Ph. D. diss. 1972.

of the fiddle' (22), expressions which point to the story of Rai
Diyach and the power of spiritual music. The same topic is taken
up in the lovely *wā'ī* which speaks of various instruments and
praises those who play them; even the *murlī*, the snake charmers'
pipe, has found a place here. The covert allusions to Sassui and
Rai Diyach (in *Sur Sōrathi*) are laid before the listener more
openly in this *wā'ī* which excels, among other fine poetical
qualities, by the clever use of long chains of diminutives ending
in *-rrī*, certainly a favorite device of women's songs.

Chapter II is interesting for its formal aspects. It is the first
literary example of a genre of folksongs that had been popular in
Indo-Pakistan for many centuries, e.g., the enumeration of
months, weeks, and days. [31] Starting from the age-old Sanskrit
form of *bārāmāsā*, the poems on the seasons, and then the twelve
months of the year, as seen through the eyes of the lover, the
poets then went on to describe what happened during a period of
so and so many weeks, or during a sequence of days. The *Ādī
Granth* contains a few examples of this poetical form, mainly
connected with the fourteen days of the waxing moon. As for
Shah Latif, he uses in his chapter only twelve days to speak of his
feelings about the Yogis, who, as is constantly repeated, 'are hidden from the people'. This is indeed true for the veritable saints:
they should be hidden like a bride, for God is jealous of them,
and does not want them to display too much of the secret of
union. In permanent boiling, *jōsh*, they become gold—we may see
in this verse an application of a current Arabic saying which was
very popular in 18th century Sind: *al-balā' lil-walā' ka 'l-lahab
li' dh-dhahab*, 'Affliction is for saintliness the same as are flames
for the gold', e.g., it purifies man completely, burning away all
impure matter. And then, he continues, 'concealed they wander
among the people'—this last sentence forms the refrain of the
whole Chapter II.

> *I heard the state of the Wērāgī on the second day:*
> *Their sacred thread dirty from dust, their hair-bands worn
> out,*
> *Those who have willingly left the hair matted, the hair
> tufts beautifully,*

---

[31] A collection of this type of poems by Dr. N.A. Baloch, *Haftā, dinhā rātiuñ ain
mahinā*; in the *Adi Granth* they occur in Ragu Ganrī, p. 424-430, 486-87, further as
The Vārs of Kabir p. 488.

They never talk about the poor body with anyone.
Naked they became happy; concealed they wander among
the people.

On the fifth day he sees them 'in the arena of love,' an expression known from *Yaman Kalyāṇ* (VI 17), and he follows them, until he sees on the ninth day:

Where the sight of the Lord is, there are their abodes,

and when he speaks of the tenth day he inserts the expression:

They have turned over the page, waraq, *of union,* wiṣāl,

and thus reminds the listener of his verses about the pages that were filled with unnecessary words and the one page with the required letter (YK V 19 ff, a similar expression Khāh. II 2). He sees them 'constantly keeping their breath' on the eleventh day, which may simply mean 'silent,' but may also be an allusion to the *ḥabs-i dam*, the long periods of keeping one's breath in meditation, which was common with the Sufis in later times and may have developed under the influence of Indian Yoga practices.

In the IIIrd chapter, Shah Latif goes on describing those whom he here, as in *Khāhōrrī II*, calls the *lāhūtīs*. He indulges in depicting the pain they have to suffer, when they take not-being on their shoulders. The *faqīrs*, with slit ears and a tiny loin-cloth, are completely annihilated, *fanā*, after having cut all relations with others and burning their beds. (6); and the smoke of grief raises from them (8). Again, the journey towards the East (3) and that to Hinglaj are mentioned (10), and eventually the saints are reported to have reached Kabul, the distant place beyond the hills (14). Important is the remark in *wā'ī I*, that the true mystical guide, the *Satgūrū*, as Shah Latif calls him, is he 'who has the *illā Allah*,' e.g., the profession of faith: '[There is no deity] save God.'

What can one do to become a Yogi? That is the problem discussed in Chapter IV. Once more the arena of love is the place where the mystic has to enter (I, also *wā'ī*), and he has to leave all greed and hatred:

4.   *Leave greed,* ṭamaʿ, *completely,*
     With the sword of patience, ṣabr, *make a massacre,*
     qatlām, *of hatred.*

The traditional warnings against the lower instincts such as greed, and negative feelings towards others are repeated, and so is the idea that the future Yogi has to follow the correct etiquette, *adab*, by accepting God's guidance (6). Annihilation, too, is required: the disciple is asked to drink the cup of not-being (*kīn = nīstī*). The imagery is closely connected with that of *Sur Maᶜ dhūrī II*, where Sassui is called to give up the burdens of the world and the body. Only by acting according to such advice, the Yogis reach the ideal state which is to live and not be alive; they lose the ego, as is the duty of the true lover who wants to enter the beloved's secret chamber.

> 12.   *What quickens the Yogis, are afflictions for men,*
> *Wounds are health for the Swamis.*

Their way of life is exactly the opposite of that normal people would hope for; they enjoy pain more than common people would enjoy health. The mysticism of suffering, expressed so forcefully in *Kalyān* and *Yaman Kalyān*, is repeated here. Their journeying east (15) and the fire of love that burns them inside (20) occur likewise.

The fifth chapter of *Rāmakalī* is without doubt the most interesting part of this *Sur*, just as the fifth chapter of *Yaman Kalyān* offered the finest description of the true Sufi. The application of Quranic words to the Hindu ascetics is quite surprising, and worth quoting in full.

> 1.   *The knees of the Sanyasis are Mount Sinais,*
> *In prostration they put on blisters.*
> *'And it was two bows' length or less'* (Sura 53/9), *thus the naked bow down,*
> *'Whatever is on it, is vanishing'* (Sura 55/26)—*there remains none.*
> *'God is the friend of those who believe and leads them from the darkness to the light'* (Sura 2/258)—*they walk in this style.*
> *'Moses fell down swooning'* (Sura 7/139)—*the groups of Yogis burn.*
> *'The eye did not rove nor did it turn away'* (Sura 53/17)—*such walking they go.*
> *Without regarding, without hearing, without meeting they sit,*

Without going, without talking do they go thus—
Sayyid says: How can you get information about
them?

The true Sanyasis are shown here as having reached the highest
level of religious experience. They have realized that 'everything
but God is perishing,' and they have steadily put their eyes on
the divine reality without becoming confused, as did the Prophet
of Islam, contrary to Moses who fainted at the sight of the Burning Bush. We may think of Jamali Kanboh's (d. 1535) beautiful
verse in honor of the Prophet:

> Moses fainted at a single manifestation of the attributes;
> Thou seest the manifestation of the Essence, and still smilest.

These saints wander from the tenebrae of worldly life towards the
eternal divine light, hidden and silent.

2. *The knees of the Sanyasins are Mount Sinais,*
   The ascetics have not taken with them existence to-
   wards the East.
   The veil of mystery is a bedspread for the homeless
   [people].
   Proximity has covered the Kaparis from head to feet.

Only those who have given up every worldly possession in their
way east, will be veiled comfortably by the divine proximity, as
God had promised in a *hadith qudsi*: 'Verily my friends are under
my domes,' or: 'under my cloak.'

3. *The knees of the Sanyasis are Mount Sinais,*
   'The seeker of the Lord is masculine'; this word they
   have brought near.
   Thinking of agreeable things of all kinds they have
   given up everything.
   The Sanyasis have, recollecting, put the alif *into the*
   soul.

The Arabic quotation in the second line is the final part of a
Sufi saying attributed to Jamal Hanswi in 13th century India. It
is the idea of the true man of God, expressed by the Arabic term
fatā, the Persian *jawānmard* or the Turkish *er*, all of them pointing to the ideal heroic fighter in the way of God. The *alif* is, as
everywhere and as mentioned in *Yaman Kalyān*, the name of

Allah, which the Yogis recollect in their never-ending silent
dhikr.

4. *Those, whose knees are a prayer niche, their body is a*
    mosque,
    Making the heart the place of the qibla, *they have*
    made circumambulation around the body.
    Uttering the takbīr *of realization they have gone away*
    from the body:
    *How should those have sin and account (*hisāb) *in*
    whose darling hearts the Guiding has descended!

The knees of the true saints are a prayer niche because they
constantly put their heads on their knees in the position of meditation, and sanctify their whole body, as was said also in *Yaman
Kalyān* (V 34). No longer bound to outward forms of worship
they have realized that the heart is the dwellingplace of the object of worship. The *takbīr* of realization may mean the call
Allāhu Akbar at the beginning of ritual prayer, but also the four
takbīr at burial, which would be in harmony with the traditional
imagery: Rumi has described in a famous passage of the *Mathnawī* how those who prayed behind a great saint were, so to
speak, sacrificing themselves when speaking the words *Allāhu
Akbar.* [32] Although the term 'descending', *ḥall*, in the last line
seems to allude to the heretic theory of *ḥulūl*, the indwelling of
God in man, it here rather means that God enters the human
heart and man becomes aware of this presence Divine in himself.

5. *The friend's face is the* miḥrāb, *the whole world a*
    mosque,
    From the writing tablet of the furqān *they deducted*
    the Quran.
    *Flying has gone their intellect and gnosis (*ᶜaql, ᶜirfān),
    Everything is the Glorious, subhān, *where those have*
    *gone who intend to pray (*niyyatī).

The idea that the Divine beauty is the only true prayer-niche,
miḥrāb, is commonplace in Sufi poetry, and even the wording
leaves enough possibilities for interpreting the 'friend's face' as
worldly or otherworldly. The mystics have read the Quran from
the pre-eternal tablet; *furqān* is, however, basically only a differ-

---

[32]   *Mathnawi* III 3140 ff.

ent designation of *Qurān*. In the experience of divine unity neither intellect—always the scapegoat of mystical poets—nor intuitive knowledge is of any avail.

6. *Those who are happy when sitting, the head put on their knees,*
    *Yogis make the pilgrimage, they have reached divine essence (*ulūhiyyat).
7. *They have reached the divine essence, who have passed through divinity (*lāhūt),
    From their bodies not a single sound is being heard.

Lāhūt, divinity, and, as we saw, also a local name, is still beneath the stage of *ulūhiyyat*, a term which is otherwise used rather by philosophically minded Sufis than in the usual descriptions of the Path.

8. *Interior fire of love, outside bellows with dust,*
    They have left and given up lie, falsehood, deception.
    Defects are not near, so many good qualities have they made;
    As they burn, is it truth, as they burn, it is beautiful.

The allusion to the blacksmith and his furnace, used in YK III 17, is repeated here to emphasize the way of silently burning in divine love until the seekers are completely purified.

9. *Leave it, to open the hair like a Yogi, do not produce smoke;*
    'And remember your Lord in your soul' (Sura 7/204)— lit fire inside.
    Those who have recognized the beloved, for them nothing is sweeter than not-being.

To show off as a Yogi, and to produce smoke of words, is not the true mystical path, as Shah Latif stresses also in *Khāhōri II*; the seeker, recollecting God in his soul and forgetting existence like a child (Asā I 16), will reach, eventually, the sweetness of annihilation and become as he was before he was. For, as Shah says elsewhere:

At this door those are successful who have lost existence (Sarīr. I, wā ʾī 2)

10. *Yogi, cut off your neck; to cut off the neck is princely;*

> *Your company, says Sayyid, with the swamis is*
> *beauty.*
> *'God leads to His light whom He willeth'* (Sura 24/35),
> *thus it is for them,*
> *This is the place for those who have left the other*
> *world.*

The allusion to the royal act of cutting one's neck points, once
more, to *Sur Sōrathi*: King Diyach is the examplar of the true
lover. But Shah inserts a similar expression also in the Sohni tale:
he quotes in Persian a line that is usually connected with the fate
of Shah Inayat of Jhok (exec. 1718):

> The head is sacrificed at the Friend's foot,
> which is in order (Sohn. I II).

The term *sohbat*, 'company,' may be taken as the technical
term for the company of master and disciple, one of the pillars of
Sufi education. Not only this world, but also the thought of the
Otherworld is a burden for the soul, and has to be discarded;
only then the Yogis will reach the light of God.

> 11.   *The Yogis leave this world, they walk the way towards*
>   *east;*
>   *The Lahutis, says Latif, having gone, wander transgres-*
>   *sing 'the rūby'.*
>   *'And God calls toward the abode of peace'* (Sura
>   16/26), *the Lord calls all those,*
>   *Woe! Woe! This skeleton has made confused everyone.*

'This skeleton' is the world, which was accused of making
man's head turn in *Yaman Kalyān* (V 9) as well. The word 'skeleton' *haddhī*, is probably used for the sake of alliteration instead
of the usual Arabic *jīfa*, 'dead body,' which occurs in the oft-
quoted *hadīth* of the world as dead body and its seekers as dogs.

> 12.   *With which desire do the Kaparis act like this?*
>   *They have neither the heart toward Hell, nor do they*
>   *wish Paradise.* [33]

---

[33]   Vaudeville, 'Kabir', Nr. 11 v. 16, p. 215:
        I have embraced hell itself,
        it causes me no terror
        For paradise I have no craving
        away from Thee, my Beloved.

> *They have nothing to do with infidels, no muslimdom*
> *is in (their) spirit.*
> *Upright they speak, the friend has been made their*
> *own.*

The Kaparis appear here as the true saints who are neither afraid of Hell nor covet Paradise; that means they follow the ideal expressed first in Islamic mysticism by Rabiᶜa al-Adawiyya. They are beyond the borders of faith and infidelity, which would lead them to Paradise or Hell, respectively, because they see and contemplate only the divine beloved.

> 13. *The Yogis are in the neighborhood, as if they were not*
> *somewhere;*
> *They have come into their dwelling-place, yesterday*
> *they have played the pipe.*

The pipe or flute of the Yogis, so eloquently praised in the first chapter of this *Sur*, reminds the lover of the spiritual truth; we may connect the image with Rumi's reed-flute which tells of the separation from its original reed bed, thus awakening the longing for home in men's heart. It is possible that the 'yesterday' in this verse means, as it does often, the covenant of *alast*.

> 14. *They have gone the way of the religious law,* shariᶜa;
> *meditation,* tafakkur, *is their spiritual path,* tarīqa.
> *They have reached the state,* ḥāl, *of truth,* ḥaqīqa;
> *gnosis,* maᶜrifa, *is their place.*
> *The planes of humanity,* nāsūt, *angelhood,* malakūt,
> *divine power,* jabarūt—*these graces they have given up,*
> *Then they have passed over divinity,* lāhūt, *and have*
> *gone to the (divine) ipseity,* hāhūt.

Here, Shah Latif exemplifies the perfect Sufi way: *shariᶜa* and *tarīqa* belong to each other; *ḥāl*, state, and *maqām* (though as in *Yaman Kalyān* not mentioned with its Arabic name), are the corresponding experiences on the Path, which finally leads to *maᶜrifa*, intuitive gnosis of divine mysteries. The four-partition of the planes of divine manifestations is perfectly in accordance with the models worked out by the Sufis from the 13th century onward. The term *hāhūt*, Divine Ipseity, can be easily derived from Ibn Arabi's system: it is the innermost essence of the Godhead as revealed in the last letter of *Allāh*, *h*, which is also the last sigh that remains audible towards the end of *dhikr* exercises, but likewise the first letter of *huwa*, He. It was this manifestation of the divine *h* which Ibn Arabi saw in a vision: the highest revelation of God who revealed Himself once through the Quranic word is possible not through a picture, but through the letter. [34]

> 15. *Having gone out of humanity,* nāsūt, *they have gone towards angelhood,* malakūt,
> *The Yogis from the sphere of divine power,* jabarūt, *have played on the road (?)*
> 16. *Those who have gone out have not understood; in sitting they find the Lord,*
> *They have seen the far distance with difficulty; in themselves is the foot.*
> *Those who have left—says Latif—the chain of the body, the Kaparis have not seen Kabul and Kashmir,*
> *Those who make the journey of truth, sitting they meet the guru.*

True journey is *safar dar waṭan*, interior journey, as Sassui was told at the end of her road. The foreign kingdoms are in the seeker's heart, and already Maulana Rumi had told his disciples about the necessity of constant wandering, but if there is no foot for travelling, the journey into one's self is better than anything else; it is here that the spiritual rubies are found. Why should one roam about in marketplaces to search for the friend? thus asks Sachal Sarmast: the friend is in the heart; He whom heaven and earth can not contain is the guest in the narrow hut of man's purified heart.

> 17. *Hopelessness is the nurture, the bedspread of the homeless,*
> *Always raining contentment, the seeker [follows] the destination.*

The true mystic does not put his hope on anything but God: he avoids what the Sufis call *ṭūl-i amal*, 'long hope,' but rather accepts with pure contentment whatever is given to him, following the eternal fate in peace.

---

[34] H. Corbin, 'Imagination créatrice et prière créatrice dans le soufisme d'Ibn Arabi', in: Eranos-Jahrbuch 25/1965, p. 171.

18. *Hopelessness is the nurture, the bedspread of the*
    homeless,
    Sometimes on the back of a horse, sometimes they
    walk below,
    The swamis swim in the ocean like gourds,
    When they fall into a crocodile's mouth to be killed
    they do not speak a word.

The true seeker knows that his 'daily bread,' *rizq*, is in the hands
of God, one of whose names is *ar-razzāq*, 'Who gives sustenance'
(Dhah. IV 7); God knows whether he will grant the seeker a royal
attire or make him walk among the humble footmen. Similar to
hollow gourds the true mystics give themselves completely to the
movement of the stream of destiny, and it makes no difference
whether they are swallowed by some monster or reach the other
shore safely. Sohni's tale comes to mind, but also one of the
most famous stories told in early Sufism about complete *tawak-*
kul, 'trust in God:' a man had fallen into the Tigris and was asked
whether he would like to be saved. He answered 'No'. So he was
asked whether he would rather like to drown? Again 'No'.
Angry, they asked him 'What do you want, then?' And he re-
plied, 'What have I to do with wanting?'. He left his fate in the
hands of God who knew whether he was to live or to die. [35] Such
overstressed tawakkul is seen here as the ideal state of the true
Yogi.

19. *Some of the jewels, who came across God, were dyed*
    in red,
    In the abyss of not-being they have made their place,
    the Adhutis,
    They have moved, the dumb ones, the whirlpool with
    their spirit.

The first line with its threefold repetition of the word *lāl* in the
meaning of 'red', ruby', and 'Beloved' = God, is difficult to translate. The reference to ᶜ*adam*, not-being, is typical of Sufi
thought: here, as in Rumi and later mystics, ᶜ*adam* is the state of
being before one is, the state of the soul before the covenant of
Alast. The Hindu interpreters explain it as *suñj*, 'Peace inexpres-
sible'. Out of this unfathomable depths of divine unity, where

---

[35]   For the problem cf. B. Reinert, 'Die Lehre vom *tawakkul* in der älteren Sufik'.

there is no movement at all, the spirit moves the world, and creates the various forms and waves, foam and whirlpools which cover the surface of the essentially immobile water. Another explanation, proposed by Dr. Jotwani, would be that they are dumbfounded by the knowledge of the 'whirling', which would mean, in Hindu interpretation, the churning of the milk-ocean.

> 20. *Humid weather, bad times, have the Yogis suffered in their souls;*
> *The Kaparis have no protection save Allah.*

The saints do not rely upon any outward protection against bad times and the vicissitudes of fate and weather; they suffer without complaint, for, as the next verse says,

> 21. *Not willing,* nā-murādī, *is their house, not-being,* ʿadam, *their hut,*
> *Contentment,* riḍā, *is their kingdom; they do not ask for other capital.*

The true Sufi and Yogi has no will of his own, and lives in the Eternal Now without change of time, as Shah Latif says in the following verses, and thus they walk the 'lordly path'. [36]

The *wāʾī*, then, is the complaint of the lonely girl whose sleep has been taken away by the Yogis, for their symbolical allusions, alike to lightnings, annihilate men completely; and the poet closes with the 'following quatrain,' as he calls it:

> *One in one have they become, they do not understand duality,*
> *Their eyes have left laziness, in the heart is no hypocrisy.*
> *'God is an odd number and loves odd numbers'—that has come for them,*
> *Enchanted by the symbols, I am burning for the mountaineers.*
> *God! says Abdul Latif, make good things with me, oh Lord!*

The allusion to the Prophetic tradition 'God is an odd number,' *witr*, e.g., One, is the most interesting aspect of the song of the maiden soul; its importance is underlined by its insertion into the

---

[36] The verses 22 and 23 are grammatically not clear.

very beginning of *Sur Asā* (I 2). This *ḥadīth* is often used to justify the odd numbers as used in the repetition of prayers or religious formulas, which are often recommended: one has to do something three, seven, 41, 99 times. But Shah Latif's interpretation that God, being One, does not tolerate the feeling of duality in those who love him, is also in harmony with the tradition, although it may lead, as often in mystical folksongs, to the simple statement that 'Everything is He.'

After this central chapter which abounds with Arabic terms and Quranic allusions, Shah Abdul Latif goes on describing the outward sufferings of the Yogis in Chapter VI. They certainly do not look attractive with their long dirty hair (3), a picture which is even more impressive in Khāh. II 26, where Shah Latif speaks of their dirty bodies, their dried-up mouths, and the old shabby rags and worn out shoes which cover them. Yet, they burn in interior fire. One is reminded of the similar descriptions of the 'true Christian' as found in the hymn:

> Es glänzet der Christen inwendiges Leben,
> obgleich sie von aussen die Sonne verbrannt ...
> Sie scheinen von aussen oft arm und geringe,
> Ein Schauspiel der Engel, verlacht von der Welt,
> Doch innerlich sind sie voll herrlicher Dinge ... [37]

Shah Latif's Yogis constantly think of Ram but speak in different tongue, e.g., they do not divulge the secret of their love or the name of their beloved. They continue their travelling without rest:

> 11. *The naked ones do not sleep,*
>   *they go, weeping, toward Ram.*

And yet, they are identified as true Muslims, for 'they read the *sūras* of the Glorious, *subhān*' (13), that means they meditate the Quran. Logically, the *wā ʾī* takes up the terminology of Sufi love mysticism with terms like *ulfat*, company, and *qurb*, proximity, and once more speaks of the company, *sohbat*, with the beloved. Then (Chapter VII) Shah Abdul Latif praises the Kaparis 'who have no greed, *ṭamʿ*, for food, *taʿām* (7), and:

> 8. Dying from hunger they ask not alms from anyone. Their

---

[37] Es glänzet der Christen inwendiges Leben, by Christian Friedrich Richter, 1676-1711.

ascetic practices are again described. They have no genealogy, neither father nor mother nor family tree (13), and they consider it proper behavior to put the Lord, *rabb*, into their spirit, *rūh*. To be sure, they do not perform the ritual ablution (*mash*, a word which technically means the wiping of the shoes with water), but:

> 15. *Those who were before Islam, they have always heard the call to prayer.*

Although they outwardly do not comply to ritual they have been faithful Muslims from the moment of the pre-eternal covenant. But as Shah Latif says, it would be wrong to concentrate upon one's worship exclusively. The journey towards the spiritual East is mentioned again (22).

Chapter VIII is a tender song of longing; it is close to the *Stimmung* in the first part of *Sur Pūrab*, to which it is connected by the imagery of journey to the East. Of special interest is the description of the *ōtāq*, the assembly room where the beloved Yogis have formerly been sitting to enthrall the audience by their songs.

In the last chapter, Shah Latif once more dwells upon the ascetic qualities of the true mystics who 'drink first' (1) and 'always face the Lord,' as he had also said in *Kalyān*. The Yogi is called here a *jabarūtī*, living in the realm of divine power (probably due to his impressive ascetic performances) (5). Hunger is a great festivity to the saints (9): the contrast between hunger and the word *ʿīd*, the festival at the end of the month of fasting, is extremely well chosen. Burning in the fire of love (17) they set out for Hinglaj (20 ff.) and experience that 'he who has the Lord has everything,' as is stated in Arabic. Then, their tongues become dumb (29), again an application of the Sufi saying 'He who knows God becomes dumb.' They obey the Quranic order 'Remember your Lord' (Sura 7/204) (33). Not those are true mystics who have clean dresses and blankets and are inwardly dirty, but those who look wretched and broken but are filled with spiritual wealth (43-44). In one of the last lines of this Sur Shah Latif turns to the central subject of unity and multitude:

> 45. *Seeing flower and flower, do not consider them to be many— This know, please: This is One.*

And he closes this chapter by summing up the qualities of the true saints, the seekers whom everyone seeks:

55. *Where there is no Divine Throne nor sky, nor a particle*
     of the earth,
     Not a rising of the moon, nor a sign of the sun,
     There the Adesis have reached their utmost threshhold,
     Beyond knowledge, they see the Lord, nāth, *in Noth-*
     ingness, nāh (= ʿadam).

As much as Shah Abdul Latif has praised the noble qualities of the heroes of faith, as much is he aware that such people can only rarely be found. He, like many earlies Sufis, and even more like his contemporaries in the big cities of Muslim India, complained that true seekers are no longer left. Instead of dealing with precious pearls, men prefer to use cheap beads, as he sings in *Sarirag* II, and who would be ready now to drink the poisoned wine of union or to pawn his head for this precious liquid?

The peacocks are gone, dying,
not a single swan has remained—
(The lake) became again the home of the liar-birds (Kar. I 29).

Perhaps the most touching expression of this longing for the true saints is found in a late passage of *Sur Mārūī* where the mystic bursts out in higly pathetic verse, asking, where the heroes and heroines of his tales have gone, and what has happened to those who willingly sacrificed wealth, honor, and life in the path of God:

Marui is no more in Malir,
   and there is no Hamir—
Punhun is no longer in Kech,
   nor is in Sind an Amir;
Mumal is no more in the hall,
   in Ganji is no faqīr,
True seekers cross the stream no more,
   for Sahar's sake without fear.
There is in the convents no Pir,
No guide in the burning place (Mar. Mut. 30).

CHAPTER SEVEN

THE ISLAMIC BACKGROUND OF
SHAH ABDUL LATIF'S POETRY

The way Shah Abdul Latif unites his descriptions of Sufis and Yogis by explaining the wondrous life of the Hindu ascetics with Quranic terminology has induced many of his Hindu admirers and interpreters to regard his poetry as a perfect blending of the two religious traditions of India. It is but natural that scholars like Lilaram Watanmal, Jethmal Parsram and recently Motílal Jotwani, who belong to his best interpreters, should have seen him predominantly in the light of their own traditions. H.T. Sorley correctly remarks about the way J. Parsram retells a story from the *Risālō*:

> His understanding is, however, tinged with the ideas of the Hindu Vedanta and a kind of theosophical universalism which is quite unlike the Islamic mysticism of the *Risālō* itself.[1]

Lilaram Watanmal, on the other hand, has tried to collect and explain all the Arabic quotations found in the *Risālō*, which means, in the first line, citations from the Quran. That is a praiseworthy attempt, and he certainly avoids mistakes like that by J. Parsram who regards the alleged, rather late, *ḥadīth* 'Man is my mystery, and I am his mystery' as a Quranic statement.[2] The tendency of interpreting into the poetry of Sufi saints too much of Vedantic philosophy is also visible in studies about the neighboring tradition, that of Panjabi mystical poetry, when studied by Hindu authors.

Lately, the Islamic background of Shah Abdul Latif's poetry has been emphasized once more, and we would largely agree with A.K. Brohi's statement:

> If Shah for this high flight is indebted to any personality or to any book, it is Muhammad and, again, the Quran; for what ever Shah Sahib may be, there is no doubt that he is the interpreter of the teaching of the Holy Quran and the standard bearer of Islam.[3]

---

[1] Sorley, 'Shah Abdul Latif', p. 259.

[2] Parsram, 'Sufis' p. 105. The *ḥadīth* occurs very frequently in Sachal Sarmast's mystical poetry.

[3] A.K. Brohi, in *Mehraṇ ja moti*, p. 104

Are not even the Yogis shown as those 'who read the *sūras* of the Glorious (*subhān*)'? (Rām. VI 13).

A survey of the Quranic verses which are quoted in their original text shows a remarkable breadth of variety, and contrary to many other mystical poets who composed their ecstatic songs in the Islamic folk tongues Shah Latif does not concentrate upon a few central Quranic verses which have been interpreted as keywords for mystical theories time and again.

Shah Abdul Latif is faithful to the pristine ascetic outlook of early Sufism in his powerful, poetic meditations about death and resurrection. Death is not only, as he often repeats with the favorite *hadīth* of most Sufis, 'dying before ye die,' it is rather something very real: 'Every soul will taste death' (Sura 3/181 a.o.)—that is a word he repeatedly inserts in the *wā ʾī* part of his poetry (thus Sarīr. III, Mūm. II). His heroines express the feeling of their sinfulness: Marui (Mār. V *wā ʾī*) speaks of the millions of grave sins and hundreds of thousands of minor sins she has committed, and the fear of resurrection, along with the feeling of sinfulness, is likewise voiced (Sarīr. III wā ʾī). For man tends to forget the grave, he is 'all forgetfulness,' *nisyān*: may we think of the old Arabic saying that the word *insān*, 'human being' is derived from *nisyān*, 'forgetting'? (Sarīr. II *wā ʾī*).

Like every Muslim, and particularly every mystic, Shah Latif is convinced that 'everything that is upon it is vanishing' (Sura 55/26) (Rām. V 1), and does not hesitate to describe dramatically the appearance of Azrail, the angel of death, before poor Sassui who, however, takes even him to be a messenger of her beloved (Abrī VIII 8); the same holds true for the two questioning angels, Munkar and Nakir, with whom she is faced (id.). Stories of a saint's meeting with the angel of death are not rare in classical Sufism. But the infidels do not believe what God has revealed about the resurrection, and Shah Latif alludes to their reaction 'Far away be what you were promised' (Sura 23/38) (Dēsī II 1), although in an unexpected place, to wit in Sassui's complaint that the camel-riders have carried away Punhun. Perhaps he means to say that this shock was, for her, as unexpected as doomsday is for the unbelievers; for separation and terrible excitement are usually called by Shah, as in other Muslim languages, a *qiyāmat*, 'resurrection.' (Dēs. I 1, IV, Kōhy. VI wā ʾī). He knows that fear that will overcome man on 'the day when

man flees from his brother' (Sura 80/34) (Sarīr. III wā 'ī), and
makes his hero ask God to protect him from the 'burning hell
fire' (Sura 101/8) (Sōr. I 9)—a passage which the learned
E. Trumpp mistranslated charmingly by regarding *nārun* 'fire' as
a Sindhi word so that the minstrel exclaims, 'Protect us from the
women ...'. Yet, Shah Abdul Latif makes the despaired Sassui
express also the hope that 'Verily God forgives all sins' (Sura
39/54) (Kōhy. III wā 'ī). In juxtaposition with the hellfire the
'gardens of Adan,' often occuring in the Holy Book, are mentioned (Sōr. I 9). It seems typical that most of these allusions are
inserted into the final part of each chapter, e.g., the *wā 'ī*, where
Shah liked to express his truly Islamic feelings. That is true also
for the allusions to the 'pure wine,' *sharāban ṭahūran*, which the
pious will be offered in Paradise (Sura 76/21), while once the
listener is admonished to forget this wine (Bil. I 8).[4] But even
without these outspokenly Islamic quotations one could easily
interpret many stories of the *Risālō*, particularly that of Marui, as
poetical elaborations of the Quranic word, 'Verily we belong to
God, and verily to Him is our return' (Sura 2/151).

But who is this God who is addressed in so many different
terms as Beloved, Sweetheart, Master, Lord, the Near One, and
whatever tender words Shah Latif puts into the mouths of his
heroines? One is almost tempted to say that he, fond of the Most
Beautiful Names of God, has invented new names for Him whom
no name can properly describe—names which are used by the
longing soul, not semi-philosophical terms which demand technical commentaries. With this approach is he in full harmony
though not with most of his contemporaries, but with the Sufis
of old; we are immediately reminded of Dhu 'n-Nun's prayer:

> In the multitude I call Thee 'My Lord!', and in solitude I call Thee 'O
> my Beloved!'[5]

That is exactly what Shah Abdul Latif does through the mouth
of the women-souls who burn in love and die in longing. But he
knows first and foremost that this beloved is The Lord—be He
symbolized in Punhun, the Baloch prince, or in Jam Tamachi, the
Sindhi ruler; and be his Presence called with the term for 'men's

---

[4]   It is further mentioned in BS III *wā 'ī* 2; Sohṇī III *wā 'ī*, Bil. I 2, III and IV
wā 'ī.
[5]   Abu Nuᶜaim al-Isfahānī, *Ḥilyat al-auliyā*, IX 332

guestroom,' *ōṭāq*. Perhaps the most beautiful account of this aspect of God is found in *Barvo Sindhī I*: It sings of the beauty and power of the Lord, which is beyond description, and culminates in the prayer: (I 19)

> *Thou a prince, Beloved, I a poor slave!*
> *I offer servantship without end, ready with folded hands:*
> *Did I ever leave Thy door, Friend, for someone else?*
> *Do not take away Thy loving grace from me, o Darling!*

God is also seen as the *khāliq*, the Creator, who can produce man out of a drop of sperm (*naṭfō*) (Pirbh. *wā 'ī* II), and it would be surprising if Shah had not returned time and again to the assertation of the profession of faith: 'He alone, who has no companion.' That is the *basso ostinato* of the *Risālō*, beginning in the very first verse of *Sur Kalyāṇ* and underlying all the other chapters. This acknowledgement of God's absolute Unity and Uniqueness leads Shah Latif sometimes to formulations which are strongly reminiscent of traditional Sufi handbooks:

> *The essence of associationism* (shirk) *is that you think you are without* shirk (Asā I 6).

The very thought of otherness constitutes in itself a kind of idolatry because it implies duality. The poet asks the soul to leave double sightedness, *dōbīnā 'ī*, and to reach the state of the *ashhadu*, 'I witness,' the true state of a Muslim (Asā IV 19), a formulation which could easily lead to the assertion of existential monism, *waḥdat al-wujūd*, as expressed in the formula *hama ōst*, 'Everything is He' (thus Asā IV 10). But Shah never uses that variant of the profession of faith that was a favorite with most later Sūfis, e.g. 'There is nothing *existing* but God'. On the whole, the traditional interplay of *nafy ū ithbāt*, denying everything besides God and proclaiming His Unity in the formula of the profession of faith, is maintained (Asā IV 12). God alone is implored by the searching soul, and Shah Latif acknowledges with the words of Sura 112 that 'He is eternal' (Kēd. III 10), and 'has not begotten nor is He begotten' (Mār. VIII 1, Kām. II 10), and that 'There is nothing like Him' (Sura 42/9) (Mār. VIII 3).

> *Even if you have a hundred thousand friends, compare none to Punhun (Maᶜ dh. V 2).*

God is the absolute Lord, who reveals Himself best, as we may understand from Shah Latif's verse, in his quality as *sattār*, the one who covers sins. It is He who is kind to slaves (Līlā II 4) rather than to the proud, and one of the finest expressions of trust into his promise to cover man's sins is the prayer in *Sur Ḍahar* (II 18-25):

God, as Thy name is, so I have great hope.
Creator, there is no limit nor end to Thy patience,
Thy name, o Lord—I have put it into the soul. (18)

Great is Thy strength, with graces art Thou filled,
Do not lift Thy kindness from me—I am Thine. (21)

As sweet as Thy name, as great is my hope,
No door is like to Thee, I have seen many other doors (22)

Do not make loose, o Lover, the relation with this poor one;
The miserable one has no salvation but Thee.
Only Thy name, I grasp it constantly (24)

Cover, o Coverer! I am naked!
Cover, o Coverer! Give me the hem of Thy protection! (25)

The lonely soul finds herself naked without God; she will freeze to death from shame if He will not cover her. And as His grace covers the sinful woman on her lonely bed, thus 'God encompasses everything' (Sura 41/54)—Sassui realizes this truth on her painful journey through the desert (Abri V 14) and she implores Him 'of lofty degrees' (Sura 40/15) to unite her with her beloved (Dēsī III 14).

It is interesting that the Quranic verses which speak of the Light of God are all found in the more 'technical,' less folkloristic chapters. The word 'God is the light of Heaven and earth' (Sura 24/35) consoles the martyrs of Kerbela (Kēd. V 10), and the Yogis experience (Rām. V 11) that 'God leads to His Light whom He willeth' (Sura 24/35), as they had been told before that 'God is the friend of those who believe, and leads them from the darkness toward the light' (Sura 2/258) (Rām. V 1). We may ask ourselves whether or not Shah Latif thought, with this quotation in the context of a Hindu topic, of the Upanishad expression according to which men are led from the darkness towards the light. Yet, the idea is so general that it may be sheer coincidence. The Sindhi variation of this Quranic saying occurs in Dēsī (VII 16). God's inexplicable way of dealing with man, 'And He elevates whom He willeth, and He lowers whom He willeth' (Sura 3/25)—is a perfect expression of the Sufi's feeling that God's greatness is revealed through the interplay of His mercy and His wrath, of His *jamāl* and *jalāl* (Kal. III 7, Pirbh. I *wā 'ī*). One of the finest verses in this connection are those in *Barvō Sindhī* (I 18), where the poet ponders the strange manifestations God shows to those who love Him:

> *Sometimes they put locks, sometimes the friends'*
> *doors are opened*
> *Sometimes I come, or I can not come,*
> *then He calls me to the high place,*
> *Sometimes I long for His call, sometimes He says*
> *secret words—*
> *Such one is, master, my Beloved!*

Another verse pertaining to this mysterious acting of God has become almost proverbial in Sindhi:

> *Thou makest the leaf drown in the stream, and makest the*
> *stone swimming* (Ḍahar II 19),

lines that have consoled many pious souls in the afflictions of life and the years of poverty and misery that came over the country time and again, and which form the title of several contemporary short stories.

Strangely enough, Shah Abdul Latif never alludes to one of the favorite verses of early Sufism, i.e., Sura 5/59 'He loves them and they love Him,' although the idea of God's preceding love, which the Sufis of the classical period tried to prove by this Quranic sentence, occupies a central place in his religious feeling: we mentioned already the lines taken over from the *Mathnawī*, in which Sassui was told that the water is as thirsty for men as they are thirsty for the water (Abrī I 8). But another verse that was central for the meditation of the Sufis occurs both in its Arabic original and in a Sindhi variation: 'We are nearer to him than his jugular vein' (Sura 50/16): God, transcendent as He is, can be found in man's own heart, closer to him than his breath, more his own than his blood. That is what Sassui experiences in Shah

Latif's interpretation of her story (Abrī I 9, V 13, cf. Mār. I 9). Yet, the poet has not, as his compatriot Abdur Rahim Girhori did, applied the words of Sura 57/4 'And He is with you wherever you are' to Sassui's journey in the desert. He rather prefers another quotation to admonish his heroine that she should find the signs of God everywhere around her and in her own soul (Abrī V 12): 'And We have put our signs in the horizons and in yourselves—do you not see?' (Sura 51/21); a Quranic verse that had served generations of mystics to express their experience of God's inescapable presence and is here logically applied to Sassui's finding her beloved in her own heart. That feeling of God's omnipresence may lead the poet to the conviction:

> *The eyes have done me much good—*
> *for they see the Friend even when I bring them in front of*
> *the evildoer* (Asā II 3).

God's signs are everywhere, in the sinner and in the beauty of the morning, in the angel of death and in the merciful rain, as many poets in the Indo-Persian tradition had witnessed.

We may agree with the Sindhi interpreter of the *Risālō*[6] that the description of the Yogis (Rām. V 5):

> The *miḥrāb* is the Friend's face,

is based on Sura 2/109: 'To God belong the East and the West—whithersoever ye turn there is His face,' although the wording itself is more reminiscent of traditional Persian poetry which, however, has derived this image from the just-mentioned Quranic quotation. The same Sindhi author, then, explains:

> The beauty of the Friend is far from seeing (Asā III 8)

as a poetical variant of Sura 6/103 'The sight does not reach Him.' For:

> *Could the metaphorical (majāzī) eyes see the real (ḥaqīqī)*
> *face?* (Asā III 3).

Shah Abdul Latif's description of God's qualities fits perfectly into the normal Sufi tradition. He has praised God as the protector and the creator of Heaven and earth (Pūrab III wā ʾī, BS II

---

[6] Pir Saᶜid Hasan in *Makhzan* p. 21 ff.

wā 'i II). Admiring God's creative work he describes Him as the one who says 'Be, and it becomes' (Sura 2/111 a.o.) (Sohṇ. VI I f); but his (as innumerable other Sufi poets') favorite Quranic allusion is that of the pre-eternal covenant (Sura 7/171) *Alastu bi-rabbikum*, 'Am I not your Lord?' That was God's address, directed to the not-yet-created beings, and by their answer *balā*, 'Yes,' they accepted all the affliction, *balā*, that will be showered upon them during their earthly lives. Shah sometimes combines the *alast*-tradition with that of the creative 'Be' (Dēsī II 3, Khar. I 2-7), but he always returns to the same idea: the heroines who seems to be closest to his heart, e.g., Sohni (Dēsī II 3), Marui and Sassui, are shown as paragons of a life that is led in perfect consonance with the pre-eternal promise of the soul:

> *In that very time I have made an engagement with the inhabitants of the jungle* (Mār. I 1).

Marui had promised their friends in Malir to remain faithful to them, as the soul has promised the Lord to acknowledge His rule till Doomsday. Sohni (Sohṇ. VI 3-10), in turn, knows that this pre-eternal love has bound her to Mehanwal, long before the souls were created: how, then, should she not swim towards him and die in the flood? It is a return into the unity before the differentiation into Divine subject and created object—

> *before the soul and moon and sun, sin and retribution, sound and flesh were created,*
> *and there was only Unity* (wahdaniyat) (Mār. I 3-7).

The heroines thus experience what Junaid had seen as the true goal of Sufism: to go back into the time before creation, when only God was, as He always was.

The Day of *alast* is, in Persian poetical language, called *dūsh*, 'yesterday,' and contrasted with the Tomorrow of Resurrection often mentioned in the Quran. Thus, when restlessness has fallen into Sassui's soul by seeing Punhun's tresses 'yesterday,' the poet thinks of the primordial enchantment through Beauty and Majesty. The tresses, then, are described as 'like [the letter] *Kāf*'; it may be licit, although perhaps too far-fetched, to see here an allusion to the letter *Kāf* by which creation began, when God spoke *Kun*, 'Be'. That would be consistent with the traditional image of the tresses as manifestations which hide the sun-like

'Face of the Beloved.' (Abrī 2-4). The remembrance of these Divine manifestations will lead her to the place of final union.

The idea of the primordial covenant is closely connected with another concept of Quranic imagery, that of the Wellpreserved Tablet, on which everything has been written by the Divine Pen. 'Say, nothing meets us but what God has written' (Sura 9/51): Mumal relies upon this word (Mūm. V 12), and all the other heroines feel the truth of this statement as well.

> *How could she turn from what is written on the Wellpreserved (Tablet)?*

is said about Sohni (Sohnī IV 4), whose strange behavior by crossing the river in cold winter days is again ascribed to her Fate:

> *Even these are the works of God—*
> *Otherwise who would step into the whirlpool?* (Sohnī VI 13).

The imagery of Tablet and Pen is found in many places in the *Risālō* and belongs to the most important aspects of Shah's teachings. He knows that union cannot be achieved through human force:

> *Where so many hours are written on the Table and Pen,*
> *there so many hours have to pass* (Maᶜ dh. V 9).

The *qismat*, the inevitable fate, is a strong fetter (Mūmal I 8-9), it is as strong as *qaid al-mā*, the 'prison of water,' which is stronger than the prison of iron; this is presumably an allusion to Solomon's putting the jinns in iron bottles and casting them in the ocean, to make sure that they cannot escape at all from their prison.[7]

But as much as Shah Abdul Latif, as every good Muslim, knows that life is ordered according to God's inscrutable will, as much does he believe that God 'does not burden a soul more than it can endure' (Sura 2/286), as he sings in his threnody on the martyrs of Kerbela (Kēd. V 7).

All his heroes and heroines are called, in a certain sense, to follow the *sirāṭ al-mustaqīm*, the straight path (Sura 1/5). Thus,

---

[7] Sachal, too, uses this word in connection with Maru ʾi, thus IV 2, 8, 9, 24, VII 6, 7, 11, and others.

God is often called by his name *al-Hādī*, 'The Guiding' (thus Mum. II wā 'ī). Sassui is the model case; she sets out for the path that leads her towards the Lord (Dēsī II 2). The poetical figures thus become the exemplars of true Muslims and *mu 'mins*, of faithful believers. 'God calls them towards the abode of Peace' (Sura 16/26), as the Yogis experience (Rām. V 11). His ideal heroes are 'those who believe and rely upon God' (Sura 41/17) (Asā IV 45), those who are addressed by the Lord in a non-Quranic saying: 'Thank me, and do not be unbelievers' (Sār. I wā 'ī). All the martyrs of love whom he describes 'struggle in the way of God' (Sura 5/59) as do the heroes of Kerbela (Kēd. VI 10). Of course, theirs is not the war against outward enemies, but rather the greater *jihād*, the Holy War against the lower self, the dangerous *nafs*, which is according to the Prophet's word, 'man's greatest enemy.' That is why they are called to use 'the dagger of *lā*', e.g., the word *lā ilāha* 'There is no deity [save God]' against the *nafs*, as the mystics had told their followers for centuries.

The poet knows that in the beginning of the Path fear is necessary, and praises him 'who fears the place of his Lord' (Sura 79/40) (Sohṇī I 12). That implies a constant occupation with prayer so that the heroes of Kerbela are praised as those 'whose marks [from prostration] are on their faces' (Sura 48/29) (Kēd. V 10). And his mystical wayfarers need also another noble quality: that of patience. Could Sassui wander through the forests if she were not patient? Could the Yogis or the faithful Sufis achieve proximity to the Lord if they were not patient under all afflictions? That is why Shah Latif gives the maxim 'And God is with those who show patience', so often repeated in the Quran, in one of the central chapters on mystical theory, e.g., *Yaman Kalyāṇ.* (VIII 13). And he calls them to show patience (BS I 13): 'And admonish each other to truth, admonish each other to patience' (Sura 103/4). The result of such a patient behavior will be, eventually, that the wayfarer reaches the station where he, or she, is called a friend of God, and these friends, the perfectly sanctified persons, live in constant security and spiritual happiness: 'No fear is upon them, nor are they sad' (Sura 10/63 and often) (Kal. I 6). The sinful soul, surrounded by the dangers of the world, may sometimes think that the beloved has forsaken her and that she, like a faithless wife, is no longer worthy of his attention. But Shah Latif reminds these souls which have been deceived by selfishness and egotism (Kôh. III *wā ᵓī*): 'Do not despair of God's mercy!' (Sura 39/54) (Sohn. I 21).

One central aspect of mystical education is mentioned several times in the *Risālō*: that is man's duty to recollect God often: 'Remember your Lord in your soul'! (Sura 7/204) says the poet, (Ram. V 9-33) and relies upon the Divine promise: 'Remember me and I will remember you' (Sura 2/147), which forms the basis for the theories of *dhikr* in Sufi education (Kal. II 13, Sar. I wā ᵓī).

> *Who has remained awake all night and recollects God, his dust becomes honored, says Latif.*
> *Millions greet him, having come into his presence* (Sarir. II 2).

The practice of *dhikr* has inspired Shah Abdul Latif to a whole chapter in the *Risālō*, although he never mentions any technicalities of the various stages and forms of the recollection, but rather takes *dhikr* as a constant occupation of the soul.

Scattered allusions to Quranic stories do not lack, like that of Mose's swooning (Sura 7/139), when the revelation came—a verse used by Maulana Rumi to denote the overwhelming experience of ecstasy (Rām. V 1). Contrary to the tradition of Persian, Turkish and Urdu mystical and even profane poetry, names of personalities mentioned in the Quran occur but rarely, thus Khalil (Abraham) and his idol-worshipping father Adhar (Asā III wā ᵓī, IV). Strangely enough we find Qābīl, Cain, as symbol for the extremely cruel beloved! (YK VI 7) Shah Abdul Latif does not, as his more sophisticated colleagues did, write out long chains of prophets with their qualities, nor does he enumerate the names of those killed by their overwhelming divine love, as for instance Sachal Sarmast loved to do. Very rarely he plays with Quranic puns, thus when he advises his listener (Kal. III 8) to turn to 'the end of *al-ᶜaṣr*' (Sura 103), which means to its last word, namely *ṣabr*, patience; the full text of this verse is (as mentioned above) given in another connection (BS I 13).

We may assume that many more allusions to Quranic verses are likely to be found in the *Risālō*; for mystics like Shah Latif must have experienced what Père Nwyia so ingeniously calls the 'Quranization of memory': the Quran was so everpresent in his mind that he could allude to certain verses and events without mentioning them *expressis verbiss*. A typical example of this style seems to be the *wā 'ī* in *Sarirāg II* with its rhyme -*ān*, which inevitably leads the listener back to the Quranic model with this rhyme, e.g., the *Sūrat ar-Raḥmān* (Sura 55).

Some Muslim scholars have tried to go deeper into Shah Latif's Sindhi verse in order to discover more Quranic allusions; but in certain cases different interpretations are possible; therefore, we do not venture into this difficult matter.

The Quranic verses selected by Shah Abdul Latif point to a traditional, mystically tinged religiosity, and the same seems to be true for the Prophetic traditions and extra-Quranic revelations (*aḥadīth qudsiyya*) which he inserts into his verse. Once more stressing God's absolute power as he saw it expressed in the primordial covenant, and in the Quranic verses about the Well-Preserved Tablet, Shah is fond of the tradition 'The Pen has already dried up', e.g., nothing ever written in pre-eternity can be changed, a *ḥadīth* (Mār. I 11-17), which was used by the Sufis very frequently, though with different interpretations. The ascetic background of early Sufism, which otherwise seems to have almost disappeared among the mystical poets of Iran, Turkey, and India, is once more recalled by Shah Latif's use of the tradition 'The world is a rotting carcass, and those who seek it are dogs,' which occurs twice (Sar. III *wā 'ī*, Maʿ dh I 9) to show that the only goal of the seeker should be the eternal and unchanging Divine reality, whereas the seekers of the world are victims of the appetites of their lower soul, *nafs*, which is often represented in traditional literature as a black dog. In an ingenious way has Shah Latif made the transition from his invitation to Sassui to give pieces of her flesh to the dogs of Kech to the motif of the soul-dog;

> *The dog chews bones, the truly generous man* (jawānmard, e.g., *the Sufi*) *chews his liver* (Maʿ dh. I 9).

This juxtaposition of the lower, dog-like instincts and the ideal 'man,' who is, at the same time, contrasted with those uninitiated who are 'like animals, no, but more astray,' (Sura 7/178) is taken up in the saying about *ṭālib al-maulā* which, though not a Prophetic *ḥadīth*, had become one of the favorite proverbs in Indian Sufism: 'The seeker of this world is feminine, the seeker of the Otherworld is a catamite, and the seeker of the Lord is masculine.'[8] This sentence, originating in 13th century India, once more praises the real 'man,' who can also be outwardly, like Rabiᶜa or Sohni, of feminine sex, as is shown by Shah Latif's use of the word; for its last part is used in *Sur Sohṇī* (I 17, 18), as well as in *Rāmakalī*.

It is natural that the ascetic basis of Shah Latif's work induced him to insert traditions about the necessity of repentance, *tauba*, into his poetry: 'Hurry with the repentance before death' is mentioned (Asā III wā ʾī), however, without its usual continuation 'and hurry with the prayer before the prescribed hour has passed.' *Tauba* is the first step on the mystical path, and constitutes the beginning of the constant struggle against the lower soul, which the Prophet had called *jihād akbar*, the Greater Holy War. Shah Latif makes use of the *hadīth* concerning man's worst enemy, e.g., the *nafs*, in an interesting comparison when he praises the just ruler (Bil. III 2, 12 ff.): here, the *nafs* is compared to a *majūsī*, an infidel Zoroastrian, who has to be slain. Even more realistic is the passage in *Sarīrāg III* where the Europeans represent the *nafs*:

> *When the pilot is not there, then the Firangis come and plunder the boat* (13)

—a reminiscence of the Portuguese attack on Thatta in 1555. For the lower instincts may deprive the boat of the soul of its precious merchandise when the mystical guide, as representative of the Prophet, does not guide it safely through the ocean of this world.

The central theme of Shah's poetry, however, is expressed by the tradition 'Die before ye die' which formed a cornerstone of Sufi theology as much as it was known to the Indian tradition that one has to become a *jīvanmṛta*, while alive, in order to become a *jīvanmuktī*, who has reached eternal salvation during one's lifetime. All his heroes, be they the Yogis or Sassui, know that by dying to one's self they will reach a new life of union with the Beloved:

> *Those who die before they die, they are not dead when they die—*

---

[8] Cf. Zubaid Ahmad, 'The Contribution of Indo-Pakistan to Arabic Literature, s.v. Jamal Hanswi.

Those will be alive who have lived before the (eternal) life
(Ma ꜥ dh. IV 7).

It would be no exaggeration to state that most of *Shāh jō Risālō* is a variation of this theme; for the fate of Sassui, Sohni, King Diyaj, and the repentance of Mumal and Lila can be seen under this aspect: all of them are purified by slowly stripping off their base qualities, dying to their Ego, and reaching a higher state of illumination and final union, for 'only the death through initiation gives access to resurrection', as H. Corbin has stated. Shah Latif knows well that God has promised that His beauty, or He Himself, will become the blood money for those whom He has killed, as he had proclaimed in the case of Hallaj; and in the light of this *ḥadith qudsī*, Sassui's death in the desert becomes meaningful.

The Friend is blood money for those who die on the Path (Abrī XI 6).
Who are killed by the Beloved, in their embrace is the Beloved (Ma ꜥ dh. VI 14.)

'There is no one intended in the two worlds [but God]', this word expresses the central feeling of the Sufi (Y. V 21), and therefore belongs to the standard quotations of Indian mystics. And the Quranic assertion 'Verily we belong to God, and to Him is our return' (Sura 2/151) is taken up by an alleged *ḥadith* 'Everything returns to its origin' (Mār. I 14), which forms the leitmotif of the story of Marui, the 'soul in exile.' Shah could have quoted in connection with her tale also the *ḥadith*, which modern Sindhi scholars sometimes apply to her: 'Love of one's native country is part of religion:' for she sacrifices everything in order to remain faithful to her original home and her first and only love.

Shah Latif also quotes the famous *ḥadith qudsī* in which God describes his hidden friends: 'Verily, my friends are under my domes' (*qabābī*, or, as he has it with a common mistake: 'under my cloak', *qabā ʾī*) (Asā IV *wā ʾī*). This saying occurs often from the 10th century onward to designate the true saints, who are hidden from the eyes of the masses, protected by God who alone knows them and conceals them out of jealousy. These friends, described in Shah's verse with Quranic expressions as well (see p. 224 f.) are those who have existentially realized the truth of the famous *ḥadith* 'Who knows himself, knows his Lord' (Abrī V 5):

with these words Sassui discovers the lost Lord and Beloved in her own heart, so that the veils of duality are eventually lifted.

Another *hadīth qudsī*, which is meant to express a similar experience, but is used only in a later period of Sufi theories, is 'Man is my mystery, and I am his mystery' (Sōr. II 5, Pirbh. *wa'ī*). It points to the closest possible relation between God and man, man being the place of manifestation for the Divine Names (as Mir Dard has repeated unceasingly). The tradition, mentioned in Rumi's *Mathnawī*, was to become one of the central sentences in later Sindhi Sufi poetry; particularly Sachal Sarmast found here the proof for his ecstatic experience of union with God and of God's all-embracing Unity. Is it an accident that Shah never alludes to this *hadīth qudsī* in his stories about the loving women, but mentions it twice in tales connected with the power of music, e.g., in *Rāmakalī* and *Phirbātī*? A similar distribution of a famous *hadīth* occurs once more in the *Risālō*. The tradition: 'God is an odd number and loves odd numbers' is used several times (Rām. V wā'ī, Asā I 2) to explain the secret of perfect unity in which even the 'I' of the mystic constitutes still a veil, nay, is an expression of his *shirk*, associationism, which makes him to think of two, e.g., God *and* man.

Dard had pondered a major problem of the mystical poet, to wit, the tension between the overwhelming unitive experience and the wish to explain it to mankind on the one hand, and the feeling that the lover is dumbfounded by the shock of this experience on the other hand. Shah Latif uses the tradition that 'he who knows God becomes dumb' in *Sur Rāmakalī* (IX 28, 29), but he never thought of using its counterpart, that the mystic 'who knows God, talks too much.' His heroes apparently did not suffer from this problem.

The reader who is acquainted with the general selection of Prophetic traditions and *ahādīth qudsiyya* in the works of later Sufis, and especially with the poetry of popular mystics in both Turkey and the Subcontinent is amazed to see that some of the otherwise most frequently quoted traditions are not found in Shah Latif's poetry, and that he rather clings to the more 'orthodox' sayings. Some of the traditions, just as the Quranic verses, are only alluded to in one or two words, and no one but the specialists will be able to detect these allusions. That is quite different from the way how Shah's younger compatriot Sachal

Sarmast dealt with the Prophetic traditions which he inserted in various forms and with very outspoken predilections into his poetry. In Shah's work, the number of traditions is small compared to that used by later Sufi poets in Sind, but also in relation to the general tendency in Persian mystical poetry.

Of course, Shah Abdul Latif uses also Arabic quotations from other sources as were generally utilized by the Sufis in their works. For many of them the exact source is by no means clear, and some amount rather to proverbial expressions. Thus the famous proverb 'Who seeks and strives will find' is attributed to Ali ibn Abi Talib; it forms a fitting motto of Sassui's story, for she was to find her beloved through constant searching (Dēsī II 3, Ḥus. VII 1). But the same heroine, before discovering her beloved in her heart, had first to experience that 'Journeying is part of hellfire' (Dēsī II 2) and that 'Separation is more difficult than death' (Abrī V 9). Stylistically, it is worth mentioning that most of these Arabic sayings are located in *Abrī* V, where not only love is described with an old Sufi saying as 'a fire lit by God' (V 15), but also the last experience of the lovers is told with a sentence that has its roots in classical Persian love mysticism in the tradition of Ahmad Ghazzali and Iraqi: 'Love is a veil between lover and beloved' (V 17). Again, in the same group of verses, one finds one of the traditional sayings of Sufism, which has come down in various forms, and has been attributed to various authors, e.g., 'I did not see anything but saw God [in it]' (V 11): did not Sassui see the messenger of the Beloved even in the angel of death? Many stories are told of Sufis who indeed discovered God everywhere: to see the cruel beloved in the person of the executioner, as did the ecstatic poet Sarmad, the Persian-Jewish convert to Islam (executed 1661) is perfectly in harmony with Sassui's experience; but when Shaikh Tahir saw God even in a camel behind which he started running we reach the border between the lofty and the ridiculous.[9] In Shah Latif's poetry, however, the experience is genuine and can also be explained from another viewpoint, namely as the attitude of the Muslim who sees God's hand in everything, and hence accepts whatever comes from Him with equal peace of mind, and even with gratitude.

---

[9]   Qaniᶜ, *Tuḥfat ul-kirām*, Sindhi translation p. 389

Sassui is the translator of Arabic sentences about love and longing; Marui, too, is made to recite two Arabic lines: she sighs from her prison: 'Here is my body, and the heart is with you' (Mār. I 10) and continues: 'The two eyes weep blood in your love' (Mār. I 13). The Yogis, finally, are consoled with the saying 'Who has (found) the Lord, has got everything.' (Rām. IX 28). And all of Shah's heroes live through the truth of the promise that there will be 'joy after difficulty,' al-faraj ba‘da 'sh-shidda, the well-known Arabic expression which is, however, found only in its Sindhi version in the Risālō, a fact that may prove how commonly used it was (BS II 12).

Based on the previous remarks we would fully agree with Sorley's general statement that 'the religion of the Risālō is thoroughly Islamic.'[10] But even more than by enumerating the Quranic passages and overt or hidden allusions to Prophetic traditions we feel this 'Islamic' attitude from the way Shah Abdul Latif treats the Prophet in his poetry. Lilaram Watanmal has made a remark which seems typical for the approach of even the most open minded and enlightened Hindu scholars when dealing with the religion of their Muslim neighbors:

> I may mention here once and for all one inconsistency at least that I have noticed in the writings of various Mahommedan Sufi authors. They try to make their belief in the prophet Mahommad consistent with their Sufi doctrines, an attempt in which they fail most ignomiously ...

After a few remarks about the method of the Dabistān-i madhāhib, a 17th century book the authority of which is more than questionable he continues:

> Shah Latif, too, has in his Risalo, in several places, impressed on his hearer the necessity of believing in Mahommad as a prophet and something more. It is true that some of the verses in praise of the prophet, somewhat vulgar in language, are not our poet's ... But it cannot be doubted that there are several genuine verses in which our poet has expressed his full belief in the prophet ... The orthodox Mahommadans might well believe him as the chief prophet of God. But the Sufis can not, consistently with their pantheistic doctrines, say that the prophet Mahommad is the only medium of salvation ...

The author, after having thus told the Sufi what he ought and ought not believe, quotes the example of Hallaj, who recognized

---

[10]　　Sorley, l.c., p. 259

ḥaq, 'Divine Reality,' everywhere, and nicely splits up 'Mansur' and 'Hallaj' into two heroes of monistic philosophy; then he asks himself why Shah Abdul Latif may have inserted such un-Sufi verses into his poetry:

> It may be that he was not so utterly indifferent to his outward body containing the divine spirit as the great Mansur and others were. Had he said anything against the prophet, it is almost certain that Mahomed Kalhoro, who was at first our poet's enemy, would have seized a pretext for causing him to be put to death. It may be that Shah Latif wanted to lead the minds of his followers slowly and gradually into higher Sufism by allowing them to believe first in their prophet, and then by degrees to ascend higher and higher. [11]

These patronizing remarks are certainly far off the mark. Whosoever has studied Sufi poetry and prose knows that it was just the Sufis who developed the love of the Prophet in various forms among the people, and the 'celebrated Hallaj' was among the first to compose most beautiful hymns about the pre-eternal light of the Prophet, which encompasses everything. [12] Whether we turn to the theories about the Perfect Man (*insān kāmil*) as embodied in Muhammad, who is the comprehensive place of manifestations of the Divine Names, or to the simple folk poetry where Muhammad is praised in unsophisticated little rhymes as the guide of his beloved community and their intercessor at Doomsday: it is the love of the Prophet which distinguishes the Muslim from every other religious community. His love is, as Constance Padwick has emphasized, the strongest binding force in the Muslim world, and everyone shares in the feelings of admiration and trust, whether one interprets him as the intercessor, the *Insān Kāmil*, the social or political reformer, the most loving human being, or whatever attracted the hearts of the masses and the élite toward him. Why, then, should Shah Abdul Latif not express his trust in the Messenger of God? All the more since the poetry written in honor of the Prophet in the Indus Valley is amazingly large. His veneration was taught in orthodox works like Makhdum Muhammad Hashim's *Qūt al-ᶜāshiqīn*, 'Nurture of the Lovers,' and was imbibed by the children who learned even in lullabies something

---

[11]   L. Watanmal, 'Shah Abdul Latif', p. 38

[12]   The best introduction is still Tor Andrae 'Die person Muhammads in lehre und glauben seiner gemeinde', 1918. For Sind in particular cf. A. Schimmel, 'The Veneration of the Prophet Muhammad, as reflected in Sindhi Poetry', in: The Saviour God, 1964

about the lofty qualities of Muhammad, and were instructed to follow his example even to the smallest detail, to obey him as the instrument of God's revelation, the executive of God's orders. The stories of his miracles (although he himself did not care at all for miracles, his only miracle being the message of the clear Arabic Quran) were known everywhere, and it sufficed to allude to them just with a little side-remark, to awaken the whole context in the listener's mind. Maulana Rumi did this as much as innumerable later poets in the eastern and western Muslim tradition. Thus, instead of regarding the loving words about the Prophet in Shah Latif's poetry as something that belongs to a lower level of experience one should rather see these verses as faithfully reflecting the traditions of mystical Islam. That is why Shah returns time and again to extolling the 'seal of all Prophets' (Bil. II 11).

'Lord, give me my people!'—this prayer of the Prophet, as quoted in Bil. I 31, offers the key word out of which the various descriptions of Muhammad develop. Indeed, the *umma* belongs to Muhammad (BS III *wā'ī* 2). Muhammad is depicted here as the leader of his community, whom he will guide in this world and for whom he will intercede at the end of days: for in this terrible hour every prophet will ask for his own salvation; only Muhammad, model of the generous 'man of God' (*fatā, jawānmard*) will ask that his community be saved.

Among the Quranic verses which are inserted into Shah Latif's poems, many point to the high rank of the Prophet. *Sur Sārang* (III *wā'ī*) contains a lovely poem in *maulūd*-type, e.g., a description of the miracles before and after Muhammad's birth:

> *The elephant immediately performed a prostration when he saw the light on [Abdul] Mutallib's forehead*

and the orphaned child was consoled by the Divine promise 'Verily God will give you ...' (Sura 93/5). Another poem mentions the 'good tidings' (Sura 39/19) which the Prophet is called to give to his people. There is no doubt—and this idea forms the center of Shah Abdul Latif's prophetology—that Muhammad was sent *rahmatan lil-ʿālamīn*, as 'mercy for the worlds,' as Sura 21/107 attests (cf. Bil. IV *wā'ī*).

It would not be exaggerated to say that a great part of Islamic prophetology has developed out of this very conviction, that the last prophet was indeed mercy for the inhabitants of this earth, and would remain so even in the other world. His intercession, though not derived from clear Quranic statements, became part and parcel of Muslim faith, and the steadfast hope in him is often expressed in Shah's verse. Who acknowledges God's unity and obeys Muhammad (as the Quran has stated it as the believers' duty, Sura 4/82 a.o.) will be brought safely home:

> *When those who said He is alone God, He has no partner,*
> *respect Muhammad the intercessor out of love with their*
> *hearts,*
> *Then [none] out of them was entangled in a place where*
> *there is no landing* (Kal. I 2-4, cf. Sar. II).

The first verses of *Sur Ḍahar* II elaborate this feeling of complete trust in the Prophet in a very ingenious style: after the description of the dried-up tree, which lacks the water of life, as found in part I of the *Sur*, the poet calls out:

> *Prince of Medina, listen to my calling,*
> *In thy protection is the journey; thou leadest the travellers*
> *to the other shore ...*
>
> *Lord of Medina! Listen to my calls!*
> *[My] hope rests upon thee, I do not think of any other help.*
>
> *Bridegroom of Medina! Listen to my calls!*
> *Please, Muhammad, come back, the sinner's hope is upon*
> *thee.*
>
> *Shah of Medina! Listen to my calling!*
> *For God's sake, make the friend arrive quickly!*
>
> *Lion of Medina! Listen to my calls,*
> *Put thy blessed feet, the sinner has hope in thee.*
>
> *Prince of Medina! Listen to my call!*
> *I am one who seeks protection; reach quickly on the journey.* (Ḍah. II 1 ff).

Sindhi interpreters have regarded *Sur Khanbhāt* as a description of the beautiful qualities of the Prophet, although only the *wā'ī* gives a clear statement pertaining to the poet's hope for his help (II wā'ī). The whole motif of the journey toward the beloved, whose beauty is higher than any description, and toward whom the camel, e.g., the soul, is driven with a hundred tricks, can as well be understood as a description of man's spiritual journey in general as it can be interpreted as a poetical version of a visit to the Prophet's resting place in Medina, the city which is also mentioned elsewhere in the *Risālō* (Bil. I *wā 'ī*). The fact that the moon is asked to kiss the friend's feet may be interpreted as pointing to a Western direction, e.g., Arabia; but Shah's geographical remarks should not always be taken at face value. The final songs, in fact, do not always exactly sum up the contents of the chapter which they follow; the hope for the Prophet's intercession is found in *Surs* as different as *Bilāwal* (I, IV *wā 'ī*), *Barvō Sindhī* (III *wā 'ī* 2), and *Sārang*. The lovely *wā 'ī* in *Khanbhat I* praises Muhammad:

> *On black doomsday, the Friend is protector* (ḥāmī).

Other poems speak of Muhammad's tent on doomsday (Sar. II *wā 'ī*), or of the whole crowd of people that will cling to him:

> *In the front will be Mustafa, in the rear the people will march* (BS. II *wā 'ī* 2),

or they express the hope of being united with Muhammad (BS I *wā 'ī*). And the faithful is warned:

> *Do not go to any door besides* [*that of*] *the unique Hashimite* (Bil. I 5)

Muhammad's *rauḍa*, his tomb in Medina, is also mentioned in *Sur Sārang* (I 15, 16), the Rain Song (a derivation of the classical rain-rāga *Mēgh*), which has been called by Sorley one of the most beautiful parts of the *Risālō*, so much so that the British scholar even seems to prefer it to Shelley's description of the clouds. Indeed, Shah's lyrical description of the earth waiting for rain, and the happiness that is felt after the cloud has distributed its precious gifts are closer to *Erlebnislyrik* in the Western sense than any other part of Shah Abdul Latif's poetry. And yet, the whole imagery serves mainly to extol the Prophet and his mercy.

To compare Divine grace to rain is a common topic in oriental cultures, where every drop of rain meant new life for the steppes, and where every shade of green was almost fore-shadowing Paradise.[13] Profane poets of ancient Arabia, such as Imrulqais, described the power of rain as much as did later poets in every part of the Islamic Empire. In order to implore God's help in times of drought a special ritual prayer, the *ṣalāt al-istisqā*, was performed by the community outside the town, and in many legends the power of a hidden saint becomes revealed when God answers his prayer for rain.

The Quran praises God, the bestower of fertility, the one 'Who makes you see the lightning in fear and longing and who produces the heavy clouds. And the thunder praises Him, and the angels, fearing Him' (Sura 13/13 f.; cf. 30/24). One of the most poignant proofs for the possibility of resurrection is the example of the seemingly dead earth which is quickened again by the spring rain (Sura 30/48). Islamic mysticism could easily take over this image. Rumi's verse is filled with spring poems which describe the overwhelming power of resurrection as it happens every year under the influence of thunder (the trumpet of Israfil), rain and sunshine; the rain bestows paradisical green garments upon the naked gardens, and invests trees and shrubs with celestial robes of honor. And the tears of the lover, says Maulana Rumi, will result in the growth of kindness in the heart of the beloved ... 'Love and rain are one thing', thus sings also Shah Latif (Sār. II 6).

Rain is called in some of the Islamic languages, particularly in Turkish and Persian, *rahmat*, 'mercy,' derived from Sura 27/64, where the clouds are described as messengers of God's mercy. That expression gave a perfect basis for the combination of rain with the person of the Prophet who is also 'mercy for the worlds.' This was all the easier since the comparison of a king or a religious leader to a rich rain cloud was common in oriental poetry, whether the psalmist describes the king of peace in Psalm 27, or a court poet sees his macenas showering gifts upon his admirers. The Mahabharata compares the *dharma* to the rain which makes everyone just and equal; but the most beautiful description of this kind is the hymn in honor of the Buddha in the *Saddharma Pundarika*, where he is seen as a large cloud, raining peace and blessings over the world.

---

[13]   For the motif cf. A. Schimmel, 'Der Regen als Symbol in der Religionsgeschichte', Festschrift G. Mensching, 1966

This background explains why *Sur Sārang* is so particularly strong in its blending of realism and mystical meaning. The poet sets out with describing the northern wind, when the villager begins his ploughing and the herdsman looks happily to his cattle, because

My beloved puts on the garment of the cloud today!

Then the black clouds with red lightnings (reminiscent in their bright red, of wedding dresses) bring big drops of rain; these lightnings are as beautiful as sunflowers (Sār. II 3). The dry wind disappears, the cattle quenches its thirst, the buffaloes have full udders (IV 5), and every twig opens its buds. It is touching to see, and very rare in the history of Islamic mystical poetry, that a poet tenderly mentions the poor villagers who have been waiting for the rainy season; and he prays that there may be plentiful rain so that the grain becomes cheaper, and the people happier; but he curses the greedy hoarding merchants who are unhappy when the poor are eased (IV 16). After describing this longing of men and nature, including the toads in the ponds and the gazelles and cows in the field, Shah Abdul Latif turns in an ingenious way to the Prophet to express his unshakable hope in him who will protect his poor followers during the Last Judgment:

My Prince will give me protection,
  therefore my trust is in God.
The beloved will prostrate, will lament and cry,
  therefore my trust is in God.
Muhammad, the pure and innocent, will intercede there for
his people,
  therefore my trust is in God.
When the trumpet sounds, the eyes all will be opened—
  therefore my trust is in God,
The pious will gather, and Muhammad, full of glory—
  therefore my trust is in God,
Will proceed for every soul to the door of the Benefactor—
  therefore my trust is in God,
And the Lord will honor him and forgive us all our sins—
  therefore my trust is in God.

The following chapters continue in this style, and offer the reader a lovely picture of the happiness during the rainy season, but also of the lonely women who long for their beloved, a topic typical of the traditional Indian rain songs in the *barāmāsa* poems, which describe the various aspects of the seasons as experienced by a loving female. The poor women feel cold without quilts, for the northern wind blows through the holes of their thatched huts, and they wait for the husband to cover them. *Sur Sārang* culminates in the passage where the poet describes the cloud of mercy in its way through the world (V 12); beginning from the desert area in Eastern Sind, the Thar Parkar, he sees it floating from Africa to China in a beautiful description of the lightnings that begin to flash as signs of Divine mercy:

> *Some get up and go to Istanbul, some turn to the Maghrib,*
> *some glitter over China, some descend on Samarqand,*
> *some roar over Rum, some in Kabul, some in Qandahar,*
> *some over Delhi, some in the Deccan, some make noise over Girnar,*
> *some tremble from Jaisalmer, and give rain to Bikaner ...*

Thus he encircles the countries, coming closer and closer to his home region until he breaks out in the prayer:

> *My Lord, be kind over dear Sind,*
> *Friend! Sweet darling! You may make the whole world happy!*

Just as the clouds bring mercy and happiness over all those countries which they touch thus the Prophet's word, too, quickens the dead hearts of men and gives them a foretaste of paradisical bliss. The tendency to describe a saint's or the Prophet's mercy in geographical terms is found here for the first time in a longer description; it became later common in the works on Sindhi folk poets who, surpassing Shah Latif in the clever, though not always poetical, use of alliterations, sometimes produced strange effects, and did not hesitate to include even England in the realm of divine mercy. [14]

Sur Sārang belongs to the most beautiful expressions of popular Islamic mysticism; it speaks out a feeling which underlies also the title of Mirza Ghalib's *mathnawī* in honor of the Prophet,

---

[14]   Cf. Dr. N.A. Baloch, *muᶜjiza ain madāḥūñ*, p. 51-59, 109 for similar 'geographical' descriptions.

Abr-i goharbar, 'The Jewel-carrying Cloud,' which was written about a century later in Delhi. Shah Abdul Latif's talent to develop religious topics out of a fine realistic observation of nature is, to some extent, reminiscent of Maulana Rumi, but is a rare quality among the urban mystical poets of India.

The intercession of the Prophet as praised in *Sur Sārang* occurs time and again in the *Risālō*. However, it would be wrong to assume that only this aspect of the Prophet is described in Shah's verse. The Sindhi poet is well conversant with the high mystical tradition and therefore uses several times the favorite pun on Muhammad's honorific name, *Aḥmad,* a pun which was common among the Sufis at least from Attar's days onward: God spoke: *Anā Aḥmad bilā mīm,* 'I am Aḥmad without the letter *m,* e.g., *Aḥad,* One.' The letter *m* with the numerical value of 40, represents in later Sufi interpretation the forty stages between man and God, as described so beautifully in Attar's *Musībatnāma.* Maulana Rumi, who uses this *ḥadīth qudsī* several times, does not yet mention this interpretation. Allusions to the *Aḥmad bilā mīm* tradition are found almost everywhere in the areas under Persian cultural influence, in Turkey, Central Asia, and Muslim India. Be it the Chishti saint Gisudaraz in 14th century Deccan, or the Uzbek ruler Shaibani in the early 16th century, or Mirza Ghalib in 19th century Delhi[15]—all of them play with this ingenious *ḥadīth* which, however, was never used in the Naqshbandi tradition. The folk poets of Sind and the Panjab were particularly fond of the tradition. Shah mentions the full *ḥadīth* in *Sōraṭhi II 4.* Combinations of *alif,* the Divine letter, and *mīm,* the Prophet's letter, were common from early times, and Shah Latif is no exception to this rule.

> *We hope in the* alif *(e.g., Allah), and have obeyed Muham-*
> *mad (Pūr. II wā 'ī),*

or:

> *Todi has more honor than others:*
> *Close to the* alif, *she has blended her spirit with the* mīm ...
> (Sohṇ. III 9).

As much as Shah Abdul Latif dwells upon the person of the Prophet in its main aspects, I wonder if one can interpret, as M.U. Daudpota does, the verse:

---

[15]   Bullhē Shah, too, uses the *ḥadīth qudsī,* see his *Kulliyāt* Nr. 9, 53, 75. Trumpp translates the quotation in Sor. IV 2 as 'Aḥmad *is* without mim'.

Do not call him lover, nor call him beloved! (Kal. I 19). [16]
as pertaining to the Prophet; the learned scholar thinks, as
many interpreters may have thought as well, that the *ḥaqīqa
muḥammadiyya*, the archetype of Muhammad, serves as a kind of
mediator between the Divine and the human sphere. Dard, too
spoke of the role of Muhammad as 'dawn' which informs the
dark human world of the eternal Sun of God, and Shah's younger
contemporary, Abdur Rahim Girhori, like Dard a Naqshbandi
mystic, offers a similar interpretation, following apparently the
statements of his master Muhammad Zaman Lanwari. In Shah
Abdul Latif's case, however, the reference seems to apply to
God, who is everything and yet cannot be called by any name.

In various places other Quranic allusions to the Prophet or
traditions about him are found: twice the poet quotes from *Sūrat
an-Najm*—the account of the Prophet's vision 'two bows lengths
or closer' (Sura 53/9) during which he remained perfectly collected so that 'his eye did not rove' becomes the model for the
vision of the true lovers of God, represented by the Yogis in
Shah's text (Rām. V 1); in *Bilāwal*, where the hero is identified
with the Prophet, it is mentioned again that 'this place (e.g., that
of perfect vision) was given to him' (Bil. II 11). The most perfected lovers can say, as did the Prophet: 'My eyes are asleep, but
my heart is awake;' their very sleep is worship (Asā IV 46), for
they are never separated from God.

Besides the Prophet, his son-in-law, the caliph Ali ibn Abi
Talib, called Haidar, the lion, is praised in several passages, and
his help is implored against the *nafs*, as he is sometimes depicted
in popular painting as lion who kills the dragon 'lower soul,' (Bil.
III 1, 4). And Shah Latif's love of the Prophet's family is manifest in *Sūr Kēdāro*, the threnody for the martyrs of Kerbela, and
probably the first *marthiya* in Sindhi. The poets who wrote in
Persian, and often came to India from the Shia Safawid Empire
during the 16th and 17th centuries, composed many dirges about
Husain's martyrdom in Kerbela, and the genre was popular in the
Shia kingdoms of the Deccan, where the king Muhammad-Quli
Qutbshah of Golᶜonda (d. 1620) is credited with the composition of the first *marthiya* in Urdu. The number of these tearful
poems grew steadily, and some of the early ones touch the reader

---

[16]   U.M. Daudpota, *Kalām-i Girhōrī*, p. 46 footnote.

still today by their heartfelt simplicity. Shah Abdul Latif's contemporary in Delhi, and later in Oudh, the great satirist Sauda (d. 1781) gave the Urdu *marthiya* its classical form by introducing the six-lined stanza, *musaddas*, which became the vehicle in which the great poets of Lucknow during the 19th century sang their threnodies in ever more detailed descriptions of the sufferings the pious family of the prophet had to undergo in the heat of Kerbela, thus consoling the Indian Muslims who were smarting under different afflictions, brought upon them by the rule of the infidels.

In Sind, some Shia writers, like Ma'il, composed Persian *marthiyas*, but it seems that Shah Abdul Latif is the first to use his mother tongue for this purpose. His *Sur Kēdāro* uses the old melody of dirge and tells in heartrending short cries the tragic fate of the beloved grandson of the Prophet about whom all creation wept. But Husain is not only the martyr of Kerbela; he becomes a model for all the martyrs of love:

> *This is no war*
> *but the manifestation of love* (II 7)

and the fact that the melody *Ḥusainī* had been used for a description of Sassui's fate, connects the loving women with the lovers who perished in Kerbela partly from their wounds, partly from thirst. To her applies the rule that those 'killed in the way of God' need neither a bath, nor a shroud:

> *Those who have been killed by* [*the friend's*] *tresses*
>   *do not need a shroud;*
> *having drunk the* [*goblet of*] *martyrdom,*
>   *they have become dear* (= *pure*)
>   *and accepted* (Abrī VI 6).

Both died on the narrow path that leads toward the Beloved, and thus fulfilled their pre-eternal promise to be faithful to the creator.

We may sum up the Islamic contents of the *Risālō*, which, it seems to me, are undeniably strong, by saying that the God of the *Risālō* is a living and loving God; not a philosophical or mystical principle, but rather the Creator, the Merciful and Majestic, the First and the Last, and always the Lord as revealed through the Quran.

CHAPTER EIGHT

TO SUM UP

Shortly before sunset, the red sandstone buildings of Mughal Delhi seem to glow for a moment in an interior fire, as though they were made of purple and crimson flames.

At the same time, the villages in Sind are covered with a veil of golden dust; the walls, built of unbaked clay, look like bronze, and the blue and white tiles which cover a lonely saint's tomb match the purity of the blue sky.

Both Mir Dard and Shah Abdul Latif are poets of the twilight of Muslim India. Their approach to the experience of mystical love and gnosis is as different as are the sunsets in their native provinces, and still, they very much belong to the same spiritual country.

Dard's mystical writings are filled with fragrant roses, whose petals fall on the dust like drops of blood; the light of the late afternoon of Indian Islam is reflected in his verse in hundreds of small mirrors as they decorate Mughal palaces, and in the brilliant white marble of imperial pavillions—just as the Rumi painters reflected the colorful Chinese pictures on their immaculately polished wall. The refined culture of Mughal India sets the stage for Dard's imagery, his music, and his almost incredible skill in handling both the Persian and the Urdu languages.

Shah Abdul Latif does not mention roses and nightingales in his verse. He sings of the plight of the poor villager, describes the grazing camels and the soft-eyed buffalo calves, gracious rain and scalding desert wind; the large, simple assembly halls in the male quarters and the lowly thatched huts at the river side, are his world; and his music, though indebted to the classical Indian tradition, utilizes the folk songs of his home province until even the cries of the desperate lovers turn into love's own melody.

Both mystics have experienced the same truth, e.g., that man's true journey is not fulfilled by walking on the outward narrow path, *ṭarīqa*, as it branches off from the highroad called *sharī'a*, 'divine law,' but by the pilgrimage into one's own heart. Dard may call this journey with the technical term *safar dar waṭan*, and may describe in highly sophisticated language his attempts to reach deeper and deeper levels of consciousness until he, united with the 'Muhammadan Spirit,' knows for sure that God is dwelling in his own heart, and that he is surrounded by the Divine Light without being dissolved in it. Shah Latif exteriorizes this journey in the stories of his heroines: his are the very realistic descriptions of the sufferings man has to undergo once he enters the forest of his own self, a forest filled with dangerous beasts, which has to be burned in the fire of asceticism until nothing is left but the barren desert. But behind the desert and the steep mountains there is the Palace of the Beloved, behind the confusing multitude lies Unity: Dard, too, saw the Divine Essence beyond the shifting sand dunes of creation.

Mir Dard is a particularly interesting case in mystical psychology since he gives a detailed description of his inner development. We can follow him almost step by step on his way through the 'intoxication' of early days and the identification with the spirits of various prophets until he becomes the true representative of Muhammad the Prophet on earth, called by God, like his contemporary Shah Waliullah, to reform the rotten Muslim society, and especially the decadent mystics who had sullied the pristine purity of Muhammad's message by their pseudo-philosophical teaching and a life style which contradicted the Quranic injunctions and the Prophet's *sunna*. Mystical autobiographies of this extent are rare in Islam. To gain a picture of a saint's development we have to rely in the early period upon the scattered sayings of the Sufis as they were collected in more or less correct form by their followers; the later biographies of the saints as composed by many a pious soul approach the problems only from the outside and tend to add much unhistorical material in order to wrap the venerated master's personality in a gown richly embroidered with legends and miracles. In other cases, such as Qushairi's and Ruzbihan Baqli's, we have records only of some extraordinary events in their mystical lives, or, as in Najmuddin Kubra's work, revealing flash lights of his visions. Sha'rani, the great Egyptian mystic (d. 1565) may be singled out as the author of a rather complete mystical autobiography if we do not prefer to go back to Ibn Arabi's numerous remarks about his experiences, and the way in which he was invested with supernatural powers.

The most interesting part in Dard's spiritual autobiography is, however, not so much the emphasis he lays upon the mystical graces by which God distinguished him before everyone else (similar expressions can easily be found in Shah Waliullah's work); it is his close relation and final identification with his father. He experienced the truth of the saying 'The *murīd* is the son of the *shaikh*' in a twofold way, being both son *and* disciple. It would be worth while to study the father-son relation in the history of Sufism, as it would be rewarding to find out how many Sufis entered the Path under the influence of their pious mothers. While in the early Chishti tradition in India the relations between the rigidly ascetic fathers and their children were apparently not very close, in later Sufism, the son often followed his father on the mystical path and continued the tradition. This happened, of course, when the leadership of an order became hereditary, although in these cases the original strength of the mystical experience is usually lost in the sequence of a few generations, as can be witnessed in many 'saintly' families. Still, the *baraka*, the blessing power, of the founder saint is venerated by the masses even in a late descendant.

A complete identification of father and son, however, is utterly rare, at least in the light of the hitherto discovered sources. The only case that comes to mind from classical Sufism is that of Jalaluddin Rumi and his son, Sultan Walad. As for Jalaluddin's relation with his own father, the mystical theologian Baha 'uddin Walad, it has not yet been studied in detail; it seems, however, that only after his aged father's death, his theology began to mean something to young Jalaluddin. Still, the dark fire of Baha 'uddin's strange mystical writings has probably helped in shaping Jalaluddin's imagery, which is certainly much weirder than the usual Persian mystical poetry with its smooth surface. Jalaluddin's son, Sultan Walad, was educated as his father's faithful follower, contrary to his 'rebellious' younger brother Ala 'uddin. He had to bring back his father's lost friend Shamsuddin Tabrizi from Syria, he had to marry the daughter of his father's second friend, Salahuddin Zarkub, and eventually handed over the leadership of the order to his father's third friend, Husamuddin Chelebi. Sultan Walad's *Waladnāme* offers Maulana Jalaluddin's biography and his central teachings in a somewhat watered-down form, and the mystical power that distinguishes Jalaluddin's work is certainly lacking in this obedient son of his, who always remained in the second rank, although he once claims that only thanks to his book, the names of his father's mystical friends have become immortal.

In Dard's case, the situation is different. As much as he considered his father's book to be his only source of inspiration, besides the Quran and the Prophetic tradition, yet, the modern student of Sufism has to admit that Dard definitely improved his father's work. Even though it is not exactly a pleasure to read *'Ilm ul-kitāb*, it is certainly more concise and realistic than the diffuse *Nāla-yi 'Andalīb*.

Dard's prose and poetry (even the 'inspired' poems) prove that he has been reared in a mystical tradition in which cerebral work played a considerable role. He utters harsh words against the followers of Ibn Arabi, but cannot avoid using the terminology coined by the Magister Magnus—as little as Ahmad Sirhindi could avoid it. His tendency to explain every spiritual experience, every movement of the soul, in a highly technicized language is typical of a person who grew up in the North Indian urban mystical tradition and tried to intellectually control his inner life as a follower of the Naqshbandi school. The tension between his goal to be nothing but a 'sincere Muhammadan' and his attempt to describe mystical cosmology and anthropology in longwinded sentences is a great as the discrepancy between his certitude to be the elect representative of the Prophet and his constant search for self-identification. In this latter quest he is a perfect example of 18th century high-cultured Indian Muslims: confronted with new developments on the political and social level, they had to learn the bitter truth that they were no longer the rulers of a vast and glorious empire, but rather had to fight against heavy odds and to lead unsuccessful wars against interior and exterior enemies under whose blows the glory of Mughal India was crushed. This shock led those of them who had ears to hear and eyes to see to question their own position. When Shah Waliullah is rightly regarded as the first theologian to analyze some reasons of the decline of Muslim power in 18th century India and to look for at least some remedy for the wounds of the society, then Mir Dard seems to be the first to express in clear statements the problem of self-identification which was to trouble the Muslims (not only of India) for the next two centuries.

Shah Abdul Latif apparently had no problems of this kind. He stands before us as the representative of that type of the rural mystical tradition in which his contemporaries in the Panjab and, to a certain extent, in the Pashto speaking areas were rooted; he can be compared also, for this reason, with the best representatives of Turkish mystical folk poetry. Living out of a deep trust in God, whose wisdom is visible even in the most terrible events, he transforms the simple heroines of Sindhi oral tradition into radiant symbols of suffering and love. Like Dard, he knows and acknowledges the central place of the Prophet Muhammad in the system of Islamic mysticism; but he sings his praise and expresses the hope for his help without entering into complicated speculations about his identification with spiritual realities, or about the archetypical Muhammad. Similar to Dard he, too, complains of the lack of true lovers; but he included in his complaint also his Hindu neighbors who had lost their former spiritual qualities as much as the Muslims had forgotten the source of their strength. Here, Shah Latif is more 'Indian' than Mir Dard who sometimes seems to dwell in a closed shell outside the stream of life, as much as his activities as an instructor of poets and mystics connected him with 'the world'. Shah Abdul Latif, as did his Panjabi contemporaries and his successors in Sind, accepted the Hindus who were striving on the way to perfection as true pilgrims in the eternal Light, and his attempt to explain, in Quranic terms, the high rank of the Yogis is revealing for the historian of religion. Shah Latif's imagery and his whole way of speaking is deeply rooted in the popular tradition of women's songs. It would be tempting to compare his mystical poetry to that of Kabir, who was inspired by a similar environment: a number of images and expressions are common to both poets, and a few of their verses are almost interchangeable. Nevertheless, Kabir's *Granthivala* in the new edition and translation by Charlotte Vaudeville is, in the long run, more 'negative' than *Shāh jō Risālō*: Kabir's imagery is much closer to the Hindu tradition, and one often feels that his final goal is complete annihilation as final salvation from all the painful experiences in this world, which he, like Shah Latif, describes so dramatically. Shah's mysticism of suffering contains, in itself, a more positive attitude: he feels secure in the divine promise of help and forgiveness even in moments of deepest despair; he enjoys suffering not because it leads to absolute annihilation but because he feels the hand of the Divine Beloved, the King and Physician, in every stroke. His imagery, and his way of describing the path of the lover is often reminiscent of Christian pietist hymns in the same 18th century. One would almost be tempted to say that Tersteegen is more his spiritual brother than Kabir. His 'heavenly Jerusalem' is the palace of Punhun in Kech, where no duality causes any more pain and suffering, and in this final port, the soul that has crossed the waves of the world under the guidance of the Pir or the Prophet is united with the center of divine life and experiences the positive aspect of *fanā*, 'annihilation,' e.g., *baqā*, remaining in God. In order to go back behind the duality caused by the Divine address to men in the covenant of *Alast*, one has to believe in the reality of this covenant.

Dard's work is an explanation of what he calls *tauhīd-i muhammadī*, the true profession of faith according to the Prophet's teaching, and as explained in the mystical tradition: God is the only Reality, He remains Lord, and man, real only in so far as the divine light illuminates him, remains His slave. Servantship is the highest goal man can aspire to reach so that he may become similar to 'God's slave' par excellence, the Prophet. This is what the mystic of Delhi repeats in unending images, in opalizing verses and ever changing reflections throughout his work. Shah Abdul Latif, too, leads his listener to the One God, and teaches the soul to become a humble slave at the threshold of the eternal King; his work is the poetical description of the way the women-soul wanders from the position of *nafs ammāra*, the lower instincts, to the state of *nafs mutma'inna*, the soul at peace. His *Surs* are connected with each other by many internal cross-relations so as to form, carefully read, a complete whole, as different as the topics of his poems look at first sight.

Both mystical writers come from Sayyid families; hence, they are particularly fond of their ancestors, the Prophet and the caliph Ali. In Mir Dard's case, his strong love of the Prophet's family is part of his theology, and his attitude may have been acceptable to his Shia compatriots who otherwise disliked the anti-Shia of the *Naqshbandiyya mujaddidiya*. In Shah Latif's case, we find even a *marthiya* on the martyrs of Kerbela, and he is related to have called himself 'something between Sunni and Shii Islam;' that means he continued in the tradition of the *tash-*

ayyu ḥasan, the loving attitude towards Muhammad's family. In this respect, Mir Dard and Shah Abdul Latif are very similar and seem to represent a tendency that can still be found among the Sufi families of the Subcontinent, as it existed also in early centuries in Iran.

Mir Dard and Shah Abdul Latif constitute two complementary aspects of Islamic mysticism and mystical poetry, in general and on the Indian scene particularly. One is the urban, sophisticated, and highly intelligent trend as it had developed in the areas under Persian cultural influence, and which is still enjoyed by every lover of refined poetry, or admired by the expert in mystical theology. The other one is the rural, simple and unassuming Sufism which uses the whole repertoire of inherited forms with great ease without burdening the images with too many theoretical interpretations. It is the kind of Sufism the masses enjoyed, for it offered them some consolation in their miserable lives. They could sing Shah Abdul Latif's poetry when ploughing or going out for fishing, picking cotton or spinning it, and thus the central concepts of Islamic mysticism—Love of God and the Prophet, and trust in the eternal divine wisdom—became part and parcel of their daily lives.

Yet, in spite of the different ways of expressing their ideals which may be called 'naive' and 'sentimental' according to Schiller's definition, our two 18th century mystics in India start from the same premises and reach the same goal: they are firm believers in God's unity and in the greatness of the Prophet. They use almost the same favorite Quranic verses and Prophetic traditions to explain their ideals: they know 'Whithersoever ye turn there is the Face of God' (Sura 2/109), and they love the tradition 'Who knows himself knows his Lord.' When the difficult journey through the forests and deserts of the Self is finished and the multi-colored forms of the created world are recognized as a mere reflection of the uncreated Light they see that the Beloved is both transcedent and immanent, both the Beyond the Beyond and the *dulcis hospes animae*. And they understand that Divine Beauty and Majesty, as revealed in human joy and suffering are only two aspects of the one Divine Perfection—may this last perfection be called Light, or Love.

APPENDIX

KHWAJA MIR DARD

Sind dies Gedichte, sind's nicht Klagen,
So sehr, wie sie das Herz zerreissen?

Von Kopf bis Fuss sind, kerzengleich, wir Zunge —
Doch wo wär' hier es möglich uns, zu reden?

Wenn immer meinen Schmerz
           ich jemand sagen wollte,
Fing er zu sprechen an
               von seinem eignen Gram.

Warum soll ich denn erzählen, wie schwer meine Lage sei?
Wenn ich die Geschichte anfing, kam dem Hörer Schlaf herbei!

Du schufst den Menschen für den Schmerz der Liebe —
Für den Gehorsam hast du deine Engel!

Was du im Dasein siehst, Dard, sich hier zeigend,
Als dem Befehl des Höchsten stets sich beugend:
Des Himmels Rücken krumm vom Niederwerfen,
Die Sonne senkt ihr Haupt, vor Ihm sich neigend.

Als ich beschaut die Welt des Ich und Wir,
Ward ich dem Wind gleich in der Wüste hier.
Wohin das Herz sein Ohr erkennend legt:
Wie eine Pauke war's voll Lärmen mir.

Immer trägt das schwarze Glück rauhes nachtfarb'nes Gewand,
Hat es eine Kerze auch, ist sie stumm und ausgebrannt.
Seufzet nur und klaget laut, trinket eurer Leber Blut:
Hat man Jugend doch die Zeit für Musik und Trunk genannt!
Wenn du Gutes für dich wünschst, gib des Irrsinns Pfad nicht auf —
Wir betrachteten die Welt: Räuber ist nur der Verstand.

Die Freiheit der Erkenntnis löst — du weisst —
Dir jede Knoten-Schwierigkeit im Geist.
Des Lebens Band, warum ist's so verschlungen?
Auch dies ein Knoten, der wohl einstmals reisst!

Für die Entwordnen ist entehrend   das Wort schon: 'Sein'!
Der Grabstein selbst — auf meiner Brust ist's   ein schwerer Stein!
Vom Denken an die beiden Welten   sei unbeschwert:
Den Rost nur scheu auf deinem Herzen,   dem Spiegel rein.
Es ist nicht nur der eine Spiegel   erstaunt, verwirrt:
Verwirrt wird jeder, der hier aufschlägt   die Augen sein.

Von diesem üblen Sein, was wünschten,   was hofften wir?
Ach Offenbarungs-Rausch, betörend   mit List uns fein ...!
Den Frieden wählte ich mit allen   in dieser Welt;
Doch Tag und Nacht bin ich im Streite   mit mir allein.

Wer 'Welt' begehrt — wann könnt' er ruhig weilen?
In wessen Herz Begierde brennt, so weilen?
Beruhigung schenkt dir die Gottes-Schau:
Siehst du die Schöpfung nicht mehr, wirst du weilen.

Kein Gotteshaus ist's und kein Götzentempel —
Wer legt sein Herz in dieses wüste Haus?
Im Nichtseins-Spiegel offenbart das Sein sich:
Im Tropfen schon wogt dieses Meer voll Braus.

Im Herzen wohnst du, doch den Augen
    war nicht vergönnt die Sicht:
Vom Hause komm bis an die Pforte —
    so weit ist es doch nicht!
Verbrennen sollten beide Welten mit einer Flamme mir:
Solche kalte Seufzer, ach, erwartet
    man in der Liebe nicht.

Als ich zur Nacht von Angesicht zu Angesicht ihn traf:
Wie einer Kerze Zunge schwand in Glut mir Wort und Wunsch.

Wohin du kommst: dein Ziel liegt weiter vorne —
Nie kehrt man um, ganz wie im Schach der Bauer.

Sei auf das Elixier so stolz nicht, o Betörter!
Besser als Alchemie ist es, ein Herz zu schmelzen!

Hartherzig wird, wer kräftig   und mächtig ward:
Steinherzig wird der Tropfen,   der Perle ward.

Am höchsten Herrschaftsplatz sitzt   ein jeder, Dard,
Der seinen Thron, wie Salomo,   dem Winde gab.

O Trennung! Es gibt keine Nacht, der nicht ein Morgen graut.
Ach, Morgen wurde es, und doch warst du noch nicht erschaut.

Komm, dass in meinem Herz dein Bild sich niederlasse!
Geh nicht nach China, denn dort malt man's nur auf Seide.

Wer dem Frühwind gleich in deine Strasse
Einmal kam, kehrt nie von dort zurück.

Wir wünschen nicht als Engel den Himmel zu erreichen!
Des Herzens Wunsch ist dieser: nur deinen Fuss erreichen.

Wir wollten gern vor deinem Haus verweilen,
Das Herz, der Fuss-Spur gleich, von dort nicht heben;

Doch wie die Fuss-Spur in der Wasserfläche,
So flüchtig ist, so nichtig unser Leben!

Gleich einer Fuss-Spur trampeln mich die Leute in den Gassen:
O mein vergangnes Leben du — wo hast du mich gelassen?

Wie auf dem Wasser eine Spur,
So unbeständig sind auch wir;
Für andre Augenschminke, und
Für unser Herz nur Staub sind wir.
Wir sind im Feuer flammengleich,
Vom Kopf bis Fuss sind Frühling wir.
Einsichtgen Auges blickt hierher:
Des Grabsteins Inschriftbild sind wir.
Wohin wir gehn, wir kehren um —
Das Echo eines Bergs sind wir.
Sei es Madschnun, sei es Farhad:
Der Freund der Liebenden sind wir.
Ach, hindre uns am Kommen nicht:
Darin sind ohne Willen wir.

> Zwar gibt es viele Liebende,
> Doch ein paar Freunde sind wir hier:
> Madschnun, Farhad, Wamiq und Dard —
> Das sind wir endlich, alle vier!

Ich war wie eine Fuss-Spur im Weg des Freundes — ach:
Vom Tritt, vom Schritt der Füsse der andern ausgewischt ...

Meine Trübe ist der Aufglanz -
> Punkt des Lichterstrahls der Reinheit —
Wie sehr ich auch Eisen sein mag —
> Stoff doch für den Spiegel bin ich.
Ist der Zustand beider Welten
> für mein Herz auch offenkundig —
Habe ich bis jetzt noch immer
> nicht verstanden: Was, ach, bin ich?
Ton und Stimme lässt die Kette
> im Gefängnis niemals hören,
Und so sehr ich in der Welt bin:
> von der Welt geschieden bin ich.
Bin der Karawanenführer
> auf dem Pfad der Alten gleichsam:
Eine Fuss-Spur, die den Menschen
> einen Weg zeigt, Dard — das bin ich.

Ob ich eine feuchte Wimper,
> abgeschnittner Rebstock bin —
Stets bin ich ein solches Etwas,
> dass ich Ziel des Unglücks bin.

Jeden Abend gleich dem Abend
        bin ich finsteren Geschicks,
Jeden Morgen gleich dem Morgen
        aufgerissnen Hemds ich bin.
Wohl hat sich der Duft der Rose
        meinem Wesen ganz vermählt —
Ach, dass die verwehte Welle
        auch des Morgenwinds ich bin!

Ganz sprachlos ist hier mit zehn Zungen die Lilie:
Denn in diesem Hage, wer könnte wohl sprechen?
O Schenke, erkenn diese Zeit als Geschenk doch:
Denn später bin ich nicht, nicht du, noch der Garten!
So habe mein eigenes Selbst ich verlassen:
Nicht träum ich von Reisen, nicht denk ich der Heimat!

Der Wasserquell ist nicht geringer als die Sonne,
O Flammen-Antlitz, wenn du dich im Wasser spiegelst.

Wie am Morgen ihren Glanz verliert die Kerze,
Floh vom Rosenhag — dich sehend! — Duft und Farbe.

Vor uns Entseelten ist beschämt jetzt
        selbst Christi Hauch:
Wann fänd' den Weg zu der gemalten Rose
        der Zephir auch?

Es nahte die Wolke, und Lenz ward im Garten —
Nun eile, du Schenke, da wir dich erwarten!

Was für Unterhaltung ging heute früh im Garten vor?
Alle Knospen waren Mund, und die Rose war ganz Ohr.

Nicht versteh ich das Geheimnis
        in des Lebens Glück und Sorgen:
Wessen denkend weint der Tau wohl?
        Denn es lacht uns doch der Morgen!

Im Weltenpark gibt's Rosen: sind wir's — und Dorn: sind wir's;
Sind Freunde da, sind wir es, sind Feinde da, sind wir's.
Sieh der Erkenntnis Meer an: wir sind die Küste ihm —
An diesem Ufer sind wir's, an jenem Strand sind wir's.
An uns ist es gebunden: Bestimmung, freie Wahl.
Vorausbestimmte sind wir, und frei an Wahl sind wir's.

Durch unser Welken welkt die Rose rot,
Der Menschen Herz erfriert durch unsre Not.
Durch uns nur wird die Welt erst anerkannt —
Die Erdenwelt wird Nichts durch unsern Tod.

Von unsrer eigenen Erscheinung
          in diesem Garten wir nichts wissen:
Nicht sehen ja mit eignen Augen
          den eignen Frühling die Narzissen.

Der Seele Frohsinn hängt nicht ab von Rosen und vom Grün:
Dort wo das Herz sich aufgetan, ist Garten voller Blühn.

Im Hag des Daseins atmeten wir hier,
Die Rose 'Nichtsein' pflückten wir dann hier —
Nicht anders als des Schlummers Farbenspiel
War Wachen, Schlaf, die wir erlebten hier.

Sieh, jetzt verbrennt und wird zu Staub und Asche
Die Rose, die des Gartens Leuchte war.

Wo du auch immer seist, dort bin auch ich —
Bist du die Rose, Lieb — dein Dorn bin ich.

Augenblick um Augenblick sieh neue Wunde, neues Mal —
Blick hierher — denn mein Brustfeld ward ein Garten allzumal.

Aus meinen Augen rinnt jetzt nur das Blut des wunden Herzens —
Das, was in meinem Herzen war, wird sichtbar auf den Wangen!
Die Knospe: ein gefangnes Herz; zerrissner Brust die Rose:
Wo könnte selbst im Rosenhag zum Frieden man gelangen?

Sei's im Land, im Meer — verwirrt von den Rosenwangen allen:
Selbst im Ozean sahn wir den Tumult der Nachtigallen.

Welch Unterschied von Ros' und Wunde,
          wenn in der Rose Duft nicht ist?
Was ist des Herzens Werk und Kunde,
          in welchem Herzen du nicht bist?

In der Versammlung sind die Einzeldinge
          der Welt nur Eins,
Denn alle Blätter einer Rose bilden
          zusammen Eins.

Ein hundertfältig zerrissenes Herz, das ist die lachende Rose —
Denn Fröhlichkeit ist und Gram in der Welt verbunden im Zwillings-Lose.

Gleich sind an Form und Gestalt
          Freude und Leiden: die Rose —
Nenn sie geöffnetes Herz,
          nenn sie gebrochenes Herz.

Für eine Zeit den Hag, den Garten sehen,
Das heisst, den Frühling und den Herbst zu sehen.
Wie lange, spiegelgleich verwirrten Blickes?
Die Augen schliesse, um die Welt zu sehen.

Den Sphären gleich ist unser Herz
        beheimatet im Reisen —
Doch weiss man nicht: wohin wird es
        sein Wille endlich weisen?

Ob auch der Wein erbraust und gärt in Funken,
In Schweigen sind die Schauenden versunken.
Sie trinken immer von dem Wein der Wogen,
Dem Wirbel gleich sind sie ganz meeres-trunken.

Wenn wir dich hier nicht Aufglanz-schenkend sehen,
Ist's gleich, die Welt zu sehn und nicht zu sehen.
Gleich einer Knospe ist mein Herz, gefangen,
Die niemand je geöffnet noch gesehen.
Heimsuchung, Plagen, Quälerei und Tadel:
Was hab in deiner Liebe ich gesehen!
Wir selbst sind Schleier vor des Freundes Antlitz —
Die Augen öffnend, Schleier wir nicht sehen!

Ein Leben lang hört ich von ferne ihn,
Im Traume nur zog an die Brust ich ihn.
Jetzt, da als Spiegel nur ich vor ihn trat,
Sah er sich selbst, nicht ich erschaute ihn.

Es ziemt sich, dass wir Aug und Ohr vor allem schliessen:
Du hast uns ganz zum Ohr, zum Auge ganz gemacht.

Die Formwelt ist kein Schleier dem Licht des innern Sinns,
Und wenn sie's ist, dann ist sie nur wie ein Lampenschirm.

Ihn — ohne den zu sehen wir nicht schlafen —,
Ihn können also wir im Traum nicht sehen ...
Wie viele Formen, in den Staub gegangen!
Schönheits-Tresore in der Erde stehen ...

Vom Strom der heissen Tränen sind alle Glieder mir
Zum Teil ganz überflutet, zum andern Teil verbrannt.

Manchmal weinen, manchmal lachen, manchmal ganz verwirrt:
Wie durch Liebe manch Gesunder doch zum Narren wird!

Wie sehr der Mensch auch Heiligkeit erstrebt:
Die Gier nur schwer er aus dem Herzen hebt.
Würd' man im Jenseits frei von Speis und Trank?
Ach, Hölle selbst das Paradies durchwebt.

Was soll man tun, ach, wohin soll man gehen?
Im Tod nur kann man diesem Gram entgehen.

Das Alter kam, die Jugend ist vergangen,
O Dard, wo ist das Leben hingegangen?

Ein andrer wird dasselbe morgen sagen —
Heut die Erzählung, wie es uns ergangen!

Sachte, wehe, Brise, über einen Freund:
Meinen Staub zu stören — bitte, lass es sein!
Seht, wie unverlässlich er, dess Herz von Stein —
In Erwartung wurden meine Augen Stein.

Genug ist, wenn auf meinem Grabe manchmal
An Kerzen-Statt ein freundlich Herz entbrennte!
Wen wundert's, wenn von meinem Seufzen, Weinen
Das Land ertränke, und der Himmel brennte?

Versprochen hat uns jemand, an unsre Brust zu kommen —
So haben gleich dem Meer wir Meerbusen rings gelegt.
Nicht Blitz sind wir noch Funken, Quecksilber nicht noch Glut:
Wir sind das Etwas, dem man stets Unrast auferlegt.
In wessen Herz sich senkte der Einsicht Form und Bild,
Der hat stets vor die Augen den Grabstein sich gelegt.

So rasch enteil ich auf dem Weg des Nichtseins:
Des Frühwinds Hand reicht nicht zu meinem Staube.

Sie sind jetzt tot, die diese Welt erhellten —
Steh auf von hier; denn alle Freunde schlafen.

Wenn wir von deiner Tür gegangen sind,
Begreife dies: dass wir gestorben sind.

Wer soll was von wem wohl wann erzählen?
Jeder wird sein Eignes doch erwählen.
So verging das eigne mir, das Leben:
Weinen, einsam sein, sich schweigend quälen.

Auch wir, wir haben Krug und Glas gesehen,
Das, was nicht ist, von Angesicht gesehen.
Wenn du die Dinge tiefer nun betrachtest:
Nur traumgleich was, was immer wir gesehen.

Ach Tor du! — wenn wir sterben, wird dies bestätigt werden:
Ein Traum war, was wir sahen, was wir gehört, ein Märchen.

Wie könnte seine Locke man beschreiben?
Sie ist so lang; das Leben ist so kurz!

Sources:
U 58, 52, 3, 87, U 63, P 79, 77, U 82, 145, 84, 144, 51, 67, 15
P 111, U 4, P 34, 13, U 65, P 5, U 95, 69, 30, 101, 42/3, 123,
49, 47, 55, 61, 73, 81, 123, 82, 45, 56, P 77, 45, U 106, P 79,
U 25, 21, 106, 126, 134, 70, 57, 97, 41, 138, 14, 142, 17, P 78,
4, P 43, U 66/7, 86, 118, 139, 137, 145, 122, 132, 47, 41,
93, 43, 140, 140, 2, 81.

SHAH ABDUL LATIF

Kalyan I 14-21

Nenne Liebender ihn nicht,
        nicht 'Geliebter' zu ihm sprich,
Nenne, Tor, ihn Schöpfer nicht,
        und Geschöpf nicht — hüte dich!
Lehre jene den Pfad, die sich von Fehlern gelöst.

Aus Einheit kam die Fülle, Einheit der Vielheit Wirren;
Die Wirklichkeit ist Eines: lass nicht die Rede irren!

Er ist ganz erhaben hoch,
        Er der tiefste Schönheitsglanz,
Er ist des Geliebten Bild,
        Er vollkommner Liebreiz ganz,
Es wird Meister, Jünger selbst,
        Er wird aller Träume Tanz,
    Und aus aller Dinge Kranz
           wird Er uns bekannt.

Er erschaut sich selber stets,
        Er ist der Geliebte wert,
Alles liebliche Geschöpf
        ist Er, und ist, der's begehrt.

Er ist dies und Er ist das,
        Er ist Gott, Er ist der Tod,
Er der Liebste, Er der Hauch,
        Feind, und Helfer in der Not.

Wo Schrei, da Gegenschrei — wer Rufes Geheimnis verstanden:
Im Hören wurden es zwei, die im Ur-Ew'gen verbunden.

Ist ein Schloß mit tausend Toren,
        Fenster jenseits aller Zahlen —
Wohin ich den Blick auch wende,
        dort seh ich den Herrn erstrahlen.

Tausende sind Deine Körper, millionenfach jeder Moment,
Leben mit sämtlichen Leben, niemals fern und getrennt.
      Wer ist es, Freund, der sie nennt,
          all Deine Zeichen erkennt?

Yaman Kalyan I 1-3

Du der Liebste, du der Arzt, du des Schmerzes Arzenei!
Hoher, siehe! Mir im Leibe Leiden vielerlei.
Herr, o gib Heilung, Meister! dem Kranken!

Du der Liebste, du der Arzt, du des Schmerzes Medizin;
Arzenei mir für das Herz: süss dein Wort erschien.
Röchelnd ruf ich; denn von anderen
    hilft kein Heilkraut hier.

Du der Liebste, du der Arzt, du zerbrochner Herzen Heil;
Du nur gibst, und du nur nimmst,
    du, Herr führst zum besten Teil!

V 1-21, 24, 31, 32

Der Sufi, fliehend die Menge, gelangt ohne Fährde ans Ziel,
Vergessend nicht Spielender Spiel,
  Des Trauten vertrauter Gespiel,
    durch Trunkenheit näher zu ihm.

Er wallt in allen Dingen, wie in den Adern Blut,
Wer nie ein Wörtchen redet, der im Gedenken ruht;
  Was öffentlich er tut,
    das wird ihm Sünde sein.

Er leidet durch das Geben: Nicht-Geben gilt ihm mehr,
  Ein Sufi wird nur der,
    wer nichts mehr mit sich trägt.

Der Sufi ohne Riten — und keiner kennt ihn nur;
Er kämpft den Kampf der Seele; sein Fuss lässt keine Spur;
  Wer ihm auch Feindschaft schwur,
    dem wird zum Helfer er.

Der Sufi wusch das Blatt des Daseins ab, ist rein:
So darf er lebend schau'n des Liebsten Schönheitsschein.

Du möchtest Sufi werden — den Sufis ist's nicht nütze:
  Du wirst's nicht durch die Mütze:
    nur vorwärts, in die Glut!

Wer auf das Haupt den Hut setzt, ein echter Sufi zu sein,
Er nehme die Schale Giftes, er trink sie pokalvoll wie Wein —
  Der Platz wird des Mannes sein,
    der mystischen Zustandes kund.

Im Leibe, für den Mächt'gen schlag auf ein heimlich Zelt;
Lass deutlich deine Zunge Ihn künden aller Welt!

Den Grössten Namen suche, den der Koran enthält —
  An andern Pforten fällt
                dir nie die Perle zu!

Von Ichsucht zerrissen, dreht, krümmt sich die Welt —
Sie selbst hat kein Wissen —
                der Zauberer spannte den Zauber aus.

Es sucht das Viel der Schönheit Quell,
                        das hat uns Rumi anvertraut:
    Wer jenen Ort geschaut,
                der spricht nun nimmermehr.

Es sucht das Viel der Schönheit Quell,
                        so haben wir Rumi vernommen.
    Woher ist der Mensch gekommen?
                Du kannst dieses Trugbild nicht sehn!

Es sucht das Viel der Schönheit Quell,
                        so sagte Rumi wieder —
    Wer hebt die Augenlider,
                dem wird die Schau zuteil.

Es sucht das All der Schönheit Quell,
                        so äussert Rumi sich.
    Zuerst verliere dich —
                dann wirst den Freund du finden.

Es sucht das Viel der Schönheit Quell,
                        ist Rumis Ruhewort.
    Wer schaut der Wahrheit Ort,
                der redet nimmermehr.

Es sucht das Viel der Schönheit Quell
                        — es ist dies Rumis Festgemach,
    Und wer der Trennung Tür zerbrach,
                dem wird die Schau zuteil.

Verbrecher nach aussen hin,
                in Einsamkeit sind sie entworden,
    Ihr Innres durchbohrte der Pfeil,
                sie fassen der Lehre Sinn,
    Sie drehen im Herzen drin
                das himmlische Zeichen stets.

Für die ist die Zeit des Schmerzes,
                die lesen die Leid-Lektion,
    Die still die Schreibtafel halten
                und schweigende Meditation.
    Wer jenes Blatt liest — als Lohn
                wird er drauf den Liebsten erschaun.

Vergessen die Lektion! Nicht weiss ich mehr den Beginn!
Dies Blatt ward bis heute schon,
          weh, niemals gelesen!

Ich habe es wohl gelesen, das Blatt der Vereinigung.
Nur Du bist darin, kein Wesen,
          als Du nur für einen Nu.

Die jener Zeile nicht denken, die mit dem A beginnt,
Sie blicken auf Blätter, die lenken
          sie ruhelos ab von dem Freund.

Doch die der Zeile gedenken, die mit dem A beginnt,
'Nur Er ist in beiden Welten das Wunschziel', werden sie denken,
    In Windung den Weg zu lenken,
          dankbar dem gnädigen Gott.

Liebender ist Azazil — alle die Menschen sind Lügner:
Er liebte grenzenlos viel,
          und Freund wurde so der Verfluchte!

O Schreiber, wie du kunstvoll das L ums A gewunden,
So ist der Freund unlösbar im Herzen uns verbunden.

Warum radierst du die Schrift aus? Warum die Tinte vernichten?
    Den Blick sollst du fernehin richten,
          dort wo alle Schrift nur entstand!

VI 1

Ein Becher — zwei Personen: so ist die Liebe nicht!
Wie soll die Nähe finden, wer immer rechnend spricht?
    Von der Vereinigung Licht
        schliesst ihn das Dasein aus.

Khanbhat II 2, 5

Aufstehend, sei der Augen Haft dem Liebsten zugewandt.
O Mond, berichte jenem Freund, dass schwach ich bin, erschlafft,
Hab weder Saft noch Kraft!

Guter Mond! Grüsse
        mir den Geliebten!
Wenn du am Hofdach
        aufsteigst, sprich süsse
    Worte — die Füsse
        streichle ihm zart!

Sohni II 3-5, 7

In der furchtbaren Flut des Flusses, wo der Schrei der Schrecken schlug,
Inmitten feindlicher Mächte —
        wohin ging der tönerne Krug!
    O Sahar, Herrscher du klug —
        so hilflos ward ich auf dem Weg!

In der furchtbaren Flut des Flusses die mächtigen Krokodile,
Gewaltige Alligatoren im Strome, unzählbar viele,
Ich finde im Leib keine Kraft mehr, getrennt von dir, o Gespiele!
    Fürst Sahar — zum Reiseziele
        lass mich, o Edler, gelangen!

In der furchtbaren Flut des Meeres, wo die Strudel tosen und toben,
Ich zwischen den Bestien bebend und immer von Feinden umwoben —
Sei gütig, Geliebter! Aus Liebe zieh deine Freundin nach oben,
    Streck deine Hand von droben,
        errette vom Abgrund mich.

VI 1, 5

Die Schönheit des Liebsten bestand,
    bevor die Geschicke geschrieben,
Noch war kein 'Es werde!' und auch nicht andere Rede bekannt,
Die Engel waren noch nicht, als Sohnis Klage entbrannt,
    Als sie mit dem Hirten verband
        die Liebe — so sagte Latif.

Als Er die Seelen fragte: 'Bin ich nicht euer Herr?'
Ward mir im Herzen zum Omen urewiges Ja, das ich sagte;
Damals ergriff ich die Liebe Mehars, ich Unverzagte,
    Dass ich zu folgen ihm wagte,
        Freundinnen, das ist mein Recht.

Ma^{c}dhuri VII 18, 19, 21, 22

O Stimme in der Steppe: als ob der Kuckuck schreit,
    Ein Jammerlied und Leid —
        es ist der Liebe Ach.

O Stimme in der Steppe: als sei's des Sittichs Sagen:
    Es ist der Sehnsucht Klagen,
        es ist der Liebe Ach.

O Stimme in der Steppe, als ob die Wildgans riefe;
    Schrei aus der Wassertiefe —
        es ist der Liebe Ach.

O Stimme in der Steppe, wie einer Geige Klang:
   Das ist der Liebe Sang —
        das Volk nur hielt's für Weibes Lied.

Desi V 7

Solche Wege ging Sassui — Helden verlören ihr Leben,
Hohe Berge — der Liebe
        sind sie wie Steppenland eben.

Husaini I 8-11

Möge die Gespielin mein nicht mit mir zur Wüste wandern!
Wasser fern, der Weg so weit, Steppe stets und Staub und Stein,
   Stürbe sie in Durstes Pein,
        würde dem Liebsten sie fluchen.

Sonne sank hinter den Bäumen, Dämmerung blutig sich rötet —
   Ach, mich hat sie getötet,
        Mutter! da nun die Dunkelheit kommt.

Sonne sank hinter den Blumen, färbte die Dämmerungsschatten.
   Die mir entführten den Gatten,
        haben das Bergland durchquert.

Sonne sank hinter den Bäumen, Dämmerungsdunst sich rötet —
   Ach, mich hat sie getötet,
        Mutter! in Finsternis!

II 14, 17, 18

Heiss sei des Tages Brand, wandere, wandre nur —
Uralte Liebe band
       an die Balochen dich.

Lebenlang lodernd brenne, kein Platz ohne Brennens Leid,
In Hitze und Kälte renne,
       zum Weilen ist keine Zeit.

In Hitze und Kälte eile, zum Weilen ist keine Zeit,
Dass dich nicht das Dunkel ereile,
       und du seine Spur nicht mehr siehst.

VII 1-5, 7

Wer heischt, wird empfangen, wird schauen den Liebsten,
Wer sucht, wird gelangen zum Hofe der Wunder.

Du, der du suchst, geh voran: dies ist kein irdisches Suchen —
Ferne ist niemals der Freund von fahrender Sucher Herz.

Nur suchen will ich, nur suchen, o dass ich den Freund nie erreichte!
Dass niemals die Unrast der Seele durch Finden ein Ende nähme!

Nur suchen will ich, nicht finden, Gefährten aus früheren Tagen,
    Die Saumlast weitergetragen,
        so zogen sie ferne ins Land.

Ich suche — mög ich nie finden! Geliebter, ferne bist du!
    Nie finde mein Herz je Ruh,
        nie werde Trost meinem Leib!

Ich suche, o mög ich nie finden! Erhöre der Liebenden Meinung!
In deiner Liebe, Geliebter, liegt meines Lebens Verneinung:
    Am Jüngsten Tag erst, zur Einung
        mag ich mich voll Ruhe erheben!

VIII 8

Hätt' ich doch ahnend gefühlt, dass einst die Trennung mich träfe,
Hätt' ich die Schrift des Geschicks von urew'ger Tafel gespült,
    Hätte dann wohl nicht gefühlt
        Leiden auf endlosem Pfad.

XI 18

Dass doch in Kach niemand wüsste, ach, meine unedle Kaste,
    Dass sich nicht schämen müsste
        Punhun, der Sippe gedenkend.

XII 1, 2

Ja, hätten sie ihn erschaut, den Freund, mit den Augen, wie ich,
'Auf, such ihn!' riefen sie laut,
        ins Bergland stürzten sie sich.

Sie haben den Freund nicht erschaut,
        nicht Tadel treffe die Trauten,
Sonst weinten wie ich sie laut,
        und bissen sich reuig die Hände.

Mumal Rano IX 6, 7

Wohin kehr ich das Kamel? Rings flutet Vollmondes Licht!
In mir die Kammer von Kak, in mir sein Platz, sein Gesicht,
    Liebster, und Liebster — und nicht
        gibt's etwas andres als ihn.

Wohin kehr' ich das Kamel? Rings flutet Vollmondes Glanz,
In mir die Kammer von Kak, Frühlingshag in mir und Kranz;

Wurde der Freund alles ganz,
    bleibt nun kein anderer Ruf.

Lila Chanesar II 1

Schauend des Schmuckes Strahl strauchelt' sie, stürzte in Stolz —
Sie kamen zu ihr und riefen 'O Schande!' und kamen vielmal,
Sie brannten und sie versengten das Herz ihr mit Tadels Qual,
    Der Jugend heiteren Saal,
        die Arme vergass ihn bald.

Marui V 2-7, 9, 10

Verloren hab ich die Schönheit, bin schmutzig anzusehen —
    Wie kann ich dorthin gehen,
        wohin nie ein Unschöner kommt?

Verloren hab ich die Schönheit, der Lieblichkeit lichten Strahl —
    Im Herzen der Qualm der Qual;
        so ward mein Antlitz beschmutzt.

Verloren hab ich die Schönheit; hierher kam ich erst jetzt eben!
    Wie kann ich den Mangel beheben?
        Die Schönheit verging mir allhie.

Verloren hab ich die Schönheit — wo ging die Vollkommenheit hin?
Wie kann ich nach Hause gelangen, so elend wie ich bin?
    Wer gibt mir der Schönheit Gewinn,
        damit ich die Hirten erblicke?

Verloren hab ich die Schönheit — wie kann ich zur Heimat kommen?
    Ich, der man die Schönheit genommen —
        wie kann ich die Hirten jetzt sehn?

Verloren hab ich die Schönheit — wie kann ich die Hirten erblicken?
    Die einst der Schäfer Entzücken —
        gestaltlos grämt sie sich nun.

Verloren hab ich die Schönheit — wer sollte mich jetzt noch empfangen?
    Nicht Freunde, kein liebend Umfangen,
        wenn die Hirten die Hässliche sehn!

Verloren hab ich die Schönheit, kam gestern in diesen Palast —
    Geschenk ist und Gunst mir verhasst —
        hier ist meine Schönheit verblasst.

X 14-16

Die Muschel in Meerestiefen: der Wolke nur gilt ihr Hoffen;
Sie trinkt nicht die salzigen Tropfen — dem süssen Regen nur offen;

So hat sie die Perle getroffen,
        da Drangsal in dunkelster Tiefe sie litt.

So lernet alle, ihr Mädchen, von Muscheln, wie Tugend tut:
  Es wechsle des Meeres Flut;
        sie stehen, die Wolke erhoffend.

So lernet der Sehnsucht Sitten, ihr Mädchen, von Muscheln nur:
Die Wasser vom Himmel erbitten,
        das Nahe aber verschmähen.

Sorathi I 1, 3-5

Auf Gott nur vertrauend, so zog er durchs Land,
Mit Bändern der Barde die Fiedel umwand,
Dem Fürsten Diyach war sein Weg zugewandt,
Er fleht' zu dem Einen, er rief unverwandt:
'Huldreichster! Lass freuen
     den Fürst sich des Sangs!'

Er wandert fern der Heimat, hierher ist er gelangt;
Nicht Speise sucht der Sänger, das Leben er verlangt:
  'Der Kopf sei schnell erlangt —
     ich kann mich nicht gedulden!'

Ich wandre fern der Heimat, nun tret' ich bei dir ein;
Du thronst so hoch am Himmel, ich bin auf Erden klein.
  Wie kann ich dich erfreun?
     Der Sänger will dein Haupt.

Ich wandre fern der Heimat; dein Ruhm reicht weit, ist gross,
Was könnte klug ich wünschen? Ich bin ganz ahnungslos.
  Du schenk das edle Los
     dem, der die Gier vergass.

Sarang I 7, 8, 10, 29, 30, 33, 34, wa͞i

Auch heute weht's von Norden,
        der Kuckuck singt sein Lied,
Der Bauer spannt den Pflug an,
        der Hirte froh die Herden sieht,
  Das Kleid der Wolke zieht
     heut mein Geliebter an.

Auch heute weht's von Norden,
        so schwarz und schwer die Wolkenwand;
Es fielen grosse Tropfen,
        dass jeder Zweig in Blüte stand,

Die Wüstenwinde wichen;
          nun löscht das Vieh des Durstes Brand,
    Es grasen Kühe, fett, im Land
        und kehren heim zur Hürde.

Auch heute weht's von Norden;
          die Wolke schwarz: sein Haar,
Und rot wie er gekleidet
          der Blitze blanke Schar.
    Den Freund, der fern mir war,
        bringt so der Regen nah.

Wolke! Um Gottes willen,
          gewähre dem Dürstenden Schutz!
Mach billiger das Getreide,
          die trockenen Tümpel hilf füllen,
    Das Land lass fruchtbar schwellen,
        dass sich der Landmann freut.

Es denken des Gewölkes
          Mann, Hirsch und Ochs und Kuh,
Wildenten warten der Wolke,
          die Kröte klagt ohn' Ruh,
Die Muschel auch im Meere
          blickt harrend auf sie zu –
    Die Teiche fülle du,
        dass sich der Landmann freut.

Die Wolke, sie ordnet sich,
          die Blitze beginnen zu zucken,
Die Regenschwangere rieselt,
          verdorrtes Flussbett zu füllen.
Die Wolken ordneten sich,
          die Blitze beginnen zu zucken,
In düsterer Wetterwand,
          entzückt hat die Züngelnde mich:
    Der Gram-Staub vom Herzen wich
        beim Rauschen und Rieseln des Regens.

Mein Fürst wird Schutz mir geben,
          so trau ich fest in Gott!
Der Liebste wird sich neigen, im Jammerruf erbeben,
          – so trau ich fest in Gott –
Fürbitten wird Muhammad für seines Volkes Leben,
          – so trau ich fest in Gott –
Wenn die Posaune aufdröhnt, wird sich das Aug' erheben,
          – so trau ich fest in Gott,
Da sammeln sich die Frommen; Muhammad, ruhmumgeben,
          – so trau ich fest in Gott –

Wird sich für Seel um Seele zum höchsten Thron begeben.
— so trau ich fest in Gott —
Der Herr wird, ihn zu ehren, uns alle Schuld vergeben!
— so trau ich fest in Gott.

IV 12

Wieder kehren die Wolken,
                gnadengefüllt bis zum Rand,
Wieder beginnen die Blitze,
                ringsum aufzuckend entbrannt.
Manche steigt auf bis Istanbul,
                manche bis Afrikas Sand,
Manche erglänzt über China,
                manche erreicht Samarkand,
Manche nach Kandahar, Kabul,
                fern nach Kleinasien gewandt,
Manche erdröhnt über Delhi,
                über Südindiens Strand,
Donnernd kommt die von Jaisalmer,
                Frucht schenkend Bikaners Land.
Manche benetzt Bhuch, und manche
                hat auch Lars Hitze gebannt,
Manche, von Amarkot kommend,
                hat Grün den Feldern gesandt.
Höchster, du öffne in Gnaden
                stets über Sind deine Hand!
Freund, o du holder Geliebter!
                Lass alle Welt neuerblühn!

Asa I 1, 8, 9, 11, 12

Suchend im Grenzenlosen
                fand ich des Höchsten nicht Grenze noch Mal,
Ist doch die Schönheit des Freundes
                ferne von Höhe, von Breit oder Schmal,
        Liebende hier ohne Zahl —
                dort der Geliebte, ruhend in sich.

Nicht hat ein Ende der Mensch — hat er doch keinen Beginn:
Welche sich selber verlieren, hat der Geliebte erkannt.

Die Hoheit von sich getan, beschreitend der Sehnsucht Bahn,
        Sie kamen zu jenem Plan,
                der Ende und Grenze nicht hat.

So du dich selber noch siehst, wo wäre wahres Gebet?
All diese Formen gib auf —
                dann erst ruf aus: 'Gott ist gross!'

So du dich selber noch siehst, wo wäre wahres Sich-Neigen?
All dieses Dasein gib auf,
          dann erst ruf aus: 'Gott ist gross!'

III 8, 9

Dort wo nicht Sein ist noch Nicht-Sein
          — Gedanke von Staubgebornen:
Die Schönheit des Auserkornen
          ist ferne, so ferne vom Sehen.

Dort wo nicht Sein ist noch Nicht-Sein
          — der Staubgebornen Gedanke,
Des Freundes Reinheit, die blanke
          ist ferne, so ferne vom Sehen.

Khahori II 1-7, 11

Sie, welche erkennen
          das Dorf der Himmlischen Hügel,
Sie lassen Felder und Tennen,
          suchend Gott nahe zu sein.

Sie, welche entstammen
          dem Dorf der Himmlischen Hügel,
Sie rollen die Bücher zusammen,
          suchend Gott nahe zu sein.

Wer nach dem Staube sich sehnt
          des Dorfs der Himmlischen Hügel,
Er hat sich des Schlafes entwöhnt,
          suchend Gott nahe zu sein.

Wer einmal den Duft erfuhr
          des Dorfes der Himmlischen Hügel,
Sehnt sich nach des Ortes Spur,
          suchend Gott nahe zu sein.

Die einmal erfassen
          das Dorf der Himmlischen Hügel,
Geld and Gut sie verlassen,
          suchend Gott nahe zu sein.

Wer einmal den Duft empfand,
          des Dorfes der Himmlischen Hügel,
Er lässt das bunte Gewand,
          suchend Gott nahe zu sein.

Das Dorf der Himmlischen Hügel,
          wer einmal es nur gesichtet,

Der hat den Körper vernichtet,
      suchend Gott nahe zu sein.

Wo Vögel den Pfad nicht mehr finden,
      da blitzt ein Feuerschein auf —
Wer könnt' es wohl entzünden,
      wenn nicht der Derwische Schar?

III 15

Dunkle Nacht, strahlender Tag
      — das ist nur äusseres Licht.
   Dort, wo des Liebsten Gesicht
      gibt es nicht Farbe noch Form.

Barvo Sindhi I 18, 19

Bald verriegelt er die Pforte,
      bald tut er die Tür mir auf,
Manchmal komm ich, komm vergebens,
      dann ruft er zum hohen Orte;
Bald ersehn ich seinen Anruf,
      bald sagt er geheime Worte —
Sieh solch ein Wesen
      hat er, mein Freund!
Du ein Fürstensohn, Geliebter,
      ich in einer Dien'rin Kleid.
Ohne Ende will ich dienen,
      steh gekreuzten Arms bereit.
Hab ich Eure Tür verlassen,
      Freund, zu irgendeiner Zeit?
Wende den gütigen Blick doch,
      Liebster! nicht ab von mir!

II 4, 5

Denk ich der Tage, die mit dem Freund ich verbracht,
Klage um Klage hebe sogleich ich an.

Wie Glied um Glied aus Eisenerz
      der Schmied zur Kette fügt,
Hat der Geliebte auch mein Herz
      dem seinen unlösbar verbunden.

III 1

Liebe ist solch eine Macht,
            dass sie selbst tapfere Helden verwirrt.
Wandern sie Tag und Nacht,
          weinen sie Nacht und Nacht,
      Stets, ob man schläft, ob wacht,
            sprechen vom Liebsten sie.

BIBLIOGRAPHY

a) SOURCES IN EUROPEAN LANGUAGES

Ahmad, Aziz, Studies in the Islamic Culture in the Indian Environment, Oxford 1964.
——, An Intellectual History of Islam in India, Edinburgh 1969.
——, Sufismus und Hindumystik, in: Saeculum 15/1, 1964.
——, Political and Religious Ideas of Shah Waliullah of Delhi, The Muslim World 52/1, 1961.
——, and G. E. von Grunebaum, Muslim Self-Statement in India and Pakistan, 1857-1968, Wiesbaden 1970.
Ajwani, L. H., History of Sindhi Literature, New Delhi 1970.
Andrae, Tor, Die person Muhammads in lehre und glauben seiner gemeinde, Stockholm 1918.
Ansari, A. S. Bazmee, Dard, in: Encyclopedia of Islam 2nd ed., II 137.
——, Sayyid Muhammad Jawnpuri and his Movement, in: Islamic Studies II 1, Karachi March 1963.
Arberry, A. J., Sufism, London 1950.
Arnold, Sir Thomas, The Preaching of Islam, 1898, 3rd. ed. Lahore s.d. (ca. 1952).
——, Saints, Muhammadan, in India, EHE X 68 ff.
Attas, Syed M. M., The Mysticism of Hamza al-Fansuri, Kuala Lumpur 1970.
Baljon, J. M. S., A Mystical Interpretation of Prophetic Tales by an Indian Muslim: Shah Wali Allah's ta)wil al-aḥādith, Leiden 1973.
Baloch, N. A., Shah Abdul Latif, the Founder of a new musical tradition, Pakistan Quarterly IX 3.
Bausani, Alessandro, Storia delle letterature del Pakistan, Milan 1958.
——, Persia Religiosa, Milan 1959.
——, and A. Pagliaro, Storia della letteratura Persiana, Milan 1960.
Browne, E. G., A Literary History of Persia, 4 vols., Cambridge 1902-1921, repr. 1957.
Bürgel, J. Christoph, Lüge und Wahrheit in der arabischen Dichtung, in: Oriens XX, 1974.
Burton, Richard, Sindh and the Races That inhabit the Valley of the Indus, London 1851, repr. 1974.
Corbin, Henri, Creative Imagination in the Sufism of Ibn Arabi, Princeton 1969.
——, L'Homme de lumière dans le Soufisme iranien, Paris 1973.
Eliade, Mircea, Die Religionen und das Heilige, Salzburg 1954.
Enamul Haq, Muslim Bengali Literature, Karachi 1957.
Ethé, Hermann, König und Derwisch, Romantisch-mystisches Epos vom Scheich Hilali, Leipzig 1870.
——, Neupersische Literatur, in: Geiger-Kuhn, Grundriss der iranischen Philologie, Strassburg 1898-1904.
Ettinghausen, Richard, Paintings of the Sultans and Emperers of India, New Delhi s.d.
Fouchécour, C. -H. de, La description de la nature dans la poésie lyrique Persane du XI ième siècle, Paris 1969.
Friedmann, Yohanan, Shaykh Ahmad Sirhindi: An Outline of his Thought and a Study of his Image in the eyes of Posterity. Montreal 1971.
——, Medieval Muslim Views of Indian Religions, in: JASOS 95/2, 1975.

Friedrich und Buddrus, Schamanengeschichten aus Sibirien, translated from the Russian, 1955.

Garcin de Tassy, M., Histoire de la Littérature Hindouie et Hindoustani, 3 vols. Paris 1870-71.

Goswamy, R. N., and J. S. Grewah, The Mughals and the Yogis of Jakhbar, Simla 1967.

Gupta, H. R., Studies in Later Mughal History of the Panjab, Lahore 1944.

ter Haar, J. G. J., De visie van Shah Wali Allah al-Dihlawi op de wahdat al-wujud en de wahdat al-shuhud en een tweetal reacties hierop, Ph.D. diss. Leiden 1974.

Hart,Capt. S. V. W., A pilgrimage to Hinglaj, Proc. and Transactions of the Bombay Geograph. Soc. III, p. 77-105.

Hasrat, B. J., Dara Shikuh, Life and works, Calcutta 1953.

Heiler, Friedrich, Das Gebet, München 5 ed. 1923.

——, Erscheinungsformen und Wesen der Religion, Stuttgart 1961.

Heinrichs, Wolfhart, Arabische Dichtung und griechische Poetik, Beirut-Wiesbaden 1969.

Horten, Max, Die religiöse Gedankenwelt des Volkes in Islam, Halle 1917.

Hotchand, Tirithdas, Pakistan's Immortal Poet Shah Abdul Latif, Hyderabad/Sind 1962.

——, The Song of the Necklace, Hyderabad/Sind 1961.

——, The Song of Kinjhar Lake, Hyderabad/Sind 1963.

Hujwiri, Ali ibn ꞋUthman, The Kashf al-Mahjub', The Oldest Persian Treatise on Sufism ... transl. by R. A. Nicholson, London 1911, repr. 1955.

Husain Khan, Yusuf, L'Inde Mystique au Moyen Age, Paris 1929

——, Glimpses of Medieval Indian Culture, London 2 ed. 1959.

Irvine, William, Later Mughals, ed. Jadunath Sarkar, Calcutta 1922, 2 vols.

JaꞋfar Sharif, Islam in India, or the Qanun-i Islam. Transl. by G. A. Herklots, ed. by W. Crooke, Oxford 1921, repr. 1972.

Jotwani, Motilal, Shah Abdul Karim, New Delhi 1970.

——, Shah Abdul Latif, his Life and Work. A Study of the socio-cultural and literary situation in eighteenth century Sind (now in Pakistan), New Delhi 1975.

Khakee, Gulshan, The Dasa Avatara of the Satpanthi Ismailis and the Imam Shahis of Indo-Pakistan, Ph.D. diss. Harvard 1972.

Massignon, Louis, La Passion d'al-Husayn ibn Mansour al-Hallaj, 2 vols., Paris 1922.

——, Essai sur les origines du lexique technique de la mystique musulmane, Paris 1928.

——, et Cl. Huart, Les entretiens de Lahore, JA 209/1926.

Mayne, Peter, Saints of Sind, London 1956.

Meier, Fritz, Vom Wesen der islamischen Mystik, Basel 1943.

——, Das Problem der Natur im esoterischen Monismus des Islam, Eranos-Jahrbuch/ 214/1946.

——, Die fawā'iḥ al-ǧamāl wa fawātiḥ al-ǧalāl des Naǧmuddin al-Kubrā, Wiesbaden 1957.

Mohan Singh, An Introduction to Panjabi Literature, Amritsar 1951.

Molé, Marijan, Les mystiques musulmans, Paris 1965.

——, La Dance exstatique en Islam, in: Sources Orientales VI, 1963.

Muid Khan, The Arabian Poets of Golconda, Bombay 1963.

Mujeeb, M., The Indian Muslims, Montreal-London 1969.

Nabi, Muh. Noor, Development of Muslim Religious Thought in India from 1200 to 1450 AD, Aligarh 1962.

Nicholson, R. A., Studies in Islamic Mysticism, Cambridge 1921, repr. 1967.

Nizami Arudi, Chahār Maqāla, transl. by E. G. Browne, London 1921.

Nizami, Khaliq Ahmad, The Life and Times of Shaikh Farid Ganj-i Shakar, Aligarh 1955.
——, Some Aspects of Religion and Politics in India during the 13th century, Bombay 1961.
Nwyia, Paul, Exegèse coranique et langage mystique, Beirut 1970.
Parsram, Jethmal, Sind and its Sûfis, Madras 1924.
Qanungo, K. R., Dara Shukoh, Calcutta 1935.
Qazi, Elsa, Risalo of Abdul Latif. Selections. Hyderabad/Sind, 1965.
Padwick, Constance E., Muslim Devotions, London 1960.
Qureshi, Ishtiaq Husain, The Muslim Community of the Indo-Pak. Subcontinent, 's-Gravenhage 1962.
Rahman, Fazlur, Dream, imagination, and ⁽ ālam al-mithāl, in: E. G. von Grunebaum and R. Caillois, The Dream and Human Society, Berkeley 1966.
Ramakrishna, Lajwanti, Panjabi Sufi Poets, London-Calcutta 1938.
Raverty, H. G., Selections from the Poetry of the Afghans, London 1862.
Reinert, Benedikt, Die Lehre vom tawakkul in the älteren Sufik, Berlin 1968.
Ritter, Hellmut, Das Meer der Seele, Leiden 1955.
——, Hat die religiöse Orthodoxie einen Einfluss auf die Dekadenz des Islam ausgeübt? in: Klassizismus und Kulturverfall, Frankfurt, 1958.
——, Muslim Mystics Strife with God, in: Oriens 5/1952.
Russell, Ralph, and Khurshidul Islam, Three Mughal Poets, Cambridge, Mass. 1968.
Rypka, Jan, History of Iranian Literature, Dordrecht 1968.
Sadarangani, H. J., Persian Poets of Sind, Karachi 1956.
Sadiq, M., A History of Urdu Poetry, London 1964.
Saksena, Ram Babu, A History of Urdu Literature, Allahabad 1927.
Sarkar, J., The Fall of the Muslim Empire, Calcutta 2 ed. 1950.
Schimmel, Annemarie, Mystical Dimensions of Islam, Chapel Hill 1975.
——, Islamic Literatures of India; Sindhi Literature; Classical Urdu Literature, in: J. Gonda, History of Indian Literature, Wiesbaden 1973, 1974, 1975.
——, Gabriel's Wing. A Study into the religious ideas of Sir Muhammad Iqbal, Leiden 1963.
——, al-Halladsch, Märtyrer der Gottesliebe, Cologne 1969.
——, The Martyr-Mystic Hallaj in Sindhi Folk-Poetry, in: Numen 9/3, 1962.
——, The Influence of Sufism on Indo-Muslim Poetry, in: Anagogic Qualities of Literature, ed. J. P. Strelka, Univ. of Pennsylvania 1971.
——, Khwaja Mir Dard, in: German Scholars on India, New Delhi 1973.
——, Mir Dards Gedanken über das Verhältnis von Mystik und Wort, in: Festgabe deutscher Iranisten zur 2500-Jahr-Feier Irans, herausgeg. von W. Eilers, Stuttgart 1971.
——, A 'sincere Muhammadan's' Way to Salvation, in: Memorial Volume S. F. G. Brandon, ed. E. J. Sharpe and John R. Hinnels, Manchester 1973.
——, Ernst Trumpp. Karachi 1961.
——, Šāh ⁽ Abdul Laṭīf's Beschreibung des wahren Sufi, in: Festschrift für Fritz Meier, herausgeg. von R. Gramlich, Wiesbaden 1974.
——, The Veneration of the Prophet Muhammad, as Reflected in Sindhi Poetry, in: The Saviour God, ed. S. F. G. Brandon, Manchester 1963.
——, Shah ⁽ Ināyat of Jhok, A Sindhi Mystic of the early 18th century, in: Liber Amicorum in Honour of C. J. Bleeker, Leiden 1969.
——, Nur ein störrisches Pferd ..., in: Ex Orbe Religionum, Festschrift für Geo Widengren, Leiden 1972.
——, Der Regen als Symbol in der Religionsgeschichte, in: Religion und Religionen, Festschrift für Gustav Mensching, Bonn 1967.

——, Mevlâna Celelettin Rumi'nin Sark ve Garp'ta Tesirleri, Ankara 1963.

——, Yunus Emre, in: Numen 8/1961.

——, Maulāna Rūmi's story on prayer, in: Yādnama Jan Rypka, ed. J. Bečka, Prague 1967.

Swartz, Merlin, The Position of Jews in Arab Lands, in: Herbert Mason (ed.), Reflections on the Middle East Crisis, Leiden 1971.

Sorley, H. T., Shah Abdul Latif of Bhit: His Poetry, Life, and Times, Oxford 1940.

Spear, Percival, Twilight of the Mughals, Cambridge 2 ed. 1969.

Spies, Gertrud, Mahmud von Ghazna bei Faridud'din Attar, Basel 1959.

Subhan, John, Sufism. Its Saints and shrines, Lucknow 2 ed. 1960.

Titus, Murray, Indian Islam, Milford 1930.

Trimingham, J. Spencer, The Sufi Orders in Islam, Oxford 1971.

Trumpp, Ernest, Grammar of the Sindhi Language, London 1872, repr. 1970.

——, Sorathi. Ein Gedicht aus dem grossen Divan des Sayyid Abd-ul-Latif, in: ZDMG 17/1863.

——, The Adi Granth, or the Holy Scripture of the Sikhs, translated from the original Gurmukhi, with introductory essays, London 1877.

Underhill, Evelyn, Mysticism. A Study in the Nature and Development of Man's Spiritual Consciousness, 1911 and often.

Usborne, C. F., Hir Ranjha, ed. by Mumtaz Hasan, Karachi 1966.

Vaudeville, Charlotte, Kabir, Oxford 1974.

——, Barāhmāsa, les chansons des douze mois dans les littératures indo-aryennes, Pondichéry, 1965.

Watanmal, Lilaram, The Life of Shah Abdul Latif, Hyderabad 1889.

Wensinck, A. J., Concordance et indices de la tradition musulmane, Leiden 1936 ff.

Zaehner, R. C., Hindu and Muslim Mysticism, London 1960.

Zimmer, Heinrich, Maya, Zürich 1952.

Zubaid Ahmad, The Contribution of Indo-Pakistan to Arabic Literature, Lahore 2 ed. 1968.

b) SOURCES IN ORIENTAL LANGUAGES

Abdul Haqq, Maulvi, Urdū kā nashw u namā meñ Ṣūfiya-yi kirām kā ḥiṣṣa, Karachi 1953.

Abdul Latif, Shah, Shāh jō Risālō, ed. Trumpp, Leipzig 1866.

——, Shāh jō Risālō, ed. Kalyan B. Adwani, Bombay 1957.

——, The Poetic Compendium of Shah Abdul Latif of Bhit, based on Three Manuscripts written in 1269 and 1270 AH, ed. by Dr. N. A. Baloch, Bhitshah 1974.

——, Poetry of Shah Abdul Latif of Bhit, a versified Urdu translation from the original Sindhi text by Shaikh Ayaz, Hyderabad/Sind 1963.

Abū Nuᶜaim al-Isfahānī, Ḥilyat al-auliyā, 10 vols., Cairo 1932 ff.

Amīr Khusrau, Dīwān-i kāmil, ed. M. Darwish, Tehran 1343 sh/1965.

Aṣlaḥ, Muḥammad, Tadhkira-yi shuᶜarā-yi Kashmīr, ed. H. Rashdi, 5 vols., Karachi 1967-68.

ᶜAṭṭār, Farīduddin, Diwan-i qaṣāᶜid u ghazaliyāt, ed. S. Nafisi, Tehran 1339 sh/1960.

——, Ilāhīnāma, ed. H. Ritter, Leipzig 1940.

——, Manṭiq uṭ-ṭair, ed. Jawad Shakur, Tehran 1341 sh/1962.

——, Muṣībatnāma, ed. N. Fisal, Tehran 1338 sh/1959.

——, Tadhkirat al-auliyā, ed. R. A. Nicholson, London 1905-1907, repr. 1959.

Bahoo, Sultan, Abyāt, ed. and transl. Maqbul Ilahi, Lahore 1967.

Baloch, N. A., Shāh jē Risālē jī tartīb, Bhitshah 1975.

——, Miyeñ Shāh ᶜInāt jō kalām, Hyderabad/Sind 1963.

——, Haftā dīñha, rātiūñ aiñ mahīnā, Hyderabad/Sind 1961.
——, Ṭhīh akhariyūn, Hyderabad/Sind 1960.
——, Ggīch, Hyderabad/Sind 1963.
——, Maujizā, Hyderabad/Sind 1960.
——, Munāqibā, Hyderabad/Sind 1960.
——, Maulūd, Hyderabad/Sind 1961.
——, Madāḥūñ ain Munājātūñ, Hyderabad/Sind 1959.
——, Morirrō ain Manjar Macch, Hyderabad/Sind 1967.
——, Līlañ Chanēsar, Hyderabad/Sind 1971.
——, Mūmal Rāṇō, Hyderabad/Sind 1975.
    (All these books are published in the Sind Folklore Series, Sindhi Adabi Board)
Baqlī, Rūzbihān, Sharḥ ash-shaṭhiyāt, 'Les paradoxes des Soufis', ed. H. Corbin, Tehran-Paris 1966.
Bayram Khan, Dīwān, ed. M. Sabir and H. Rashdi, Karachi 1971.
Bēdil, Mirzā, Kulliyāt, 4 vols., Kabul 1962-65.
Bēdil Rohrīwārō, Dīwān, ed. Abdul Husain Musawi, Karachi 1954.
Bēglārī, Idrākī, Chanēsarnāma, ed. H. Rashdi, Karachi 1956.
Bilgrāmī, Āzād, Subḥat al-marjān, lith Bombay 1903.
Bullhē Shāh, Dīwān, ed. Faqir M. Faqir, Lahore 1960.
Burhānpūrī, Rashīd, Burhānpūr kē Sindhī Auliyā, Karachi 1957.
Dārā Shikōh, Sakīnat al-auliyā, ed. Jalali Na ʾini, Tehran 1344 sh/1965.
Dard, Khwāja Mīr, Asrār-i ṣalāt, lith. with Ahmad Sirhindi's Mabdaʾ wa maʿād on p. 69-92, Delhi s.d. (ca. 1892).
——, Dīwān, ed. Muhammad Habibur Rahman Shirwani, Delhi s.d. (with an important introduction).
——, For his other works see the list of abbreviations.
Daudpota, M. U., Kalām-i Girhōṛī, Karachi 1956.
Fakhrī Harawī, Rauḍat as-salāṭīn, ed. H. Rashdi, Hyderabad/Sind 1968.
Fānī, Muḥsin, Dīwān, ed. G. L. Tikku, Tehran 1342 sh/1963.
—— (wrongly ascribed to), Dabistān-i madhahib, transl. D. Shea and A. Troyer, London 1901.
Faizi, Abu'l-Faiz, Sawāṭiʿ al-ilhām, Lucknow 1306 h.
Firāq, Nāṣir Nadhīr, Maikhāna-yi Dard, Delhi 1344 h/1925.
Furūzānfar, Badīʿuzzamān, Aḥādīth-i Mathnawī, Tehran 1334 sh/1955.
Ghālib Mirza Asadullah, Collected works, 17 vols., Lahore 1969.
Ghazzālī, Abū Ḥāmid, Iḥyā ʾ ʿulūm ad-dīn, 4 vols., Bulaq 1289h/1872-3.
Ghazzālī, Aḥmad, Sawāniḥ. Aphorismen über die Liebe, ed. H. Ritter, Istanbul 1942.
Hoshyārpūrī, Ḥafeeẓ, Mathnawiyāt-i Hīr Ranjhā, Karachi 1957.
Ibn ʿArabī, Fuṣūṣ al-ḥikam, ed. A. A. Affifi, Cairo 1954.
——, Tarjumān al-ashwāq. A Collection of Mystical Odes by Muhyī ʾuddīn ibn al-ʿArabī, ed. and transl. by R. A. Nicholson, London 1911.
Ibn ʿAtā Allāh, Miftāḥ al-falāḥ wa miṣbāḥ al-arwāḥ, Cairo 1961.
Ibn Khalliqān, Wafayāt al-aʿyān, ed. M. de Slane, Paris 1838-42.
Ikrām, Shaikh Mohammad Armaghān-i Pāk, Karachi 1953.
——, Rūd-i kauthar, Lahore 4 1969.
Jāmī, ʿAbdur Raḥmān, Nafaḥāt al-uns, ed. M. Tauhidipur, Tehran 1336 sh/1957.
——, Lawā ʾiḥ, Theran 1342 sh/1963 and often.
Kalīm, Abū Ṭālib, Dīwān, ed. Partav Baidawi, Tehran 1336 sh/1957.
Jalbānī, Ghulām Ḥusain, Shāh Walīullāh jī zindagī, Hyderabad/Sind 1973.
Khalīl, Makhdūm Ibrāhīm, Takmila Maqālāt ash-shuʿarā, ed. H. Rashdi, Karachi 1958.
Makhzan, Collection of articles on Shah Abdul Latif, Hyderabad/Sind 1954.

Mehrān jūñ maujūn, Karachi ca. 1956 (collection of essais on Sindhi culture, and of short stories).

Mehrān jā mōtī, Karachi 1959 (a similar collection).

Niẓāmī, Khalīq Aḥmad, Shāh Walīullāh kē siyāsī maktūbāt, Aligarh 1950.

——, Malfūẓāt kī tārīkhī ahammiyat, in: Arshi Presentation Vol., ed. Malik Ram, New Delhi 1961.

Qāniᶜ, Mīr ᶜAlī Shīr, Maqālāt ash-shuᶜarā, ed. H. Rashdi, Karachi 1956.

——, Maklīnāma, ed. H. Rashdi, Karachi 1967.

——, Tuḥfat ul-kirām, Sindhi translation, Hyderabad/Sind 1957.

Quddūsī, Iᶜjāzul Ḥaqq, Tadhkira-yi ṣūfiyā-yi Sindh, Karachi 1959 (the same author has collected biographies of the saints from the various regions of Pakistan: Panjab, Frontier, Bengal).

Quraishī, ᶜAbdur Razzāq, Mirzā Maẓhar Jānjānān aur unkā kalām, Bombay 1961.

——, Makātīb-i Mirzā Maẓhar, Bombay 1966.

Rāshdī, Sayyid Ḥussāmuddīn, Sindhī Adab, Karachi s.d. (ca. 1954).

——, Shāh kāfīa jō mūjid na ahē, in Mehrān jūñ maujūn.

Rūmī, Maulānā Jalāluddīn, Mathnawī-yi maᶜnawī, ed. and transl. by R. A. Nicholson, 8 vols., London-Leiden 1925-1940.

——, Dīwān-i kabīr ya Kulliyāt-i Shams, ed. B. Z. Furuzanfar, 10 vols., Tehran 1336sh/1957 ff.

Sachal Sarmast, Risālō Sindhī, ed. Othman Ali Ansari, Karachi 1958.

——, Siraikī Kalām, ed. Maulwi Hakim Md. Sadiq Ranipuri, Karachi 1959.

Saᶜīd Ḥasan, Pīr, Shah Abdul Latif (about Quranic allusions in his work), in: Makhzan, Hyderabad/Sind 1954.

Sanā ʾī, Abū ʾl-Majd Majdūd, Dīwān, ed. M. Rizwi, Tehran 1341sh/1962.

——, Ḥadīqat al-ḥaqīqa, ed. M. Rizwi, Tehran 1329sh/1950.

Sarrāj, Abū Naṣr, Kitāb al-lumaᶜ fī ʾt-taṣawwuf, ed. R. A. Nicholson, London-Leiden 1914.

Ṣuṣud, Ḥasan Luṭfī, Islam tasavvufunda Hacegân hanedanī, Istanbul 1958.

Tafhīmī, Ḥāfiz Sājidullāh, Sharḥ-i aḥwāl ū āthār-i fārsī-yi Shaikh Bū ᶜAlī Qalandar Panīpatī, Ph. D. diss. Karachi 1975.

Thattawi, Muḥ. Aᶜzam, Tuḥfat aṭ-ṭāhirīn, ed. B. Durrani, Karachi 1956.

ᶜUrfī, Muḥammad, Kulliyāt, ed. A. Jawahiri, Tehran 1336 sh/1957.

Walīullāh, Shāh, Ḥujjat Allāh al-bāligha, ed. as-Sayyid Sābiq, Cairo s.d. (ca. 1960).

——, at-Tafhīmāt al-ilāhiyya, 2. vols., ed. G. M. Qasimi, Hyderabad/Sind 1967, 1970. ——

——, Hamaᶜāt, ed. G. M. Qasimi, Hyderabad/Sind 1964.

Yunus Emre, Divanī, ed. Abdulbaki Gölpīnarlī, Istanbul 1943.

Dr. N.A. Baloch, Maulana Jalaluddin Rumi's influence on Shah Abdul Latif, Paper at the International Mavlana Seminar Ankara, 1973.

INDEX OF QURANIC QUOTATIONS AND *HADITH*

INDEX OF PROPER NAMES AND TECHNICAL TERMS